The G N Devy Reader

'Devy's theses go much beyond literature and literary criticism in touching uncharted areas of sociology, of literary ideas and practice, and the whole web of interdisciplinary information underlying any sociology of literature. Devy's book—*After Amnesia*—is so important that one would wholeheartedly recommend it to anyone with any concern about contemporary Indian literary culture.'

Dilip Chitre, *The Times of India*

'Devy's conviction is that literature is something rooted in the soil and is understood in terms of the whole gamut of experience in a given language.'

C. T. Indra, *The Hindu*

'His quest for a quintessential Indian discourse has seen him traverse some problematic domains, especially in cultural and literary studies…he makes quite a statement while putting forward various arguments of his current work on violence.'

Narendra Pachkhede, *The Indian Express*

'*After Amnesia*…is truly a benchmark by which literary criticism in India will be judged for many years to come.'

R. Parthsarathy, *Sahitya Akademi awardee*

'No single person in the modern history of India has done so much and so effectively for the articulation and conservation of tribal imagination and protection of their cultural identity.'

Mahasweta Devi, *Author*

The G N Devy Reader

After Amnesia
'Of Many Heroes'
The Being of Bhasha
Countering Violence

with a Foreword by Rajeswari Sunder Rajan

Orient BlackSwan

THE G N DEVY READER

ORIENT BLACKSWAN PRIVATE LIMITED

Registered Office
3-6-752 Himayatnagar, Hyderabad 500 029, Telangana, India
e-mail: centraloffice@orientblackswan.com

Other Offices
Bengaluru, Chennai, Guwahati, Hyderabad, Kolkata,
Mumbai, New Delhi, Noida, Patna, Visakhapatnam

First published 2009
Reprinted 2014
This paperback edition 2023

ISBN 978-93-5442-471-7

037711

Typeset by
Trinity Designers & Typesetters
Chennai 600 041

Printed in India at
B.B. Press, Noida 201 301

Published by
Orient Blackswan Private Limited
3-6-752 Himayatnagar, Hyderabad 500 029, Telangana, India
e-mail: info@orientblackswan.com

Contents

Introduction

When I opted for English Literature as the subject of study for B. A., I had no idea that such a study was generally geared towards preparing students as office assistants or clerks. I started suspecting during my years as an M. A. student, that the study was crafting a career in academics and teaching for me. My perspective changed as I moved on to my doctoral work. Those years of slogging in libraries made me aware for the first time that study of literature in India is primarily aimed at producing review-writers, or what may be euphemistically called 'literary critics'. The study of English literature had one strange effect on me. The encounter created in me a rather strange sense of alienation from the literatures in the Indian languages that I know. As the effect deepened, I observed that my links with the prosody and style elements of Marathi literature, that I had studied and enjoyed during my school years, had snapped.

When I joined a British university as a student of English literature, I noticed that while I found reading poetry and drama in English an exhilarating experience, I had started developing a sense of remorse for losing my touch with Marathi. A. K. Ramanujan was one of the Indian English Poets I had studied. In many of Ramanujan's poems I found an echo of my own experience. One of his poems that I read in those days, with a somewhat amusing title, was 'An Amnesiac's Memory'. The title, not so much the poem, made a deep impression on my mind. Several years later, while reading the *Bhagvadgita*, which has its own analysis of loss of memory—anger leads to confusion, and confusion to amnesia—Ramanujan's play with memory in his poems flashed back in my own memory. It was at this point in time that I first started thinking about the phenomenon of amnesia. By then, my suspicion that institutional study of literature is meant more for producing literary scholars rather than any literary talent had been amply confirmed by my growing awareness of what I and others in my profession had been doing. I was trying to revive my contact with Marathi literature, and was newly taking interest in literature in the Gujarati language. As an experiment in self-examination, basing my scrutiny on Ramanujan's rather amusing insight, I keenly observed the Marathi and Gujarati literary scene. A few years prior to my engagement with the scrutiny, I had become interested in a literary debate that was the rage of the day in Marathi literary circles. The debate revolved round the stand that a small but vocal group of literary critics had taken, and the movement was called *desivad* or nativism. Therefore, when I sat down to write an essay on the state of literary criticism—really my own condition as a teacher of literature—I felt compelled to use the rather long title 'Tradition and Change in Indian Literary Criticism After Amnesia'. When I was writing it, I had no idea that it would be a 'book', and much less that it would be read so widely. But on its publication, I noticed that it managed to attract the attention of critics in many Indian languages. Since then I have often wondered if the title of the essay had been somewhat different, say, 'Colonialism and Literary Criticism in Some Western Indian Languages' or some such thing, the 'book' would have at all been noticed. Of course, this was an after thought, and it would be pretentious on my part to say that I was not pleased with the attention that the essay received. Being acutely aware that the essay was not a complete statement, that in it I had not gone much beyond myself, I felt it necessary to write an essay that would form an appropriate sequel to *After Amnesia. Of Many Heroes*, published by Orient Longman in 1997, was the essay in which I had taken up the question of literary history—as previously I had taken up literary criticism—in India. However, in that essay I had not confined myself to Marathi, Gujarati or any particular Indian language. The idea was to show how limiting is any idea of literary history in the context of Indian literature. The essay was not about what happens to contemporary historiography while dealing with the question of Indian literature; it was about how a variety of styles of remembering had been developed in various phases of Indian history, and how divergent these had been, making 'history' itself an elusive proposition.

Writing *Of Many Heroes* gave me a taste of what it is to write about 'Indian' literature. A synchronic study of literature in all Indian languages, or at least the more known among them, is in itself an intellectual challenge. To think of literature in all those languages historically, and the languages that have been, is quite a daunting task. In *Of Many Heroes,* I was trying to trace the history of literary historiography in the subcontinent. However, the material that I examined did not allow one to construct any history in the Hegelian sense, that is, not in terms of a cause and consequence series. I had to stay content with merely placing in an arbitrary manner interpretation of one historiographical text after another. And, I had to introduce explanatory sentences such as, "This situation however changed." The difficulty did not arise merely because there was shortage of supporting historical material, such material is available in plenty, but it arose rather out of the fact that the history of languages in India is as yet an unfinished project.

After Amnesia takes up the question of 'knowledge' as constituted by a historical experience, such as colonialism. I have argued in that essay that colonialism induced in the Indian thinking a distortion in memory because the self-image had undergone a substantial degree of distortion. But I had not been able to fully understand, while writing that essay, how a culture remembers its past even when many tensions between the past and the present keep building up for any given civilization. While writing *Of Many Heroes,* I started understanding that remembering and forgetting are not mutually exclusive acts in a psyche but rather interdependent and even complementary to each other. For a while, I thought I would be able to locate some satisfactory explanation for the degree of interdependence between the two in one or several historical periods by providing economic analysis. I had made a tentative beginning in *After Amnesia* in that direction by pointing out, albeit somewhat adventurously, that the poor conditions of roads and communications at the beginning of the second millennium had initiated emergence of modern Indian languages. After examining for myself such a method carefully, I came to the conclusion that economy alone cannot be causal to imagination and linguistic expression; instead, imagination—and more particularly, the political imagination—can be causal to the rise of a new economy. In other words I had started suspecting that the role that language plays in the Indian society is somewhat different from the role that has been conceptualised in the established Western linguistic theory. In my personal experience of encountering various linguistic communities in and outside India, I had vaguely noticed that various speech communities relate to their respective languages in diverse ways. Some communities have a greater emotional attachment to the languages they use; some communities have languages that permit them a more complex sense of humour or irony than languages of other communities allow to their speakers. However, I had not come across any device of measuring or assessing a speech community's engagement with its language. This question attracted my thoughts to examining phenomenological positions on language and consciousness. It is, of course, futile to raise questions as to the precedence of language over the consciousness, or the priority of consciousness over language. I must admit that my inclination towards thinking of language in terms of what it does to one's consciousness led me to the thinking of language as a vital force rather than a merely objective social system.

While I had been engaged in writing *After Amnesia* and *Of Many Heroes*, I had been gradually gravitating towards social activism. My activism was not triggered off by an ideological understanding of the society, it was also not born out of my altruistic or charitable instinct. Quite strangely, it developed out of my fascination for languages other than the ones sponsored by the state. The Indian Constitution has provided a mechanism of the state sponsorship to languages by creating the Eighth Schedule. While working at Baroda University, I had started looking closely at the communities that spoke languages other than Gujarati or Hindi. I found many such speech communities in close vicinity of Baroda. As my interest in them intensified, I noticed that a large number of such language communities exist in India, and that most of them are designated as tribals. For a while, I kept wondering if languages spoken by caste Indians have any radical difference from the languages spoken by tribal Indians. Soon, however, I dropped that line of inquiry because I realized that the distinction between caste and tribe in the Indian context is an easily challengeable distinction. It is of course true that the literary traditions in practically all tribal languages have remained oral in nature to this day. But, there are oral traditions in the languages of the castes as well, and their presence is substantial enough for any literary observer to be overwhelmed by them. Therefore, I decided to look at the oral traditions in languages spoken by tribal as well as non-tribal communities of India. In order to acquaint myself properly with these traditions, I decided to step out of the academic, institutional set-up.

Beginning with the movie songs that form a large part of the emotive matrix of contemporary Indians, the *bhajans*, *kirtans*, episodic narratives and truncated myths and legends that any average Indian knows is an amazing collage of oral tradition that forms the substratum of personality for us. It may be possible to argue that in examining language as a vital force or energy, it is essential to first look at the Indian understanding of oral rendering of imaginative and creative expression. Such a scrutiny may not yield much unless one gets rid of the straitjacketed notions of literature as distinct from folk literature or oral literature. The disjointed notes that appear in this *Reader* under the caption *The Being of Bhasha* is an attempt to articulate the interplay between consciousness and orality in the Indian context.

Following the notes on oral traditions in *The Being of Bhasha*, I have chosen to place a long essay on the theme of violence in Indian society. The essay contains a discussion on various known theoretical perspectives of violence that analyze its sources. I have brought the essay here, entirely unexpected in a publication that will be seen as 'literary criticism', in order to integrate the three different questions raised in *Amnesia*, *Heroes* and *Bhasha*: What is 'knowledge' in a postcolonial society? What is the strategy to reconstruct the past knowledge in order to assess its necessary irrelevance or occasional relevance to the present? What is the bind between the consciousness that forgets as well as remembers the past and the oral transaction of imaginative expression? In the essay on violence, I have suggested that in a postcolonial society with an amazingly long history, demanding its recognition in the present, and even more amazing diversity of languages, contributing to the wealth of imaginative expression, it is necessary to identify and recognize the 'local' in order to avoid any imposition of the 'global'.

The *Bhagvadgita* explains the loss of memory as a result of the violence in the psyche: *krodhat bhavati sammoh, samohat smriti-vibramah*, literally meaning, anger makes one bewildered, and bewilderment leads to amnesia. Without any disrespect to the *Gita* I have sought to reverse the causal sequence. I have suggested that it is an amnesiac society that has lost the ability to read history in its own terms, the society which feels confused by the plethora of languages becomes essentially violent. Therefore, I thought a discussion of violence in our time in India should form a necessary component of any study of aesthetics in the Indian context. If aesthetics is, as the term originally meant, a description of 'aesthesis' or the ability to draw or understand pleasure out of the senses, one's understanding of aesthetics is likely to remain inadequate unless the forces that cause pain are not taken into consideration.

What is presented in the *Reader* is a graph of my intellectual engagement that has kept changing over the last three decades. I hope readers of this volume will show generosity by reading it as an account of a solitary thinker's journey rather than as a cohesive single argument.

Orient Blackswan, formerly Orient Longman, have been indulgent towards my writings and have published them when other publishers would have hesitated in treating my inadequately developed essays as books. My thoughts go to the late Sujit Mukherjee who first suggested to me that I send my writings to Orient Longman. I am grateful to Priya Adarkar who decided to publish *After Amnesia* in 1992, to Vidya Rao and Hemlata Shankar for bringing together these works as a *Reader,* and to Deepa Krishnamurthy for suggesting ways of improving my texts.

G. N. Devy
Vadodara
October 2008

Foreword

I feel greatly honoured to have been invited to write a foreword to this collected volume of G. N. Devy's works, but rather overwhelmed at the prospect. I am conscious of being less suited for the task than almost anyone else Dr. Devy might have asked. In contrast to his scholarship in the many literatures of India, mine is limited to English and Anglophone literatures. Ideologically too I belong to a different school, being somewhat wary of the 'nativism' that he proposes as the response to the cultural impasse that confronts postcolonial India. I am constrained further by my sense that his renunciation of an academic career in favour of full-time commitment to social work is a reproach to those of us who pursue our careers in greener pastures abroad. If he thought that I might be able to usefully preface his writings with some observations of my own despite these many disqualifications, I take it as a sign of his interest in reaching out across intellectual divides. I will also treat it as permission to depart from the conventions of a foreword by engaging his work in the more critical spirit of dialogue.

By bringing together four of his essays within the covers of a single volume—two earlier publications, *After Amnesia: Tradition and Change in Indian Literary Criticism* (1992) and '*Of Many Heroes*': *An Indian Essay in Literary Historiography* (1998), and two other book-length new essays, *The Being of Bhasha* and *Countering Violence*—Dr. Devy and Orient Blackswan have done readers a service. This handy collection enables us to trace the evolution of Devy's thinking over the past fifteen years or so. There is a logic that leads this former professor of English from a critique of colonial English and its critical frames to a survey of the traditions of Indian literatures in his first two books, and from there, in his most recent work, towards a plea for acknowledging the rich oral literatures of India to be found among the Adivasi peoples. His concept of an 'Indian literature' extends beyond the dead Sanskritic high tradition to include the multifarious living bhashas in their dynamic contexts. The privileging of literatures in the bhashas over those in English *and* Sanskrit was the polemical argument of *After Amnesia,* the critical work for and which he was awarded the Sahitya Akademi award in 1993. It is his subsequent discovery that the 'being of bhashas' is dependant on the dialects that 'presage their emergence,' that led him to the study of literary creativity in the Adivasi languages. His involvement not only in the Adivasi *cause* but also in Adivasi *culture*—or more accurately in the one by way of the other—makes him one of the few scholars in India to present, describe, transcribe, translate, and theorize, oral literatures.

The intellectual energy he expends on this task of understanding an'other' knowledge is not a mere theoretical exercise however. It is instrumental in furthering the cause of Adivasis, the most discriminated against and oppressed of India's 'minorities.' Devy seeks to rescue their cultures from 'aphasia,' the loss of speech. It is *language* that marks us as human, not writing, he reminds us, and speech (too) is language that must be respected and preserved. The most radical and challenging argument he makes in *The Being of Bhasha* is to propose that speech and script occupy entirely different and opposed cognitive worlds: 'speech is threatened by script'. Devy's speculations can be productively read alongside Derrida's *Of Grammatology,* though obviously his are impelled by a civilizational crisis different from the logocentrism of European metaphysics that provoked Derrida's work. The theoretical propositions presented in these opening sections of *The Being of Bhasha* are profound and unsettling. Devy divorces script from language as such since he speculates that the basic purpose of human scripts was counting, founded in a pastoral economy that 'needed to mark the quantity of surplus invested.' He associates script therefore with the capitalist drive (the acquisitive economy) and with the privileging of the imagination, and hence of 'fiction'; by contrast speech is pre-capitalist (characterized as a distributive economy) and is transmitted through memory, hence linked to truth or realism. 'The acquisitive ideology privileges intellect and imagination. The distributive ideology gives primacy to sensation and memory', he sums up. Despite the temporal schema of the *pre*-capitalist that grounds and explains the opposition, speech communities are not to be regarded as an anachronism. Devy's mission is to show, on the contrary, the relevance and value of the Adivasi world view in contemporary India. It is his role as mediator and translator between the two worlds that gives rise to the complex meditations that constitute this new work.

It is fitting that the *Being of Bhasha* and *Countering Violence* should be a transcription of Devy's lectures at various forums, as opposed to a written book. The powerful argument he makes for speech and oral knowledge transmission in the book is in consonance with the impatience he expresses with writing, and especially academic prose. It is of course ironic that the lectures had to be reduced in this fashion: 'reduced' in both its senses, as 'written down' but also as 'diminished.' It is easy to see that the strengths of his ideas would emerge most forcefully in spoken form. Devy prefers to offer a series of quick illuminations in his lectures by way of aphorisms, provocations, essentialist formulations, throwaway ideas and speculative thoughts, rather than undertake the more tedious tasks of elaboration, argument, qualification, and documentation that are the conventions of academic writing. This leaves us wishing sometimes that he had developed his insights in more conventional ways and at somewhat greater length—not merely that he might persuade us but also so that he might instruct us better.

There are also the more obvious facts about writing that gives it leverage over speech (at least under present day conditions): its permanence and reach. Hence the activist and scholar, whether seeking to disseminate or preserve oral literatures or make public his own lectures, must do so by taking recourse to writing, that is, by transcribing and printing them. Such necessity can no doubt be ironically acknowledged, but can it be overcome? Devy does not take up the question whether audio-visual media and the performing arts today belong to the oral tradition, or if they emerge from a different conjuncture. In any case would it be possible to record, preserve and disseminate the songs, stories, and other forms of Adivasi speech for posterity by means different from writing and more closely allied to the spoken medium? In thinking about speech and writing we are called upon to reflect on their respective *technologies* in addition to the *ideologies* they represent.

The seminal ideas about oral cultures put forward in this book could also be helpful in thinking about illiteracy in India, not in the usual way as the absence of scriptural skills (and consequently as a problem of development), but as an alternative knowledge and a counter-culture. Similarly it might help us understand performative genres like theatre, dance, songs, recitations and story-telling, which continue to draw large audiences in many parts of even urban India. (D. Venkat Rao's work on the Telugu revolutionary poet Gaddar, for instance, offers profound insights about the communitarian nature of song cultures, and of genres like the 'mourning' song, which Gaddar taps into).

Countering Violence develops a set of concerns, relating to violence, its origins, meanings, manifestations, causes and antidotes. Here Devy is in the good company of Ashis Nandy in his analysis of the pathologies of modernity, the materialism of 'the West', the violence of (Western forms and modes of) knowledge, the anxieties of masculinity, and the example and teachings of Gandhi. Interesting and important as these ideas are, this portion of the book feels less focused, reflecting perhaps Devy's understanding of violence at several levels: as universal and inherent to human nature, with a distinctive socio-biological basis, but also as historical and culturally specific in its meanings. The contradictory and protean aspects of violence apparently make it difficult to be tackled as a phenomenon in anything but a generalized way.

The Being of Bhasha develops the thoughts on Adivasi culture and the Indian state's failures of development that Devy first formulated in his landmark anthology of Adivasi literature, *Painted Words* (2003), and then in the collection of essays titled *A Nomad Called Thief: Reflections on Adivasi Silence* (2006). But the essay is also related along another axis to Devy's earlier writings on more narrowly disciplinary literary critical and literary historical subjects with which it is juxtaposed in this volume. Devy probes Indian literary traditions to uncover their deep roots in oral forms and emphasizes their survival via oral transmission. He builds on the profound observation that 'in Indian traditions of creative expressions, the 'literary' includes the written as well as the oral', pointing to the numerous ancient and medieval texts (including *bhakti* poetry) which have come to us 'without the mediation of writing, but with the grammar of memorizing them'. 'Indian manuscript traditions are not solely traditions of writing,' he reminds us. *The Being of Bhasha* thus throws light on the historical 'origins' and the theoretical underpinnings of the bhasha literary traditions. This is the logic that connects it with Devy's early academic writings.

At the time of the publication of *After Amnesia* in 1992, the ferment—or 'crisis' as it was more dramatically referred to—in English literary studies in India was beginning to find expression in a few volumes published in India. Around the same time, and increasingly since then, serious and scholarly work on Sanskrit and the different bhasha literatures began to appear in English, breaking out of the disciplinary frame of traditional Indological or area studies. Vasudha Dalmia, Francesca Orsini, Harish Trivedi, Sudipta Kaviraj, Rosinka Chaudhuri, Udaya Kumar, Stuart Blackburn, Sheldon Pollock, Venkat Rao, D. R. Nagaraj, David Shulman, Velcheru Narayana Rao, Milind Wakankar, Rashmi Bhatnagar, Simona Sawhney (listed in no particular order) are some of the established and younger critics, literary historians, translators, and sociologists of literature whose works are beginning to populate the field. They could not all have been known to Devy at the time of course. But the mere fact of the existence of such works today, even apart from their excellence, is a validation of the revisionary Indian literary history and criticism that Devy was developing twenty years ago.

There is still much to be done of course. Devy's critique was primarily an internal one addressed to Gujarati and Marathi literary communities and more generally to indigenous Indian scholarship and pedagogy. Perhaps in these domains change has been slow to happen. But even within Indian institutional sites there are now unmistakeable signs of invigoration, as seen in the increase in translation activity for instance; or in the visible growth in comparative literary studies; in the pioneering efforts of critics like Meenakshi Mukherjee (reflected in her landmark work *Realism and Reality*, as well as her edited collection of critical essays on the early Indian novel); also in the historical scholarship on caste, reform, gender, and left cultural movements which has turned to literary texts in the bhashas as an important resource. All these developments, however few and scattered, are to be welcomed. One of G. N. Devy's strengths as a thinker is to be at the forefront of change. It is entirely likely that his engagement with Adivasi cultures at multiple levels, as educator, anthologist, translator, critic and theorist will similarly initiate a trend.

Devy is right in perceiving his new writings as heterodox, but that is only another word for originality. His ideas are born out of deep reflection, itself the painful product of his grappling with the realities of Adivasi struggles for livelihood, legal rights, identity, dignity and cultural space. He seeks to understand as much as to explain. His activism pushes the bounds of his thought. And the thoughts, once set in motion, do not come to rest in conclusions—they are instead torn out of their comfortable parameters, restlessly pursued, revisited, revised and only provisionally settled, always subject to re-opening on another occasion. Even as readers survey the body of his past and current work collected in this volume, they are bound to be looking ahead already to Devy's next project, with the anticipation of again encountering the radical interrogation and revelation that they have come to expect from his writings.

Rajeswari Sunder Rajan
June 2008
Bangalore and New York

AFTER AMNESIA

Tradition and Change in Indian Literary Criticism

For Surekha

A Mahatma and his wife came along, bringing a *sarivina* with them. They plucked at the string and began to sing a song.
As they began to sing, the Mahatma sang one *raga,* his wife sang another *raga*, and they played the instrument in a third *raga.*
And the Gosavi said, "Die, you miserable wretches!"
And they kept silent.
Then the Gosavi left.

Sri Govindaprabhu Caritra, AD 1392

* The translation from the original Marathi Mahanubhava text is by Anne Feldhaus (*The Deeds of God in Rddhipur*, 1984). I have taken the liberty to reinstate *sarivina* and *raga* in the place of 'a stringed instrument' and 'song' used by her.

Acknowledgments

An initial outline of this essay was discussed with the late Professor Suresh Joshi, a few months before his death in September 1986. The first draft was prepared during my tenure as a Commonwealth Academic Staff Fellow at the University of Leeds between October 1986 and July 1987, and was read by the late Mr. Arthur Ravenscroft (Leeds), and Dr. John Stachniewski (Manchester). Parts of it were read by Dr. Chandrashekhar Jahagirdar (Shivaji University), Dr. Shirley Chew (Leeds University), and Mr. Jyotirmaya Sharma (Hull University). Valuable suggestions were made by Mr. S. K. Rana and Dr. Deval Dharker (University of Baroda) while the typescript was prepared. This work has benefited much by the comments offered by Dr. Sujit Mukherjee. I thank them.

I wish to thank the Indian U. G. C. and the M. S. University of Baroda for nominating me for the Commonwealth Fellowship and for relieving me from my teaching work at Baroda. Prof. John Bernard, the then Chairman of the School of English at the Leeds University, provided me a stimulating academic environment to work in. Mr. and Mrs. Ravenscroft and Dr. Shirley Chew made my stay in Leeds enjoyable. I thank them.

The basic motivation for this work has come from my former teacher Professor Shantinath Desai, currently the Vice Chancellor of K. V. P. University of Shimoga. I am infinitely grateful to him. I also wish to appreciate the constant support and encouragement that I received from my wife while I was busy writing this essay between April 1986 and March 1989.

G. N. Devy

Contents

1

Introduction

This essay is about literary criticism in contemporary India. It is an attempt to describe what is recognized by common agreement to be a crisis in Indian criticism, and to explain it in historical terms. It does not aim at offering an analysis of theoretical positions in vogue. I believe that it will not be possible to formulate fresh and meaningful questions of a theoretical nature in the context of contemporary Indian literature without having established first the historical parameters of this field of activity. A perspective of literature and literary criticism with a greater self-awareness, a more accurate knowledge of native traditions, and an insight into their modern transformations, are preconditions for initiating relevant and useful debates about the function and practice of literary criticism. That perspective will make it easier for Indian critics to propose theoretical formulations.

It is commonly assumed at present that traditional criticism has been completely displaced by modern Western criticism, which is regarded as a new current in Indian literary and aesthetic sensibility. But did or did not the earlier current leave behind it any silt which modified the new current? Besides, was the old current a single mainstream, or was it made up of several tributaries of which we have lost sight now? Was the displacement of the indigenous by the alien a simple and unified phenomenon? These questions await satisfactory answers. But there is an even greater question which needs to be looked into in order to understand the precise nature of the crisis in Indian criticism. That question relates neither to the Sanskrit tradition of poetics nor to Western literary thought. It relates to literary criticism in the modern Indian languages, or, to use the traditional Indian term, the bhashas.

Each bhasha has a tradition of literature which can be described in all fairness as a mature tradition. Some bhashas like Kannada and Tamil have literary histories of more than a millennium; others, like Marathi and Gujarati, of seven or eight centuries. The bhashas were rapidly moving away from Sanskrit poetics, and it was not for several centuries that they were exposed to Western aesthetics. That exposure came in the wake of British colonial experience. But, whereas Marathi literature, for instance, is believed to have made a glorious beginning in the thirteenth century, literary criticism in Marathi is considered to begin with the mid-nineteenth century 'prefaces' by Dadoba Pandurang (1865), Parashuram Tantya Godbole (1867) and Mahadev Moreshvar Kunte (1869).[1] Similarly, in Gujarati the literary tradition is considered to have begun with the lexicography and poetry of Hemachandra (1088–1173), who also wrote distinguished criticism in Sanskrit; but the critical tradition is traced back only up to Navalram (1836–88) and Govardhanram (1855–1907).[2] It is quite inconceivable that the bhashas produced great literatures for half a millennium or more without developing literary criticism, in however crude a form. Or is it that Indian literary history has been insensitive to that development?[3]

If a more reliable literary history is to be postulated, a more accurate description of the bhasha traditions will have to be offered. It will be necessary to examine closely the role played by printing technology in increasing the volume of critical articulation as distinct from its impact on critical sensibility. Similarly, the process of assimilation of Western 'modernity' into Indian 'tradition'—a process which lends every alien intellectual tool a ritual status before internalizing it—calls for careful scrutiny. Naturally, a reorganized historical perspective, if it is sufficiently realistic, will contribute towards evolving a more useful description of literary criticism in India, and rid it of the static images of Western criticism and Sanskrit poetics.

Any discussion of literary criticism—or other forms of literary activity—in modern India, involves the use of the terms 'India' and the 'West'. The term 'India' may be valid in the pages of an atlas, but as a cultural label it is hopelessly inadequate and simplistic. A product of colonial historiography, the term brings with it a politically coloured self-image and the suggestion of cultural amnesia. It can be said that colonialism gave rise to an equally false image of the West in India, an image that is larger than life, static and apparently invincible. Accordingly, the Indian view of the West has remained fraught with idealization, arbitrary fragmentation and unhistorical reductions.[4] This disfiguring colonial epistemology has created false frameworks of cultural values and has stratified knowledge into superior (Western) and inferior (Indian) categories.

An attempt has been made in this essay to establish how these false images can create profoundly mistaken modes of literary criticism. The term 'India' as used within the pages of this essay presupposes no cultural unity or integration of the subcontinent. It is certainly more meaningful to speak in terms of specific linguistic traditions and regions than to speak of an imaginary cultural unit and unity. Instead of using the long and cumbersome expression 'literature in the modern Indian languages,' I have used the traditional term bhasha. Thus, bhasha literature or bhasha criticism; but the label merely indicates a manageable group of many different literatures. It should be understood in the same manner as labels like 'European literature' and 'Commonwealth literature'.

In discussing the crisis in contemporary literary criticism in India caused by what has been described here as a lapse in cultural memory, I have drawn illustrations from several bhashas; but I have depended mainly on Marathi and Gujarati, the bhashas I follow, and occasionally on Indian English criticism. There are numerous bhasha critics who write criticism in English as well. Bilingualism in critical and literary writing has been a traditional feature of Indian culture. It needs to be seen as a matter of cultural strategy of a people brought up on the dialectics of the *marg* and the *deshi*, a great tradition and little traditions, rather than in terms of a superficial linguistic choice. However, the main concern of this essay is bhasha criticism.

I have made a conscious attempt to minimize, as far as possible, Western paradigms of intellectual enquiry and to draw as much as one can on what could be called, unpretentiously, the modern Indian intellectual discourse. This discourse seems to have been gradually emerging in recent years through the collective effort of intellectuals like M. N. Srinivas (in sociology), Romila Thapar and Ranajit Guha (history), Anil Seal and Partha Chatterjee (political science), Sudhir Kakar (psychology), Ashis Nandy (cultural history and psychology), and Meenakshi Mukherjee and Bhalchandra Nemade (literary criticism). Though gradually ascendant, it has numerous gaps which make crudeness unavoidable in an argument dependent on it. Yet to lean on it, rather than on the excessively sophisticated but Eurocentric Western theory, seems to me to be a desirable cultural and critical strategy in this essay which views criticism as a cultural subsystem rather than a web of abstract theoretical constructs.

There is no point in merely running down the Indian tendency to imitate the West. Even the most original of the twentieth century Indian thinkers—Sri Aurobindo, M. N. Roy and Mahatma Gandhi—could not escape the impact of Western thought. Cultural forms and intellectual institutions do keep changing continuously, and no postcolonial society can claim to have come unscathed out of the colonial period. The colonial past cannot just be wished away. But it is desirable to question the efficacy of the intellectual tools produced during that past.

Colonial experience releases several conflicting tendencies in the colonized society. One obvious tendency is to imitate the colonizers and to win their approval. But it may also give rise to nationalist feelings and create the tendency to resist the colonial influence. It creates simultaneously a revivalistic romanticism and a hard-headed political pragmatism. This simultaneous release of several conflicting tendencies results in a strange, superficial cultural dynamics. A colonized culture becomes violently progressive and militantly retrogressive, and in consequence tends to remain static. In order to understand this cultural immobilization an appropriate historiography is of prime importance.

A wishful, revivalistic re-creation of history increases the gap between the cultural changes as they are and the modes of intellect used to perceive them. Similarly, an ideological, and arbitrary, conception of the processes of modernization as a unified progression cannot satisfactorily explain intellectual institutions—such as literary criticism—which do not seem to fit into ideological paradigms of tradition or change. The present essay is a modest and tendentious attempt to describe some prominent features of the crisis with reference to literary criticism in India.

Each literature demands its own kind of literary historiography. In India this field has remained almost totally neglected.[5] A major consequence of this neglect is that the general framework of assumptions about Indian culture and literature postulated by European Indologists like William Jones, Albrecht Weber, George Grierson, Maurice Winternitz[6] and so on, continues to be in operation. This is not to say that no writing in the area of literary history has been done by Indian scholars. But these writings have retained the general Indological framework, including its basic assumption that the beginning of modern Indian literature is synonymous and synchronous with the British colonial period. Sir William Jones, the founder of Indology, declared in his 'Third Anniversary Discourse' in 1786 that 'in all these inquiries concerning the history of India, I shall confine my researches downward to the Mohammedan conquests at the beginning of the eleventh century, but extend them upwards, as high as possible, to the earliest authentic records of the human species.'[7]

Under the influence of this view, classical India became 'glorious' and British India became 'progressive', but the intervening centuries became, culturally, a period of continuous vulgarization. This methodological convenience has turned into a historiographical convention, and has come to be accepted as an undisputed principle of Indian literary history. Criticism developing from such misleading historiography is naturally ill-equipped to break new theoretical ground. This essay, therefore, moves from a description of the crisis in criticism towards proposing a tentative historiography of Indian criticism.

2

Tradition and Amnesia

The cultural forms developed in classical India from the third to the tenth centuries started undergoing momentous changes at the beginning of the present millennium. The most fundamental of these was the emergence of new languages—bhashas—all over the Indian subcontinent. The new bhashas expressed regional and heterodox aspirations in protest against the hegemony of Sanskrit and the culture developed through that language, *sanskriti.* A similar movement occurred in the south with respect to Tamil which, after a continuous history of two thousand years, branched into Telugu (eleventh century). Earlier, Kannada had already become an independent dialect of Tamil (fifth century). Nine hundred years later, Tamil and Kannada jointly gave birth to Malayalam (fourteenth century). In the north, the regional dialects known as Apabhramsha asserted themselves as independent languages. Consequently, the Middle Indo-Aryan dialect in the east split into Bangla and Oriya (tenth century). Subsequently, Bangla gave birth to Assamiya (thirteenth century). The northwestern dialect developed into Kashmiri (thirteenth century), Sindhi (fifteenth century) and Panjabi (fifteenth century). The western Apabhramsha of Middle Indo-Aryan distributed itself into Hindi (which till the beginning of the nineteenth century existed as several distinct dialects), Gujarati (eleventh century) and Marathi (eleventh century). The Hindi family of dialects developed autonomy in the fourteenth century. It also interacted with the

Islamic languages—Persian, which was spoken in India from the thirteenth to the nineteenth centuries, and Arabic, in use from the eleventh to the nineteenth centuries—and produced a cantonment language, Urdu (thirteenth century), which later became a great literary language. Urdu was developed as a language of military camps of Arabic soldiers in South India, particularly in Gulbarga.

The origin of some of these languages can be traced further back to earlier centuries. We are told that Gujarati and Marathi for example, existed in rudimentary forms as found in stray inscriptions and isolated verses dating from the eighth century.[1] Their known literary traditions, however, do not seem to emerge until a century or two after each language assumed a distinct identity. In any case, all bhashas had become literary languages by the end of the fifteenth century. These literary traditions have survived two phases of prolonged alien rule; and many of them have claims to a large number of great literary works and major authors. The emergence and survival of mature literary traditions in so many languages is the greatest phenomenon in Indian cultural history.

The earliest prose work in Marathi is Mhaibhata's *Lilacharitra* (completed in 1278). The earliest surviving poetic work is Mukundaraja's *Vivekasindhu* (exact date disputed);[2] Jnanadeva's *Jnaneshvari* (completed in 1290) was the first Marathi classic to be critically acclaimed. The Gujarati literary tradition was inaugurated by Hemachandra, poet-saint and grammarian, who lived about the mid-twelfth century. At the time these new literary traditions were emerging, literary criticism was already a highly sophisticated and well-developed intellectual discipline in Sanskrit, and to some extent in Tamil. Sanskrit had a rich literary tradition spanning some sixteen centuries—from Vyasa in the fifth century BC to Bhoja in the eleventh century AD. This great tradition of creative literature had helped Sanskrit criticism in becoming an extremely sophisticated system of literary thought.

Sanskrit grammarians, scholars and writers had thought profoundly about language and linguistics (Panini—fourth century BC; Vararuchi—first century AD; Patanjali—second century AD), metrics, style and diction (Vamana—eighth century; Bhoja—eleventh century), drama, dance and theatre (Bharata—fourth century), metaphor, symbol and diction (Anandavardhana—eighth century; Abhinavagupta—eleventh century), genre and form (Bhamaha—fifth(?) century), sociology of literature (Rajashekhara—tenth century), and so on.[3] The thoughts of these critics were expressed methodically and in a manner acceptable to Indian systems of logic, and were preserved through manuscripts. Theory relating to drama and poetry was taught in universities, commented upon by scholars, and considered seriously by philosophers. For instance, the linguistic theory of *sphota* figured prominently in Sankara's philosophy of Advaita Vedanta in the ninth century. *Sphota,* which means a sudden explosion, was used as a hypothesis by linguists to explain the mechanism which transforms a verbal image into a semantic concept. Sankara adopted this theory of linguistic meaning, and used it to explain his emphasis on *brahman* in the context of the meaning of existence.[4] Sanskrit critics had a very fine conception of the whole field of literary criticism, which they had divided into several subgenres. Rajashekhara mentions the following nine types of criticism in his *Kavyamimamsa:* i) *sutra*—aphoristic and logically formulated idea in prose; ii) *karika*—aphoristic and logically formulated idea in verse; iii) *vyakhya*—elucidation; iv) *vrtti*—elucidation and illustration; v) *bhashya*—comprehensive summary of a point of view and commentary on it; vi) *tika*—assessment; vii) *mimamsa* — analysis; viii) *samiksha*—review; ix) *shastra*—theory of literature related to other theories of knowledge.[5]

Hemachandra, the Jain monk who initiated Gujarati into a poetic tradition, was a poet, lexicographer and theorist. His *Kavyanushasana* (completed in 1140) is considered to be a valuable contribution to Sanskrit poetics. It was written in Sanskrit, and was scholarly more than it was original in thought. The fact that Hemachandra brought the whole tradition of Sanskrit poetics to the threshold of Gujarati literary tradition is endorsed by his modern commentators. A recent evaluation of Hemachandra states:

> His work is perhaps the most eclectic of this period, whose spirit is often dominated by eclecticism. Without committing himself to any doctrine (even the *rasa/dhvani)* Hemachandra

> succeeds in giving a circumstantial account of the various topics of *alamkarashastra,* and also of the *natyashastra.* His work approaches, in other words, the standards of modern scholarship . . . [He] lays himself open to the charge of compilation. In balance though, his net was very broad, especially in the area of illustrative verses (some 1500 from various authors), and he seems to have possessed also a comprehensive scepticism rare among Indian *shastris.*[6]

Like Hemachandra, Mukundaraja, considered to be the first Marathi poet, had an intimate knowledge of Sanskrit intellectual traditions. A critic comments:

> Mukundaraja is the immediate predecessor of Jnanadeva for whom he paved the way by his two works, the *Paramamrta* and the *Vivekasindhu,* an exposition of the Vedanta written in the peculiar intellectual style of the Vedantin. It is strange that Marathi literature should begin where other literatures generally end. But it is a fact, and the reason is the long tradition of the Sanskritic lore that was behind Marathi and which it was trying to rejuvenate after the lapse of Apabhramsha.[7]

Marathi and Gujarati had the advantage of founding their own literary traditions upon intellectual developments in Sanskrit. Other bhasha literatures too had the benefit of contact with Sanskrit.

The emergence of bhasha literatures coincided with, even if it was not entirely caused by, a succession of Islamic rules in India. The Islamic rulers—Arabs, Turks, Mughals—brought with them new cultural currents to India, and provided these currents legitimacy through liberal political patronage. Their languages—Arabic and Persian, mainly, and Urdu which developed indigenously under their influence—brought new modes of writing poetry and music. This intimate contact with Islamic cultures created for the bhasha literatures new possibilities of continuous development.

From the middle of the eighteenth century the British followed a policy of active political interference in India. Once political domination was well established, the British rulers decided, during the nineteenth century, that it was their historic duty to educate India. More pragmatic concerns of colonial rule strengthened this faith. The education designed for India by British colonial officers was founded on the British idea of civilizing the less civilized races. As Lord Lawrence put it, "in doing the best we can for the people, we are bound by our conscience and not by theirs."[8] A new education system based on and spread through the English language was introduced, and with it was introduced English literature as a civilizing influence. It may be noted in passing that during the Victorian period of British history the British universities themselves did not consider English literature a subject fit for study in civilized institutions of learning. English literature earned that privilege in Britain itself just about half a century ago.[9] In India, however, it was introduced in the middle of the nineteenth century along with industrial products developed through British colonial expansion.

English literary education brought with it new literary models and critical concepts—initially from English, then from the continental languages through the medium of English. They found their way into Indian literature and Indian literary sensibility. To what extent they 'civilized' India is difficult to determine. However, it can be said with certainty that the violent intrusion of alien literary pressure produced many undesirable tendencies in bhasha literature. The most damaging effect of this phenomenon has been a cultural amnesia, which makes the average Indian intellectual incapable of tracing his tradition backwards beyond the mid-nineteenth century. And even when traditions are traced back, the sense of discrimination in that act appears to be largely absent.

Colonialism creates a cultural demoralization. It creates a false sense of shame in the minds of the colonized about their own history and traditions. This pattern of influence has deprived Indian critics, since the period of high colonialism in India, of a healthy relation with the past of the bhasha literatures. Trapped between an undiscriminating revival of the past and an uncritical rejection of it, between Sanskrit poetics and Western critical theory, bhasha criticism today has ceased to be an intellectual 'discourse'. And as a combined result of amnesia and disorientation, bhasha literatures, with literary histories ranging from five to ten centuries, seem to suffer damage from what is obviously an acute crisis in Indian literary criticism.

The Crisis in Literary Criticism

Let us list some of the more prominent symptoms of the crisis facing modern Indian literary criticism. They are: a proliferation of nonproductive commentaries on Western critical positions and thinkers; lack of initiative in modifying critical concepts, tools and criteria in the process of importation; inappropriate use of critical terminology developed in the West, mostly out of its original context, in an undisciplined way and without sufficient justification to use it; lack of scholarly material to support critical pursuits—want of literary biographies, bibliographies, translations of Indian and foreign works, editorial scholarship and relevant critical debate; inability to relate literature to other arts, the media and social and cultural phenomena; uncritical and uninformed attitudes to influence; absence of self-awareness and of tradition; arbitrary and mostly alien critical standards. These failures may not be peculiar to Indian criticism alone. In a neo-colonial world based on exploitative political structures and fascist cultural paradigms, the situation may be just about the same in any culture with material disadvantage. Yet, in the Indian context it assumes a special seriousness because here this situation cripples sensibility cultivated through long-standing and rich literary traditions. The somewhat chaotic list of failures in the field of literary criticism given above does not imply any pre-formulated paradigm of literary criticism. Though a prescription to remedy the situation can easily be hazarded from the list, it is not intended to be prescriptive. It is a summary of a vast range of comments made by numerous bhasha critics in the present century, and merely lists the major themes of self-censure by these critics.

Let us take some examples from Marathi and Gujarati literary criticism. In Marathi the critics who have concerned themselves with the study of literary culture—from the late-nineteenth century critic K. B. Marathe to the contemporary trend-setting novelist

Bhalchandra Nemade—have invariably expressed a bitter sense of disappointment at the lack of proper critical standards. In his essay, 'Concerning the Theatre and the Novel', K. B. Marathe wrote in 1872, "not even one in a hundred of these writers is acquainted with the principles and rules."[10] He then proceeded to formulate the principles of fiction and drama which on his own admission he had borrowed "from the essays of Addison, Scott and Macaulay and . . . from the science of *Alamkara.*" This 'synthesis' did not help Marathi literary criticism much. And so, in 1902, V. K. Rajawade had to ask, while discussing fiction criticism in Marathi: "What kind of wisdom is it that picks up what the foreign writers say about their own literature and applies it verbatim to our own situation?"[11] Eighty years later, Bhalchandra Nemade attributes the state of vitiated literary culture to the mindless fiction criticism in Marathi. In conclusion to a bold and radical revaluation of the novel in Marathi (1980), Nemade states: "Unless the next generation revolutionizes criticism and helps up the sunken literary taste in Marathi the situation is little likely to change."[12]

It needs to be stated at once that there is no dearth of self-congratulatory evaluations of Indian literary criticism. One comes across samples of this type in census-like surveys of Indian literary achievement. In 1965, Manasukhalal Jhaveri credited some fifteen Gujarati critics with "important" contributions—whose standards "are very high", for they "refuse to be satisfied with anything less than perfection."[13] Similar claims were pressed in a survey of Indian literature published in 1986.[14] Sahitya Akademi has given the award for literary excellence eight times so far to critical works in Gujarati. The claims put forward for Marathi achievement in literary criticism by Anant Kanekar in 1965 and Sudhir Rasal in 1980 are no less impressive.[15] Marathi critics also seem to believe, in an inexplicably credulous manner, that Marathi criticism has made an important contribution to the field of general and literary aesthetics.

R. B. Patankar, whose contribution in making recent criticism in Marathi a self-conscious activity is significant, has analyzed the development of Marathi literary criticism since 1940 in an extended article (1984). After explicating the basic principles of aesthetics as a discipline and discussing the logical inconsistencies in the theoretical positions in Marathi criticism, Patankar concludes:

> Now that we know something definite about the nature of aesthetics, it should not be difficult for us to see and evaluate what the Marathi critics and aestheticians have been able to do, and what they have not been able to do. Theories of beauty grow in the womb of art traditions, they begin to become explicit in criticism, and if there is a strong intellectual tradition in the community, they can be formulated with logical rigour. If we resist the temptation of indulging in self-glorification and decide to face reality, we shall have to admit that nothing significant has been done in any of the three fields: aesthetics, criticism and creative writing. It is a saddening realization that this all-round poverty is not a recent phenomenon in Maharashtra; it has been there for decades. That there should spring into existence new aesthetic theories in this atmosphere of poverty seems almost impossible. We will have to come to the same conclusion about the disciplines that are given the general name of 'Humanities'. It is only when society is vibrating with life and vigour in all its aspects, traditions and institutions that the possibility is created for the emergence of new theoretical systems. Great problems arise in such a living society; and the traditions in that society throw up men endowed with genius to tackle them. No such problems have arisen in our art-traditions, and we have not produced great geniuses to tackle them.[16]

Self-denigration is an element of the Marathi sense of humour; and these comments are likely to mislead a credulous outsider into believing in Marathi's 'all-round' critical bankruptcy. But, making due allowance for the element of self-censure, it has to be accepted that Patankar's harsh indictment is in consonance with the reality of the predicament.

A similarly harsh, but necessary, indictment of Gujarati literary criticism is found in Suresh Joshi's contention that the standards applied to literary works in Gujarati are "no literary standards", and that "the inhibition ridden society had turned rubbish into art and art into rubbish"[17] in what he saw as an essentially post-cultural era of literature. His *Chintayami Manasa* (1981) was offered the Sahitya Akademi award for 1983. But Joshi turned it down, claiming that his book was no more than a collection of "stray critical articles". One tends to agree with Suresh Joshi's views, considering that Gujarati criticism has not tackled in any disciplined manner even the most basic problem of critical terminology.

The performance in Indian English criticism is no better. The following comment by S. K. Desai made in the preface to the only anthology (at the time of writing this) of theoretical criticism in English by Indians may demonstrate the state of underdevelopment in this area:

> In India there have been no native schools or movements of criticism . . . no Indian critic has ever been aware of a modern Indian critical tradition. In a sense, the history of the twentieth century Indian critical theory is nothing but a chain of fresh beginnings. Almost every critic seems to have played the role of a pioneer, the needle of whose compass points towards an unrelated critical tradition distant in time (ancient Indian poetics) or in culture-space (Western critical theory). However, there is a common pattern of failures . . . and it is this common pattern of failures that underlines the brief 'tradition' of modern Indian criticism.[18]

It is possible to go on endlessly in this manner enumerating instances of censure of modern Indian criticism. These instances make it very clear that the claims to great achievement made from time to time need not be considered seriously. If bhasha criticism has failed, as argued by the critics cited above, what are the critical grounds on which it fails? It is in answering this question that we are required to describe the essential character of the crisis in bhasha criticism.

One of the first points that is likely to strike even a casual observer of the Indian critical scene is the obsessive interest in theory. Perhaps this interest can be explained with reference to the Indian habit of depending on authority, perhaps it is a genuine capacity to live amidst abstractions. Whatever the reason, it is true that many Indian critics have displayed an uncommon anxiety over the problem of critical theory. Sri Aurobindo (1872–1950)[19] attempted to propose a theory of poetry, while B. S. Mardhekar (1908–56)[20] tried to build a theory of aesthetics on the basis of several Western theories belonging to different ages. Patankar laments that contemporary Indian society is incapable of producing a theory.[21]

Scholars of Sanskrit, like Krishna Rayan (c.1966), Nagendra (c.1983),[22] etc., think that literary theory available in Sanskrit can be applied to modern bhasha literature. On the other hand, the Dalit (protest) and *gramin* (rural) literary heterodoxy finds the present 'formalistic' theory of literature hopelessly outdated. Common to all these critics and their views is the feeling that literary theory in modern India needs major innovations to give it efficacy. No critic finds contemporary critical practice satisfactory; but no critic seems to be hopeful of being able to break through the crisis. The attempts to forge a modern Indian theory have so far depended heavily on existing theories—past (Sanskrit) or present (Western)—often in an indiscriminate manner. For instance, Mardhekar gave as much importance to Aristotle as to Clive Bell. Besides, he also engaged his intellectual energy in correcting Aristotle's theoretical formulations which had very little relevance to literature produced in Mardhekar's rapidly changing Bombay of the Quit India years. The Indian obsession with literary theory can be compared, perhaps, with the Indian obsession with worship of a multitude of godheads. R. B. Patankar frequently refers to the writings of Immanuel Kant, Suresh Joshi to those of Sartre and Maurice Merleau-Ponty, Krishna Rayan to Anandavardhana, and Nagendra to Bharata. All these writers and critics sharing a common present can nonchalantly refer to so many different traditions and past ages. Rarely does one find instances of systematic efforts at understanding contemporary literature on the basis of knowledge embedded in native literary traditions. Among these exceptions one can count Bhalchandra Nemade and his associates in the nativistic school of criticism.[23]

It is not intended to suggest here that literature has no universal values, or that theories of literature are incapable of making cross-cultural transitions. But such transitions need to be filtered through a clear awareness of cultural differences in order to be meaningful and useful. Since bhasha literatures and the various theories forcibly applied to them originate in substantially different cultural contexts, there inevitably exists a gap between them. It would be grossly erroneous to claim, however, that a gap between theory and creative literature did not exist in Sanskrit or Western literature. In fact, commentators of Western criticism like Murrey Krieger read the whole text of Western critical tradition in terms of a succession of such gaps. Krieger (1976) describes the development of Western criticism as a fruit of the incompatibility between the creative writer and the critic, and speaks of "the theoretical impatience that accompanies any major critic as he confronts the complexity of his peculiar experience and its resistance to theoretical universals that are supposed to govern it."[24]

But the incompatibility between literature and literary theory in India has a different character. It presents not only philosophic and aesthetic problems but also problems emanating from the politics of culture. The 'universals' of literary theory used in India from the mid-nineteenth century have been those postulated in Europe, and more recently in the USA as well, and they have the self-assured Eurocentric assumption of being the only 'universals'. An awareness of the rift between theory and creative literature (which is characteristic of but not peculiar to the Indian critical scenario) and the inability to mend the breakdown in critical discourse by creating a new and viable critical theory where the present intellectual vacuum exists, constitute the two basic elements of the crisis in Indian literary criticism of this century.

It is the recognition of this crisis that one finds in the themes and tone of self-censure outlined above. Throughout this century the nature of the crisis, its symptoms in the field of practical criticism, and the Indian critics' sense of exasperation at this cultural condition have remained relatively unchanged. There is little qualitative difference between K. B. Marathe's contention that Marathi writers were ignorant of literary principles (1872) and R. B. Patankar's charge that Marathi critics do not understand the basic issues of literary aesthetics (1984). The specific targets of their attacks and the degree of sophistication in their arguments have changed, not the perception of the crisis.

That India has been in its recent past a mere consumer of Western forms of intellectual substance needs almost no saying. That this importation has had an unhealthy and crippling impact on native creativity in the field of literature and literary criticism, is also a generally recognized fact. The crisis in literary criticism is of as grave a nature as the crises in other fields of intellectual life in India at present. And yet, one likes to ask whether there is not something as much wrong with the contemporary attitudes to Indian culture as there is with the culture itself. The object involved in the crisis is literary criticism. The subject involved in it is the consciousness of the critic who recognizes it as a crisis. In order to investigate the exact site of the crisis, therefore, it would be necessary to review the actual critical practice as well as the nature of the perception of that crisis. This perception, however, is not an isolated awareness of an unrelated phenomenon. It is conditioned by a web of perceptions which define the modern Indian intellectual's self-identity. For instance, it would be possible to conclude on the basis of the comments of self-censure about Indian literary criticism that an unspelt literary idealism is at work behind these comments. The continuous censure presupposes what criticism should be and should not be. An ideal state of criticism in particular and of culture in general seems to be set deep within the Indian consciousness. This idealism remains unspecified so far, mainly because of the uncertain sense of tradition. In order to probe a little further the web of attitudes guiding the general assumptions about literary criticism in the Indian consciousness, it may be useful to discuss in some detail the prevalent attitudes to: i) tradition, ii) Western thought, iii) Sanskrit literary tradition, iv) the impact of colonialism, and v) the bhasha literature. Together, they may add to our understanding of the crisis.

Tradition

The English term 'tradition' is often used in informal or semiforma literary discussions in many Indian languages. The formal use o the concept calls for a term derived from Sanskrit, *parampara,* which is now nativized in the bhashas. Though the two terms are used interchangeably, the underlying conceptual structures are not identical. In fact, they are quite opposite in meaning. The term 'tradition' means, according to the *Oxford English Dictionary,* "handing down, or being handed down", or more specifically, "the body of experience and usages of any branch or school of art or literature, handed down by predecessors and generally followed". *Parampara,* a compound of *param* and *para,* means "distant, further, enemy, afterwards, beyond, other, stranger, next, yonder, belonging to the other side, second, far off", or more specifically, "something that is very conspicuous and very remote, almost on the other shore of the current of time, inaccessible."[25]

In the sense of *parampara,* the way to continue tradition is to increase its longevity. The characteristic Indian sense of pride in family and community tradition is of this type. Useful or not, *parampara* must be of ancient origin, and must be perpetuated by continuous family succession. This sense of tradition as *parampara* came in direct collision with the Western sense of tradition as *useful* conventions when Lord Dalhousie (Governor-General of India from 1848 to 1856) introduced the Doctrine of Lapse. This Doctrine enabled Dalhousie, within specific political contexts, to take possession of the Hindu states whose rulers had failed in providing direct heirs. Under ordinary circumstances these rulers would have adopted a person to succeed to the throne, who then could continue the family *parampara.* It would be interesting to speculate whether this collision of values was in any way directly responsible for the military conflict of 1857.

The Western concepts of tradition and culture, interrelated through the common underlying idea of 'growth', have influenced Indian literary sensibility to a great extent;[26] and since 1857 (also the year in which the first three English-type Universities were founded in India) the Western and Sanskrit concepts of tradition have clashed within the Indian consciousness. The entire debate between *sanatana* (of ancient origin) and *nutana* (of modern origin), which characterized late-nineteenth and early-twentieth century cultural life in India, indicates the persistence of this clash.

Neither concept seems to have scored a final victory. That is why in discussions related to bhasha criticism, 'tradition' is sometimes used to mean the pre-British heritage and at other times to mean the new beginnings made during the British period. In other words the meaning of the concept 'tradition' in contemporary bhasha usage wavers between conformity and change.

The uncertainty of meaning attributed to the concept of tradition, the clash between the traditional and the modern associations of significance related to the concept, and the consequent ambivalence, are important constituents of modern Indian sensibility. However, one should be aware of the dangers involved in the simplification of this process. The view that modern Indian sensibility is reared on both traditions appears uncontroversial in the light of the known cultural traits of Indian history: eclecticism, multilingualism, multiculturalism, etc. However, the simple dialectical opposition between 'Indian' and 'Western' is too neat to indicate that there is also a conflict and an opposition within the category 'Indian'—between the cultural forces associated with Sanskrit and those associated with the bhasha.

The traditional sense of *parampara* in India contains two essential components: *Marg*—the metropolitan or mainstream tradition, and *Deshi*—regional and subcultural traditions. Indian culture has a very long history of exchange and tension between the two. It would be appropriate to maintain that the addition to this relationship of a 'Western' intellectual tradition extended the relationship, without altering it radically. Thus, the modern Indian sense of 'tradition' should be described as a tripartite relationship involving *deshi-parampara, marga-parampara* and Western tradition, each of which conflicts and collaborates with the remaining two in a variety of ways.

At the time the bhashas emerged from Middle Indo-Aryan and Tamil, the concepts related to time, language and self underwent fundamental changes. In a cultural movement of turning away from classical formalism, the bhashas humanized these concepts. The process brought about a conflict between the cosmic and the human, the metaphysical and the aesthetic, and the metropolitan and the vulgar. It was a conflict that involved a clash between an idealistic world view and a pragmatic world view.

Conflict between tradition and change, therefore, was not an entirely novel phenomenon when British rule brought Western intellectual traditions to India. The cultural dialectic produced by the juxtaposition of Indian tradition and Western tradition was not entirely unforeseen. It follows, therefore, that Indian culture was better prepared for absorbing the alien impact than is generally acknowledged. This perspective may also help to explain the complex patterns of collaboration and confrontation in India's relationship with the culture that came with British rule.[27] A sharp, diametric opposition of a 'Western–Indian' type is, therefore, perhaps more imaginary than real.

The work of sociologists like M. N. Srinivas (1966), Milton Singer (1971) and Edward Shils (1961) has established that the process of cultural osmosis in Indian society is highly complex.[28] Singer's study of a community in Madras, in particular, shows that alien cultural features are accepted by Indian society after a careful process of selection, and by giving these features a traditional appearance. Singer's findings show that there is an inherent talent in Indian society for controlling alien influences and manipulating them to its advantage. In other words, traditional Indian culture shows a remarkable talent for adjusting to new situations on its own terms. The process of such adjustment, or manipulation, does not necessarily involve a clash. It follows, then, that the current debate about tradition versus modernity, which had also occupied much of nineteenth century intellectual life in India, displays but a partial understanding of the processes of social change in the country. The bipolar conflict is perhaps a consequence of the faulty perception of cultural relations, a perception shaped during the colonial period.[29] It is now inherited by literary criticism. The discussion about cultural opposition—Indian against Western—in the field of literary criticism is often presented in a highly theatrical manner, making the whole exercise futile and misleading.

Indian critics have frequently tried to juxtapose the conceptual patterns implicit in Sanskrit poetics with those in Western critical theories (Bharata–Aristotle: Kantak, 1984; *Hasya*–Meredith: G.

S. Amur, 1976; *Dhvani*–T. S. Eliot: Krishna Rayan, 1965; *Karuna*–Tragedy: R. B. Patankar, 1967, etc.).[30] The assumption in these juxtapositions is that the contemporary Indian critic is at the cross-roads, and must consciously choose his literary value-scale within the structure of binary opposition. For instance, V. Y. Kantak's brilliant essay on the Indian dramatic mode as presented in the *Natyashasastra* considers Bharata's theory in the light of Aristotle's theory of drama:

> To try to probe the basic conceptual patterns implicit in *Bharata Natyashastra* the Aristotelian Poetic is a convenient starting point—a sort of jumping off plank for a risky dive into the *Natyashastra's* dark serene waters. For one thing, the conceptual tools we use today are themselves derived from Western tradition of thought largely initiated by Plato and Aristotle. Again, the Aristotelian Poetic offers a kind of model—in many ways a sharply contrasting formulation in reference to which those features that are peculiar to the *Natyasastra* view could be set off and identified.[31]

With such clarity and lucidity, the critic conducts us through the 'dark, serene waters' of Sanskrit dramatics, and leaves us to answer the question: "Could it be... that our theatre is shuffling between Aristotle and Bharata and is at the crossroads?"

The manner in which Kantak poses the alternatives, Bharata and Aristotle, and suggests this binary opposition as the essence of the predicament of Indian theatre, is closely reminiscent of the nineteenth-century debate about education in which Sanskrit and English were presented as the only alternatives. The same assumption is at the base of the revivalistic trend and the Westernizing trend in modern Indian criticism. These two trends, which are the two most predominant trends in contemporary criticism, assume that critics and writers in bhasha literatures have easy access to Western and Sanskrit traditions of thought.

Modern Indian Intellectuals and Western Thought

There is a misconception that modern Indian intellectuals have access to Western traditions of thought as a consequence of British education, which was introduced in India in the nineteenth century. There is no doubt that British education delivered knowledge of enormous value, and made familiar many thoughts developed in Europe. But the system did not encourage exchange between traditional Indian knowledge and modern European knowledge, or a synthesis between the two, or even a meaningful participation by Indian intellectuals in European traditions. One of the greatest intellectual stimulations to European scholars during the colonial period came with the discovery of Sanskrit and other Oriental languages. And it was accepted by most of them that Sanskrit had produced a great literature. Yet, when Europe thought of extending its literary horizons in the direction of comparative literature, it scrupulously avoided including Oriental literatures within the scope of the new discipline. Thus, for instance, when Matthew Arnold advocated a comparative perspective, he wished to extend it merely to Continental literatures.[32] Given the colonial context, it was natural that Europe decided to seal off Indian literature with the label 'Orientalism'[33] or 'Indology' so that it would not contaminate the purer and culturally superior European literature!

The aim of the British educators of India was purely pragmatic.[34] The aim was not to 'educate' Indians so that they became cultural equals of the British. It was to educate Indians just enough to make them 'useful' to the empire. However, the culturally demoralized Indian intellectuals were willing to accept British culture as superior to the decadent Indian culture, and so had no difficulty in embracing the 'fairness' of British education, administration and law. This acceptance led to the belief that European culture was an 'open system', and that participation in it on a basis of mutual exchange was possible if Indian intellectuals met the minimum requirement of excellence. This wishful idea of participation and exchange needs no countering in the light of the continuing and one-sided dependence on Western ideas available to India through the English language.

The continued acceptance of ideas from the West cannot be fully attributed to the intrinsic worth of those ideas. Indians did not start accepting the cultural superiority of Western knowledge *after* examining the intrinsic worth of that knowledge. On the contrary, they started studying Western ideas *because* they had already accepted the superiority of British culture (as much as it was reflected in the lifestyle of the plundering colonial official). The military and technological superiority of the British had already been accepted, before the English language and British-style education were introduced in India. It is not surprising, therefore, that many Bengali intellectuals in the late-eighteenth and early-nineteenth centuries pleaded in favour of education through English. Offering India the opportunity to have it was one of the last, not one of the first, acts in securing cultural colonization. An examination of various statements related to the education debate would reveal that the intention to introduce English education in India was not so much to 'civilize' India, as to institutionalize the British view that India was in a bad state of civilization, and to salvage from it some obedient Indians to help run the empire.

Given the exploitative nature of colonial rule, it was natural that the English language should have played an important role in the politically motivated structuring of the fields of knowledge. It is a known socio-linguistic phenomenon that the language variety of a politically dominant minority is treated as superior by the politically dominated majority. Similarly, the 'knowledge'—which includes cultural and technological developments, the world view, means of controlling nature, etc.—of a ruling minority, tends to be accepted as superior by the majority, even when the kind of knowledge involved is utterly irrelevant to its own needs. It was this kind of political framing of values that Indian literary sensibility had to pass through during the colonial period.

Intellectual traditions are culture-bound. They come into existence because of the specific needs of the society and the period that give them birth. When these traditions are transplanted, they tend to lose their authenticity and even their utility. Sudhir Kakar has argued, in his psychoanalytical study of childhood and society in India,[35] that many Western paradigms of psychology believed to be universal in application need careful scrutiny and adaptation before they are used in a non-Western cultural context. He clearly shows how different the nature of childhood and upbringing in India is when compared to childhood and upbringing in the West, and establishes the need for a culture-specific psychology:

> Because I have lived, worked and been trained in Europe and the United States as well as in India, these 'other' cultures with which I compare India are mainly those of the West. I have, however, been necessarily mindful of the autonomy of each society. It has not been my purpose to evaluate one society, whether Indian or Western, in terms of the other. I have not interpreted a particular psychological trait in members of one society as a neurotic symptom or as an unfortunate deviation from some universal norm incorporated only by the other. I have proceeded, rather, on the assumption that both societies offer distinctive solutions to universal dilemmas, that both (in secular psychological terminology) have specific normative conceptions of what constitutes the 'healthy' personality and of how social relations should be organized to achieve this elusive goal.[36]

What Kakar says about psychology is, by the same logic, also applicable to literary criticism. And so I further quote his explanation:

> The tenets of ego psychology and psychotherapy in the West, for instance, postulate a highly complex personality which constantly works to create a common solution for the strivings of all its psychic sub-structures, a process which demands a maximum of synthesizing and integrating activity on the part of the ego. In India, on the other hand, the ideal of psychological wholeness or 'maturity' . . . is quite compatible with an ego which is relatively passive and less differentiated. Any ideal of psychological maturity which presumes to translate experiences and practices in one society into universal norms for others should give us pause. I am reminded of the Indian fable of six blind men and an elephant in which one man, after touching the animal's tail, sought to impose on the others his absolute conviction that the elephant was a snake.[37]

This warning should be equally, or even more, valid for literary criticism which has to deal with more tightly organized sets of signs and symbols than psychoanalysis does.

During the colonial period a vast number of literary and critical concepts were accepted by Indian writers and critics, and were assimilated in the educational process, as inherently superior concepts. Once introduced into the educational process, particularly in India where the system is based on a near-blind acceptance of authority, they get transfused from generation to generation. In reality, however, these concepts may simply have been Eurocentric. An instructive example of this damaging process is the concept of epic poetry. The genre is as old in India as it is in Europe. In India it has been more fortunate in finding able theoreticians from the seventh century Dandin to the eleventh century Bhoja who studied in detail its formal and thematic structures. The *Kavyadarsha* and *Shringaraprakasha* are admirable theoretical formulations on epic.[38]

The epic developed through Sanskrit as well the bhashas, and evolved many sub-genres such as *adikavya* (literary epic—the *Ramayana), mahakavya* (oral epic—the *Mahabharata), sargabandha* (modern epic during the classical period—the *Raghuvamsha), champu* (long narrative in mixed verse and prose), *akhyana* (character-based narrative), and other regional varieties of heroic narrative of epic magnitude. English education brought with it the epics of Milton, and European epics in English translation. And with these works came the European epic criticism, meagre in comparison with the epic criticism in India, but in a position of advantage under the benediction of colonial education. Familiarity with the European epics was in itself an enriching experience for Indian literature; but European criticism of the epic form of poetry was not necessarily in agreement with the native expectations of an epic. Had structuralism been the reigning critical fashion during the British colonial period, perhaps Dandin's fine concept of *sargabandha*, with an intricate structure defining its theme, would have got a second lease of life. But due to the influence of the insufficiently developed epic criticism of England, Indian critics gradually became less sure of what they had to say of the Indian epics.

The process of intellectual importation in India created an imbalance in cultural trade as well as a rift between knowledge and reality. The blind acceptance of modes of knowledge shaped in a distant island has resulted in a wide variance between life as it is lived and the modes of perception used to study it. Literary criticism is no exception to this anomaly. The concept of modernism offers a good example to illustrate it. 'Modernism', a term used to refer to a more or less specific period of European literature and culture, has acquired stable—though varying, and sometimes conflicting—meaning in Europe. Thus Kafka, Thomas Mann, James Joyce, Andre Gide, and Ernest Hemingway, writers with different individual styles of writing, can all be described as essentially modernist writers. In Indian literature the influence of European modernism has created literary movements which at times can be radically different in character from European modernism. Indian literary criticism, however, does not recognize the need to distinguish between European modernism and its Indian avatar. Since the cross-cultural metamorphosis is not taken into account by literary criticism in India, its expectations from literature are guided by Western fashions. How can an Indian critic brought up on the Derridan sense of differance do justice to literature produced in a society which has never experienced the anxiety resulting from logocentricism?

Clearly enough, colonial and postcolonial bhasha criticism has accepted the hierarchic structure of knowledge created during the colonial period for political expediency. Once created, this structure becomes self-supportive. It induces the colonized to follow the path of conformity. It leads the colonizer, on the other hand, to view any departure from his value system as taboo or, worse still, as an anthropological curiosity. As time passes, the conformist colonized subject also starts looking at his own culture without experiencing a sense of organic relationship with it. In 1826 James Mill wrote the following comments in his *History of British India:*

> [The *Ramayana* and the *Mahabharata*] describe a series of actions in which a number of men and gods are jointly engaged. These fictions are not only more extravagant, and unnatural, less correspondent with the physical and

> moral laws of the universe, but are less ingenious, more monstrous, and have less of any thing that can engage the affection, awaken sympathy, or excite admiration, reverence, or terror, than the poems of any other, even the rudest people with whom our knowledge of the globe has yet brought us acquainted. They are excessively prolix and insipid. They are often, through long passages, trifling and childish to a degree, which those acquainted with only European poetry can hardly conceive. Of the style in which they are composed it is far from too much to say, that all the vices which characterise the style of rude nations, and particularly those of Asia, they exhibit in perfection. Inflation; metaphors perpetual, and these the most violent and strained, often the most unnatural and ridiculous; obscurity; tautology; repetition; verbosity; confusion; incoherence; distinguish the Mahabharat and Ramayan.[39]

It was but natural that Mill, as an agent of the Empire building process, should maintain such ill-founded views. But if, as a consequence of the influence of the colonial bias, an Indian critic finds himself out of sympathy with the past of Indian literature, the situation needs a radical cure.

The anthropological tone, which, when not aided by compassion reduces living cultures to merely a set of analyzable objects, is overwhelmingly present in most Western responses to India. That tone is a colonial legacy, and can be discerned even in the best intentioned and apparently complimentary statements such as the following one by the formalist critic Susan Langer. Commenting on the *rasa* theory of drama in her monumental book *Feeling and Form* (1953), Langer writes:

> The Hindu critics understand very much better than their Western colleagues the various aspects of emotion in the theatre, which our writers banefully confuse . . .[40]

Does Langer want to refer to Bharata of the fourth century? Or does she want to refer to Abhinavagupta of the eleventh century? And to which specific theory of the theatre does she want to allude? The Hindu critics had names, had specific relations with a dynamic history of one and a half thousand years of literary theory, and they belonged to specific stages in the development of that theory. Langer overlooks all these contextual references, and presents a flat and ahistorical image of 'the Hindu critics'. Such ahistorical images of India created by the West in turn influence India's self-perception.

The fact that fields of knowledge have been politically stratified does not, by itself, create much of a problem in modern Indian criticism. The crisis is created, and perhaps made catastrophic, by the self-perception of modern India through Western registers of cultural thought. Yet, as said before, the idea that Indian intellectuals have 'access' to Western traditions of thought is a romantic delusion. It should be interesting for students of modern Indian culture to speculate if this crisis created by the historical situation is not in some profound way related to the immense popularity of the concept of platonic love in modern India.

Ashis Nandy (1983) has used the metaphor of a man–woman relationship to explain the psychology of colonial confrontation.[41] According to him, in a colonial situation, the colonized culture (represented as female) tries to imitate the colonizing culture (represented as male), and ends up by becoming neither (represented as androgynous). Nandy's metaphor explains to some extent the intellectual 'impotency' of the modern Indian intellectual, particularly in the area of literary criticism. It is not necessary to add that the tendency to imitate Western models is the chief reason for the predicament. Nandy's discussion brings out the non-productive nature of the colonial cultural relationship. What that relationship produces at all is false self-images of the colonized as well as the colonizer: In harbouring the illusion of access to Western thought, the Indian intellectual seeks to endorse his self-image created by the colonial rule, and, thereby, chooses self-deception. Western traditions of thought are not inaccessible in descriptive terms, or in principle; but they remain so in practice, owing to the unequal partnership and the one-sided relationship which survive as colonial legacies.

The Sanskrit play by Kalidasa (376–454?), *Abhijnana-shakuntalam,* which inaugurated the modern phase of the cultural relationship between India and the West through Sir William Jones's translation of it into English (1789), may provide us with an effective metaphor to describe the complexity of India's self-deception. King Dushyanta, the hero of the play, meets Shakuntala while he is on a hunting expedition *(mrigaya)*, and marries her secretly. This could be read as an archetypal representation of modern colonization, since it centres round an exploitative relationship. He returns to his kingdom, promising to send for her later—a promise he does not keep. When Shakuntala arrives in his court, on her own initiative, he fails to recognize her; and she fails to prove her identity, having lost the signet ring given to her by Dushyanta. Thus, Shakuntala is neither accepted by her husband, nor can she go back to her (foster) father. She has lost the sign of her identity (the ring), the cultural context that gave her significance (her father's hermitage), and the possibility of any relationship. But most important of all, she has lost the right to share a universe of discourse. One may add to this bald summary that Dushyanta's failure to recognize Shakuntala springs from a curse that makes him lose his memory temporarily. The colonial nature of the initial encounter, the loss of memory and discourse are the elements in the plot of this play that should make it an interesting text for modern analysis. One could speculate why Sir William Jones chose this play, rather than some other, like Shudraka's *Mrichhakatika* (a realistic comedy in which the heroine is a strong and active character), to present India's image to the western world. The West, as well as Westernized Indians, have so far closely collaborated in preserving that image in its most static form. Meanwhile life and literature have moved ahead.

Modern India and the Sanskrit Tradition

The links between modern Indian literature and Sanskrit literary traditions are tenuous. Among the causes responsible for their being so are: i) the inner weakness of Sanskrit literary tradition, ii) repeated waves of foreign influence and colonial rule that provided non-Sanskrit literature with official patronage, iii) continuous social transformation and growing linguistic heterodoxy, and iv) centuries of deliberate neglect. Sanskrit literary and critical traditions are accessible to the modern intellectual only as imaginary possessions. The modern Indian critic *can* say that India *had* a glorious tradition of literary criticism a thousand years ago. But, having said this, he is unable to use this tradition as a living tradition which shares a frame of reference within which his normal intellectual activity takes place. In other words, the possibility of projecting the past into the present, and often projecting the present into the past, still exists for modern Indian intellectuals, but no organic connection exists between the past and the present.

In an excellently documented study of Indian attitudes to the past, Madhav Deshpande (c.1979) has shown that imagining an archaic benefaction for things of recent origin is an essential part of the Indian epistemology of time. This argument is supported by sociological researches in recent years by Milton Singer, to which a reference was made earlier. The essence of Deshpande's argument lies in the following passage:

> The most important part of this hierarchy of authority is the assumption of lost Vedic texts and law-texts to practices of later times which are not contrary to the older authority. This presents to us very different conception of history. A modern researcher looks at the Vedic texts and says that certain things existed in Vedic times since they are mentioned in Vedic texts. However, as far as the things which exist now and are not mentioned in the Vedic texts are concerned, a modern historian cannot say that those things also existed in Vedic times. However, the classical Indian tradition used a device like 'the benefit of doubt' to project the present in the past. The Vedic Aryans were supposed to have behaved exactly like their mediaeval and modern Indian successors. Justification for the present was sought in the past, but in this process, often an imaginary past was built to justify a concrete present.[42]

This appears to be a fairly accurate description of the general Indian attitude to history and time, though it may be possible to show several variations on it in different periods and among different religious groups and sects. In the field of literary criticism the tendency to provide every new technique with an archaic past is seen actively at work in twentieth century India. During the present century Indian criticism has witnessed innumerable attempts to prove the greatness of Sanskrit criticism by locating in it thoughts and theories which European critics have been able to think only in modern times. Among those who have made such attempts are some of India's most gifted critics: Ananda K. Coomaraswamy (1877–1947), G. S. Amur (c.1976), Krishna Rayan (1966) and K. Krishnamoorthy (1969). However, since the past is creatively interpreted, or intentionally falsified, it does not correspond with the past as it really was. That past has ceased to be a part of the present perception of the past. The relation with it is romantic, and thrives on fantasy.

On the other hand, the misconception about the complete inertia of Sanskrit intellectual tradition, poetics included, is an Indological product. There is, of course, no possibility whatsoever of that tradition being recycled into a system of living and vigorous thought. But, at the same time, it is necessary to accept that it is historically inaccurate to maintain with Indology that Sanskrit intellectual traditions were abstract and static suspensions in Oriental cultural space. It was such a view that Sir William Jones had intended to present in his famous lectures on Hindu culture. In a 'Discourse' delivered before the Asiatic Society at Calcutta in 1786, Jones announced that in his project of ransacking Indian history he would go to remote antiquity but restrict his researches up to the eleventh century.[43] He thus introduced a scholarly breach between ancient Indian culture and mediaeval Indian culture. After Jones, every Indological enterprise has invariably sought to make this historical distinction by which ancient India is isolated as the repository of a 'pure' cultural condition of Hinduism.[44]

The Indological view of India was expressed through scholarly works; but the perspective it presented had other ingredients in it than mere disinterested scholarship. It had received more from its immediate political and social context than it was prepared to show. V. G. Kiernan and Edward Said have demonstrated that even the apparently non-political academic projects related to the Orient had, during the colonial period, strong political motives.[45] Western responses to India display in ample degree a sense of bewilderment while encountering a culture like India's. When young Macaulay arrived in Calcutta he felt that the book in his hand was fast turning into a disintegrating object.[46] A century later, Thomas Mann in his *Death in Venice* depicts the Gangetic plains crowded with tigers!

The sense of bewilderment, the subsequent lack of organized comprehension, and the tendency to project the exotic Orient as panacea for Europe's spiritual problems (as in T.S. Eliot's simple use of '*Shanti*' to conclude his *Wasteland),* are the other constituents in Europe's responses to India.

European scholars have done remarkable work in the areas of Indian history and culture. And it is true that modern Indian scholarship owes a debt of gratitude to Indology. Yet, the attitude to history implicit in Indological works ranging from Halhed's *Grammar of Bengali* (1780) to Max Muller's *India: What Can It Teach Us?* (1882), considers the Indian heritage as a once glorious but now decadent force. It refuses to see any connection between ancient India and modern India, and tends to study cultural phenomena as "museum pieces removed from the current of history. It romanticizes the past, and views it from an entirely ahistorical perspective. Such a perspective, because it was presented by European scholars, has seriously impaired India's own attitude to its past. A similar attitude is implied in Europe's non-scholarly response to India, from Goethe's spontaneous reception of Kalidasa's *Shakuntala* (in translation, 1791) to Arthur Koestler's disenchantment with yoga *(Lotus and Robot,* 1967—banned in India).

What is difficult to understand is how India's self-knowledge was so readily and radically affected by an alien intellectual influence. Apparently, Indology ought not to have been in a position to exert so powerful an influence, for in the debate on education the Indologists (known at that time as the Orientalists) had lost to the Anglicists. The official education policy of the British in India encouraged Anglicism in preference to Orientalism. Therefore the pressure to imitate Indological attitudes was not so powerful. It came, however, from within Indian culture. Acceptance of alien influences is dictated by the inner dynamics of a culture as much as it is guided by forces operating on it from outside. As such, not everything British was accepted by India. For instance, though the British military organization and cricket were accepted from the British, their music and Christian religion were not accepted. Acceptance of the Indological perspective of history was made possible, therefore, by some element within Indian culture itself.

The attitude that the past was all glory in contrast to the stark present fitted well the traditional Indian view of time progression as maintained by the Samkhya school of Indian philosophy.[47] Samkhya considers human evolution as a movement from the Golden Age to an age of disintegration, from *satyayuga* to *kaliyuga*. That this view was a mere fantasy, that Indian traditions had not weakened much when Indology made its first appearance, is ironically evident in the fact that Indology was easily assimilated into the Indian tradition, the tradition of believing in a steady cultural decline. Nonetheless, the acceptance of an eccentric view of Indian history by a society which in fact had been moving away from its old idealistic world view to a pragmatic world view created a further inflection in its self-image.

I have argued so far that modern Indian critics delude themselves into believing that they have access to Western traditions of thought, whereas in reality what they have is but a two-dimensional 'virtual' relationship with those traditions. The relationship is both hierarchic (in which the Indian critics have to take a lower place) as well as one-sided. On the other hand, their links with the Sanskrit intellectual heritage are weak; but while they believe in its complete decline, they may be continuing some of it unknowingly. A diagram of these two attitudes is given below.

The diagram will suggest that though the tendency to draw on Western criticism and Sanskrit poetics, together or separately, is widespread at present, it does not exhaust the possibilities of modern Indian criticism. The diagram indicates a general distribution of trends in the field of literary criticism with respect to the sense of tradition. Since the terms 'Sanskritization' and 'Westernization' have been used here, it is necessary to clarify that they are *not* used in the sense given them by the sociologist M. N.

Srinivas.[48] In Srinivas's use 'Sanskritization' refers to the social mobility created by internal forces in Indian society, and 'Westernization' refers to that created by external forces. These sociological connotations have been avoided here. In the context of literary criticism 'Sanskritization' should indicate the tendency to return to, or to revive, Sanskrit poetics, and 'Westernization' should mean the tendency to imitate, or to draw upon, Western criticism.

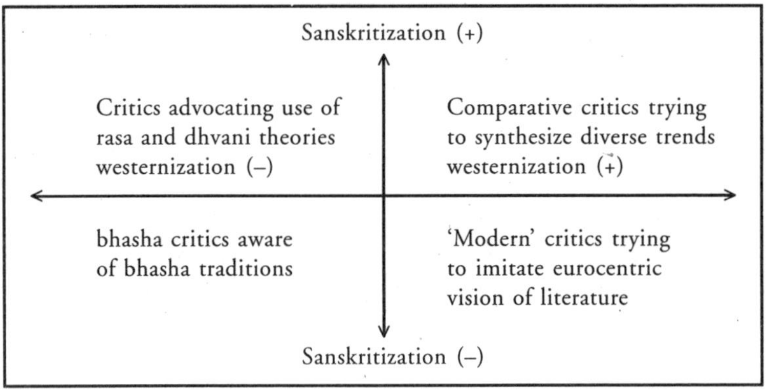

The diagram shows that there is a section of Indian critics which believes that it is possible to meet the present literary-critical needs by following exclusively either Western criticism or Sanskrit criticism. There is another section which believes that it is possible to meet the needs by combining the two trends. Most of the influential scholarly work seems to point in the direction of the last choice, that of 'synthesizing' West and East, and is exemplified in *Indianism and the Indian Synthesis* (1962) by Suniti Kumar Chatterjee, *The Hindu Society at Crossroads* (1961) by K. M. Panikkar and *Common Indian Poetics* (1984) edited by C. D. Narasimhaiah. Ananda Coomaraswamy's *The Dance of Shiva* (1948) is, of course, the classic example of the tortuous logic in such a 'synthetic' argument. I have argued that it is unprofitable for Indian critics to relate themselves to either the Western or the Sanskrit tradition of criticism, or to any kind of combination of the two. These wild cravings for distant traditions need to be moderated by an awareness of the bhasha traditions; critics should learn to confine themselves to traditions closer at hand if criticism is to break through the present crisis.

The Colonial Impact

One of the interesting paradoxes in modern India's self-awareness is that it accepts Western intellectual influence as a useful impetus to modernization of Indian culture, but rejects Western colonialism as pernicious. It is worth speculating whether there was nothing common between the culture that produced English literature and the culture that produced the colonial plunderers. Apparently, of course, there is nothing that connects figures like Lord Dalhousie and Lord Tennyson, or Rowlatt (famous for his draconian attitude towards the Indian press) and Ruskin. But at a deeper level there must be some connection in the cultures that produced them.[49] In the Indian imagination, however, the two are completely separated. Western creative literature, and creative expression in general, is seen as progressive, liberal and 'good'; the political attitudes are seen as imperialistic and 'evil'. Correspondingly, all progressive developments in Indian literature are attributed to the influence of Western literature, and all failures are attributed to the colonial influence. That this differentiation is arbitrary is pointed out by M. D. Hatkananglekar in a recent study (1986) of the Western influence on Marathi literature from 1950 to 1975.[50]

Hatkananglekar opens his argument by referring to the hopes expressed by B. S. Mardhekar, the central figure in twentieth century Marathi poetry, about Marathi's literary development. In 1941, Mardhekar had said, provocatively, that self-reliance of Marathi literature could not be thought of before it imbibed enough from Western literature. Hatkananglekar alludes to this sentiment of Mardhekar expressed half a century ago, and shows its futility by analyzing the consequences of the Western impact on Marathi literature. He maintains that the impact has been so intimidating that Marathi literature has become incapable of transforming it creatively. He finds that the influence hinders its creative use. His study supports my observation that it is erroneous to imagine a distinction between Western influence and the colonial impact. It is wrong to regard the two as opposites.

Macaulay's Minute on Education (1835) offers a classic case of the argument which combines advocacy of Western literary influence on the Indian sensibility with advocacy of colonial coercion. While it is true that the Minute has become a convenient target for any attack on cultural colonization (and such attacks are often merely sensational), it is still worth quoting from it to see the combination of piety and vulgarity in it:

> I am quite ready to take the Oriental learning at the valuation of the Orientalists themselves. I have never found one among them who could deny that a single shelf of a good European library was worth the whole native -literature of India and Arabia . . . I have certainly never met with any Orientalist who ventured to maintain that the Arabic and Sanscrit poetry could be compared to that of the great European nations. But when we pass from works of imagination to works in which facts are recorded, the superiority of the Europeans becomes absolutely immeasurable. It is, I believe, no exaggeration to say that all the historical information which has been collected from all books written in the Sanscrit language is less valuable than what may be found in the most paltry abridgement used at preparatory school in England. In every branch of physical or moral philosophy, the relative position of the two nations is nearly the same . . . It is said that Sanscrit and Arabic are the languages in which the sacred books of a hundred millions of people are written, and that they are, on that account entitled to peculiar encouragement. Assuredly, it is the duty of the British Government in India to be not only tolerant, but neutral on all religious questions. But to encourage the study of a literature admitted to be of small intrinsic value, only because that literature includes the most serious errors on the most important subjects, is a course hardly reconcileable with reason, with morality, or even with that neutrality which ought, as we shall agree, to be sacredly preserved. It is confessed that a language is barren of useful knowledge. We are to teach it because it is fruitful of monstrous superstitions . . . I would at once stop the printing of Arabic and Sanscrit books, I would abolish the Madrassa and the Sanscrit college at Calcutta.[51]

The attitude towards Indian literature and culture explicit in these statements has been too frequently commented upon. With minor variations, it makes its appearance throughout the colonial period. Just as it shaped the British policy of education in India, it also shaped the Western view of Indian literature. In spite of British contact with India for nearly two centuries, the impression about Indian literature, even among well-educated Britishers, is that Indian literature is written mainly in English! The vulgarity of views about Indian literature in Macaulay's colonial perspective is a common element in the modern (and 'progressive') West's general response to India. In other words, the colonizing West and the creative West have many interior connections.

Historians of modern India have discussed in detail the development of the British education system in India, and have studied its post-independence transformations and subversions. A student of modern Indian culture, therefore, is well acquainted with the physical aspects of this high cultural drama. The works particularly by Arthur Mayhew (1926), J. P. Naik (1965) and R. K. Mookherjee (1967)[52] provide a clear perspective on the Indian tradition of education, the debate between Orientalists and Anglicists, the gradual takeover of education by the British government in India from its traditional custodians and Christian missionaries, the disproportionate emphasis on insular British standards, the encouragement given to adopting the facile aspects of English social manners, and a continuous demoralization of native social and literary values. What has not received enough attention so far, however, is the nature of the cross-cultural transformation of the so-called 'British education' after it was introduced in India, or even during the process of introduction itself. That the system of education introduced by the colonial British was by no means a monolith is generally overlooked by its critics. The 'system' was introduced in small portions, after much hesitation on the part of the rulers; and all that was introduced under its name was not of one vintage. The sociology of education on the 'Anglo-Indian' side had diverse cultural and ideological strands. Some of those who taught in India were Irish, others Scottish, and some others Australian, though Indians themselves outnumbered foreigners in teaching. Educational institutions were run by a variety of religious denominations, often at cross-purposes with the colonial government. On the Indian side, the response to the 'system' was by no means uniform. It differed from region to region, and from community to community. Similarly, the impact of this new education was not felt equally all over the subcontinent. The divide in the impact can be seen not only in the obvious terms of 'main centres' and 'hinterlands', but also in terms of individual bhasha cultures. Besides, the education given to India was not exactly the education given in the schools and universities in Britain at that time. This last point needs some elaboration.

During the initial phases of colonial rule the British believed they needed to change the prevalent modes of education for administrative purposes. It is worth noting that while in Bengal there was considerable Indian support for the new policy, in Maharashtra the idea of education through English was not well received. Even an advocate of elitist education like Sir Thomas Munro (1761–1827) had to concede, in his Minute on Education (1826), that the standard of schools in the Bombay area was "higher than in most European countries at no very distant date".[53] He had counted 12,498 such schools imparting education through Marathi and Gujarati, an average of one school for every 500 people. Hence, he decided not to recommend "any interference whatever in the native school. Mountstuart Elphinstone (1779–1859), unlike Munro, was an advocate of education through the mother tongue.

So long as education in British India was treated as a state affair and was not centralized, Elphinstone had enough freedom to implement his ideas in the Bombay presidency. So, in spite of opposition from his own Council, and indifference from the East India Company's Board of Directors, Elphinstone decided to emphasize primary education as a priority. He also made the use of the regional language for education an important part of his policy. His views, and the willing reception of those views in the Bombay region, made Lord Auckland modify (1839) Macaulay's policy (1835) in favour of vernacular education. Similarly, the Rev. J. Wilson, who became Vice Chancellor of Bombay University in 1868, was a consistent champion of education through people's languages. The attitude that the colonial administration adopted in the Bombay region was a result of its knowledge, of the region and of the sentiment of people in it.

As against Maharashtra, Bengal was a willing participant in the Anglicization of education. There, the colonial administrators as well as the 'intellectuals', described by the term *bhadraloka* (gentlemen),[54] advocated the use of the English medium in schools and colleges. The Hindu College, with which the names of David Hare (1775–1842), Henry Derozio (1810–34) and Rammohun Roy (1772–1833) are associated, was established in 1817. By 1842, the year in which its founder, David Hare, died, it had enlisted, we are told, as many as 10,000 students for degree courses.[55]

In considering the influence of the colonial education system in India it is necessary to accept that the system suggested by Macaulay, and modified several times by his successors, was far from being an exact replica of the education system in Britain during the corresponding period. It was a system devised by administrators, and conditioned by a 'cantonment psychology', which had its own unique tensions, cross-currents and motivations. Moreover, Indian culture during the nineteenth century was not 'static', though that is the image of the period generally accepted.[56]

It is difficult to see how Indian society in the nineteenth century could be static if it had moved from the mediaeval political ideology of Raghobadada Peshwa (late eighteenth century) to the nationalistic philosophy of the Indian National Congress (founded in 1885). In fact, it would be quite appropriate to consider nineteenth century Indian culture as a dynamic culture, which witnessed and survived unprecedented cultural catastrophes, and underwent an amazing metamorphosis in the process. Therefore, it would be reasonable to assume that Macaulay's system did not directly impose undiluted British culture upon India. The framework within which the influence was exerted was created by regional and social conditions, and by specific economic realities. The whole process had a highly complex interface determined by conflicting traits and political motives of both the colonized and the colonizers.

The difficulty in understanding the nature of the colonial impact arises from the absence of appropriate paradigms for studying cross-cultural influences. In India no theory of cultural influence has so far been evolved, apart from Nandy's somewhat speculative paradigm of the sexual relationship as a metaphor for colonial relations. It does not enable us to proceed beyond a primary, though important, insight in this area. The Western theories, such as Harold Bloom's theory of literary influence (*Anxiety of Influence*, 1972), or Max Weber's theory of social change ('Civilizational dynamics in traditional society', 1958), are designed to work within the framework of a direct temporal progression. This temporal scheme creates special problems while using the theories for analyzing the British impact on India or the social changes taking place due to that impact. In order to explain the nature of this difficulty, it is necessary to use the term 'Renaissance', which is generally (and in a misleading way) used for a part of the British period in Indian history, roughly 1800 to 1920, or from Rammohun Roy (1772–1833) to Mahatma Gandhi (1869–1948). It is ironical that the so-called Indian 're-awakening' or new 'self-discovery' should have coincided with the Indian experience of British colonialism. The Renaissance in Britain had chronologically followed the alien Norman rule, whereas the Indian Renaissance and colonial rule were concurrent. Colonialism had taken away cultural freedom during the period of Indian Renaissance, while the Renaissance was opening up new possibilities of freedom within the context of colonialism. They negated each other perfectly, and made the situation culturally non-productive. It is no surprise, then, that not a single major critical text was produced during the entire nineteenth century in India. This is, however, not to say that the society did not move at all during this period. As argued earlier, the nineteenth century was indeed a dynamic period in Indian history. But the nature of that dynamism was such that it could not result in any great creativity. The complexity of social dynamism, which combined non-progression within an overall context of metamorphosis,[57] makes temporally-based Western theories of influence inadequate for interpreting the colonial situation in India.

A serious misconception of the colonial influence lies behind the view that the British period is a watershed in Indian cultural history. This exaggerated view of the colonial impact has given rise to two antithetical beliefs: that the colonial encounter has produced in Indian culture all that is modern and progressive, and that it has taken away all that was sacred and valuable in Indian culture. The colonial rule is believed to have ushered in a golden (modern) age, or to have ended an already existing golden (traditional) age in Indian history. Either way, undue importance is attached to the colonial rule. Therefore, a statement like Macaulay's is seen as marking a great historical moment in India's history, a moment either of 'fall' or, alternately, of 'emancipation'. These immodest views show a perception of history which is far removed from the historic reality.

Percival Spear, the historian, maintains that there was a direct historical continuity between the age of Akbar (1542–1605) and the age of Gandhi (1869–1948). Indian literary criticism has not as yet explored the possibility of using this argument, nor examined its validity for literary criticism. If literary criticism is considered a subsystem of culture, and not an autonomous system of thought, its correspondence with other subsystems of culture cannot be negligible. In the introduction to his history of India, Spear writes:

> [In this history] the Mughal and British periods have been taken together because much misunderstanding has been caused in the past by their separate treatment. A concentration on the British period presents Indian regimes and institutions only in decay, leading easily to the assumption that this was the state they were in. Placing the Mughal period beside the British reveals to the reader that India had its going political concerns as viable as those of British in India. In addition to this consideration, there is an organic connection between the two which separate treatment misses . . . and it is certain that British India would have been a very different place had the Mughals never ruled before them.[58]

It would seem to follow from this testimony of a historian that in literary history the colonial period would be better understood if treated in continuation of the bhasha past. Modern literary criticism in India has blown up the importance of the colonial period to such a magnitude that critics have been viewing it as an altogether fresh beginning rather than as an interlude in literary history. What colonial rule brought to Indian criticism is substantial by any standard. But its substance is exaggerated by confusing the impact of printing technology with the impact of colonial rule.

Just as it is historically inaccurate to maintain that the modern period in Indian literature is unrelated to its precursors, so it is to maintain that the past of the bhasha literatures is relatively more static (or less dynamic?) than the colonial period. It is necessary to break the entire history of each bhasha literature into several shorter periods, and to view each as a cumulative product of all preceding periods, but modified by contemporary forces. Similarly, it is necessary to regard the colonial period as a succession of brief phases, each with its own cultural complexion. The whole span of British rule, from about 1800 to 1947, does not show a single, consistent and linear graph of literary influence. Influenced by a variety of forces—liberalism, nationalism, modernism, industrialization, urbanization, revivalism, etc.—it shows constant fluctuations.

Anil Seal (1962) and John Gallagher (1982), in probing studies of the political development of the raj, have argued that the Empire did not constitute a steady growth, that it can be understood better if seen in terms of several shorter spans, each of which shows changing patterns of both collaboration and confrontation.[59] A close scrutiny of literature belonging to that period would reveal that the colonial impact on literature was not a uniform and unidirectional body of influence trying to force itself into the Indian literary sensibility. Bhalchandra Nemade has demonstrated that the influence was fragmented into a variety of trends in the Marathi novel. It might even profit us to speak of colonial 'influences'. At present Western influences are separated in an arbitrary manner from colonial influences, and the entire colonial period is seen as a single unit of literary history. It would be an appropriate historiographic strategy to regard colonial influences and Western influences as interdependent, and to perceive the colonial period as a sequence of phases.

Bhasha Literatures and the Modern Attitude

Though a common expression, 'pre-British past', is sometimes used to indicate the period between the emergence of the bhashas and their subsequent domination by English literary influence, the period is not of equal length for all of them. There is such a wide variety of chronology involved here that any common historiography is likely to be immediately frustrated. It may be useful to glance over the relevant dates that mark the period for each bhasha. In the table below are given dates of the earliest known author or text of merit, dates when printed works were becoming available in the language, and dates of the first novel in each language. The dates of the first novels are selected only as a means of arriving at a common structure, and not as an indication of modernization of literature. The two need not be confused.[60]

Language	Literary beginning	Colonial impact
Assamiya	AD 1300, Hemasaraswati, *Prahladacharitra*	Printing: 1838; Novel: 1894, Rajanikanta Bardaloi's *Mirijiari*
Bangla	Eighth century, *charyas*	Printing: 1800; Novel: 1865, Bankim Chandra's *Durgeshnandini* Nobel Prize, Tagore: 1913
Gujarati	Eleventh century, Hemachandra	Printing: 1800; Novel: 1866, Nandakishor Mehta's *Karan Ghelo*
Hindi	Fourteenth century, Kabir (Early forms)	Printing: 1800; in Bengal, 1836–38 elsewhere; Novel: Govindanarayana Mishra's *Devrani Jethani ki Kahani*
Kannada	Ninth century, *Kavirajamarga* (critical text)	Printing: 1566 in Goa; Novel: 1899, Gulbadi Venkata Rao's *Indira Devi*
Kashmiri	AD 1200, Sitakanta Acarya's *Mahayanaprakasa* with parts in Kasmiri	Printing: 1819; Novel: 1950, Amin Kamil's *Gati Mabi Gash*

Language	Literary beginning	Colonial impact
Malayalam	Fifteenth century, Cherusseri's *Krishnagatha*	Printing: 1713; Novel: 1887, T.M. Appu Netungati's *Kundalata*
Marathi	Thirteenth century, Mukundaraja	Printing: 1775; Novel: 1857, Baba Padmanji's *Yamunaparyatan*
Oriya	Fourteenth century, Saraladasa	Printing: 1775; Novel: 1901, Fakir Mohan Senapati's *Chha Mana Atha Gunha*
Panjabi	1538: Guru Nanak's *Gurugrantha*	Printing: date not know; Novel: 1897, Bhai Vir Singh's *Sundari*
Sindhi	Seventeenth century, Shah Abdul Latif (1689–1782)	Printing: date not known; Novel: 1890, Karamananda Mevaram's *Zinat*
Tamil	1000 BC, Sangam poetry	Printing: 1710; Novel: 1879, *Prathapa Mudaliar Charithram*
Telugu	Eleventh century AD Nannaya Bhatta's *Mahabharata*	Printing: 1796; Novel: 1872, Narahari Gopalkrishna Cetti's *Sri Rangaraju Charita*
Urdu	Amir Khosrau (1253–1325)	Printing: 1875; Novel: 1878, Ratan-nath Sarsar's *Fasana-e-Azad*

These bare chronological details show that the beginnings of various bhasha literatures vary from 1000 BC (Tamil) to the seventeenth century (Sindhi). They also raise a doubt about the relation between technology and modernization, between printing and changes in literary forms. They show that the introduction of printing technology did not bring with it an immediate or an inevitable acceptance of Western forms of literature. In Urdu the gap between the introduction of printing technology and the publication of the first novel is just three years, in Kannada it is three hundred and thirty-three years. In Marathi the first novel appears a century before the first novel in Kashmiri appears. Can we, then, set any mechanical equations between the introduction of printing and the beginning of modern literature in any Indian language? Clearly not. Similarly, any mechanical equation between the emergence of the novel and the beginning of the modern period will prove too rigid to be acceptable. The most important observation that can be made on the basis of the above table, however, is that the beginning of modern literature in each bhasha is a result of the indigenous dynamics of that bhasha rather than a product of the exogenous cultural pressures. In other words, though the impact of British literature on Indian literature is not quite insignificant, the bhasha seem to have their own continuous histories, guided by their own inner dynamics.

Literary criticism and literary history in India have been insensitive to the conclusions that can be drawn from a comparative perspective of bhasha literatures. In fact a comparative and historical perspective in itself can offer several useful starting points for postulating isolated strands of a theoretical nature about literature in the bhasha, which can eventually be gathered into an Indian theory of literature. A blind acceptance of the cliche that Indian culture is eclectic, and the belief that the British came, were seen and immediately accepted, are detrimental to the theory as well as history of literature in India. It is necessary to remind ourselves that much of the literature of the pre-British bhasha period is still a living heritage in India. The poetry of Namadeva (1270–1350) and Tukaram (1598–1650) in Marathi, that of Narasimh Mehta (1408–80) and Akha (1615–1675) in Gujarati, of Kabir (1440–1518) and Surdas (1483–1567) in Hindi, of Guru Nanak (1469–1539) in Panjabi, and so on, have formed an inalienable part of the Indian consciousness. Tukaram, Mira, Kabir and Basaveshwar, among others, have been some of the dream-images of India's cultural unconscious. They still guide the hands of modern poets like Arun Kolatkar, A. K. Ramanujan and Gajanan Mahadev Muktibodh. Yet, the cultural amnesia from which the modern Indian intellectual suffers, creates highly confused attitudes to the period—or periods—of these poets. The common term used to describe the above named pre-British poets is *bhakti,* devotionalism, or saint poetry. The term covers a vast period extending from the last part of the thirteenth century (Jnanadeva) to the early part of the nineteenth century (Tyagaraja, 1767–1847).

It is like combining European poetry from Dante to Blake under one inexpressive label. It is certainly not very perceptive of literary historians to pack great works from five centuries into a straitjacket of a single insensitive critical category.

The colonially sanctioned hierarchic structure of literary values accepted by modern Indian critics leads them to think that the 'real' literary and critical issues can be found in Western literary traditions. There is a deep-seated sense of inferiority in their minds, a feeling of being impostors in these fields.The fact is that in British, American or Russian literature there is nothing comparable to the school of Tukaram, Mira and Kabir, or to modern Dalit writing. Indian literature has its own kind of excellence. Western literatures have their own kinds of excellence. But, because of the incurable sense of inferiority, the bhasha critics tend to lose emotional touch with the pre-British bhasha literatures, for appreciating which there are no readymade Western formulas, since they were not approved by Western Indology. They wish that the bhasha pasts had Shakespeares, Drydens and Fieldings, and in consequence tend to neglect their Tukarams, Kabirs and Miras. There is, then, a conscious activity of repressing images from the culture's collective unconscious, and banishing them to the deepest recesses of the unconscious. That is how the greatest poets of India's bhasha literature make their appearance in the unguarded segments of the social discourse, segments reserved for 'folk', women, children, idiots, the 'irrational' ones. In the intellectually institutionalized *bhadralok* discourse they are not fashionable.

In discussions of Gujarati criticism the period known as *Pandita Yuga* (roughly 1880–1920) seems to define the outermost historical sweep of the critics' memory. Anything prior to that period is considered to belong to the domain of the mediaevalist. In a survey of Gujarati criticism, Manasukhalal Jhaveri writes:

> Literary criticism in Gujarati can be said to have developed roughly through four ages. The first covers the period from 1860 to 1880; the second from 1880 to 1920; the third from 1920 to 1950; and the fourth and the current stage commences from the year 1950. There is, of course, nothing rigid or sacrosanct about these dates. Nor do they

> coincide with publication of books that could be regarded as landmarks in the history of literary criticism in Gujarati. The year 1860 is roughly the time when the first sprouts of literary criticism were observed. 1880 is the year by which Gujarat, for the first time, confronted the critical thought of University graduates. The year 1920 witnessed the period by which Gandhiji's influence came to be recognized as a steady force under which the life and letters underwent a metamorphosis . . .[61]

Having made out these four periods of Gujarati criticism, Jhaveri goes on to state that nothing much happened in the first period. No comment is necessary on the sense in this historiography.

Jhaveri expresses an idea of literary history accepted by a large number of Gujarati critics. He is typical and not alone in his views. Therefore, even without raising a single doubt, Jhaveri assumes that the university graduates of the 1880s brought a better critical sense into operation. It is true that these graduates had obtained degrees under British benediction; and a writer of Govardhanram's talent belonged to this generation. But did the graduates go to schools and universities imparting English education with minds that were totally blank slates? They had inherited a literary tradition of six or seven centuries, a tradition which, as argued earlier, was still alive and continuous. The Gujarati literary sensibility they had inherited had built-in mechanisms of dealing with alien cultural forces. Can we say that in Govardhanram's generation this culturally inherited ability to deal with outsiders was suddenly lost? Surat, which had the longest experience of British residence of all Indian cities, was the city where Narmad, Gujarati's first modern poet, worked. Is it possible that the folklore of Surat had no impact on the life of Narmad? That Manasukhalal Jhaveri's typical historiography is short-sighted is very unfortunate; but any colonial interference with the culture's self-image can create such defects in historical sight. The modern Indian critic seeks legitimation of his amnesia through a multitude of ways, the chief among them being a faithful reliance on the criteria of some imaginary 'universals' which in reality are merely Western.

Through the benevolent mediation of Indology between Europe and India, Europe came to accept the antiquity of the Sanskrit heritage of India. But neither Indology nor the British colonials paid any attention to the classical period and the British period. Today's Indian critic too feels emotionally in tune with the 'great' Sanskrit classics. Indology was not, unfortunately, gifted with a good literary sensibility. And as such the modern tuning in with Sanskrit classics is done quite indiscriminately. In literary criticism, particularly, every Sanskrit critic from the highly original Bharata and Anandavardhana to mere commentators like Vishvanatha and Appayya Diksitar are considered 'great' theoreticians. Sanskrit theories are paraded with pride in national and international forums. In Gujarati, important critics like Rasiklal Parikh, Dolarray Mankad, Ramprasad Baxi and Nagindas Parekh have devoted themselves to unearthing Sanskrit critical texts and theories. This trend is not peculiar to Gujarati. In Marathi too similar attempts have been made by R. S. Jog, W. L. Kulkarni, R. S. Walimbe, S. K. Kshirsagar and D. K. Bedekar. In Indian English criticism, Krishna Rayan, Krishna Chaitanya and K. Krishnamoorthy belong to this type. It is not intended here to question the scholarly worth of their work, only its cultural propriety.

If modern India can connect itself emotionally with ancient India, whereas it cannot—or does not want to—relate itself to the pre-British past, the phenomenon will have to be described as a disorder in the culture's psyche. The view of tradition held by the general run of modern Indian critics is voiced by Sushil Kumar De in his history of Bangla literature (1919). De thinks that "the time of birth of modern Indian literature was the first half of the nineteenth century." And this view is accorded almost an axiomatic value. The argument such as De's is put forward as a 'historical' argument, and is expected to meet with general agreement, and not as a literary-critical view intended to precipitate a redefinition of the tradition. This inflexible view of bhasha literatures indicates nothing but a failure of memory.

Two distinct types of critical methods have evolved in bhasha literature study: one for the so-called 'modern' period, another for the 'mediaeval' period. The method used for 'modern' literature is derived from various branches of literary linguistics developed in the West. The method used for 'mediaeval' literature is derived from Western theories of historical linguistics and anthropology. In other words, the critical apparatus used for analyzing 'modern' works is 'critical' in nature, whereas that applied to the study of 'mediaeval' works merely presents facts and details without any assessment. This 'positivistic' method of study used in the case of pre-British literature in the bhasha reveals an uneasy relationship between the modern critics and the pre-British literary traditions. The relationship is not sufficiently critical, the critics being either awestruck or indifferent towards those traditions. The job of merely describing the past tradition of a literature is in itself highly demanding, for it presupposes a range of scholarship combined with mature critical sensibility; but the bhasha critics, because of the uneasy relationship, deliver their critical judgement of the past literary traditions even before they have begun a critical scrutiny.

The history of the bhasha literatures has been recorded with praiseworthy scholarly care. In Marathi the work of S. G. Tulpule, V. B. Kolte and G. B. Sardar, and in Gujarati the single-handed efforts of Harivallabh Bhayani, can compare well with the best achievements of literary history and scholarship in any other language. However, literary criticism in the bhasha has not made sufficient use of the preparatory work by these scholars in order to establish well-informed and critical links with the past traditions. Literary critics have neither evaluated nor established the importance of the emergence of so many new languages and literatures in India's cultural history. Literature can indeed be a key to opening the heart of mediaeval Indian culture, a means of connecting modern India with pre-British India, and thereby decolonizing the modern Indian sensibility. But the impassive archaeological and historical evidence presented in a positivistic manner by the mediaevalist is not adequate to answer the question: "Why is it that languages can change so fundamentally in India as they did at the beginning of this millennium?" Unless some of these basic aspects of linguistic transactions in India are sufficiently discussed, literary criticism and history are likely to remain seriously underdeveloped. Bhasha criticism has not so far taken up the challenge and faced it imaginatively.

It would be instructive to examine some specific instances of literary history. A four-volume history of Gujarati literature has been produced by the Gujarat Sahitya Parishad. The first of these four is devoted to 'old' literature, the second to 'mediaeval' and the last two to 'modern' literature. The volume assigned to mediaeval Gujarati literature embraces a vast span of four centuries: 1450–1850. In its key-note chapter, '*Madhyakal-na Sahitya-prakaro*', Chandrakant Mehta states:

> According to the well-established scholarly view, the mediaeval period in Gujarati literature extends from the twelfth century, that is from the time after Hemachandra's death, down to the nineteenth century, till the death of Dayaram.[62]

This periodization does not seem to have any concern for literature as a dynamic social institution, or for the extraordinary agility of the Gujarati language which stabilized itself as a language of literary discourse while its sister branches such as Rajasthani and Hindi sprouting from the common Indo-Aryan parent, were still in a state of flux. Since the dynamism of Gujarati is totally discounted, the 'history' of its literature is reduced by the Parishad volume to a school-text level inventory of authors, forms and calendar events. A history of literature which has no critical inwardness to the period to be historiographed can easily miss the vital spirit of its subject. It can fail in conveying to its readers the feel of the total presence of literature. The socio-cultural unconscious of literature, its linguistic subconscious and stylistic self-consciousness, as well as the transitions in the cultural *episteme* of those four centuries of Gujarat's history are all essential aspects of the Gujarati mediaeval history. It is not possible to portray all these in the absence of a self-confident critical sensibility.

Marathi literary history is more fortunate in this respect. In the 1950s literary historiography in Marathi was the subject of a major debate. Some of the more important documents related to this debate have been anthologized by Dattatraya Punde in a collection of essays on literary historiography (1986).[63] The main issue involved in this discussion was the literary history project undertaken by the Marathi Sahitya Parishad. The original proposal for an exhaustive survey of Marathi literature was drafted by S. M. Mate.[64] He had planned it in eleven volumes, of which five were to be devoted to the mediaeval period, from 1350 to 1820. These were planned to match five author-based epochs: (i) 1350–1600: Eknath epoch, (ii) 1600–1700: Tukaram epoch, (iii) 1600–1700: Ramdas epoch, (iv) 1600–1800: Pandit-poets and chroniclers epoch, and (v) 1600–1820: narrative prose and poetry epoch. In this scheme there was a crude combination of the principle of periodization, author-based epochs, and formal distribution of history. A more sensible plan was suggested earlier by S. V. Ketkar (1932), in which sixteen volumes each were assigned to literature of the pre-British and British periods.[65] Of the first sixteen, four volumes were to be assigned to literature before Eknath, and twelve to 'mediaeval' literature. Ketkar's distribution of material was mainly genre-based, and had more space for the social context of literature; but it showed clearly the hand of an encyclopaedia-writer at work. Besides, Ketkar's plan was never considered seriously while the Parishad was finalizing its project.

Mate's plan was opposed by D. K. Bedekar and G. B. Sardar, both with leftist leanings, on the ground that history is no mere chronicle, it must also reflect the growth of literature. It calls for a critical analysis of historical data and scholarly researches. Bedekar and Sardar suggested three volumes for the mediaeval Marathi literature—1350–1680: middle-mediaeval period; 1680–1800: final-mediaeval period; and a volume for analytical conclusions and a survey of the transition from the mediaeval to the modern period.[66] The analysis was to have a mild Marxist orientation. The periodization in this scheme was bound to political events, 1680 being the date of Shivaji's death. This view was accommodated by the Sahitya Parishad, and it modified the original idea of an eleven-volume history to a nine-volume history. Though the volumes published by the Parishad are scholarly, they leave much to be desired in terms of specific critical orientation towards the pre-British Marathi literature.

The tendency to interpret the entire mediaeval span in terms of a 'unified temporal entity', which prevails in Gujarati, can learn a valuable lesson from the neighbouring Marathi historiography's subtler periodization. Imposing one common scheme of interpretation on the entire period from Hemachandra to Dayaram would result in an incorrect evaluation of the entire period. In Marathi literary historiography the temporal arrangement is satisfactory; but the mediaeval period of Marathi literature also admits, and even demands, a sociological and thematic distribution in terms of the folk, the popular and the elite, in order to avoid the confusion caused in applying the same critical yardstick to an elite Moropant, a popular Tukaram and a folk Honaji. Besides, distinctions in the style and diction need to be established in terms of the Sanskritic, the Persianic, and the native, new Marathi. The history of mediaeval Marathi literature should be a story of its amazing progression from literature with paper and script technology to that with printing technology and university sociology.

Cultural Amnesia

In our discussion of the prevalent Indian attitudes to Western ideas, to the colonial impact, to Sanskrit heritage, and to bhasha literature, we observed that the modern Indian critic feels a false emotional proximity to Western and Sanskrit ideas, while he tends to repress the bhasha tradition and to overlook the 'colonial' side of the colonial experience. In reality the relationship with Western and Sanskrit ideas is but a virtual and idealized relationship, not an organic one. Western ideas entered India during the colonial period, and were guided and conditioned by the colonial context. It would be necessary, therefore, to view Western ideas and the colonial context as constituents of a broad spectrum of an alien graft on Indian culture. Similarly, the Sanskrit heritage has percolated into the modern Indian consciousness after being filtered through bhasha literature and bhasha culture. Hence the Sanskrit heritage and the bhasha heritage need to be seen in terms of a single historic continuity. Not to do so is to introduce distinctions which have no historical basis, and, moreover, they delude Indian critics into believing in the chimera of a non-contextual 'universal' theory of literature and literary historiography. It is difficult to say whether some inexplicable idealism creates this distorted perception of history, or whether it is the faulty perception which gives rise to that idealism.

The misplaced emotional affinity with Western and Sanskrit ideas experienced by modern Indian critics is likely to have the following two sources:

One source, more ancient than we may suspect, is the Janus-faced relationship that the Indian mind has with *marg* traditions and *deshi* traditions, the 'pan' traditions as against the 'local' traditions. The experience of being stretched ambivalently between the two may create an identity crisis, and, worse still, give rise to self-contempt and self-pity. Most currents of Indian philosophic thought have been more like bridges spanning intellectual divides rather than currents with independent origin and direction. Even at present, the chosen political structure in India continues the tradition by being at once unitary and federal, making room for both the *marg* and the *deshi*. The continuous fluctuation of priorities, and the profound ambivalence involved in the situation, create, as noted by M. N. Srinivas, self-censure, an agony that is by no means new to Indian culture. Srinivas traces this characteristic in Indian elite culture back to the later Vedic times.[67]

The other source of faulty cultural perception is the cultural demoralisation caused by the colonial experience. A colonial encounter teaches the colonized a new intellectual idiom, impairing, in the process, the natural native style of thinking. By coercively introducing an alien value structure in the existing value structures of its subjects, colonial domination causes serious dislocations and fragmentations in the intellectual discourse of the colonized. It canonizes alien, and usually irrelevant, systems of intellectual 'totems', and deprives the rhythm and syntax of previously existent value systems of their charm and meaning. This disorder manifests itself in the form of cultural repressiveness and amnesia. Projecting static images of the past, inaccurate and inflexible concepts of literary traditions and history, and non-productive affinities with remote but idealised traditions—all are symptoms of this disorder.

The current affliction of cultural amnesia is compounded by the traditional Indian anxiety over the loss of memory. It is, of course, idle to speculate if amnesia has been a constant malaise of the Indian psyche. It would also be idle to speculate if the longevity of Indian culture has any direct connection with this anxiety, for the biological method of cultural anthropology tends to carry the metaphor of culture as a person beyond the domains of logic. However, one can find a variety of examples of the fear of amnesia, and indeed of amnesia itself, in aspects of Indian culture ranging from the profane to the sacrosanct. The most interesting example is to be found in the method of learning by rote which is still in use in this age of the printed page. Ananda Coomaraswamy, in an illuminating and authoritative essay on the place of memory in Indian culture and psyche,[68] points to a multitude of sources in Brahminical texts discussing memory. God needs no memory, argues Coomaraswamy, for He never forgets; but for human beings Truth and Self have to be approached through memory, through a recollection of what has been forgotten. Amnesia is, thus, considered by Brahminical texts as the basic attribute of human consciousness, and memory as a power that is independent of intelligence. Invoking the *Chandogya Upanishad* in evidence, Coomaraswamy states:

> Memory (*smara*) is more than Space (*akasa,* the medium of hearing). Accordingly, even were many men assembled, not being possessed of Memory, neither would they hear any one at all, nor think (*man*), nor recognize (*vijna*), but if possessed of Memory, they would hear and think and recognize. By Memory, assuredly, one recognizes (*vijanati*) children, recognize cattle. Revere Memory . . . The subject of Memory is discussed in *Milinda Panho,* 78-80. It is first shown that it is not by thinking (*citta*) but by Memory (*sati=smrti*) that we remember; for we are not without intelligence even when what was done long ago has been forgotten (*pamuttham=pramrstam*). It is then asked, "Does Memory arise (*appajjati*) always as an over-knowledge state (*sabba . . .abhijananta*) or is Memory factitious (*katumika=kritirna*)", and answered that "Memory occurs in an over-knowledge state, and is also factitious."[69]

Coomaraswamy argues, with an impressive range of evidence by his side, that "Memory is a kind of latent knowledge," and that by implication amnesia is a given, if reversible, condition of the human mind. His explanation for the inevitability of amnesia is that memory transcends space and time; and while entering this life the soul enters these limits and loses memory. The argument is based on the metaphysical assumption of an all-knowing Soul, or Self, *purusha* being an *a priori* reality. Memory and amnesia become, in Coomaraswamy's interpretation, symbolic representations of 'an omniscient Self' and 'the contingent Ego', respectively.[70] The contingent ego, which is the human ego, must 'recollect' its own nature as the omniscient Self, must learn as a child about its father. The metaphysics of amnesia, with its attendant argument of a hierarchic structure with divine sanction, has hints in it that lead us to the descriptive catalogue of amnesia offered by the experimental psychology of Sigmund Freud.

Amnesia is related, as understood by experimental psychology, to violent unconscious repression of memory. In his *Psychopathology of Everyday Life,* Sigmund Freud claims that there exists a definite relationship between the loss of memory and the nature of the memory lost. This relationship can be merely superficial or complicated and profound. On the basis of this relationship, Freud presents the typology of what he calls "the concealment of memory". I quote from his text which by now has become a classic in the psychology of memory:

> [In the given example fully analyzed], I particularly emphasized a peculiarity in the temporal relation between the concealing memory and the contents of the memory concealed by it. The context of the concealing memory in that example belonged to one of the first years of childhood, while the thoughts represented by it, which remained practically unconscious, belonged to a later period of the individual in question. I called this form of displacement a retro-active or regressive one. Perhaps more often, one finds the reverse relation—that is, an indifferent impression of the most remote period becomes a concealing memory in consciousness, which simply owes its existence to an association with an earlier experience,

> against whose direct reproduction there are resistances. We would call these *encroaching* or *interposing* concealing memories. What most concerns the memory lies here chronologically beyond the concealing memory. Finally, there may be a third possible case, namely, the concealing memory may be connected with the impressions it conceals, not only through its contents, but also through contiguity of time; this is the *contemporaneous* or *contiguous* concealing memory.[71]

Freud's formulations need to be amended when used in the context of a culture that has created a pervasive mythology of memory transcending death and retaining itself into another life—probably as a fantasy to counter the culture's perpetual fear of forgetting. But for such amendments we must wait for an Indian genius in experimental psychology. Meanwhile, it should be useful to argue on the basis of Freud's concept of the concealing memory—though only in a haphazard and tentative form—that cultural amnesia is an inevitable consequence of colonialism. It is caused when a dominated culture, or its constituent features, are branded as inferior by a dominating culture, and are accepted as being as such by the subject culture. If this amnesia destroys the native perception of the immediate past, it also helps as a strategy to preserve the self-respect of the dominated culture as well as to win approval from the dominating culture.

The superior modes of production, efficiency in military organization, and the material success of an intruding alien force can easily intimidate a colonized culture into experiencing a sense of embarrassment for its immediate past. It is this repression which, then, creates an oversize dream image of its distant past. Or to use another Freudian concept, the colonizing force is seen in the role of a parent, hated and feared and imitated, by the colonized culture, which starts perceiving itself as a 'child' who fears its own impotency and fantasizes about the productive power of the 'parent'. The intimidated child then engages itself in acts to win the approval of the parent to enable itself to define its own new identity. This is where history ceases to be history and becomes an extended spectrum of fantasy and amnesia.

The leaders of the so-called Indian Renaissance considered the processes of modernization as a kind of 'national rebirth'. There is ample sociological and historical evidence to establish that modernization was quickened by the colonial rule, but not introduced as a totally new feature in Indian culture. The Renaissance, therefore, was not a rebirth but the attainment of maturity in a process that had been initiated at the beginning of the present millennium. However, the idea of rebirth was consistent with this new image of India as a 'child' that takes periodic births. The Indological studies and the revivalistic tendencies were a corresponding form of 'recollection'. The Indian Renaissance and Indian nationalism had thus tacitly accepted cultural amnesia as an indispensable condition for progress.

It is possible, on the one hand, to enumerate several novels and poems written since the time of Macaulay on the theme of amnesia and the fear of forgetting, and, on the other hand, to show amnesia in operation from the beginning of Islamic regimes in India. We will, however, see here only some examples from the colonial period in order to keep the argument within the confines of our present concern. We will see three examples, one each from the area of language, painting and technology.

When the various central-northern dialects were consolidated into what is now known as Hindi in the early part of the nineteenth century, the impetus came from the East India Company and not from the speakers of those dialects. Curiously enough the 'consolidated' Hindi emerged from the printing press at Fort William, and its founding father was an officially appointed 'writer', Lalluji Lal (1763–1825). His job in the Company Government was to prepare printed texts in Hindi.[72] But while performing the clerical job of putting a language in print, Lalluji Lal performed a creative act by preparing a Hindi rendering of the *Bhagawata Purana* in Khari Boli—the R.P. of Hindi. This rendering, *Premasagar* (The Ocean of Love, 1805–06) became the principal textbook for European students of Hindi throughout the nineteenth century and became a source book much relied upon by Indians too. Lalluji Lal's selection of a *purana*—a history told mythologically—for using the new medium and technology of script in print is a case of the typical Indian response to new technology. On the one hand, he traditionalized the technology and endowed it with a ritual status, on the other, he expressed his urge to remember the Indian past and displayed his uncertain sense of history. It is not implied that he himself was aware of this tension. We have the advantage of hindsight.

The above reading of Lal's consciousness seems to have at least some substance in it when we support it with evidence from the field of painting. When the practice of using a straight brush (in place of the curved brush of native tradition), synthetic pigments and the naturalistic technique of painting arrived in India with the British, they touched the genius of a painter like Raja Ravivarma.[73] Ravivarma (1848–1906), modern India's first notable painter, saw a European painter at work at the court of Travancore. Greatly impressed by the technique of portrait drawing, known in his days as 'archaeological' drawing, he started creating portraits of gods, heroes and mythological personalities, giving them substantial body and colour. His goddesses were particularly healthy. His fame spread all over India, and his lithographed works adorned houses all over the country. Even Tagore praised his work. What constituted the peculiar appeal of his work? He certainly did not follow the archaeological method of re-creating the past faithfully, for his gods and heroes bear little likeness to the details given in Hindu sacred books. He was not following 'naturalism', for his themes came from a world of fantasy. It is possible that the superior, Western technology of painting disturbed Ravivarma's memory of the past, but it was a distant past full of dream images. Ravivarma could not gather images and themes for his work from the experience of the Black Hole of Calcutta or the mutiny of 1857. His kind of amnesia can be put in clearer relief when we note that during the initial phase of the contact with the British—before India had accepted complete military defeat at the hands of the British—the painters at Kalighat could freely draw on their immediate environment.

Another instance of this tendency is to be found in the way in which the printing technology was used in its early days. M. N. Srinivas tells us that the majority of books published during the initial years of printing in India were 'revivalistic':

> the manipulation of Western technology does not mean that the manipulators have accepted a rationalistic and scientific world view . . . There are instances, moreover, where Westernization has given birth to forces which are mutually at cross-purposes . . . The introduction of printing, for instance, made possible the transmission of not only modern knowledge but also the knowledge of traditional epics, mythology, the lives of saints, and other religious literature . . . In the political and cultural field, Westernization has given birth not only to nationalism but also to revivalism . . .[74]

Srinivas's comments generalize on a pervasive social process that he has termed 'Westernization'.

In India, Westernization has brought with it a regressive tendency of Sanskritization, in the sense of reviving a distant past and repressing the immediate past. This fantasization of the past, the loss of capacity to see that the distant past has reached modern times after passing through a complex process of mutation at the hands of the immediate past, and the uneasy relationship with recent history, are all consequences of the cultural amnesia into which Indian culture has regressed during the colonial period. The worst part of the colonial impact was that it snatched away India's living cultural heritage and replaced it with a fantasy of the past. This amnesia, which has affected our awareness of native traditions which are still alive, is perhaps the central factor of the crisis in Indian criticism.

3

A Never-ending Transition

Cultural Archaeology

The present state of amnesia in Indian literary criticism underlines two urgent needs: i) to re-examine the British impact on Indian literary traditions, and ii) to formulate a pragmatic literary historiography for bhasha literatures. Problems of literary theory cannot be understood in isolation from the problems of literary history, particularly at the present juncture of Indian literary criticism. Therefore, a redefinition of cultural identity becomes necessary before an attempt is made to articulate the existing value-structures in criticism or to formulate new theoretical positions.

R. B. Patankar hints at the two needs mentioned above in an essay, 'The Three Alternatives',[1] which is perhaps the first attempt to relate modern literary criticism to the native bhasha traditions. He suggests that the study of the sixteenth or seventeenth century 'roots' of Indian criticism is the key to understanding modern poetics in Marathi. By extension his argument is valid in the context of other bhasha literatures too. Patankar also puts forth the idea that India might have brought itself to the threshold of modernity even without the British impact. He writes:

> We cannot hope to find or create *our* literary framework in a seminar where ineffectual angels flap their borrowed Western and ancient Indian wings in a void. We must shed these wings and assert ourselves as First Class

> citizens. I am not suggesting that we should seal off our borders in space and time. We should arrive at an intellectual articulation of our literary sensibility as it was before the British advent. Sixteenth or seventeenth century would serve as promising starting points. We shall find there poetry preoccupied with ethical problems, problems of daily life without losing sight of the problems of eternity. Let us then move from there to the modern times with their new problems, try to visualize how people with that value structure and sensibility would have tackled them, see if there were adequate techniques of production, whether they would have ploughed their surplus back into production instead of directing it towards conspicuous consumption or charity, whether they would have recognized the due importance of *Artha* and *Kama* and taken steps to organize these two aspects of life. Perhaps we would have been required to assimilate ideas from abroad, and the ancient past; but we would have then assimilated and not been dominated by them. Had not the British violently arrested our natural growth probably we might have, on our own, developed into a modern nation.[2]

The concluding part of the argument is futile, an idle speculation. But the idea of going back to the bhasha past can be immensely fruitful for evolving a more relevant historiography. However, this cultural archaeology presents its own peculiar difficulties. The lack of scholarly material related to and belonging to the pre-British bhasha past is one difficulty. The more daunting problem is the fact that much of the material related to the seventeenth century emanates from records left behind by casual, non-literary European observers such as merchants, travellers and administrators. Most of them were slow to learn Indian languages, and were hardly interested in bhasha literature.

When the Orient was still a new discovery for Europe, a feared and mysterious primitive being rather than a domesticated animal, Orientalism was almost a genre of creative writing.[3] Milton's numerous references to Ind in *Paradise Lost* and Dryden's play *Aurengzebe* belonged to this genre.[4] Understandably, therefore, the seventeenth century European reports on India were written in keeping with accepted stereotypes. The fiction of India that Orientalism created in the seventeenth century has percolated to documents on which the history of that period is based. Indian historiography which developed during the nationalistic phase was a reaction to these fictional accounts. Indian historians tried to assert the virtues that the Orientalist reports had denied India. Therefore, those assertions too need to be questioned thoroughly. Here are some typical samples of the source material of Indian history.

James Forbes (1749–1819) observed, after spending several years in Gujarat, that the Asiatic people "attended very little to the fine arts."[5] Unlike his namesake, A. K. Forbes (1821–65) who contributed in several ways to the development of Gujarati language and literature,[6] James Forbes could not appreciate the poetry of Narsimh Mehta and Akha, which was a living presence in Gujarat, as much during Forbes's times as it is today. His insensitive opinion survived two centuries and found its echoes in Sir George Grierson's report in his monumental work, *Linguistic Survey of India* (1894–1927). Grierson declares, "Gujarati has not yet produced a great poet, approaching in excellence the mediaeval Masters of Hindustan."[7] He obviously missed such major poets as Premanand and Dayaram.

The fountainhead of the European views of India was the report by a Frenchman, Francois Bernier, who spent fourteen long years in the Mughal court and in travelling through India, and wrote a compendium of 'information' on Indian life and culture. His account of India (1656–68) was influential throughout Europe in forming an image of India, more particularly that of the Oriental despot. The appeal of this strange and simplified image led Dryden to write his play *Aurengzebe* (1675).

A modern-day critique of India by V. S. Naipaul pales in comparison with Bernier's testimony on the sociology of Indian art and literature:

> Can it excite wonder that, under these circumstances, the arts do not flourish here as they would do under a better government, or as they flourish in our happier France? No artist can be expected to give his mind to his

> calling in the midst of a people who are either wretchedly poor, or who, if rich, assume an appearance of poverty, and who regard not the beauty and excellence, but the cheapness of an article, a people whose grandees pay for a work of art considerably under its value, and according to their own caprice, and who do not hesitate to punish an importunate artist, or tradesman, with the *korrah* . . . The arts in the *Indies* would have long ago lost their beauty and delicacy, if the Monarch and principal *Omrahs* did not keep in their pay a number of artists who work in their houses, teach the children, and are stimulated to exertion by the hope of reward and the fear of *korrah*. . .
>
> A profound and universal ignorance is the natural consequence of such a state of society as I have endeavoured to describe. Is it possible to establish in Hindoustan academies and colleges properly endowed? Where shall we seek for founders? Or, should they be found, where are the scholars?[8]

It was this kind of simplified and fictional perception of India, to a large extent divorced from the social reality of that period, that was later recycled through the writings of scholars and administrators. European Indologists of the late eighteenth and nineteenth centuries did make some impressive scholarly forays into the ancient past of India, but their vision of the contemporary Indian society retained the element of dark humour introduced by Bernier.

The British period of India's history stands between modern Indian scholars and the pre-British past not as a temporal episode alone but also as an epistemological stumbling block. In order to see beyond it, one has to see through it. It would have been easy to weed out the politically biased and mischievous European reports on pre-British India from the historical source material, had it not been for the subsequent legitimation bestowed upon them by the British education system. The worst hit victim of the epistemological inflection created by the erroneous Indology is the past of bhasha literatures. Hence, the need to disabuse Indian literary history of the idea of a Dark Age, and also, at the other end of the spectrum, that of a Golden Age, can hardly be overstated.[9] The actual starting point of our enquiry into the problems of contemporary literary criticism is obviously the period in which bhasha literatures made their beginnings. However, a closer look at the situation in the seventeenth century does throw some useful light on the crisis in criticism today.

Seventeenth century India presents a record of highly impressive achievements in the arts and in literature. The contributions to music, painting, dance, architecture and poetry made during this period form a glorious chapter in India's cultural history. Yet, no simple formula of the relationship between living cultural traditions and great social problems can explain the entire period satisfactorily.[10] One encounters here a paradox difficult to explain. Side by side with the emergence of a novel Marathi poetics in Tukaram's (1598–1649) redefinition of the Hindu world view, one finds Jagannatha (1620–65)[11] concluding the long, tired line of Hindu poetics in Sanskrit. On the one hand is seen the development of a novel literary genre like the Assamiya *Buranji,* on the other the faltering progress in Hindi of the Bhakti school created so ably in the preceding century by Mira (1498–1573), Kabir (1440–1518) and Tulsidas (1532–1623). It was in the seventeenth century that Panjabi produced a great poet like Waris Shah, and Gujarati the equally great Premanand and Akha; but the same period saw a rapid decline in Telugu literature in spite of ample patronage given to the arts in Andhra. In other words, the century was characterized by the decline of the Hindu intellectual tradition of poetics, even while, politically, Hindu nationalism was in the ascendant.

Jagannatha's *Rasagangadhara,* a comprehensive work on literary style or *alamkara,* as Sanskrit poetics termed it, is considered by his twentieth century commentators to be comparable to the best in the *alamkara* tradition. It is also considered to be original to some extent. Jagannatha had studied grammar and philosophy under distinguished specialists, and was himself an erudite scholar and a gifted poet and stylist. However, he chose not to live in the Hindu milieu in which his learning, poetry and philosophy had been developed. He sought patronage at the Mughal court in

Delhi, moving from his native Telugu to Assamiya, and then to a Persian linguistic milieu. He wrote poetry in Sanskrit, which by his time was no more a language related to life, but his subjects were not necessarily from the Sanskrit world. *Asafavilas,* an elegy that Jagannatha wrote, had for its subject a relative of Shahjehan. His poetry and poetics, thus, admitted of a social, metaphysical and linguistic fragmentation.

The great Marathi poet Tukaram was Jagannatha's contemporary. So were two other major figures of the Marathi poetic tradition: Mukteshvar (late sixteenth century) and Ramdas (1608–81). While Jagannatha was composing verses on Mughal courtiers in the tired metres of Sanskrit, Tukaram had been creating a new religious discourse. His *abhangas* brought together diverse social groups and creeds, but, more important, they integrated the diction of Marathi poetry with the language of the common people and gave great expressive power to both. Tukaram's vibrant and socially oriented poetry, written in a living language, contributed substantially to the growing Maratha nationalism. When we juxtapose Jagannatha with Tukaram, within their shared cultural context, it would be possible to formulate the following two questions: i) What was the exact historical sequence of the decline of Sanskrit poetics and the emergence of bhasha literatures? and ii) What was the nature of the relation between the Great Tradition and the newly emerging little traditions, between the *marg* and the *deshi?* In following up these two questions it should become possible to move a little further in our search for the value structures in bhasha criticism.

A Never-ending Transition

I

If one were to adopt the principle of a sequential periodization of bhasha literatures, following the European models of 'continuous motion' from one literary epoch to another or 'oscillation' between polarities, one would find it a frustrating job to propose any useful historiography. By drawing on these models, now firmly ingrained in the Indian literary sensibility, it would be logical to expect that bhasha literature was matched by a decline of Sanskrit poetics and a corresponding rise of criticism in the bhashas themselves. The temporal sequence of events in the process of transition ought to have been: (i) decline of Sanskrit as a literary language, (ii) emergence of the bhashas, (iii) decline of Sanskrit poetics, and (iv) emergence of bhasha criticism. But history as it was defies this logic.

The two most important deviations from this logical sequence are (a) Sanskrit poetics does not show signs of decline several centuries after the emergence of bhasha literatures, and (b) no significant criticism in the bhasha traditions is in evidence. Hence the process of transition from Sanskrit poetics to bhasha criticism appears to demand a fresh and more adequate historiography.

It may amaze a student of Indian literature that though India had in the past, and continues to have in the present, literary traditions in a great many languages, no ancient, mediaeval or modern Indian language has produced a well-developed poetics, with the solitary exception of Sanskrit. The British impact and the Western influence resulted in some writing in the nature of a theory of literature; but much of this has been 'poetics' only in an academic sense, with no organic links with creative literature in modern India. A look at the available statistics about languages in India may be instructive. There are one hundred and eight languages at present in India, each of which is spoken by a minimum of ten thousand people.[12] Many of these are literary languages, with well-established traditions of creative literature. Others may not have written literature, but do have a rich heritage of song and drama. On the other hand, some languages are spoken by a smaller number and yet have developed written literary traditions. English, for instance, takes sixty-seventh place in the numerical strength of speakers claiming it as their first language, but it has a rapidly growing body of creative literature to its credit. Besides these living languages, there have been several that had rich literary traditions at one time, though they are now extinct. In other words, the number of languages that ought to matter in a historical perspective of Indian literature is indeed very large. However, most Indian languages have never cultivated literary theory as an intellectual discipline or genre.

Perhaps the only exception (leaving aside Sanskrit) to this pervasive absence of a theory of literature is the system of poetics in Tamil.[13] The 'system' comprises three original texts and several subsequent commentaries. These three source texts of Tamil poetics are: the *Porulatikaram* of Tolkappiyar (approximately AD 450), Iraiyanar's *Kalavilaya* or *Akapporul* (fourth to sixth century), and Aiyanar Itanar's *Purapporulvenpamalai* (eleventh century). Among the commentaries, the most important is Nakkirar's commentary on *Kalavilaya.* The most original contribution of *Porulatikaram* is its classification of poetry into two main genres—*akam* (poetry dealing with the subjective world) and *puram* (poetry dealing with material themes). This division has been seminal to all subsequent developments in Tamil poetry. However, it does not seem to have influenced Sanskrit poetics. Rather, it seems to have assimilated the Sanskrit theory of *rasa*, which in Tamil became *meyppatu.*

The other strong rival to Sanskrit in intellectual fields was Pali (which is a label given by modern linguistics to a group of dialects).[14] As in Sanskrit, in Pali too there were well-developed philosophic traditions. It had acquired political patronage, a background of vibrant social debate, and had developed traditions of creative literature. Since it was the language of Buddhist literature, it was not bound by the Indo-Aryan and Sanskrit world view. Yet, it has no achievement to boast of in literary criticism. The only critical treatise found in Pali was written by the Sri Lankan scholar Sangharakkhita in the latter half of the twelfth century, eithteen hundred years after the language became accepted for use in philosophic discourse. Commentators feel that Sangharakkhita was dependent on Sanskrit models from which his technical terms are borrowed and adapted.

The only text of Sangharakkhita's considered to have some originality is *Vuttodaya,* his book on Pali metres; but the entire terminology, and with it the linguistic assumptions of Sanskrit poetics, enter his work, depriving it to that extent of its claim to originality. Sangharakkhita had no successors in Pali.

Among the modern Dravidian languages, Telugu and Malayalam had developed some stray aspects of lexicography, but it was Kannada that produced critical works of some significance.[15]

Of these the most valued is *Kavirajamarga* (ninth century) by Nrpatunga or Srivijaya. The next in importance is Nagavarma's *Kavyalokana* (eleventh century). *Kavirajamarga* was an attempt at transplanting critical concepts from Sanskrit to Kannada, and in the process it laid down the guiding principles of Kannada syntax, style and metre. *Kavyalokana,* on the other hand, reversed this process and moved closer to the Sanskrit tradition, and while offering numerous illustrations from Kannada verse to explain styles and genres, it depended too heavily on the authority of Sanskrit poeticians like Vamana, Rudrata, Rajashekhara, etc. Between this eleventh century text and B. M. Srikanthaiah's *Kannadigarige Olleya Sahitya* early in the twentieth century, Kannada produced some of the greatest poetry in the world, but no critical theory. Yet, Kannada's achievement in literary criticism seems to be far better than that of Hindi which too had equally great poetry. Hindi has some isolated comments on the concepts like *nayaka-nayika-bheda* (intermixture of elements of plot and character), and *shringara* (treatment of man-woman relation in poetry), in its old Brajbhasha form. It also shares with the neighbouring Bangla the development of the concept of *bhaktirasa,* adding one more *rasa* to the repertoire of aesthetic emotions well established in Sanskrit. However, most of the works in Brajbhasha were digests prepared as educational aids, and were predictably unoriginal. They were in fact ordinary school textbooks. This tendency is still rife in Hindi.

Bangla has been a leading literary language since its exposure to British influence in the eighteenth century. But before that its development was not what one would expect it to be. The development of criticism in Bangla is best summarized by a recent history of Bangla literature in the following words:

> [P]re-modern Bengali literature was characterized by a complete lack of any theoretical writing on literature, poetics, aesthetics or stylistics. In other words, it did not create any codified aesthetic canon of its own which would help the poet to learn to write and their audiences and readers to discern between 'good' and 'bad' literature. It will suffice to recall numerous Sanskrit works on poetics

> and their innumerable rules to realize how different the situation was in Bengali. On the one hand, Bengali poets simply followed the example of their predecessors and were led more or less by their poetic instinct, on the other, some of them who were acquainted with Sanskrit literature made free use of various Sanskrit works on poetics, especially that by Rupa Goswami, and to a certain extent adapted some of their rules to Bengali. Literary criticism of any kind was similarly absent in pre-modern Bengali literature and could have hardly been compensated for by a few anthologies of Vaishnava poems which at least indicated what the general consensus held to be the best achievements in this particular branch.[16]

The story of criticism in Gujarati, Marathi and Oriya is no different. It is possible to argue that the lack of political freedom was responsible for the absence of intellectual disciplines like literary criticism. This is, however, too specious an argument. Besides, it is not uniformly true of all the bhashas and for all the centuries of foreign political domination. It would be highly instructive therefore to examine criticism in the Islamic languages—Arabic, Persian and Urdu—which enjoyed political patronage and also had poetic excellence, enabling literary criticism to develop in them.

Persian was accepted as the official language of the Mughal administration by Akbar in AD 1582; though Turkish was more popular than Persian, owing to the 'low' sociological associations of Turkish, it was in Persian that the Islamic literature of India found its great efflorescence. Its impressive line of poets is inaugurated by Amir Khosrau (1253–1325), and is ushered into the modern period by the great masters, Ghalib (1797–1869) and Iqbal (1875–1937).

Here it is important to note that unlike in many of the bhashas, the Islamic languages had well-developed forms of discursive prose. Of particular interest for the present study are the works on medicine prepared under the leadership of Mian Bhawan (executed in 1512),[17] on law by Molla Giwan (d. 1717),[18] and on lexicography by Gamaluddin Husain Ingu (1623),[19] soon after Persian became the official language. A culture's self-awareness in terms of its law, medicine and grammar is an important precondition for awareness of its aesthetics. In order that this statement is not misunderstood I should like to add that the knowledge of medicine—a system of management of pain, of anaesthetics, of birth and death—is interrelated to the knowledge of poetry—a system of management of pleasure, of aesthetics and of creation. Law as an activity involving ethical abstractions is closely similar to criticism as an activity involving aesthetic abstractions. And grammar does for a language what criticism does for literary language. However, though these three disciplines made significant progress in Persian, there was no attempt made to develop a theory of literature in that language.

The culture associated with and developed by the society that used Persian was rich in architecture, music, dance and painting. It had developed intellectual disciplines like astronomy, historiography, and philosophy. It had an independent world view derived from its Islamic religion and its political position of advantage. Since this differed radically from the Hindu world view evolved through Sanskrit, literature in the Persian language had every reason and opportunity to look for a new system of literary canons. But Persian denied itself this opportunity. The literary career of Khosrau,[20] the first great Persian poet in India, forms an eloquent example of the low priority given to literary criticism in Persian.

Born of a Turkish father and a mother of Indian extraction, Khosrau was trained in the craft of poetry, and had a very wide exposure to various literary styles used in northern India at the time. His contributions to the *gazal* form of poetry and to the *tarana* and *khyal* styles of singing deserve to be considered as some of the greatest by any single person. He seems to have been a prolific writer, to judge by the ninety-two books that he wrote on Indian life, customs, political affairs and personal history. His knowledge of Indian life, culture and history was extensive. He is also believed to have written a treatise on music, which indicates his ability as a theoretician. Considering his scholarship and interests it was more than probable that Khosrau was familiar with Sanskrit poetics, which had witnessed a remarkable efflorescence in the two centuries preceding him. It is not improbable that Khosrau knew the *dhvani* and *alamkara* theories. Yet, he did not venture to introduce that branch of literature into Persian. His successors during the five centuries that followed maintained his precept.

From the examples discussed above it may be safely deduced that no theory of literature of any consequence was produced by and for the bhasha literatures until they were exposed to British literary influence in the nineteenth century. It is, however, conceptually impossible to imagine so many poetry traditions without their own poetics—whether articulated or not—just as it is impossible to think of consciousness without language. It is therefore necessary to consider whether the absence of poetics—or more appropriately, well-articulated poetics—in the bhasha literatures was not the absence of only a certain kind of poetics rather than poetics of any kind what ever. It is perhaps possible that the history of bhasha literatures does not conform to a pre-formed notion of poetics or theory of literature. In the next part of this section we will try to probe into this question as far as it is possible on the basis of evidence available to us.

II

An enquiry into the social context of the period when the bhashas started emerging in India would reveal large changes in the value structures on which classical Indian society was based. Historians have noted that during the eleventh century—the century that saw the rise of Marathi, Gujarati and Bangla—the political structures, the concepts of law and the organization of the economy had started undergoing rapid changes.[21] The arrival of Islam in India was a radical cultural experience for the generations involved in the earliest encounter with this alien force. Literature of that period clearly shows the growth of regionalism as well as deviation from Hindu orthodoxy. This was happening all over India.

Of all the changes, the most remarkable and conspicuous was the shift from Sanskrit to the bhashas as the medium of literary creation. Perceiving the historical situation in this light, one would expect corresponding shifts in the modes of perceiving literary excellence as well, particularly since literature remained an essential part of theology and of university education throughout India's history.[22] Therefore, it becomes difficult to understand why Sanskrit poetics was not replaced by the bhasha poetics during the first few centuries of this millennium; why, on the contrary, it continued to hold its own for centuries after the bhasha literatures replaced Sanskrit as a living literary tradition.

Islamic adventurers had started invading parts of India in the eighth century. But the first serious Islamic blow was dealt to the classical structure by Mahmud of Ghazni in AD 1001. After repeated aggressions, he occupied the Punjab in 1025. The three centuries between Ghazni's first raid on the Somnath temple and the completion of the first great Marathi classic, Jnadeva's *Jnaneshvari,* in 1290, show a great transition in Indian history.

Surprisingly, but by no means accidentally, a wide range of theoreticians, from Abhinavagupta (eleventh century) to Vagbhata (fourteenth century), did significant work during the period when the bhashas were consolidating their literary foundations. These theoreticians included such important names as Bhattanayaka, Kuntaka, Mahimbhatta, Bhoja, Kshemendra, Mammata, Ruyyaka, Vagbhata, Hemachandra, Jayadeva and Vidyadhara. This simultaneous growth of Islamic political domination, literature in the bhashas, and literary theory in Sanskrit, throws overboard all simple formulas of the relationship between socio-political and cultural structures. It shows that the emergence of the bhasha literatures and the decline of Sanskrit poetics are not temporally sequential episodes. What is more important, it shows that in respect of literary theory, the bhasha literatures were not born 'innocent'. All this clearly points to the fact that the evolutionary model of literary historiography, which considers the progression from one unified epoch to another as the essential principle of literary history, is inadequate to explain this situation.

The near-absence of theorizing about literature in the bhashas might have been due to too much knowledge of Sanskrit poetics rather than too little of it. Hemachandra in Gujarati and Khosrau in Persian demonstrate the bhasha writers' unwillingness to adapt

Sanskrit poetics to literatures in their own languages. The feeble attempts at such adaptation made by Sangharakkhita in Pali and by Nrpatunga in Kannada, found few successors, and their legacy did not find acceptance in the respective languages. On the other hand, Sanskrit poetics continued to develop, undeterred by the Islamic political invasions and the bhasha literary invasions.

One way of explaining this anachronism, and I think a rather superficial way, is by pointing out the tradition of multilingualism built into the system of Sanskrit poetics. Sanskrit poetics shows an extraordinary sensitivity to regional linguistic variations. Most of the Sanskrit linguists and poeticians were polyglots. For instance, Vishvanatha (1300–1380) illustrates multilingual poetry by citing his own *Prashastiratnavali,* a poem he wrote using sixteen different languages.[23] One imagines, therefore, that Sanskrit poetics did not feel threatened by linguistic heterodoxy. Multilingualism had been an accepted practice in creative literature too. For instance, in the early classical drama, different languages and language dialects were used for characters belonging to different social classes.

The Sanskrit plays using several languages or language dialects in one scene implied a social hierarchy. In that hierarchy the bhashas (or their various predecessors) were considered as being socially inferior to Sanskrit. The new literatures in the bhashas challenged this hierarchy. Jnanadeva called his Marathi a language sweeter than nectar; and two centuries later, Eknath clearly asked:

> If Sanskrit was made by Gods, was Prakrit born of thieves and knaves? Let these errings of vanity alone. Whether it is Sanskrit or Prakrit, wherever the story of God is told it is essentially holy and must be respected. God is no partisan of tongues. To Him Prakrit and Sanskrit are alike. My language, Marathi, is worthy of expressing the highest sentiments, and is rich-laden with the fruits of divine knowledge.[24]

As against this increasing linguistic heterodoxy, Sanskrit poetics was becoming more rigid in its outlook, and hair-splitting in *alamkarashastra* (stylistics). Abhinavagupta's famous text, *Abhinavabharati,* and Ghazni's attacks on the Somnath temple came at the same point of time in Indian history. With Abhinavagupta the tradition of Sanskrit poetics gained immensely in sophistication, though, or perhaps because, it started losing contact with contemporary literature.

Ever since Indology revived scholarly interest in Sanskrit culture, scholars have tended to look at Sanskrit poetics more as a subject of scholarship than as a component of the living literary culture of classical India. Indology considered the whole tradition from Bharata to Jagannatha as one unified tradition. It is more realistic, however, to view it as a long sequence of continuous changes. Ashok Kelkar, who presents Sanskrit poetics from this perspective, distributes the tradition into three distinct phases, each with a specific theoretical emphasis.[25]

The three phases, according to Kelkar, are: (i) Dandin (AD 700–750), Vamana (AD 800), Bhamaha (AD 700–750) and Udbhata (AD 800), and their *rasa-guna* and *rasa-alamkara* theories; (ii) Anandavardhana (AD 890), Dhananjaya (AD 700–750), Kuntaka (10th century), Rajashekhara (AD 900–950), etc., with their *dhvani* and *vakrokti* theories; and (iii) poeticians from Abhinavagupta (925–1025) to Jagannatha (1600–1650) with their synthesis of earlier theories and their tradition of producing textbooks. This historical approach is helpful in understanding the 'civilizational dynamics',[26] as sociologists would call it, of the Indian tradition of literary theory.

Anandavardhana's *Dhvanyaloka* came, we are told, as a culmination of a lively debate which was going on for the two preceding centuries. It then became accepted as the central critical statement of classical Indian culture. Its relation with other disciplines like philosophy and linguistics, with social forces and political developments, and with the new religious awareness of its time contributed to its becoming the centre of an intellectual tradition. The contemporary view of Sanskrit poetic tradition considers Abhinavagupta as Anandavardhana's direct successor. The two are separated by a chronological gap of a century and a half; and by the standards of the time-scale to which Sanskrit poetics belongs, this gap does not appear to be very substantial. But what seems to be forgotten is that by the time Abhinavagupta, with his thousand followers, walked away from society into a cave in the Himalayas,[27] the vital links between poetics and the society producing it had snapped. In Abhinavagupta's lifetime Sanskrit had started accepting its cultural marginalization. The fact that Anandavardhana and Abhinavagupta used common critical terminology is not enough to bind them together in a common epoch of Sanskrit poetics. The two should be treated as belonging to two distinct phases of a tradition. What would have been considered as heresy in Anandavardhana's classical India had already started receiving acceptance in Abhinavagupta's post-classical India. It is true that Abhinavagupta and his successors in the Sanskrit critical tradition brought to it greater intellectual sophistication. Usually this sophistication is misconstrued as an indication of development and growth. But it is more than likely that the sophistication observed in the post-Abhinavagupta tradition of poetics is related to its orthodoxy and alienation from the extant social concerns.

The transition in Sanskrit poetics occurring during Abhinavagupta's period can be understood properly if poetics is treated as a subsystem of culture rather than as an autonomous intellectual activity. So far, no social history of Sanskrit poetics has been written by any modern scholar. We have to make a beginning, therefore, by proposing some crude hypotheses in this direction, with the help of social history. Sociologists like Max Weber, Louise Dumont and Samuel Eisenstadt[28] have offered some general observations about the processes of social change in India. Of these attempts, Eisenstadt's explanation of what he calls 'the civilizational dynamics' comes closest to offering useful guidelines for analyzing the transition in the Indian literary culture at the beginning of this millennium. He sees at the source of the increasing heterodoxy, manifest in the emergence of several new cults, sects and cultural practices, an ever increasing tension between the metaphysical ordering of the universe and the ethical ordering of existence. In other words, a perceptible gap between god's world and man's world caused the transition from the classical to the post-classical Indian society. Having described the general character of this tension, he goes on to comment on its consequences:

> An almost unavoidable by-product of this perception of tension between the transcendental and the mundane was the development of various versions of 'salvation'—i.e. means of resolving the perceived tension. Most such versions focused on the need for the reconstruction of human personality and behaviour in accordance with precepts of the higher moral or metaphysical order. Other visions went beyond this, demanding reconstruction of the entire socio-political and economic order.[29]

To the extent that it is valid for the period it deals with, this analysis implies that the tradition of Sanskrit poetics too had perceived, and it was required to take into account, the tension between the metaphysical assumptions of literary theory and the social dynamics of the literature it concerned itself with. The development of the tradition of poetics and its capacity to amend itself to suit the needs of changing times, depended on its clear perception of this tension. It would be useful to see how the tradition of Sanskrit poetics conducted itself through this period of transition.

In its early stages of development,[30] Sanskrit poetics had evolved the concept of *lokottara,* which conceptualized the aesthetic experience in terms of a transcendental delight. Bharata maintained that the aesthetic experience is very similar to the experience of spiritual delight. Care, however, was taken not to identify *kavyananda* with *brahmananda,* aesthetic delight with metaphysical ecstasy. The formulation of the *rasa* theory of poetry and drama clearly showed the awareness that the theatre was basically a *lokadharmi natyadharma* (socially-oriented dramatic art). The next major step in the development of Sanskrit poetics was the formulation of the *dhvani* theory, which preserved Bharata's distinction between the symbolic and the realistic, the worldly and the other-worldly, the soul and the body of sound. But the distinction starts getting blurred in Abhinavagupta's post-classical India. In fact, the whole thrust of the last phase of Sanskrit poetics is towards imposing an artificial synthesis on concepts so meticulously evolved, defined and separated by Bharata, Anandavardhana and Kuntaka. Vishvanatha wrote his *Sahityadarpana* after the bhashas had established their literary traditions and the Hindu polity was completely replaced by an Indo-Islamic polity. By the time Vishvanatha wrote his *opus,* in the fourteenth century, even the distinction between poetry and drama was more or less lost; or more appropriately, the critical perception of that distinction was lost. In his terse definition of verbal art, "*vakyam rasatmakam kavyam*" (poetry is aesthetically pleasing linguistic structure),[31] he clearly intended to cover both poetry and drama. Similarly blurred was the distinction between an autonomous *loka*—sphere of existence—of sound and its physical manifestation in terms of *sphota*—revelation of meaning by describing all poetic *dhvani* as emanating from a divine sphere, as *rasatmakadhvani.* The original treatise on *dhvani,* Anandavardhana's *Dhvanyaloka,* had taken great care to establish a distinction between *vastudhvani* (signification), *alamkaradhvani* (suggestion) and *rasadhvani* (evocation), all of which constitute *pratiyamana* (implied meaning) as against *vacya* (stable meaning).

Vishvanatha was not the only major representative of this tendency towards regression and the trend of decline seen in the destructive synthesis of finely evolved concepts. This tendency is seen in every theorist from Abhinavagupta. And the decadence can be seen setting in Sanskrit poetics with respect to every concept and genre discussed in it. Dandin and Bhamaha had, for instance, used two categories, *arthaguna* and *sabdaguna,*[32] to describe separately the thematic character and the stylistic and structural character of epic poetry. Three centuries later, Bhoja continued to employ these two categories; but he also added one more of his own, namely, *ubhayaguna* (composite properties of structure and theme of an epic).[33] He described five of these composite characteristics as being essential to the epic form: i) *rasarupa-sandharbhatva* (correspondence between aesthetic emotion and the form in any given part of the work), ii) *patranurupabhasyatva* (correspondence between the dignity of a character and the dignity of his speech), iii) *arthanurupacandastva* (correspondence between the substance and metrical patterns), iv) *samastalokaranjanatva* (entertaining to all audiences), and v) *sadalamkaravakyatva* (well-embellished structure and diction). Dandin's original definition of *sargabandha* (episodic or epic poetry) had not ruled out the close interdependence of epic style and epic theme; but he had established it less pedantically. His concept of epic was finer. It had suggestively outlined the thematic content of an epic and the stylistic features of episodic narrative, and it only hinted at the correspondence between the theme and the structure in a completely non-prescriptive way. In short, the tradition of Sanskrit poetics from Abhinavagupta onwards indicates, through its increasing sophistication of terminology and synthesizing of concepts, an uneasy awareness of the tension between the *lokottara* and the *lokadharmi.* In this conflict, which starts to loom large towards the beginning of the Islamic age in India, the Sanskrit theorist perceived his role as the keeper of the *lokottara* view of art and literature, of the transcendental order established in classical India. The numerous textbooks on poetics produced during the first three centuries after Ghazni raided Somanath, reveal Sanskrit theorists fighting to save the orthodoxy in poetics. Arising from the fear of disintegration of their *lokottara,* world view, is their obsession with the idea of synthesis. Meanwhile, life, and the bhasha literatures, had moved conclusively away from Sanskrit and *sanskriti.*

Rajashekhara's literary career (ninth/tenth century)[34] forms an eloquent example of how poetics had started disintegrating as a meaningful cultural discourse in the tenth century. Born in Maharashtra, he migrated to Kanauj, as many of his learned contemporaries did, to become counsellor to two generations of princes. He is mainly remembered for his monumental work on poetics, *Kavyamimamsa,* which classifies various branches of knowledge, defines literary concepts like *sutra, bhashya, vritti, paddhati, tika, samiksha* (all of which were branches of criticism), and with illustrations explains other concepts like literature, syntax, metre, genres, semantics and linguistics. But mainly, Rajashekhara's *Kavyamimamsa* comments on the social purpose of literature and the sociological context of the writer. Its range of references is characteristically impressive—from writers like Kalidasa, Bharavi,

Harishchandra, and linguists like Panini, Pingala, Vararuchi, to critics like Avantisundari (Rajashekhara's wife), Palyakirti, Bharata, Mangala, Rudrata, Vakpatiraja, Vamana, Shyamadeva, Surananda, and so on. He is also known to have written poetry himself; and he has been described as being an excellent polyglot—*sarvabhashachatura.* His diplomatic career suggests that he knew some Latin, Arabic, Persian and an African dialect (known in India at that time as Romaka, Yavana, Parasika and Barbara, respectively). He certainly knew many of the Prakrit dialects. In *Kavyamimamsa* he offers detailed analyses of literatures in Paishachik, Vidharbhi, Gaudiya, Panchali and Kaku, and a careful catalogue of various geographical regions, their dialects, intonations, socio-linguistic particulars and literary conventions. He himself wrote in two languages: his *Kavyamimamsa* was written in Sanskrit, but *Karpurmanjiri,* a farcical play belonging to the *shattaka* genre, was in his native Maharastri, the precursor of Marathi.

Rajashekhara's life and critical work show that the need to take into account the new social forces, particularly the spirit of regionalism, prompted him to bend his theory towards a greater social realism, thus reflecting the tension between elitist poetics and populist literature, between Sanskrit and Prakrit. His enquiry into the sociology of writing, quite reminiscent of Bharata's analysis of the sociology of drama, indicates the beginning of the humanizing processes of Sanskrit poetics. The trend did not develop any further, for the Sanskrit language had become the target of the heresy institutionalized by the bhashas. Consequently, Rajashekhara himself remained within the traditional framework of Sanskrit poetics. He did not propose a theory for the new *deshi* traditions of literature with which he was closely acquainted. In a curious way, Rajashekhara's criticism is suspended between critical orthodoxy and literary heterodoxy. His *Kavyamimamsa* is the first Indian text in literary criticism to initiate what I have called the never-ending transition. This transition originates, to change Eisenstadt's terminology slightly, out of a tension between the *marg* and the *deshi* views of literature. To the extent that such a transition continues to exist as a cultural process even today, Rajashekhara can be claimed as the precursor of bhasha criticism.

III

If Sanskrit criticism had attained a state of suspended animation, or more appropriately if it had been surviving on artificial respiration, and if the bhasha literatures had started gaining strength, it is difficult to understand why no bhasha ever developed the discipline of literary criticism. Considering, however, that the *bhakti* movement in bhasha poetry—that covered a period extending from the fourteenth century to the seventeenth—had its own literary aesthetics (or 'poetics'), a new class of audience, new modes of 'publishing' poetry, and its concept of *bhakti* as a *rasa,* it becomes necessary to ask: Why did the bhasha literatures produce no critical document or text? There is no easy answer to this question, but the following comments may provide part of the explanation.

It has long been recognized that languages and regionalism have been interrelated in India, and that the relationship of any one region to Sanskrit on the one hand, and to its own bhasha on the other, have been different in nature.[35] Sanskrit, used only for the purpose of higher pursuits ever since the Aryans naturalized themselves in India, was distributed all over the country, including those parts that were using Dravidian languages for the business of this world. It was spread horizontally in a sense, all over India, without taking strong roots in any specific region. Only small groups of individuals in any particular area used it as a 'living' language. It was understood by only a small minority of the total Indian population. During the Indo-Islamic centuries, the prestige of Sanskrit, and its use, were further undermined. Communication through Sanskrit, therefore, took place in extended geographic space but was confined to small pockets of communities surrounded by non-Sanskrit speakers. Sanskrit did not have the same speech culture as the bhashas had. In such a situation, the spoken Sanskrit word was always in danger of perishing fast.

The Sanskrit writer or scholar was often engaged in carrying on a dialogue with the past. Sankara 'spoke' to Buddha and Vyasa,[36] Abhinava 'spoke' to Bharata,[37] and so on. I may add, in parenthesis, that some of the secrets of Indian culture lie hidden in the linguistic structure of the past tense in the Sanskrit language, a study of which should form a fascinating field for scholars of cultural anthropology. Here, it is necessary to note that the demands of scholarly disciplines, developed in Sanskrit over a millennium or more, and the need to communicate across rarefied social space, made the composition of texts and their preservation in manuscript form imperative. The regional languages were free from these two compulsions, for they were 'living' languages, and communication through them was intended for a living and compact society. The distinction thus drawn between Sanskrit and the bhashas has a further evidence to support it in the form of details related to the technology of writing during the bhasha period.

During the age of classical Sanskrit literature, literary texts were passed on from generation to generation by committing them to memory. The ability to memorize was encouraged at school and university, and considered an essential part of knowledge acquisition. Remembering old texts was the criterion of one's learning, and the ability to remember conferred social dignity on a person. However, the texts were preserved in written form too. They were periodically duplicated in manuscripts made of bark or dry leaves. With the advent of the bhashas these methods underwent a sociological as well as a technological change.

The sociological change occurred because the class and caste structures came under heavy attack from new sectarian movements, which, reflected in *bhakti* poetry, did not accept theological knowledge as a purely brahminic monopoly. Many non-brahmins started preaching their own realization of religious knowledge, through their poetry. In Marathi, Namadeva (1270–1350) was a tailor by caste. He was surrounded by Gora Kumbhar (potter), Samvata Mali (gardener), Chokha Mahar (untouchable), Sena Nhavi (barber), and Janabai (a maid). Either because some of these poets themselves were illiterate or because they composed poems for the benefit of the illiterate classes of society, they preferred 'publishing' the poems as oral compositions rather than as written texts. They sang their poems to large gatherings in temples, in places of pilgrimage or in the streets. The function of the text, and its place in the literary culture, had changed.

The technological change came with the use of paper for writing. Paper was known in India by the twelfth century. By the early fourteenth century, during the reign of Muhammad-bin-Tughluq (1325–51), India was exporting paper and books to Iran and other Islamic nations. Historians tell us that this trade made the Iranian merchants in Delhi very prosperous.[38] It was now possible to make copies of texts easily. It was easier to write with ink on paper than with herbal dyes on leaves. The result was that during the bhasha centuries of Indian literature, preparing written texts had become a common practice. Perhaps the most famous example of this practice in Marathi is that of the rigorously scholarly edition of Jnanadeva's *Jnaneshvari* prepared by Eknath (1585). The new technology was probably used more by the elite Sanskrit writers whose appeal was limited to small numbers of readers. Thus, the new technology widened the gap that already existed between elite poetry and popular poetry.

Before the introduction of paper as a literary technology, the distinction between elite literature and folk literature was based on the clear criteria of 'written' poetry and 'oral' poetry. The poetry of the bhashas, i.e., their mainstream poetry, was neither entirely written nor entirely oral. It was certainly consciously composed, and though many poets continued to operate orally, some actually wrote down their own verse. Moreover, bhasha poetry did not replace completely either the Sanskrit 'written' poetry or the regional 'folk' poetry. It was a cross between the two, and was an altogether new category of poetry. But it is necessary to add that the entire range of bhasha poetry was not of this type. It is possible, and also appropriate, to think of the three trends as smaller trends within bhasha poetry itself. A tabular representation of bhasha poetry may make the position clear. The categories accepted for classification are not adequate to describe the complexity.

However, here I have used them for the sake of methodological convenience.

Tabular representation of Marathi poetry between introduction of paper technology (13th century) and introduction of printing technology (18th century)

Type	Elite	Popular	Folk
Text	Written, and reproduced in written form.	Sometimes written but usually reproduced orally.	Oral. Recorded in written form subsequently.

Type	Elite	Popular	Folk
Themes	Myths from Sanskrit literature, generally from the *Ramayana* or the *Mahabharata,* but with scope for erotic descriptions, *shringara.*	Moral, philosophic and practical philosophy of life. Social themes, devotion.	Magic, racial memory, fantasy, etc. Heroics. local history chronicles.
Forms	*Chandas* and *vrttas* derived from the Sanskrit *Chandashastra;* episodic narrative, *Akhyan.*	*Ovi, abhanga, bhajana, kirtana,* lyrics or lyric sequences.	*Lavni, powada, bharud, tamasha,* songs.
Orien-tation & influences	Oriented towards Brahminic traditions; influence of Sanskrit poetry and Sanskrit metric. Revivalistic.	Oriented towards contemporary society, progressive and revisionistic; influenced by Sufi mysticism to some extent, and by Maratha nationalism	Oriented towards entertainment, local history and sub-regional themes. Later influenced by Persian *gazal* and diction.
Poetics	Articulated by Sanskrit poeticians, conventional.	Not articulated. But conventions of style, form, poet-audience relation, etc., were consciously evolved independent of Sanskrit traditions.	No articulated poetics. Conventions not very strong But in folk-drama and bardic poetry traces of old Sanskrit poetics can be located.
Represen-tative poets	Mukundaraja (13th century) Moropant (18th century)	Namadeva (14th century) Ramdas (17th century)	Honaji Bala (18th century)

The table shows, with reference to Marathi the relationship between the mode of writing and publishing poetry, and the kind of poetics implied by each tendency. It also shows the field of poetry distributed and fragmented on the basis of the method of communication, metrical patterns employed, and the poetics evolved by each of the tendencies tabulated. Between the introduction of paper technology (thirteenth century) and the advent of printing technology (eighteenth century), poetry developed in a great variety of unrelated ways, making a unidirectional poetics inoperative; and so critical discourse also became fragmented. It is possible to show, by taking examples from literature in the other bhashas that the pattern is detectable in those languages too. Thus, the poetics of the classical period of Sanskrit poetry could be applied to elite, Sanskritic bhasha poetry, but was grossly inadequate for non-Sanskritic poetry.

The Marg and the Deshi

The nature of literary fragmentation can be understood properly in the light of the fact that Indian society had developed a sophisticated cultural apparatus of intricately balancing various subcultures in relation to the mainstream culture. Perhaps the use of the terms 'horizontal' and 'vertical' may help us in understanding this relationship.[39] The 'horizontal' culture and literature operated as the overarching patterns, within which individual 'vertical' patterns of culture were accommodated. In Sanskrit as well as in the bhasha, the term used for the overarching, horizontal pattern was *marg*; for the local, vertical and subsumed pattern, *deshi.*[40] Etymologically, the distinction is believed to have originated in descriptive linguistics; linguistic geography described the regional languages or dialects and the language varieties as *deshi,* the standard language as *marg.* Later, these terms were transferred to sociology and poetics. By the tenth century, they had come to be used as definite aesthetic categories. An important example of their use as aesthetic categories is to be found in Matanga's *Brhaddeshi,* a tenth century treatise on music.[41] Matanga classifies music into five types of *marg gitis (shuddha, bhinna, gaudi, raga* and *sadharani)* and in several other categories under the general heading of *deshi.*

But this distinction was not based merely on variations between the national and the regional. Matanga used the term *marg,* we are told, to refer to "the ancient traditional musical material, whereas *deshi* refers to the music practices then current in the provinces."[42] Thus *marg* was not only the mainstream but also the traditional, and *deshi,* not only the regional but also the contemporary. The relationship between the two was based on the principle of a healthy exchange. During its heyday, Sanskrit poetics had acknowledged the importance of regional variations in poetics and dramatic styles. Even a decadent Sanskrit theorist like Vishvanatha (fourteenth century) describes *deshi* styles such as *gaudi, vaidarbhi* and *maharashtri* in the ninth chapter of his *Sahityadarpana.*[43]

A major classic on *deshi* language traditions is Hemachandra's *deshinamamala* or *deshishabdasamgraha* (a dictionary of Prakrit) called *Rayanavali.* The dictionary lists 'provincialisms' of three types: (i) words not traced to Sanskrit origin, (ii) words of Sanskrit origin but with Prakrit semantic additions, and (iii) words of Prakrit origin and conventions. This passage from a recent commentary on Hemachandra illustrates the extent to which *deshi* coexisted harmoniously with *marg* during the twelfth century:

> The *deshinamamala* is accompanied by a Sanskrit self-commentary of great merit, in which Hemachandra endeavours above all to explain his reasons for including or omitting certain words and for adopting or discarding certain spellings and meanings. Though this involves a good deal of polemics, he seldom divulges the names of the authorities with whom he is in harmony or at variance; those referred to specifically are the Prakrit lexicographers Abhimanacinha (with his scholiast Udukhala), Gopala, Devaraja, Drona, Dhanapala, Padalipta, Rahulaka, and Silanka, the Prakrit poets Avantisundari and Satavahana, the Sanskrit writers Bharata and Bhamaha, and the Kalapas or Katantra grammarians, two anonymous quotations being from Halayudha's *Abhidhanaratnamala.*[44]

This impressive list of Hemachandra's intellectual debts should show a sense of belonging to both *marg* and *deshi* traditions.

Traditionally, the exchange of ideas and intellectual or cultural movements between the *marg* and the *deshi* traditions, or between one *deshi* tradition and another, took place through a system of cultural diffusion evolved all over India. The country's geography has been a crucial factor in determining its history and culture; and in this system of cultural transfer too, geography played a central role. The system has been described by geographers as "network oriented cultural geography".[45] Cities, universities, princely courts, places of pilgrimage, itinerant ascetics and scholars, and the armies constantly on the move, together performed the function of transfusing ideas from the *marg* to the *deshi,* and the other way round. But the network structure also made cultural centres and intellectual conventions vulnerable to alien influences and threats.

This network of cultural transfusion nearly broke down when Mahmud of Ghazni started his raids on India.[46] The threat of disintegration was intensified by an almost simultaneous decline of three powerful dynasties: the Palas, the Pratiharas and the Rastrakutas. Their armies had fought one another long enough to drain their treasuries, leaving the highways and roads in bad repair. In the changing political structure, the number of feudal vassals had increased enormously. This growth in the levels of middlemen, characteristic of eleventh century politics, left both king and peasant—at either end of the chain linking production with administration—weaker than ever before. The damage to the communication network meant the assertion of regional cultures and languages over the dominant culture and language, and, at the same time, a self-defensive rigidity in the *marg* tradition. Thus, with the advent of Islam in India, the *marg* intellectual traditions stopped growing, though they survived in decadent forms for several centuries. On the other hand, the *deshi* traditions started growing in an unprecedented way, creating a new identity and a new cultural space for themselves. However, the aesthetic categories denoted by the terms *marg* and *deshi* did not change so rapidly, though the traditions themselves had reversed their roles. This new situation had two very important consequences, which influenced the development of the bhasha literatures up to the arrival of the British.

The first consequence was an increasing dialogue among various regional literatures. While the possibility of cultural domination and mediation by Sanskrit was diminishing, the bhasha literatures established direct channels of communication with one another. Hence, we see many bilingual poets during these centuries: Namadeva (Marathi and Panjabi), Vidyapati (Maithili and Bangla), Mira (Hindi and Gujarati) and so on. For these bilingual writers, both the languages that they wrote in were of equal social status. Communication between the *marg* and the *deshi,* on the other hand, was limited to mere translation or transliteration, as is indicated by the existence of several versions of the *Ramayana* and the *Mahabharata* written during the early centuries of the bhasha literatures. Similarly, there are numerous episodic poems based on themes from Sanskrit literature written in heavy conventional style. But this communication was no longer a living dialogue. The exchanges between one bhasha literature and another were more vital, and resulted, eventually, in the finest chapter in the story of Indian literature, namely, *bhakti* poetry.

The second consequence of the reversal of roles between the *marg* and the *deshi* was the emergence of a hierarchy of literary values. This hierarchy was over rigid and out of tune with the changing reality. Traditionally, the *marg* traditions established literary criteria and aesthetic values for elitist literature. *Deshi* designated rustic and vulgar literary expressions. Because of the growing rigidity of the self-defensive *marg* traditions, the values associated with the national and the regional did not change in keeping with the changes in the significance of the traditions themselves. Thus, the stigma attached to *deshi* as vulgar stuck even after major literary works were produced in the bhasha literatures. Sanskrit poetics had now to defend itself not only against the Indo-Islamic cultural invasions but also against the bhasha threat. Its instinct for self-preservation—in essence, the self-preservation of the brahminic class with which it was linked—helped Sanskrit to survive in a state of suspended animation till the seventeenth century. Inevitably, such anachronisms do enter a society that accommodates intellectual discourses fragmented by anomalous cultural pressures of the past and the present.

During the first millennium of Sanskrit poetics, critics like Bharata and Anandavardhana had respected *lokadharmi,* or art related to socially sanctioned gestures, and had shown a lively intellectual interest in the *deshis*. In the remote past, at a time when Sanskrit had been a language spoken by the people, it was close to labour and life. *Ila*, a word for speech in the *Rigveda,* also meant 'food', and *Vak,* a name of the muse *Apas,* meant 'hard work'.[47] This rootedness of the language in productive life was naturally reflected in the poetics it developed. The openness of that system of poetics had already diminished with the late-classical formalism evident in the hair-splitting analysis of *dhvani* in the eleventh century. The post-classical decadence made the system more closed, and in consequence, the hierarchic value-structure became increasingly rigid. The vested interests of the brahminical intellectual classes were no less responsible for increasing the rigidity of the hierarchy and perpetuating the importance of *marg* traditions, without counteracting their decadence in any creative way.

During the Indo-Islamic period, the *marg* traditions were dominated by the Islamic cultural influence, and subverted by the rebellious sectarianism of the *deshi* traditions. But during the initial phases of the British colonial rule in India, the *marg* traditions received some very vigorous but artificial respiration from the European Indologists. There was obviously a consistency between the political bearings of the *marg* traditions and those of Indological cultural history. The hierarchic structure of values, in which a lower place was given to the self-respecting and rebellious bhashas, suited both well. On the other hand, the movement for freedom by the *deshi* traditions and the bhasha literatures was, ironically, a movement towards a greater regionalism, unaided by scientific progress or the development of a rational self-analysis. The transition, therefore, from the *marg* to the *deshi* in the field of literary criticism remained unfinished.

Devotionalism and Discourse

A unique strategy evolved by the bhasha literatures to subvert the rigid conventions of over-stylized Sanskrit poetry, to confront the Brahminic monopoly of metaphysics and ethics, and to assert the identity of regional aspirations, was the aesthetics of *bhakti.*

Developed through poetry of extraordinary spontaneity, and in several bhashas, *bhakti* brought with it a radical social philosophy, and new metaphysics and aesthetics. It was, however, a movement and not a system. It had its own dynamics; but it never attempted a systematic theorizing of the values it upheld. In no other period in the entire history of Indian literature has literature been so intimately related to social life, or so fundamentally influenced it, as in the *bhakti* period. In reversing the established relation of hierarchy between the *marg* and the *deshi* traditions, it rattled the bones of an already ossified society, and substantially changed its complexion.

It has been argued by two great modern Indian thinkers, Ananda K. Coomaraswamy and Sri Aurobindo, that at the heart of Indian civilization is an aesthetic principle.[48] Their own work was directed towards the search of this principle: Coomaraswamy pursued it through his study of Indian arts and crafts, Sri Aurobindo through his exploration of mysticism. Taking up their line of argument, one can maintain that at the centre of Vedic society was the concept of *vak* (speech as an act and as abstraction) and its capacity to regulate the material universe. Similarly, during the late classical period, the philosophy of Advaita Vedanta was organized around the concepts of *sphota* and *dhvani* (explosion and suggestion of meaning, or Meaning), especially in Sankara's (b.788) *Brahmasutrabhashya.* His pronouncement, *vacarambhanam vikaro* ('creating is seizing with speech')[49] has been commented upon by innumerable Vedantins. Sankara's own comments on it are:

> Of what nature then is the 'word' with a view to which it is said that the world originates from the 'word'? – It is the *sphota*, the *purvapaksin* says. For on the assumption that the individual gods, and so on, originate from the eternal words of the Veda could not in any way be proved since the letters perish as soon as they are produced . . . it follows that the *sphota* is the word. After the apprehending agent, i.e., the *buddhi,* has, through the apprehension of the several letters of the word, received rudimentary impressions, and after those impressions have been matured through the apprehension of the last letter, the *sphota* presents itself in the *buddhi* all at once as the object of one mental act of apprehension . . . As that *sphota* is

> recognized as the same, as often as the word is pronounced, it is eternal; . . . From this eternal word, which is of the nature of *sphota* and possesses denotative power, there is produced the object denoted, i.e., this world which consists of actions, agents, and results of action.[50]

Sphota was thus one of the most crucial concepts of Sankara's philosophy, which in turn was the most characteristic intellectual product of classical India. Like *vak* and *sphota* in the earlier millennia, *bhakti* came to occupy the centre-stage of Indian culture for nearly five centuries—from the fourteenth to the eighteenth. However, both *vak* and *sphota* were products of the *marg* tradition, whereas *bhakti* originated in *deshi* traditions of the *bhasha* literatures. With it, the established cultural hierarchy is turned upside down.

An insight offered by the French scholar, Louis Renou (1896–1966), in his study of Mammata's poetics, helps to appreciate the magnitude of the changes implied in the *bhakti* movement. In his study of Mammata's *Kavyaprakasha,* an eleventh century work on poetics, Renou establishes that there was a close correspondence between the grammatical forms employed by Mammata and the substance of his poetics.[51] Extending this argument, it follows that the continuous linguistic changes, and the continuing emergence and decline of languages in India, indicate a continuous and corresponding transition in the world view. The emergence of *bhakti* poetry simultaneously with several new languages can, therefore, be seen as reflecting fundamental changes in India in the social, aesthetic and philosophical connotations of basic concepts like Time, Language and Self.

Prior to the emergence of the bhasha literatures, the concept of Time in Indian tradition had two interpretations—one philosophic, the other mathematical. The philosophic conception is present in innumerable myths relating the creation and the progress of life, and also in philosophic treatises such as the fourth century Jain thinker Kundakunda's *Pravacanasara.* He defines Time, with great sophistication, as a relative phenomenon:

> As the dimensional points of space, so are the dimensional points of other substances (except time). The atom has no dimensional point, but hence is explained the developments of dimensional points. But a moment has no dimensional point. It occurs when a substance with a single dimensional point crosses a dimensional point of space.[52]

As a mathematical measure, Time was presented both as a crude poeticism of cyclic progress (unfortunately thought to be the only perception of Time in India) as well as schematic and scientific linear progress. Perhaps the best record of these concepts is to be found in the memoirs of Al Beruni, an eleventh century Arabic thinker. Al Beruni recorded with amazing accuracy most of the intellectual developments in India around the year AD 1030. His areas of special interest were mathematics and astronomy. In a chapter entitled 'On the Dominants of the Different Measures of Time both Religious and Astronomical Relations and on Connected Subjects,' he mentions the prevalent schemes of measuring time in India:

> Duration, or time in general, only applies to Creator as being *his* age, and not determinable by a beginning and an end. In fact, it is his eternity. They frequently call it *the soul,* i.e. *purusa.* But as regards common time, which is determined by motion, the single parts of it apply to beings beside *the soul.* Thus *kalpa* is always used in relation to Brahman, for it is his day and night, and his life is determined by it. Each *manavantara* has a special dominant called *Manu,* who is described by special qualities, already mentioned in a former chapter. On the other hand. I have never heard anything of dominants of the *caturyugas* or *yugas.*[53]

The last reference in Al Beruni is to the Samkhya view of the 'inverted' process of human evolution, from *satyayuga* to *kaliyuga,* from a luminous age to a dark age. It is worth noting that after the eleventh century Samkhya undergoes a revision in which the original concept of time is abandoned.[54] On the other hand, the emergence of the bhashas brings with it a new outlook to time. *Pasayadana,* the concluding section of *Jnanesvari,* expresses a strong hope for a better future for every human being. An accentuated sense of the future and the past as being distinct from the present moment start developing with the new languages. Historians tell us that a new kind of historical writing had started arising at this juncture from even small geographical areas, as for instance, Kashmir and Nepal.[55] Kalhana's *Rajatarangini* (twelfth century, Sanskrit), and Hemachandra's *Parishishtaparvan* (twelfth century, Sanskrit) are well-known examples of history-based narratives. The arrival of Islam in India strengthened this interest in history to such an extent that we have an extraordinarily brilliant piece of historiography in the fourteenth century Ziaud-din Barni's *Tarikh-i-Firuz Shahi* (1357).

The new interest in history can be seen to indicate the new bhasha culture's attempt to situate itself in a new and more pragmatic relation to Time and, thereby, to tradition. In a similar way, the *bhakti* era made radical revisions of the concepts of language and the self. The main thrust of bhasha culture was towards humanizing these and other related concepts. *Devabhasa* (divine speech), Sanskrit, was discarded by literatures in favour of *matrbhasha* (mother tongue), the vernaculars. The impersonal philosophic conception of the relation between *Brahman* and *atman* (the Universal Principle and the Self) proposed by Sankara was replaced by a more personal and intimate relation between the divine and the human, whereby a saint-poetess like Mira could claim the cowherd god, Krishna, as her only mate *(Mere to Giridhara Gopala, dusaro na koi).* Even the matters of one's inner life were perceived in terms of a family structure: Krishna became the husband or the lover, Vitthal as well as Jnanadeva became the mother, *mauli,* and the devotees became at times children, at other times playmates to Krishna.

The concept of *bhakti* has received close attention in a recent psychoanalytical study of Indian society. Sudhir Kakar has commented on Krishna-*bhakti* at length in his study of Indian childhood, in which he interprets *bhakti* as a means of releasing the chaotic instincts from the inner world:

> The psycho-social meaning of *bhakti* is that is provides for, and actually uses, 'democratic' fantasies in which the

> inner and outer repressions exacted by life in a rigidly structured and highly stratified social order are lifted. Traditional codes of conduct, and relationships between social groups, between generations, and especially between the sexes, are abrogated in Krishna worship.[56]

Kakar sees Krishna symbolism as a device for releasing anarchic and instinctual forces from the psyche, and also of fulfilling the fantasies of a Utopian social order. This interpretation makes it clear that the tremendous wave of *bhakti* poetry, which swept India across all linguistic boundaries and over an extended temporal span, selected its central symbolism by no accident. It was a choice that vindicated the vertical, regional, and *deshi* elements of culture against the hegemonic, and over-rigid *marg* traditions. Of course, Krishna-*bhakti* was not the only kind of devotionalism prevalent during that period. Poets like Tulsidas in Hindi and Ramdas in Marathi felt inspired to follow Rama. The Sufi poets wrote about an idealized feminine principle; and in Marathi a strong tradition of Datta-cult literature also emerged. However, it cannot be denied that the charismatic child god, Krishna, provided the main paradigm for devotionalism.

During the *bhakti* period, many local variations on Krishna-*bhakti* became popular in different regions of India. Various myths related to Krishna 's life were enshrined in cults developed round the important geographical focuses, Vrindavan and Mathura. In Maharashtra, the local form of Krishna, Vitthal or Vithoba, was worshipped. It was around Vithoba, the god in Pandharpur, that the *varakari* sect grew, and assimilated in its body of scriptures the poetry of Jnanadeva, Namadeva, Eknath and Tukaram, by far the greatest Marathi poets. In most bhashas the story of Krishna's life, and isolated episodes from it, particularly those that symbolized free play of libidinal and subconscious impulses, became a source of inspiration to poets. Numerous poems were written, for instance, on the romantic episode of Krishna's wedding with Rukmini. This tremendous upsurge of *bhakti* literature was the visible index of complex but fundamental changes taking place in Indian society during the high tide of Islamic rule. *Bhakti* was not a movement restricted to one area of life. It was a composite concept and a pervasive movement, which mediaeval India posed as an alternative to the hegemony *of marg* traditions and to the excessively sophisticated system of Sanskrit poetics.

The development of *bhakti* poetry was a natural consequence of the emergence of the bhasha literatures. *Bhakti* unleashed an emotionalism which classical Indian literature had held under the strict control of conventions and rigidly defined social ethics. In revolting against them, and in turning to an unrestrained emotionalism, *bhakti* made itself incapable of developing intellectual systems founded on rational thought. It had a revolutionary social and literary drive; but this spirit blossomed through symbolism and mysticism, and could not find the rational strength necessary to formulate intellectual discourse. Not surprisingly, therefore, *bhakti* had few theoreticians to systematize its poetics. There were some feeble attempts at introducing *bhakti* to the gamut of *rasas* established by Bharata in the fourth century, much before India had known gunpowder, paper and Islam.

In his *Natyashastra* Bharata had proposed eight *rasas* as types of aesthetic emotion evoked by drama and poetry. The later Sanskrit theorists had started including to them the ninth *rasa*—the *shanta*—as the originative state of all *rasas* which an epic like the *Mahabharata* could evoke. As a part of the 'Sanskritization process' of *bhakti* poetry, carried out by writers and mystics who felt emotionally closer to the Greater Tradition, attempts were made to include *bhakti* in the list of established *rasas.* The most important among the commentators who gave *bhaktirasa* a distinguished status was Rupa Goswami (1470–1554). In his *Bhaktirasamrtasindhu* (1541–2)—the ocean of *bhakti*-nectar—Rupa Goswami proposed *bhakti* as aesthetic delight attained through *madhurarati,* the ecstasy of love and union with Krishna. In describing the new *rasa* he used the entire apparatus of theory provided by Bharata and interpreted by Abhinavagupta. Predictably, therefore, no new theory of poetry was created from this extension of an old theory which was formulated originally twelve hundred years before Rupa Goswami's times. During the long interval the the meaning of most basic concepts had undergone several changes. For instance, Bharata had used *shringara* (eros, or the man–woman relation) as one of the aesthetic emotions. In his time, elopement was accepted as a legitimate mode of *shringara*. *Raksasavivaha*, a forced marriage, which must have been a relic of the colonial confrontation during the early centuries of Aryan advent in India, was accepted as a form *of shringara*. But, by the time Ala-ud-din Khilji died (AD 1316), the violations perpetrated by the alien armies had turned the substance of *shringara* into that of *karuna*, or more correctly *shoka*, bemoaning. When *shringararasa* was conceptualized, the man-women relationship had a certain degree of natural freedom in society. But this freedom was almost lost during the early Islamic period which saw an increase in the crimes against woman. *Raksasavivaha*, *Gandharvavivaha*, etc., were the subject of the *shringara* poetry previously. Now, however, such a *vivaha* could only be a violent or tragic experience. To use the apparatus of the *rasa* theory in this radically changed cultural context was a futile exercise. Needless to say, Rupa Goswami's theory did nothing more than to grant a Sanskritic legitimacy to *bhakti* literature. In the words of P. V. Kane, "Rupa Goswami was inspired... to place the doctrine of *bhakti* concentrated on Krishna into the garb and phraseology of the *rasa* theory."[57] His discussion of *rasa* was limited in scope and intent, and had no power to replace the earlier *rasa* and *dhvani* theories of Sanskrit poetics.

Since the sole aim of *bhakti* poetry was to challenge the *marg* traditions, traditions of logically rigorous philosophic systems, its attitude to theory was one of indifference. It tried every kind of experimentation with style and diction, and replaced every established convention of poetry; but it never tried to formulate a statement of the new conventions of poetry. When such statements were made at all, by scholars reared on Sanskrit intellectual traditions, they were too inclusive and theoretically weak. Madhusudan Saraswati's *Bhaktirasayana* was one such statement. Commenting on it, R. B. Patankar points out that it obfuscates the concept of 'universalization' *(sadharanikarana)*, which was well defined in classical Sanskrit poetics. Patankar writes:

> In everyday life we see Dusyanta as an individual; in dramatic experience we apprehend the universalized Dusyanta, that is not Dusyanta at all but man as such. But what universalization is conceivable in the case of Krishna, who, even outside the domain of poetry and

> drama is already universalized? *Bhakti* with Krishna as its object automatically becomes *bhaktirasa;* a *bhakta* automatically becomes a *rasika.* If unmixed pleasure *(ananda)* is made the distinguishing mark of literary experience, *bhaktirasa* becomes the supreme *rasa*, because Krishna, as the ultimate substratum of the universe, is of the nature of unmixed *ananda.*[58]

Bhaktirasa, therefore, could have become a viable literary theory in the context of *bhakti* poetry, had it solved the problem of 'universalization', as Bharata had done earlier with reference to other aesthetic emotions. The theoreticians of *bhakti* poetry did not have that philosophic rigour. Their aim was, restricted to using the traditional Indian device of turning all new experiences into archaic stuff, a device of extending *parampara,* the hoary tradition.

As a consequence of the theoretical ineptitude of *bhakti* literature combined with the rigidity of Sanskrit poetics, literary criticism in India has ceased to be a unified field of intellectual discourse ever since the emergence of the bhasha literatures. It may be necessary here to define the term 'discourse', since it is variously used in current critical diction. I find the oldest definition of the term, offered by Panini is his *Sutrapatha* (4th century BC), adequate for the present purpose. It is implied in the following debate:

> *Purvapakshsin:* What is meant by *upadishta?*
> *Siddhapakshin:* Uttered.
> *P.*: How does it come to mean that? . . . By whom uttered?
> *S.*: By the *shishthas.*
> *P.:* Who are the *shishthas?*
> *S.:* The grammarians.
> *P.:* How so?
> *S.*: The character of a *shishtha* is conferred upon one by the knowledge of the science *(shastra);* and the grammarians know the science (of grammar).
> *P.:* If a man is made *shishtha* by the science, and the science depends on a man's being *shishtha,* this is reasoning in a circle. An argument in a circle does not hold . . .
> *S.:* Well, then, the character of a *shishtha* is conferred upon one by the country in which he lives.[59]

What Panini says here is that knowledge does not gain its status as knowledge unless it has a social sanction to acquire that status. Intellectual discourses are socially legitimated systems, which are also *'upadishta'* or well-ordered. Panini's discussion is about the system of knowledge of languages. He mentions three minimum conditions of a discourse: it must contain knowledge about something outside itself, it must be well-ordered, and it must receive social legitimacy as a system of knowledge. Accepting this as an adequate definition of 'discourse' it can be said that literary criticism attains the status of an intellectual discourse when it stands on the point of intersection of an existing body of literature, a logically formulated theory, and a society's acceptance of the correspondence between these two.

The *bhakti* movement generated a substantial body of literature marked by an intense devotionalism without a self-conscious intellectual discourse of criticism originating from it. The movement did not initiate a new theory of literature, primarily due to a breakdown in the intricate network of the *marg* and the *deshi* traditions. Sociologically, devotional poetry was a challenge posed by the oppressed classes to the brahminical monopoly of cultural and scriptural knowledge. The challenge, however, did not make a dent in the formal system of knowledge transmission.

All through the middle centuries of Indian history, as in the classical period, formal education in schools and centres of higher learning was under the control of brahminical classes. This grip was tightened in reaction to the upsurge of *bhakti.* During the preceding ages, Indian philosophies and intellectual movements had sought and secured a respectable academic status. For instance, thinkers like Panini and Sankara had carefully laid down the pedagogic methods to be followed to transmit their thoughts to the future generations. As against this scrupulous academic interest, the *bhakti* poets thought of formal scholarly training as a stumbling block in the way of perceiving the truth of life, and as a rigid outmoded form that was unwilling to assimilate the new perception of life. One of the innumerable examples of this irreverent attitude to formalized education is to be found in Ramdas's *Dasabodha.* In the hauntingly beautiful verses (forty-one in all) of the tenth section of the second book of his *opus,* the seventeenth century Marathi saint-poet describes the attributes of *padhatmurkha,* a person embodying knowledge without wisdom. Here is one: *"Nahi bhaktice sadhan, nahi vairagya na bhajan, kriyevina bole brahmagnana, to eka padhatmurkha"* (a bookish fool is one who knows all mapped knowledge without an iota of *bhakti, vairagya, bhajana* and deed).[60]

The prevalent patterns of patronage intensified this class war in literature. The political structures dominant during the *bhakti* centuries were feudalistic, and, though dissent within the overall central structure of the subcontinent was a constant feature of political history, dissent at the popular level was dreaded equally by all rulers. *Bhakti* literature, therefore, was not welcomed by the class capable of providing political patronage to literature. One extreme example of this political opposition to *bhakti* literature is that of Sikh extermination after Nanak inspired his people through his poetry. The other, preceding it by five centuries, is that of the cruel feudal attacks on the Kannada Virsaiva sect inspired by Allama Prabhu and Basavanna. In many of Basavanna's poems we get glimpses of the tyranny:

> I went to fornicate,
> but all I got was counterfeit.
> I went behind a ruined wall,
> but scorpions stung me.
> The watchman who heard my screams
> just peeled off my clothes.
> I went home in shame,
> my husband raised weals on my back.
> All the rest, O lord of the meeting rivers,
> the king took for his fines.[61]

It would be more appropriate, perhaps, to say that the *marg* tradition accepted only the theological content of *bhakti,* neglecting its rebellious spirituality. Hence, the ruling classes continued to provide uninterupted patronage to Sanskrit-based formal education all through the middle centuries. Persian and Arabic were added to Sanskrit when the patronage was administered by the Islamic rulers. In other words, formal education belonged to *marga,* while the experience of life's complexities was perceived and articulated through *deshi* idiolects.

The gap between lived experience and formalized knowledge was at the root of the non-emergence of critical discourse relevant to *bhakti* literature. Literature was being produced in the bhasha, criticism continued to survive through Sanskrit and the fragmented community of writers and scholars came to value in both that which was convenient to value. The modern mind, reared on Western paradigms of literary history, may find this situation difficult to grasp. The established view of this situation describes it in terms of a failure, a sickness, a vacuum, and an inability. However, given that thc bhashas produced first-rate literature and they were not entirely innocent of criticism as a discipline, it would not be correct to maintain that Indian literature had lost, for a period of half a millennium, its critical sensibility. It would be more appropriate to say that criticism did not become a discourse, a monolingual system of intellectual premises about literature; but it remained a multicultural and multilingual enterprise. Multiculturalism and multilingualism need not be seen as symptoms of a great cultural failure and sickness merely because they have no parallels in Western literary history. They were at first political and social necessities, and were invested with legitimacy and practical utility by devotionalism. This has, in fact, been a unique contribution of the *bhakti* period to Indian literary sensibility. *Bhakti* literature itself was perfectly at ease with such multilingualism. The sense of guilt attached to it is an element that was introduced in the Indian sensibility during the British colonial period, particularly after English education was introduced in India. However, at the time of the initial contact with the British, the Indian mind considered multiculturalism and multilingualism as natural conditions of existence, and continued to strive to maintain them as such even during the high period of Indian nationalism which was inspired by Europe's monolingual monocultural nationalism. We will now see how Indians collaborated with the British so as to preserve the native tradition of multiculturalism and multilingualism.

Colonial Structure: The City and the Cantonment

A distinctive feature of the British colonial rule in India was its reluctance to penetrate the interiors of Indian land and society. The colonial British valued the pragmatic concern of preserving their own cultural identity more than the idealistic concern of captivating Indian culture. When cultural influences were exerted in a conscious way, the reasons were always pragmatic and material. On the other hand, Indians developed their own insidious and subversive ways of receiving the alien influence, again for pragmatic reasons. The cultural encounter, therefore, was an elaborate pattern of collaboration and confrontation. The most essential feature of the Anglo-Indian colonial structure was its tolerance of dualities and unwillingness to make extreme choices.

In the initial stages of the East India Company's expansion (1616–1757), the British settlements were restricted to coastal trading posts such as Surat, Bombay, Cochin, Madras and Calcutta. Bengal came under the Company's indirect rule with Clive's success at the battle of Plassey in 1757. It should interest students of colonial culture that the system of government established by Clive was known as the dual system, under which the administrative power was in the hands of the Nabob, and the military and free trade powers in the control of the Company. Duality continued to be characteristic of many subsequent encounters during the entire colonial period. The British dominion over India was conclusively established by 1818, the year that marks the end of Maratha resistance. Yet, a large number of independent princely states, only indirectly controlled by the British, continued to criss-cross the map of British India. The British retained this political division during the ninety years of the high colonial rule—from the revolt in 1857 to Independence in 1947. During this phase, the territory of India was divided into British India, governed directly by the British administration in India, and princely India, consisting of 362 states with whom the British had drawn political treaties of various kinds. Though the princely states have been merged with the Union of India after 1947, the federal structure of government, which distributes authority between the Union and State governments, continues to show clear links with the dual system of Clive. When it was first introduced in Bengal, the dual system was not an established Western idea, and the idea was not to be found in any European textbook of political economy. It was worked out indigenously, in the crucible of colonial Bengal—a joint venture between the colonial British and the colonial Indians, and to that extent an Indian concept. No other British colony developed such an idea. It became a possibility due to the Indian contribution to it through a willing collaboration.

This collaborative relation came to an end with the revolt of 1857, and the encounter acquired a complex character of collaboration as well as confrontation. Prior to that, the relationship between the colonial British and the ruling Indian classes was one of equal partners/rivals in trade and plunder, in which both sides had decided not to interfere with each other except at the level of certain pragmatic concerns. It would be wrong, however, to conclude that the colonial context provided a coexistence that was free of cultural tensions. In fact, it was bound by an utter distrust of each other. The typical colonial British never could trust Indians, or those other British who trusted Indians. James Mill thought, for instance, that William Jones had no learning on Sanskrit, that he never read the *Ramayana* though he praised it so lavishly.[62] Indians, on the other side, never ceased to treat the British as alien people. William Hawkins, the first emissary of the Company, stationed at Surat, was despised by the local inhabitants and on occasion had to lock himself in to protect himself from Mughal soldiers.[63]

Early in the encounter, both the Indians and the British seem to have decided to build a relationship that was merely functional—a mixture of indifference and distrust—and to have no relationship beyond the merely economic and military. A self-consciousness about the nature of this relationship, in which both sides collaborated, resulted in a cultural relation which can be described aphoristically as 'city and cantonment structure'. It may be added in passing that English dictionaries describe the word 'cantonment' as being of Indian origin.[64] Like the dual system, to which it is ideologically related, the cantonment style of town planning is a distinctive feature of the British colonial rule in India.

It was evident from the very early stages of the colonial encounter that the British had little sympathy for Indian art and architecture. Sir Thomas Roe, writing to the Archbishop of Canterbury, strikes the keynote of this attitude;

> The buildings are all base of mud, one story high, except in Surat, where there are some of stone. The Emperor's own houses are of stone, handsome and uniform. The great men build not, for want of inheritance; but as far as I have yet seen, live in tents, or houses worse than cottages.[65]

Had he been less unsympathetic, he could not have missed the use of the *pietre dure* inlays in the royal buildings, designed after some of the most splendid buildings at Florence. A few decades later, Bernier (the French traveller referred to previously) could not stop wondering at "jaspers, *jachen,* or jade, as well as other stones" embellishing Indian architecture.[66] The negative attitude continued to dominate the British view of Indian housing till the days of James Mill and even John Ruskin. Mill reproduced Roe's letter on the first page of his *History of British India* (1826),[67] and Ruskin was left cold by the intricate embellishments of Indian art.[68] The result was that the British introduced their own style of architecture, of which the cantonment style was the more pragmatic manifestation.

Architecture is, with painting and literature, an area to which the British made a substantial contribution in India. But the colonial architecture was not a result of the pure love of that art. The Mughals had been magnificent builders; and architecture was in an advanced stage of development when the British came to India. However, most palaces, public buildings and fortified posts of district and state administration built by the Mughals, Marathas and Rajputs before the arrival of the British, were left almost completely unused by the British. In Delhi itself, the Red Fort built during the seventeenth century was not occupied by the British (except for some symbolic administrative functions) in the same way as it was occupied by the Mughals before them. Instead of occupying the traditional Indian office buildings, the British created cantonment areas. The British rulers never saw themselves in the role of 'new Mughals', though they imitated the traditional pomp and held occasional *durbars*. Total captivation of Indian culture and society had never been their aim. Thus, British architecture and town planning were organically linked with their political enterprise in India.

Another area in which the British jealously guarded their racial identity was sex relations. The Islamic rulers took as many wives as they could in India. The British, on the other hand, tried to prohibit, to the extent it was possible, sexual contact between the ruling race and Indians. Special laws were made, and were strictly enforced, for this purpose. If we mix Nandy's metaphor of sexual politics, used to describe colonialism, with the actual attitude of the British to sex, it can be said that the British displayed a keen interest in making the cultural relation completely non-productive.

One of the most embarrassing episodes in the social history of the raj was the case of Fanny Epstein[69] which attracted wide public attention in 1891. Through circumstances stranger than in fiction, Fanny arrived in Bombay, leaving behind a worried father in London. In Bombay's Kamathipura area she settled down to the life of a common prostitute. There used to be European girls specially encouraged to engage in the trade for benefit of the white races. But Fanny opened her doors to the natives of Bombay too. This act agitated the Bombay government so much that she was promptly repatriated to London. This fear of sexual relation with the native operated not only in the area of relationship between British females and Indian males, it also governed the area of relationship between British males and Indian females. After all, the total 'Anglo-Indian' population (or 'Eurasian' population as it was called before the first census in 1891) was minuscule, considering the length of the contact between the British and the Indians, at the time the British left India. The British fear of establishing sexual relations with Indians, correctly reflects the British unwillingness to participate in the ongoing cultural processes within the colonial India.

Kenneth Ballhatchet has made a probing study of race and sex relations during the British colonial period in India. He records:

> The cantonments provided an ordered environment, within which the British soldier could be protected from unsettling contact with Indian life. Most soldiers seem to have accepted the situation, and to have assumed within their world the privileged role of the member of the ruling race. They employed Indian servants, and felt the sexual jealousy characteristic of males of dominant group . . . the military police would as a matter of course turn Indian males out of brothels used by British soldiers; it seemed only proper to do so. Some soldiers, however, defied convention to the extent of declaring their intention of marrying Indian or Eurasian women. But to the end of British rule the authorities would discourage such unions. All members of the ruling race were supposed to keep their distance.[70]

Not taking Indian wives, not taking over Indian houses and buildings, segregation, and cantonment structure—all were facets of one basic attitude towards India. It was a wholly amoral, dehumanized and pragmatic attitude in which India was no more than a source of continuous economic gains. The Indian mind, trained by the multiculturalism of preceding centuries, saw through this game with clarity, and with an equal degree of pragmatism learnt to play the game to its advantage.

It is generally believed that the demand for English education came from Indian leaders like Rammohun Roy. Likewise, it is known that the nineteenth century witnessed an active debate centering round the theme of tradition versus Westernization. But a study of the sociological and psychological reasons for this has not been attempted. It is certain that though Indians asked for English education, they did not do so for a thorough Westernization. To have it was to have, figuratively speaking, an access to the life in cantonment. Arthur Mayhew, a sharp observer of Indian psychology, states this while commenting on education and Indian culture:

> When we think of what, through our instruction, the Indian can do and must do to gain a livelihood, we imagine him in his government or mercantile office, pleading in the law courts, practising in the hospitals,

> and even doing in executive council or ministries the work that, for a century, has been reserved to the 'Heaven-born' of the civil service. Here he is Western and one with us. . . . If we follow the clerk home from his office, or the agricultural labourer, who has achieved literacy in the village school, home from the plough, and watch . . . we shall find the Oriental, not the Occidental. It is not merely a change from professional attire to the loin cloth of domestic life. Practically everything is shed that has been acquired at such cost from school and college and contact with the West. . . . You may talk with the educated Hindu pleasantly and profitably about his official or professional life . . . but the ordinary European will fail to find out what he really cares for as a man, what essentially gives value to his life as a whole, what constitutes his real self. . . The professor of English will not talk about his personal and intimate debt to that literature. For it does not intrude into his personal and domestic life.[71]

Mayhew's comments make it clear that the city-cantonment structure of the colonial culture suited the Hindu Indian as much as it did the colonial British administrator. The collaboration of the two in developing and preserving the structure is the theme of many perceptive works of fiction written about colonial India. In E. M. Forster's words, what connected the city and the cantonment was just 'the overarching sky'.[72]

The cantonment mentality was no mere quirk of the British mind. It was a calculated strategy to control the vast country with a minimum of expense on administrative machinery. All through the colonial period the British presence in India was very small in number. Nearly a century after Hawkins landed at Surat, the entire British population at a major trade centre like Madras was only one hundred and fourteen civilians and some three hundred soldiers. By the middle of the eighteenth century it was "more or less a settled policy that India should be a closed land to British subjects having no official connections."[73] British-born subjects were prohibited from holding land in India after 1766, and required a licence to go to India after 1783 according to laws passed in the British Parliament. In 1833, the exact number of

British soldiers in India was 36,422; that of civil servants 1,055; and of private civilians a mere 2,687. In 1931, when a vast popular movement threatened the British empire, there were 100,000 British in India, of whom the army personnel accounted for 70,000 and civilians 30,000.[74] In order to control a vast country like India with the help of such a small number of British persons, it was necessary to project a frighteningly masculine image. The colony was always like a war camp, where only the young and fit-to-fight were sent. Edmund Burke had once remarked that "there was one sight never seen in India, and that was the grey head of an Englishman."[75]

The cantonment thus became the symbol of youth, vitality, masculinity and power. It was the colonial symbol of the dominating male ego. But the cantonment was no 'home'. One died there fighting, not in a bed. There was therefore, no need to strike deep roots during the transitory cantonment existence. The city, on the other hand, had come to be the symbol of defeat, demoralization, weakness and femininity. It had its own ways of meeting the challenges to its identity and existence posed by the cantonment. Ashis Nandy has employed the metaphor of sexual politics to analyze the colonial psychology. He argues that the British worked within an epistemological structure of biologically stratified relations, and that India did not change the bipolarity of this relation but only the stratification implied. He comments:

> It was in this sense that Gandhi wanted to liberate the British as much as he wanted to liberate Indians . . . he challenged first the ideology of biological stratification acting as a homology of—and legacy for—political inequality and injustice . . . the colonial culture's ordering of sexual identities assumed that . . . manliness is superior to womanliness, and womanliness to femininity in man . . . Gandhi used two orderings, each of which could be invoked according to the needs of the situation. The first, borrowed intact from the great and little traditions of saintliness in India . . . was that manliness and womanliness are equal, but the ability to transcend the man-woman dichotomy is superior to both. Gandhi's

> second ordering was invoked specifically as a methodological justification for the anti-imperialist movement. . . the essence of femininity is superior to that of masculinity, which in turn is better than cowardice.[76]

The city and cantonment structure, with its politics of sex, race and culture, formed the essential typology of cultural relations in colonial India. Indians, with their experience of multiculturalism in the past, were able to face the colonial situation with maturity. The dual system of values itself became their weapon to fight colonialism in every area of culture, including literary criticism.

The Duality of Law

It would be instructive to study a specific example of how Indians used the stratified dual structure for their own benefit, particularly an example that has a bearing on literary criticism. The example that I wish to present is that of the legal system, for it may form an apt analogy for criticism which is a system of principles legislating literature. One of the first problems that the East India Company faced, after taking over from the Nabob, was related to the kind of legal system to be put in use. Nathaniel Halhed was asked, therefore, by Warren Hastings to prepare a special English commentary on Hindu law. Halhed's rendering was published in 1776 under the title *A Code of Gentoo Law.*[77] And less than four months after taking charge of his position in Calcutta, Hastings himself prepared what is known as the Judicial Plan of 1772, according to which, "in all suits regarding inheritance, marriage, caste, and other religious usages, or institutions, the laws of the Koran with respect to Mahometans and those of the Shaster with respect to Gentoos shall be invariably adhered to."[78] This was a pragmatic legal principle. But it would have proved economically unprofitable had it been applied to land disputes too. Hence, with respect to land and property disputes, the Company decided to accept law derived from the existing British model.

Since India already had well established administrative and fiscal law, when the Company established its government the problem of making a choice between the Indian legal system and the British legal system had to be faced. As a commentator remarks:

> "The impact of Western civilization," says W.A. Robson, "in the shape of the officials of the East India Company, on these ancient and divinely inspired systems of Hindu and Muhammedan law, formed one of the most dramatic juridical conflicts ever witnessed by the modern world." Obviously this was the logical sequel to the Battle of Plassey which ultimately established British political authority and brought in its wake the British judicial system as well."[79]

As stated above, the Company government settled for a dual system of law. The legal system inherited by free India has its origin in the late eighteenth century Bengal.

From among the studies of Indian legal system from a sociological perspective made in recent years, Oliver Mendelsohn's contribution[80] is highly relevant to our discussion. Mendelsohn builds his argument on two earlier studies, by Bernard Cohn[81] and Robert Kidder.[82] Cohn has argued that in attempting to introduce British procedural law into their Indian courts, the British confronted the Indians with a situation in which there was a direct clash of values of the two societies; and the Indians, in response, thought only of manipulating the new situation, and did not use the courts to settle disputes but only to further them. Kidder has argued, on the other hand, that the legal system inherited from the British does not adequately reflect Indian values, and therefore, fails to be effective. Mendelsohn, while deviating from both these views, points to the land factor involved in the bulk of the legal disputes and suggests that it is "the character of land relations in Indian village society which has inhibited the Western-style courts from effectively settling these disputes."[83] By using a case study to support his argument, he establishes that the Indian peasant uses the communal law when quick results are expected, and the Western-style court when the results have to be delayed:

> The distinctive character of the Anglo-Indian judicial system emerged through the medium of the most

> cherished foundations of British law, the rigorous procedures designed to promote justice. British, indeed all Western style, courts are essentially cautious institutions: they are authorised to give judgement for one or the other party—there can never be a compromise . . . only after each side had an opportunity to put its case. It is these procedures and rights which have been systematically distorted in the Indian case.[84]

What is suggested here, through a sociologist's observations, is an image of the Indian peasant as a successful manipulator of the city and cantonment value scale in the legal sphere to suit his practical needs in life.

A recognition of the Indian capacity to manipulate two distinct legal structures would reveal the ability to accommodate bipolar cultural systems, and to use them according to convenience. This traditional capacity to accept cultural duality has been finely sharpened by the colonial experience. It may indicate that the fear-psychosis and the sense of crisis, with which Indian criticism is gripped, and the tension caused by being 'torn' between 'Westernization' and 'Sanskritization', are epistemological rather than ontological features of Indian criticism.

4

After Amnesia

The Tripartite Relation

The key terms that appear in any account of modern Indian criticism are 'colonialism', 'Renaissance', 'modernity' and 'Westernization'. The logic behind the use of these terms is that colonialism triggered off the Indian Renaissance, and that one impact of Westernization on literature was to endow it with modernity. It is assumed that the colonial impact caused the Indian attempt at a grand synthesis of the East and the West, now termed 'Renaissance', and that the assimilation of Western literary forms and critical paradigms led to the assertion of self-identity and modern self-awareness in Indian literature. In order to examine the validity of these assumptions, first it would be necessary to distinguish their utility in the sphere of creative literature from that in the field of literary criticism. The reason for this distinction is that while creative literature in India has been continuously flourishing, criticism shows little signs of catching up with it. That has been the Indian experience from the beginning of the bhasha literatures. In the context of literary criticism, the accepted assumptions about the relation between colonialism and Renaissance, and between Westernization and modernity, need to be challenged. Had the Renaissance effected a real transformation and produced an organic synthesis, the modern Indian critic could have thought in terms of a modern Indian tradition of literary criticism. The synthesis was, in reality, a hotchpotch of ideas drawn from a wide range of cultural and chronological sources. This haphazard mixture of ideas acquired value within the colonial context. It is in this sense that colonialism and the Renaissance were interrelated.

In a study of modern Indian aesthetics, S. K. Nandi[1] has discussed the literary aesthetics of Rabindranath Tagore, Brajendranath Seal, Sri Aurobindo and Abanindranath Tagore. Uniformly in the critical thought of all four, Nandi finds kinship with "the ancient Indian ideas on art and beauty", as also with Spinoza, Croce and others in the West. His concluding remarks are:

> Thus the philosophies of art and beauty as found in the two Tagores, and in Brajendranath and Sri Aurobindo were very much allied in their fundamentals as they borrowed from the same storehouse of Indian civilization and culture . . . these Indian thinkers line up with the most ardent logical minds of the West who ever thought and wrote on aesthetic problems in recent past.[2]

The four critics studied by Nandi belonged to the Indian Renaissance period, the historical boundaries of which have not yet been thoroughly debated or defined. It is difficult not to admire the quality of intelligence that has gone into the making of their critical writing. How is it that, in spite of their individual talents, they attempted a synthesis that was bound to fail? To answer this question it would be more fruitful to study the process of value acquisition at work in their writing than to examine the ideas employed there. It will be useful to see what made them undertake the synthesis, or select the specific cultural form of criticism.

It is an accepted principle in cultural anthropology as well as in economics that generally whatever is useful acquires value. The significance attached to literary criticism in the total spectrum of a nation's culture by the English critics Matthew Arnold and F. R. Leavis was an outcome of a long tradition of the usefulness of criticism in English society. As Joan Simon points out in a study of the social origins of English education, the education of the seven 'liberal' arts—grammar, rhetoric, logic, arithmetic, geometry, music and astronomy—was a device of self-transformation for the mediaeval English society.[3] Though grammar and classical literature were taught in mediaeval England at the university level, literary criticism came to be recognized as an area of study only after land ceiling acts of seminal importance started disrupting the society to create sharply divided class structures. It was towards the middle of the eighteenth century that literary criticism acquired the status of a valued cultural form in England. In a radical reinterpretation of the English critical tradition, Terry Eagleton has shown how criticism was a tool of social protest in the eighteenth century, and then how it acquired the status as a class 'possession'.[4] Like him we can say that criticism was of vital importance to Arnold and Leavis because of its ideological placement and usefulness. To this argument it is possible to add one more strand from the Indian perspective. Eagleton says about the rise of 'English' as an academic discipline:

> 'English' as an academic subject was first institutionalized not in the Universities, but in the Mechanics' Institutes, working men's colleges and extension lecturing circuits. English was literally the poor man's Classics . . . [with] the emphasis on solidarity between the social classes, the cultivation of 'larger sympathies', the installation of national pride and the transmission of 'moral' values . . . indeed the rise of 'English' is more or less concomitant with an historic shift in the very meaning of the term 'moral', of which Arnold, Henry James and F. R. Leavis are the major critical exponents.[5]

In fact, the expansion of British colonial power is as important a reason for the gain of status by 'English' as the social conflict inherent in the class structure. English criticism, which was a feeble branch of English literature up to the beginning of the nineteenth century, subsequently acquired great significance because the colonies provided a ready and vast market for critical texts. English was after all a basic theme in the imperialistic enterprise as it was in the Victorian class rift. In order to educate the colonies in the finer points of English literature it was necessary to export a large number of commentaries on English writers. The steady decline in the philosophic substance of English criticism, from Shelley's *Defence,* through Arnold's *Study,* to Leavis's text/author based assessment, has to be ascribed to the rising need in the colonies for critical commentaries on authors and texts. A historical perspective shows that English literary criticism, and by extension European literary criticism, developed and acquired value due to its usefulness. During the colonial period it became a valued marketable commodity, a pragmatic cultural form.

The nature of 'value' that literary criticism had in England underwent a major shift when 'English' was introduced in the Indian education system. From being merely a valuable commodity it now became a value-giving acquisition. Education in English literature lent value to the person who had received it, who himself became a commodity in the job-market created by the colonial government. While the intention of the Indian leaders who sought English education was to gain access to the English mind, the objective of the British in providing it was to win loyalty from their colonial subjects. Neither succeeded fully. But this collaborative effort certainly enhanced the value of English literary education and, thereby, the discipline of literary criticism. Since education worked as a channel to draw the 'natives' into the colonial market system, creating a class of culturally displaced Indians, such a displacement came to be valued. Imitating Arnold, Leavis, etc., this class then started maintaining that literary criticism is an index of a healthy culture. Thus, in India, literary criticism of the Western type was pressed into use *after* it came to acquire value.

Critical theories and trends in the West had originated in their specific local contexts. Their spread through the machinery of the colonial education system created a climate of literary views which seems, in retrospect, quite absurd. For instance, the Romantic prose writers had received some moderate praise from their contemporaries for the individuality of their prose styles, but apart from being highly interesting they had not contributed much to the tradition of English literature in terms of a new diction, syntax or concept of literary language. But these, particularly Thomas Carlyle and Charles Lamb, were taught in India as models of prose writing. Framed in colonial pedagogy, these 'interesting' writers of English became 'good' prose writers of universal significance. Drilled in Carlyle and Scott, the Indian writers of bhasha literature too, started writing in that style, producing prose that was hardly readable. Thus, the inadequacy of the concept of prose style in English—which continued till the time of the Russian Formalism and French Structuralism—was nicely packaged and sold to the colonial literary market as a substance of great value.

The colonial framework created one more absurdity—a thoughtless anachronism in critical practice. Western criticism has passed through four major stages of development, as M. H. Abrams argues: (i) Mimetic, with theories focusing on the relation between literature and the cosmos (ii) Pragmatic, with theories focusing on the relation between literature and the audience (iii) Expressive, with theories focusing on the relation between literature and the writer (iv) Autonomous, with theories focusing on literature as a sovereign ontological object.[6] This progression of Western theories took place within a time frame of nearly two thousand years. Since the colonial background invested everything Western with a positive value, Indian literary criticism started employing components of all four types of literary theory without regard to the history of their origins.

We can see in the bhasha criticism of the colonial period a simultaneous presence of the mimetic ideas of structure, the pragmatic ideas of style, the expressive ideas of the poetic imagination, and the autonomous ideas of form. Since all these ideas were Western, they were thought to be universally useful and valuable. In reality, these ideas had originated in the context of divergent metaphysical and social perceptions. The mimetic theories were formed within the framework of Platonism, the didactic concepts were based on the Ptolemaic cosmogony. The expressive aesthetics came as a culmination, even as a reaction, to Newtonian physics and Bacon's logic.[7] And the autonomous poetics had developed out of a growing relativism in physics and pluralism in philosophy. These obvious distinctions were overlooked by the colonial Indian critic not because he had no intellectual capacity to notice them but because the theorizing about literature was seen as a sign of cultural vitality.

Most of the Indian critical talent has been wasted in pursuit of theory, much of which has been totally irrelevant to literature in India. The value attached to it was only a 'reflected value', for literary theory was esteemed for its 'cultural significance' more than its usefulness. In terms of the psychology of colonialism, to theorize is the special prerogative of the colonizers and to mime the effort is the strange fate of the colonized. To theorize is to structure the universe of literature, to establish a desirable order, to discipline history, to play the dominating male, the father figure. Colonial success and imperialistic fortunes created a special role for theoretical criticism in the West. The colonial Indian critic, in the inevitable attempt to play his role of a cultural 'female', child, a person deprived of his history, a 'civilized', 'disciplined' being, tried to ape the Western trend of literary theorizing. His need to do so was an imposed need, a transaction guided by the laws of 'reflected value'.

The most crucial factor in this transaction was the attempt to define the 'self' of Indian criticism in terms of 'the other' of Western criticism. This was not just a simple comparative enterprise caused by the shrinking of the globe. In fact, the possibility of a meaningful comparison of Western literary texts/trends and Indian literary texts/trends has been seriously questioned in recent years.[8] The constant reference to 'the other' was the central feature in the self-definition of Indian criticism. Here are some instances, all belonging to the twentieth century: The opening sentence of G. S. Amur's highly scholarly essay on laughter in Sanskrit poetics, "Meredith's theory that the East has no sense of the comic comparable to that of the West does not do justice to Sanskrit literature and literary theory . . ."[9] Krishna Rayan writing on *rasa* and objective correlative, quotes from T. S. Eliot's essay on *Hamlet*, and remarks: "This could be Anandavardhana in the ninth century judging a play or a poem in terms of *rasa-dhvani.*"[10] V. K. Gokak's 'Indian Perspective' on poetry begins thus: "Carlyle defined poetry as musical thought. . ."[11] B. S. Mardhekar's opening remarks in his essay discussing the nature of aesthetic judgement:

> There is a mass of literature which, either directly or indirectly, bears on our problem. On the philosophical

> side, we may start with Plato and come, if we care, right down to Prof. Collingwood, with Kant and Croce obviously outstanding in their contributions. On the psychological side, experimental work, which began with Fechner in the last century, has been carried on by a succession of psychologists including Legowski, Yokoyama, von Allesch, Weber, Buhler, Wertheimer and others.[12]

The insistence on referring to Western scholars, on defining self-identity in terms of the Western other, on reading the universe of aesthetic experience through the mediation of the prescribed text of Western developments in that field of knowledge—all are characteristic of the colonial impact.

The Indian process of self-definition had its counterpart in the Western definition of Indian identity. Indology, the discourse which offered this definition in the field of literature, was not an isolated development, it was an integral part of a global programme of literary ordering congenial to Western imperialism. In this global order, a hierarchic structure of literary categories was postulated with Europe at the top, followed by the white colonies, the Orient, and Africa, in that order. Different methods of literary study were reserved for each category. Thus, the method appropriate to the study of European literature was comparative literature and literary theory, the one for the Orient was Orientalism or Indology, and that of African literature was anthropology. We have already referred to William Jones's project of Indological study. Here I will add comments by a scholar of anthropology about the evolution of his discipline. In a provocative essay, 'Skeletons in the Anthropological Closet', William S. Willis comments:

> White rule with its color inequality is the context in which anthropology originated and flourished, and this context has shaped the development of anthropology. The formalization of anthropology in the nineteenth century coincided with the shift from 'booty' colonialism to imperialism, which stressed profit from the control, exploitation, and preservation of cheap colored workers and consumers. The persistent distinction between "primitive" and "civilized" has been made falsely to

> coincide with the pervasive color bar. This distinction has ignored colored individuals and societies that satisfy the criteria of civilization; on the other hand, this distinction has ignored white individuals and societies not meeting these criteria . . . To a considerable extent, anthropology has been the social science that studies dominated colored peoples—and their ancestors—living outside the boundaries of modern white societies.[13]

As anthropology was the method of literary study, and cultural investigation of peoples condemned to a permanent state of primitiveness, so was Indology a method of cultural study of a nation that was condemned to a perpetual decline and linguistic vulgarization. Since the premise of cultural decline was firmly ingrained in Indology, the European scholars engaged in it valued Sanskrit poetics but did not consider the bhashas fit to evolve literary theories. Indology was received hospitably by Indian scholars; and once again poetics that had lost its usefulness four or five centuries ago was lent 'value'. Coomaraswamy, Hiriyanna and such other Indian critics who wrote about Sanskrit poetics with great enthusiasm and reverence collaborated with the Indological value scheme in literary criticism. Implicit in Indology's theme of decline was the unwillingness of the West to recognize Indian society's full and present identity. The rise of Indology was concomitant with the rise in Europe of an acute awareness of history as the past. Indology, therefore, could not perceive Indian culture as a dynamic force.

The leaders of the Indian Renaissance tried to counter the Indological unwillingness to permit Indian culture a complete status; but 'their way to do so was to emphasize the presence of all European virtues in Indian society and culture. The essays on '*pratibha* and imagination', '*rasa* and objective correlative', 'Aristotle and Bharata', that one finds in a large number in Indian critical literature of this century are a fall-out of the Renaissance reaction to Indology. Thus, the attempt at self-definition and establishing a native identity in the field of literary criticism involved either catching up with the West or vying with it in claims to ultimate answers to problems in literary criticism.

The process of 'Westernization'—in the sense of opening up to the West for the purpose of self-definition—in literary criticism was by no means a single and unified process. It had numerous strands and themes in it. It was quickened by a variety of agents. The Christian missionaries brought with them printing technology, lexical traditions of their scriptures, European medicines, elementary schools that gave education through the medium of the bhashas, and coercive conversions. Their appeal was mainly to the lower castes and to the poorer sections of Hindu society. The Indologists carried out historical researches, studied linguistic connections, produced translations of Sanskrit texts and wrote commentaries on them. They interested the class of pundits and mullahs that was away from the centres of power. It was Indology that floated the myth of spirituality as the essence of Indian culture. The colonial administration influenced the land division and revenue structures, introduced 'Western'-type university education, and introduced the 'English' component in education. Mostly it was the middle class brahmin population that was affected directly by Western literary influences released through the administrative channel. Nationalism was a response to the work of the Indologists, the missionaries and the British administration. This collective response, because of the nature of its genesis, freely combined liberal values, orthodoxy and cultural chauvinism. Hence, nationalism in the field of literary criticism involved acceptance of liberal Western ideas and paradigms of literature, together with the revival of Sanskrit poetics. An ideal imitation of the West in this field would have been to orient Indian criticism to the bhasha literatures just as English criticism was oriented to English literature. But colonialism produced tolerance for inappropriate models, a liking for theorizing, and a loss of self-confidence. In the field of literary criticism, Westernization has taken the form of submission to the forces of colonization. Hence, the modern period of Indian culture has transformed the bilateral relationship of the *marg* and the *deshi* traditions into a tripartite relationship between the *marga,* the *deshi,* and the colonial, with respect to literary criticism.

It is generally believed by historians of modern Indian literature that Westernization/modernization' marks a radical breaking away from 'tradition' in Indian criticism. Our discussion of the fate of the Western type of contract-based law, in the previous chapter, would indicate that Indian critics can manipulate both to their convenience. Sociological studies of modern Indian society too point to a similar conclusion. A recent sociological study of 'modernization' in India states:

> The indigenous centres and networks of the Little and Great Indian traditions function sometimes independently and sometimes also as bearers of the Little and Great traditions of modernization. In the contemporary processes of cultural change in India both syncretic and separate existence of tradition and modernity, which often seems enigmatic to many, can be explained by these processes. Culturally, therefore, we may find in India three important ramifications: the traditional, the modern, and the traditional-modern.[14]

The traditional–modern aspect of culture is what another sociologist, Fred Riggs, describes as 'prismatic',[15] or what we have called in the previous section 'transitional'. It is true that colonialism brought with it Westernization in literature and colonial tendencies in literary criticism. But it is not correct to mainain that it replaced the earlier process of incomplete transition. What it did was merely to introduce one more, and very powerful, element in the value-relationship that had earlier conditioned the bhasha criticism. Rather than bringing in an altogether new discourse, it actually brought with it a new, and an even more formidable, hindrance to literary criticism's completing the hermeneutical circle. For the last hundred and thirty years the body of Indian literary criticism has been trying to accommodate this third element, and has, thereby, become an expression of a tripartite relation of the *marga,* the *deshi* and the colonial. The relation consists of various patterns of collaboration as well as confrontation of these three traditions with one another. The colonial experience has also created an ideology of literary criticism which specifies what criticism should be and should not be. It has affected the Indian perception of the significance of literary criticism, and also provided criticism with an economic basis.

We have referred to Eagleton's account of the rise of 'English' as an academic discipline in England. There its aim was to keep the lower economic classes in their position. That certainly was the aim in India too, in the context of the colonizers-colonized relationship; but in the exclusively Indian context, English education and knowledge of English literature meant higher positions in the government. Acquisition of some knowledge about English literature was also acquisition of the means to social climbing. The modern Indian universities, which are at present the centres for reception and emulation of Western trends in literary criticism, are also centres for seeking material betterment. It is the class of people who benefited by the study of Western forms of knowledge, that controls the education system, publishing industry and the administrative hierarchies of knowledge. Naturally, therefore, Westernization in literary criticism is a matter of vested interest for this class.

The fear of an endless crisis in the field of literary criticism felt by the twentieth century Indian critics is the consequence of the class-based and 'Westernized' perception of the functions of criticism. While the field remains fragmented by the tripartite relation, an ever increasing emphasis is given to a steady Westernization of criticism. As we have argued, Westernization of Indian intellectual tools has merely perpetuated colonization instead of initiating modernization. The only means at our disposal to modernize literary criticism is, in fact, to allow it to complete the transition which had remained incomplete during the pre-British centuries of the bhasha literatures, and which had become all the more difficult to complete during the colonial period. It is a delusion to believe that Westernization of literary criticism in India has given it a new vitality. On the contrary, by inducing Indian critics to undertake an imitative activity of mindless theorizing, it has created a set of literary premises and critical frameworks into which bhasha literature is coercively being fitted. The colonial perceptions of the history of the bhasha literatures, and the subsequent cultural amnesia, have made modern Indian critics incapable of appreciating the pragmatic wisdom of the bhasha literatures in refusing to submit to the authority of the *marg* criticism. We will try to read the structure of this amnesia in the text of some selected literary theories produced by some of the most outstanding Indian critics of the present century.

Sri Aurobindo, Rabindranath Tagore and Ananda Kentish Coomaraswamy are the three most influential literary critics of the Indian Renaissance. All three had profound knowledge of literary and cultural traditions of the East as well as the West, fluency in several languages, and a self-conscious nationalistic spirit. Coomaraswamy and Sri Aurobindo had been educated in the best British universities; Tagore and Coomaraswamy had an understanding of fine arts other than literature too; and Sri Aurobindo and Tagore were poets of great stature. All three engaged themselves in the pursuit of theory. Tagore's literary theory, mostly of a comparative nature, was presented through lectures and essays. Coomaraswamy turned to Sanskrit poetics and spoke in terms of a perennial philosophy of art and literature. In comparison, Sri Aurobindo was more consistent and original, for he tried to present a systematic theory of futuristic poetry. We will analyze some of Sri Aurobindo's critical ideas here as representative ideas of the Indian Renaissance.[16]

Sri Aurobindo (1872–1950) received his entire education after the age of seven in England, where he studied with absorbing interest European classical languages and literature. Matthew Arnold and Oscar Wilde were the literary heroes, and the theme of "the civilizing influence of literary study" was dominant, in the years that Sri Aurobindo spent at Cambridge. He was, therefore, totally estranged from Indian culture and the Indian literary heritage when he returned in 1891. Initially he attempted to fashion his poetry and poetics after the English or European models. One can see that the aesthetic notions scattered through his early writings are lifted straight from Plato and Shelley. But, after his return home, Sri Aurobindo seems to have become self-conscious about the colonial influence. Soon after he settled down to a teaching career at Baroda, he acquainted himself with Indian metaphysics, began writing poems based on Indian myths, took part in nationalist politics, started thinking about Indian art, literature and languages in a serious way, and tried to reassess his own literary values. In an early essay, 'The Sources of Poetry',[17] written when he was barely thirty, we see Sri Aurobindo arming himself to reject the European idea of the poet as creator. With the traditional Indian concept of the poet as a seer, he asserts in this essay that poetry is a revelation of something that exists eternally. It is here that he introduces the Sanskrit terms *satvik, tamasik* and *rajasik* to describe various levels of poetic inspiration. The essay shows the nationalistic tendency of reviving the Indian past as well as the colonial compulsion to theorize. This essay should form an interesting first document[18] of the amnesiac modern Indian criticism which shows how concepts prompted by *bhakti* poetry had to confront simultaneously the revivalistic spirit and the colonial influence.

The essay proposes a skeletal conceptual framework to understand the nature and kinds of poetry. According to it, poetry is essentially revelation, which, passing through the consciousness of the poet in the form of inspiration, manifests itself as an individual poem. The implication is that poetry must strive towards the condition of revelation in order to be perfect. The essay suggests that revelation is attained by overcoming the poet's personal preferences and by minimizing the role of his personality. Perfect poetry makes evident the intuitive reason, the intuitive judgement and the intuitive intellect of the poet. These are the higher functions of the poet's mind. There are also some lower functions—the realizing mind, and the observing and reasoning intellect with its aids, fancy and memory.

The intuitive intellect receives poetry/revelation, the intuitive reason and the intuitive judgement mould the revelation. Revelation-Inspiration-Manifestation is a continuous process. Revelation belongs to that part of the consciousness which is in touch with an undivided, unstructured reality beyond appearances, and beyond the grasp of the intellect and emotions. When, from this flux, revelation enters the poet's consciousness and language, it comes under the operation of reason and judgement. These mental faculties restructure it. Sir Aurobindo classifies poetry into three types—*tamasik, rajasik* and *satvik*—in terms of the interaction between the revelation and the conscious mind. What makes poetry great is the indissoluble link of the mind's response to the flux of reality. This intense and integrated response of the poet's mind can be termed as the quality of saintliness, for it silences personality and has the quality of prophecy. All great poetry is inevitably saintly in character.

The instances used by Sri Aurobindo to illustrate the kinds of poetry in this essay are mostly from English poetry. The terminology employed is from the Samkhya epistemology. The poetic virtue outlined, however, immediately brings to mind the long line of eminent poets of the bhasha traditions. In another essay, written in 1907, Sri Aurobindo introduces a different set of Sanskrit terms: *rasa, bhoga, ananda* to describe the nature of poetic delight. The nationalistic essay is characteristically called *The National Value of Art.*[19] It is an attempt to describe the aesthetic principles at the centre of Indian civilization, an interest that Aurobindo shared with Coomaraswamy. In a famous letter written to his Anglicized brother, Mono Mohan Ghose,[20] Sri Aurobindo attempts a passionate defence of Indian art and art values, and suggests that if one had the right sympathy Indian literature would no longer appear a volley of grotesque and crude folktales but would seem full of a spirit of harmony and delight. Here he was clearly reacting to the Indological conception of Indian literature. His need to 'Indianize' himself and to decolonize his critical idiom are fully evident in his early critical comments. However, a close study of his early aesthetics shows that he found it difficult to free himself from his English upbringing and the aesthetic ideas he had inherited from the English critics. In essence, his was a colonial critical consciousness.

The Future Poetry, a collection of essays serialized in the *Arya* from 1917 to 1920,[21] is a survey of English poetry conducted with a view to showing how most of English poetry falls short of the ideal of poetry as "the *mantra* of the Real". The criteria that Sri Aurobindo employs to assess the achievements of English poetry are "revelation of spiritual reality", "intuitive intellect" and "intuitive vision". His indictment of English poetry, which he finds generally lacking in spirituality, implies an unstated comparison between the English poetic tradition and the Indian poetry of the *Vedas* and the *Upanishads.* The attempt is to turn the hierarchy established by Indology upside down; however, the hierarchic framework is retained. Within that framework, *The Future Poetry* chalks out the principles that would bring future poetry in English in line with ancient Indian poetry. These principles mattered to Sri Aurobindo because he himself was engaged in an experiment of Indianizing the tradition of English Romantic poetry. This attempt at synthesis is the focal point in Sri Aurobindo's literary aesthetics presented in *The Future Poetry.* At the beginning of his argument he poses a basic question about the nature of poetry:

> In order to get a firm clue which we can follow fruitfully in the retrospect and prospect we have proposed to ourselves it will not be amiss to enquire what is the highest power we demand from poetry; or let us put it more largely and get nearer the root of the matter—what may be the nature of poetry, its essential law, and how out of that arises the possibility of its use as the *mantra* of the Real.[22]

The theory of poetry that Sri Aurobindo proposes in response to this question can be succinctly stated as follows: Poetry expresses the soul of man and embodies in the word whatever power of beauty the poet 'sees', when the creation is 'ideal' and suffused with the spiritual insight into the poet's Self and Nature. Poetry achieves greatness when it effectively combines the highest intensity of rhythmical movement, with the highest intensity of verbal form and thought substance and the highest intensity of the soul's vision of truth. Poetry endowed with these three intensities voices a supreme harmony of five eternal powers: Truth, Beauty, Delight, Life and Spirit, the five 'Suns of Poetry'.

The emphasis on the visionary quality in poetry indicates Sri Aurobindo's preference for traditional Indian poetry of the *marg* tradition. But it is guided by his High Romantic inheritance. In order to highlight the spiritual aspect of poetry, Sri Aurobindo tends to twist Sanskrit poetic terms. The most interesting example of this tendency is his use of the term *rasa,* which he employs in its original, Vedic, sense to mean 'a liquid', 'a divine food', 'a moving entity' and 'the sap of a plant'. He uses it to explain the nature of the creative process rather than the experience of the art by the audience. Thus, the term is pressed into use for forming his artist-oriented, expressive, theory of poetry. Another instance is that of the description of *ananda*. Sanskrit poetics had used the concept of *brahmananda* in an analogous manner, as a metaphor to explain the aesthetic experience. Sri Aurobindo takes the metaphor too seriously and equates *brahmananda* with *kavyananda* in a literal way. This confusion between poetic delight and spiritual delight that he makes is an instance of nationalism joining hands with Indology—while one sought some good in the Indian past, the other claimed that the good in the past was restricted to the spiritual. But this confusion can also be found in the aesthetics of the High Romantics like Keats, Blake and Shelley, who saw poetry as a resolution of Truth, Good, Beauty. In fact, though Sri Aurobindo reverses the colonial hierarchy of cultures, the whole structure of his *Future Poetry* is designed after Shelley's *A Defence of Poetry*. The primary sections of both concentrate on defining poetry by distinguishing it from science, philosophy and logic. The middle sections of both are devoted to a tendentious survey of poetry—European poetry in the case of Shelley, and English poetry in the case of Aurobindo—and the concluding sections of both essays harp on the possibilities that poetry can explore under ideal circumstances. It is possible that as a personal preference Sri Aurobindo found the High Romantic aesthetics perfectly in keeping with ancient Indian poetry and poetics, and perhaps he thought that the two could be accommodated in one common system of poetics that his *Future Poetry* was to found. This attempt at synthesis was also an exercise in cultural self-definition. The motivating force behind the work was a passionate nationalism. Sri Aurobindo had an exceptionally good command over the Sanskrit language; and, even if he had not read Sanskrit poetics—there is no evidence in his writing to prove the contrary—he had a firsthand knowledge of Sanskrit literature, he knew several Indian languages and had acquaintance with the bhasha literatures. And yet, when he came to think of developing a new system of literary criticism, he found himself cut off from the Indian literary situation and the historical changes in the critical tradition. In his poems like *Ahana,*[23] he has celebrated *bhakti*; how is it then that in his criticism no trace of a bhasha awareness is to be seen? The answer to this question can be had by considering Sri Aurobindo as a 'colonial' critic, an enterprising intellectual belonging to a demoralized, amnesiac society desperately trying to revive a culture almost gone to seed. His failure was inherent in the attempt to synthesize, in creating a pattern of collaboration where a confrontation would have been fruitful, in accepting a framework of nationalism that was in essence colonial, and in becoming theoretical where the need was to be historical.

Sri Aurobindo belonged to the generation of Indian Romantics, whose assumptions about literature we tend to reject from our 'superior, 'modernistic' point of view. It is instructive to see what happened to literary criticism in India after modernism reached the Indian shores. 'Modernism', which in Europe was a product of a genuine social upheaval and cultural breakdown, reached India through literary models rather than through economic developments and social crisis. The first phase of modernism in Europe had been initiated by the revolutions of 1848; the second, more self-conscious phase had begun around the first world war. Indian 'modernism' made its beginnings in the 1930s; this period saw several developments in different directions. The doctrine-bound left-wing writing called the 'Progressive Movement'; nationalistic writings which combined fantasy and history; Gandhian literature which had a stylized idealism at the centre; formalistic writing that praised style for its own sake; poetry that employed various techniques like surrealism, symbolism, imagism; and fiction that employed techniques of cinema narrative as well as those of the avant-garde European fiction—all these were vying for a place in mainstream Indian literature. In a sense, Indian 'modernism' was more cleverly imitative of the Western models than Indian romanticism was. In criticism, therefore, modernism brought with it the trend of pseudo-theorizing, for most of it was theory based on alien theories without any relevance to Indian traditions.

Bal Sitaram Mardhekar (1909–56), Marathi 's first 'modernist', is one of the most significant critics of the modernistic period. He wrote his critical works both in Marathi and in English. His first critical book, *Arts and Man,* was published in England in 1938. It was followed by a book in Marathi, *Vangmayin Mahatmata,* and one in English, *Two Lectures on an Aesthetic of Literature,* in 1944. After his return from England, Mardhekar wrote and lectured on literary aesthetics extensively. All his critical writings in English were brought under one title, *Arts and Man,* published posthumously in 1960, and those in Marathi published as *Soundarya ani Sahitya* in 1956.[24]

The problem central to Mardhekar's literary aesthetics is that of the perception of beauty which connects an objectively existing work of art to a subjectively realized value judgement. He finds his inspiration in Clive Bell's theory of significance, of significant form, and in Russell's logical method of philosophic enquiry. Mardhekar tried to be original by attempting to bring the two together. Since his aim was to construct a comprehensive general theory of aesthetics, he took up such fundamental issues as the nature of aesthetic judgement, aesthetic emotion, and aesthetic organization. The central tenet of his theory is that aesthetic experience is a matter of direct, unmediated knowledge perceived through a series of absolute, qualitative sensations, and that beauty—which in all its manifestations is a rhythmic pattern of harmony–contrast–balance—is independent of its perceiver. Aesthetic judgement is an outcome of the aesthetic emotion evoked in the mind of the perceiver by the rhythmic form; and unless it so results from a direct experience, it is no aesthetic judgement. Mardhekar illustrates this aspect of his theory by examining the premise, "The Ajanta frescoes are beautiful". The text of this premise by itself would not form an aesthetic judgement unless the context provides that it is based on an individual's firsthand experience. The moment it is expressed by another, Mardhekar tells us, it ceases to be an aesthetic judgement. The cumulative rhythm of harmony–contrast–balance is what an artist creates through his specific medium.

Deriving a corollary from his central theory, Mardhekar makes a distinction between 'medium' and 'means' of art. In his opinion, the two are fundamentally different. In painting, pigments are the 'means', whereas colours are the 'medium'. Similarly, in poetry, sound is the means of organization and the meaning is the medium. Taking up I.A. Richards's distinction between the cognitive meaning and the emotive meaning, Mardhekar further subdivides the emotive meaning into 'aesthetic' and 'poetic', the aesthetic meaning being absolutely emotive, and the poetic meaning only contingently emotive. Under this classification poetry, by virtue of its use of contingently emotive meanings, gets relegated to a lower position in Mardhekar's hierarchy of the fine arts.

Mardhekar's theory has been continuously discussed, disputed, and readjusted by Marathi critics since its first publication.[25] In fact, it has become almost the central critical document of the Marathi modernist tradition. It is possible to argue, as has been done by Marathi critics a number of times during the last forty years, that Mardhekar's theory is logically, philosophically or metaphysically inadequate. It is also possible, on the other hand, to prove that he was a highly original critic who thought about fundamental issues related to art and literature. What concerns us here is not the consistency of argument or its logical uniformity in Mardhekar's theory, but the logic of its existence. Had he considered his own assertion that aesthetic judgement is an unmediated experience more carefully, he would have realized the futility of two types of mediation—of theory, and of alien intellectual traditions and concepts. In the light of his theory, both these become redundant. His range of Western references is impressive: Clive Bell, Collingwood, Russell, Aristotle, Kant, Croce, Freud, Eliot, Coleridge, Abercrombie, T. E. Hulme, Bosanquet, Herbert Read. Confronted with the Ajanta frescoes, any one of these would have pleaded his inability to pass an aesthetic judgement, for Ajanta art has its source in aesthetic assumptions and art philosophy of a type radically different from that which Western criticism is equipped to deal with. Yet Mardhekar proceeded to build a theory in the naive belief that art theories are universal in import and utility, and that intellectual formations of Europe can be safely put to use in defining the sense of beauty in India. Mardhekar's theory does not refer to any part of Sanskrit poetics. But the faith in the universality of theory implies, in fact, an attempt to synthesize.

Mardhekar was the first important poet in Marathi to introduce a post-Romantic vitality, an awareness of language, diction and metres that the Romantic period had blunted. His poetic idiom was Marathi and it had the context of a living native tradition. He wrote on modern themes, but the awareness in his poetry was inherited from the *bhakti* school. The poetry of Mardhekar, therefore, was suffused with the spirit of rebellion. This spirit of rebellion was the essence of *bhakti* poetry. However erudite and well-construed, Mardhekar's criticism lacked the context of the tradition and the spirit of revolt. Even when he tried to point out errors in Aristotle's philosophy of poetry, Mardhekar had no plans of moving out of the Western canon of criticism. It can be said that in Mardhekar's literary criticism, as in Sri Aurobindo's, the bhasha tradition of revolt against orthodoxy and authority was consumed and stilted by the colonial trend of theorizing. Sri Aurobindo tried to move away from the colonial paradigms and into the world of ancient Indian poetry. Mardhekar threw the *marg* traditions overboard, and wedded himself intellectually to the colonial tradition. The motivating force in both was the urge to create something new, to nativize and to vitalize. That urge was inherited from the bhasha traditions. Sri Aurobindo and B. S. Mardhekar are two prototypical modern Indian critics. To the extent that they represent the field, it can be said that literary criticism in India displays patterns of the tripartite relation of the *bhasha,* the *marg,* and the colonial traditions, and that, conditioned by a cultural amnesia, it still remains a fragmented discourse.

Nativism

Nativism, a recent critical trend in Marathi is an attempt to free Marathi literary sensibility and criticism from the prison of the tripartite relation described above. It views literature as an activity taking place 'within' a specific language, such as Marathi or Gujarati, and bound by the rules of discourse native to the language of its origin. It understands writing as a social act, and expects of it an ethical sense of commitment to the society within which it is born. It rules out the colonial standard of literary history as a series of epochs, and the *marg* claim of the mainstream literature as being the only authentic literature. Nativism is a language-specific way of looking at literature. It rejects the concept-specific method of 'universal' criticism. As such, it gathers its main critical issues and themes from within the tradition of the literature it examines, instead of approaching it with preconceived notions of good and bad literature. At the same time, it refuses to glorify history and tradition, and values realism. The principal advocate of nativism in Marathi is Bhalchandra Nemade. However, there are several other trends in Marathi such as the literature of regional sensibility, caste sensibility and dialect sensibility, that converge onto nativism proper.

Bhalchandra Nemade (b. 1938) shot into fame with his first novel, *Kosala* (1963), which set a new stylistic trend and a level of realism in Marathi fiction. His other novels—*Bidhar, Jarila* and *Jhul*—have received much appreciation. He has written consistently on issues related to literary culture, style and language, translation and influence. He has also worked on the problem of the influence of English on Marathi prose style. Combining his knowledge of the English influence and his knowledge of Marathi prose style, he produced an extended essay on the Marathi novel in 1980. This has come to be regarded as a critical document of seminal importance in Marathi. It was published in an English translation in 1986.[26] At the very beginning, Nemade offers a tentative description of his variety of nativism:

> The present generation must have an unfailing nativistic awareness that the novel in Marathi is a creation of Marathi writers, who, in turn, are product of the Marathi society. Further, the Formalistic, unintelligent practice of picking up all and sundry works of art from languages all over the world for a comparative assessment of artifacts in Marathi—a tendency rife in our criticism—has to be avoided. It is dangerous for criticism to enter the comparative field without making a deep study of both cultures compared. Culture is not a hot house, but a soil-bound process; literature is not a theoretical construct but a living phenomenon.[27]

With this awareness of literature as a phenomenon 'born within its own language', nativism avoids seeking self-definitions by referring to the 'Western other'.

Nemade's essay presents an account of the novel in Marathi. In order to describe the various tendencies manifest in the Marathi novel, he devises three critical categories, all of purely descriptive nature: '*riti*', '*kriti*' and '*pratikriti*'. *Riti* is used to denote design-consciousness, and a formalistic, affected style; *kriti* is employed to mean action on the part of the novelist; and *pratikriti* is used to indicate illusion or image. Nemade avoids the colonial compulsion to theorize about these terms. Using them descriptively, he finds apt illustrations in works of fiction in Marathi. Thus, he traces three dominant tendencies in the nineteenth century Marathi novel: *Muktamala* (1861) by Laxmansastri Moreshwarsastri Halbe, which is the first *riti*-oriented novel, typifies the *Muktamala* trend; *Yamunaparyatan* (1857) by Baba Padmanji, which is a *kriti*-oriented novel (and also the first novel in Marathi), typifies the *Yamunaparyatan* trend; and *Mochangad* (1871) by R. B. Gunjikar, which is a *pratikriti*-oriented novel, typifies the *Mochangad* trend. Nemade sees these three trends as the basic trends in the Marathi novel. *Yamunaparyatan* expresses, in his opinion, the basic drive of the Marathi society. It shows a strong inclination towards realism and a social morality. On the other hand, *Muktamala* expresses the colonial domination in style and theme, and *Mochangad* shows a penchant for eroticism and fantasy that are characteristic of the punditic *marg* tradition. Thus, Nemade's classification of the Marathi novel displays a clear awareness of the tripartite relation which constitutes the modern Indian literary discourse. His preference, naturally, is for the novel of social realism and *kriti*. He describes the history of the Marathi novel in terms of a composite interaction among the three basic trends, and on the basis of this historiography draws a chart of Marathi novels after 1950. The chart is presented here (see p. 132) in a tabular form.

The essay presents an incisive analysis of numerous Marathi novels that serve to illustrate Nemade's classification. But what he values most in Marathi fiction is the nativistic awareness that the novel is a social, linguistic and artistic activity and, therefore, it has a moral responsibility towards the Marathi society. Commenting on the nativistic, ethical novel, he writes:

> The new novel, which originates in *Yamunaparyatan,* has an intimate relation with reality. It considers *kriti* to be an indivisible aspect of creation, and presents a new value scale about man in life. As such it distinguishes itself from the other trends by virtue of its new morality. It believes in selecting its subject matter from contemporary life and world, and in providing a thematic dimension to its style.[28]

Nemade's essay has provided a new direction to criticism of the novel in Marathi. It has created a general awareness that criticism is not a universal game of concepts and tools, but a serious investigation of native literary traditions.

The Novel Spectrum

Unrealistic

<table>
<tr><td rowspan="4">Pratikriti-oriented Mochangad trend</td><td>1</td><td>Historical</td></tr>
<tr><td>2</td><td>Mythological</td></tr>
<tr><td>3</td><td>Biographical</td></tr>
<tr><td>4</td><td>Fantasy</td></tr>
<tr><td>Riti-oriented Muktamala trend</td><td>5</td><td>Sexual</td></tr>
<tr><td>Regional</td><td>6</td><td>Regional</td></tr>
<tr><td rowspan="3">Kriti-oriented Yamunaparyatan trend</td><td>7</td><td>Sub-community subculture based</td></tr>
<tr><td>8</td><td>Problem based</td></tr>
<tr><td>9</td><td>New morality</td></tr>
</table>

Realistic

What Nemade's essay offers is not a systematic theory of fiction; it suggests a new style of critical thought. However, it is doubtful whether literary criticism in Marathi will fully assimilate this new style of thinking. Already, it is being seen as a new 'theory' of fiction, and there have been attempts to present 'theoretical' statements about nativism. It is also seen by some commentators as a new statement of nationalistic revival.[29] Nemade himself is aware that criticism is not valuable in itself but acquires value to the extent it contributes to the development of the literary culture. In the conclusion to his essay he reminds the reader that literary criticism in Marathi will have to devote itself to thinking about literature produced in Marathi:

> [I]t has become necessary for Marathi criticism to devote itself to creating an atmosphere congenial to creative literature. Or else such surveys as the present one do not reach even a good bibliography . . . Our cultural responsibility is not fully discharged in merely discussing what has grown; to sow properly, to tend it and to destroy the pestilence of destructive tendencies are activities of greater cultural value. They are more deserving topics for discussion. There is little possibility of the situation changing for the better unless the next generation revolutionizes criticism and cures Marathi of its present poverty of taste.[30]

Nemade's essay is an excellent, though solitary, example of nativism in literary criticism. It has opened the possibility of rooting criticism in the bhasha tradition. It shows a way out of the tripartite relation that has kept Indian literary criticism fragmented and abstract. It is too early to say if nativism will become the central force in Marathi criticism and end the transition that began with Rajashekhara a thousand years ago. But it is certain that literary criticism will benefit immensely if it cultivates a nativistic awareness of Indian literary tradition.

India is a vast country with numerous linguistic cultures. These linguistic cultures have their individual ways of viewing literary creativity. The functions that literature performs in India are not necessarily what the European sociology of literature stipulates. The range of literary transactions in India is wide. These transactions cannot be classified in the accepted Western typology of the main stream, the popular and the folk. A study of the bhasha literatures may show that literature in the Indian languages has been a matter of revolt and heresy rather than that of imposition and authority. In the minimum, Indian literature has ingrained in it a spirit of multilingualism and multiculturalism. Critical models, tools, standards evolved in Europe in small, monolingual and (comparatively) monocultural nations during the period of colonial expansion for the purpose of 'civilizing' the 'primitive' nations have, therefore, limited utility in the bhasha context.

Criticism is not an isolated and autonomous activity. It needs support and sustenance from larger assumptions about life, language, meaning and society. A visible critical theory or statement always stands above a vast invisible structure of a society's 'metaphysics' which, in turn, is conditioned by its specific geography, history and linguistic range. In order to be meaningful, criticism has, of necessity, to share the same basic assumptions with its target literature. Literature growing out of one type of underlying linguistic and metaphysical structure cannot be understood and studied by criticism growing out of another and alien type of underlying linguistic and metaphysical structure. At present, the situation in Indian criticism is very similar to the one described in the epigraph to this essay: three different *ragas* are being 'sung' by our critics—the *marg,* the *deshi* and the colonial. To add to this undesirable fragmentation in the field of criticism, the colonial period has introduced an amnesia in Indian criticism, which has distorted its memory of the bhasha literary traditions. Owing to the amnesia, the loss of self-confidence, the anxiety to postulate new theories and the fragmentation of criticism, the Indian critic is gripped with a fear of a crisis in criticism. In fact, that fear itself is the true crisis. Indian criticism will have to come out of it; and that is possible only through a nativistic self-awareness. A recovery of the memory of native literary traditions will reduce the anxiety about the absence of theory. What Indian literatures need at present is a realistic historiography and not so much of a theoretical discussion. If this essay has succeeded in making the point that cultural amnesia is the central problem of Indian criticism, then it also implies that what should come after amnesia is nativistic history.

5

Epilogue

Function of Criticism

Re-reading this essay a year and a half after I completed writing the previous section, I find it necessary to add one more brief section to it. I have chosen the title 'Function of Criticism' for it. The rich body of Western criticism is replete with essays with this or similar titles. My aim here is not to take issue with any of those. The aim is to make an honest statement of what I perceive to be the role of criticism in the context of India's contemporary literary culture.

There is no fixed correspondence between the cultural well-being of societies and the literary criticism that they produce. No culture will perish for want of texts of literary criticism, nor will a society show nobler human qualities if it also happens to produce important critical documents. The equation between progressive cultures and progressive literary criticism is not logically valid. The fact that such an equation does enjoy a wide popularity in postcolonial societies needs to be explained with reference to their political history, the history of domination by European societies that used literary criticism as a means of cultural propaganda.

There is also no fixed correspondence between the well-being of creative literature and literary criticism. Linguistic creativity is an inevitable consequence of language being a human skill. Human communities will continue to mould language creatively so long as they use language as a means of communication. Literature was produced in times when literary criticism had still not acquired the status it enjoys today. The history of any given literature tells us that a sudden growth in critical activity does not necessarily bring about a corresponding growth in creative literature. The correlation between creative literature and critical writings, and theories of their interdependence, are not, therefore, logically valid. That such theories do exist and enjoy prestige has to be explained with reference to the history of the politics of literature.

The history of Indian literature is highly instructive in this regard. It shows that very fine criticism could be produced, as it was in Sanskrit from the eleventh century onwards, without having a corresponding body of living literature. It also shows that very great literature could be produced, as was the literature of devotion, without having a corresponding body of active criticism. This lesson of history is well worth remembering while thinking about the function of criticism.

Literature is a kind of knowledge, the knowledge about human existence with reference to the cosmos, nature, society, and the inner mental processes of human beings. Besides, it is presented in a manner that is aesthetically remarkable. But literature also tends to become 'power', because it is a form of knowledge. It becomes power when it is treated as 'magic', as in primitive societies, or as a class possession, as in stratified societies. The need to transmit, from generation to generation, this knowledge that is power generates the need to develop various forms of critical discourse. The main function of criticism is, therefore, to be a useful tool in the process of education. In its most essential form literary criticism is a classroom register of thought which initiates 'childish' readers into the world of powerful and adult *rasikas*. Critical reviews, essays, books and periodicals, scholarly research in the field of literature, high speculation and theorizing about literature, are all post-forms of the class room register; and they all return to it in order to make it increasingly more sophisticated and powerful. Hence, societies which do not teach literature in and through their formal or informal channels of education do not find it necessary to formulate critical premises. This does not mean that they do not have these premises; but these are not separated from the very act of literary enjoyment. They are not gathered in language and expression either before or after the act of literary enjoyment.

The actual act of literary enjoyment can be compared to the moment of union between lovers or that between God and the seeker, for all these are modes of entering which also admit being entered into. They are acts which rise above the duality of passivity and activity. In societies which value possession of women as if they are material objects, and production of children as means of greater material prosperity, the grammar of love gets impersonally articulated. *Kamasastra* is an instance of this tendency. The same is true of societies which value the 'discovery' of and communication with God as symbols of social status. Religious dogma and orthodox theology are the temporally subsequent forms of pure spiritual experiences. In societies which value literary art as a means of consolidating class/caste authority, literary criticism comes to acquire importance. The rise of literary criticism is bound by forces that exist before and after the actual moment of the reader entering literature or literature entering the reader.

Literary criticism as a system of thought or as a style of thinking can be, and has been, fascinatingly sophisticated. But the test of its validity is its logical and philosophical consistency within the frame of references it uses for its expression. But in this light, literary criticism is a branch of philosophy. There it transcends the division between sense and nonsense. As a branch of philosophy its primary need is to be logical, systematic and to belong within the established parameters of the intellectual discourse defined for it by social conventions. Its ultimate function and aim is to deliver itself to the teacher of literature who can use it as a ready classroom tool for the teaching of literature. And this teaching is in a larger part about the tools themselves. These intellectual tools, and an awareness about them, offer the learner an entry into the select group of adepts that claims a special authority.

If literary criticism is, as argued here, a teaching aid, and if it originates in the teaching procedures adopted by a society, then probably, many of the problems of criticism should really be the problems of literary education. In India they are indeed so. In monolingual and monocultural societies, only one language-literature is taught as a living literature. In England and France, for instance, English and French literature are taught, respectively, as living literatures. All other literatures are taught as 'foreign' or 'ancient' literatures. The result of this one-track literary education is that the style of thinking about literature in these countries is a common style that has a wider acceptance as the dominant critical discourse. All oppositions to it, or tensions within it, emerge with reference to the commanding discourse. Consistent and commonly accepted dominant discourses tend to acquire value and self-confidence over a period of time, and crystallise into 'major' theories. The situation in multilingual and multicultural societies is different.

In India, in any given university, several literatures are taught as living literatures. Several 'foreign' and 'ancient' literatures are also taught without the attendant awareness of their being foreign and dated. Indian teachers of English literature and world literature adhere to the critical norms relevant to English literature and world literature. Those who teach Sanskrit literature adhere to Sanskrit poetics. Teachers of regional literatures have their own set of critical beliefs. But all these teachers, and by extension those reviewers, essayists, scholars and philosophers who ultimately return their knowledge to teaching, constitute the Indian community of 'literary critics'. Naturally, no single critical discourse can claim the dominant place in this community. There are fragmented communications and exchanges, distrust and fear, tension and strife in the intellectual transactions of this community. All these stand in stark contrast to the situation in monolingual and moncultural literary communities. If the Indian community of literary scholars had pledged its singular devotion to one literature, whether Sanskrit, Hindi, English or any bhasha literature, it would have made some contribution to the theoretical and philosophic contemplation of literature. Alternatively, if Indian universities start teaching a fictitious discipline designated 'Indian Literature', and stop teaching regional literatures separately, perhaps, new theorizing will arise, for, in that case, a commonly shared dominant discourse of criticism will become necessary. But there is no need to despair. The three-language formula, and multilingual literary education, have been conscious decisions of the Indian society. They are in fact a strategy to come to terms with Indian national history. What needs to be fought is not the apparent confusion in literary criticism, but the lack of self-confidence and the cultural amnesia.

The problems faced by Indian intellectuals today are not problems peculiar to India alone. Similar problems are faced by many other postcolonial societies. In a review of the Latin American writer Eduardo Galeano's *Memory of Fire,* Sham Lal writes:

> By recreating the past with its midsummer madness, its ravenous greed, sadistic cruelties, pious lies, dark superstitions and gnawing anxieties, Galeano hopes to give back to the people their lost memory.[1]

Other Latin American writers have also dealt with the problem of amnesia in their works, the most famous instance of which is Gabriel Garcia Marquez's *One Hundred Years of Solitude.* In it, Marquez depicts the loss of linguistic memory—carried to the ridiculous extent where people have to write down names of all objects in order to remember them—as a Latin American cultural problem associated with the colonial experience. An American thinker, Velikovsky, has made a probing study of cultural amnesia in his book, *Mankind in Amnesia.*[2] He interprets amnesia, collective amnesia that is, as a result of a sense of guilt about the past. He writes:

> A victim of amnesia may live adjacent to neighbours who are completely unaware of his plight. He may be employed, he may be married, he may behave on the surface like anybody else. But he has forgotten everything before a certain date. He does not know his name and he assumes a new name to hide his own perplexity; he does not remember his childhood and adolescence or maturity prior to that date; he does not know the town or city from which he came and how he got to his new habitat; he does not know whether he was married formerly nor

> whether he has children. If he comes into conflict with the law, as for instance for bigamy, he may wind up in a psychiatric clinic . . .[3]

What would happen if he came in conflict with the law for polygamy? In the Indian critical community, each critic pledges his loyalty to one or the other of the literatures taught in India, while in reality he is 'married' to several literatures. There is no need to compare this situation with that prevailing in the Western countries. In fact, multilingual, multiliteral education is the greatest strength of Indian culture at present. Multiculturalism and multilingualism have been the strength of Indian society from the twelfth century. That multiplicity was seen as degradation in the past, and is seen as weakness today. We need to get over the sense of guilt through an open-eyed approach to history in order to build a modern Indian critical discourse.

Notes and References

Introduction

1. For an exhaustive survey of literary criticism in Indian languages, see *Comparative Indian Literature,* edited by K. M. George (Macmillan, Bombay, 1984–86).
2. *Gujarati Sahityano Itihas,* 4 Volumes, Gujarat Sahitya Parishad, edited by Umashankar Joshi, Anantrai Raval and Yashawant Shukla, Vol. Ill, *Dalapatramthi Kalapi* (Ahmedabad, 1978).
3. In the introductory chapter of *Dalapatramthi Kalapi,* Yashawant Shukla writes: "The convention to consider the beginning of the modern period of Gujarati literature synchronous with the completion of the British domination of Gujarat, i.e., in 1818, is well established. The late Govindbhai Hathibhai Desai, who wrote a volume on Gujarati literary history, followed his contemporary historians and maintained that the modern period commences with the establishment of the Islamic rule. But no one would find this view acceptable now." (p. 1). [Quotation translated by G. N. Devy.]
4. See Ashis Nandy, *Traditions, Tyranny and Utopias: Essays in the Politics of Awareness* (New Delhi, 1987).
5. The only notable publication on this subject in Indian English is Sujit Mukherjee's *Towards a Literary History of India* (Simla, 1975) and the only book in Marathi is the one edited by Dattatraya Punde, *Vangmayetihasachi Sankalpana* (Pune, 1986).
6. For an excellent bibliography of all Indological histories of Indian Literature, see Sujit Mukherjee (1975), pp. 92–103.
7. Sir William Jones, 'Discourse', from *Works of Sir William Jones,* Vol. I (pp. 19–34), reproduced in *A Reader in Nineteenth Century Historical Indo-European Linguistics,* edited by Winfred P. Lehmann (Bloomington & London, 1967), pp. 7–20 (p. 12).

Tradition and Amnesia

1. Shankar Gopal Tulpule, *Classical Marathi Literature, A History of Indian Literature,* edited by Jan Gonda, Vol. IX, Fasc. 4 (Wiesbaden, 1979), p. 312.
2. Though it is certain that Mukundaraja preceded Jnanadeva, the exact chronology has not yet been established. Tulpule (1979), p. 25.
3. For an exhaustive analysis and history of Sanskrit poetics the following titles are useful: P. V. Kane, *History of Sanskrit Poetics,* fourth edition (Delhi, 1971); S. K. De, *History of Sanskrit Poetics,* second revised edition (Calcutta, 1960): both published originally in 1923; Edwin Gerow, *Indian Poetics, A History of Indian Literature,* Vol. V, Fasc. 3 (Wiesbaden, 1977).
4. Eliot Deutsch and J. A. V. van Buitenen, *A Source Book of Advaita Vedanta* (Honolulu, 1971).

5. P. V. Kane (1971), pp. 208–18.
6. Edwin Gerow (1977), p. 279.
7. Tulpule (1979), p. 326.
8. *Modern India and the West,* edited by L. S. S. O'Malley (London, 1941), p. 587.
9. See W. H. G. Armytage, *Four hundred years of English Education,* Cambridge University Press (Cambridge, 1964); *Educational Documents: England and Wales – 1816 to the Present Day,* edited by J. Stuart Maclure, Methuen (London, 1965/86); Edward Hulmes, *Educational and Cultural Diversity,* Longman (Essex, 1989).
10. K. B. Marathe, *Naval va Natak Yasambandhi Nibandha* (Kolhapur, 1872), as quoted by Anant Kanekar, 'Literary Criticism: Marathi', in *Writing in India,* pp. 114–20 (p. 115).
11. V. K. Rajawade, 'The Novel' (1902), translated by Shanta Gokhale, *Journal of Arts and Ideas* 8 (1984), pp. 74–88 (p. 87).
12. Bhalchandra Nemade, *'Kadambari',* in *Marathi Sahitya: Prerana va Svarup,* pp. 13–56 (p. 53), translated from the Marathi by G. N. Devy, *Setu: Journal of Indian Literature in Translation,* Vol. II, 1(1986), pp. 29–71 (p. 68).
13. Manasukhalal Jhaveri, 'Literary Criticism: Gujarati', in *Writing in India,* edited by Nissim Ezekiel, The Seventh P.E.N. All-India Writers' Conference (Bombay, 1965), pp. 77–83.
14. *Comparative Indian Literature,* Vol. II, edited by K. M. George (Madras, 1986).
15. Anant Kanekar, 'Literary Criticism: Marathi', in *Writing in India,* pp. 114–20; Sudhir Rasal, *'Samiksha'* in *Marathi Sahitya: Prerana va Svarup,* edited by G. M. Powar and M. D. Hatkananglekar (Bombay, 1986), pp. 322–64.
16. R. B. Patankar, 'Aesthetics: Some Important Problems', *Journal of Arts and Ideas* 6 (1984), pp. 43–66 (pp. 64–5).
17. Suresh Joshi in an unpublished interview with John Stachneiwski (1985).
18. *Indian Critical Thought,* edited by S. K. Desai and G. N. Devy (Delhi, 1987), p. 2.
19. Sri Aurobindo, *The Future Poetry,* Birth Centenary Library, Vol. IX (Pondicherry, 1972).
20. B. S. Mardhekar, *Arts and Man* (London, 1937); *Saundarya ani Sahitya* (Bombay, 1955).
21. Patankar, 'Aesthetics: Some Important Problems' (1984), p. 65.
22. Krishna Rayan, *Suggestion Today* (London, 1966); Nagendra, 'All Time Relevance of the *Rasa* Theory', paper read at the First Conference of Comparative Indian Literature Association (Delhi, 1984).
23. A school of criticism, designated 'Nativism', has emerged in Marathi literature during the last fifteen years. It is led by the novelist-critic Bhalchandra Nemade, and has become widely influential. The main emphasis of this school is on evolving the standards of criticism from the native cultural context and on minimizing formalistic 'universal' standards in assessment of fiction.
24. Murrey Krieger, *Theory of Criticism: A Tradition and its System* (Baltimore and London, 1976), p. 54.

25. M. Monier-Williams, *Sanskrit-English Dictionary* (Oxford, 1899); R. C. Turner, *A Comparative Dictionary of Indo-Aryan Languages* (London, 1965).
26. Bhalchandra Nemade (1986) maintains that the concept of culture is expressed in Marathi through the term *'sanskriti'*, though the meaning intended is growth and development. In colloquial Marathi, Gujarati and Hindi, and perhaps in other bhashas, the term 'culture' and the term *'sanskriti'* are used as interchangeable terms.
27. An excellent account of the patterns of political collaboration as well as conflict between the British colonial power and the Indian political consciousness is given by John Gallagher in *The Decline, Revival and Fall of the British Empire* (Cambridge, 1982), and Anil Seal in *The Emergence of Indian Nationalism: Competition and Collaboration in the Later Nineteenth Century* (Cambridge, 1968).
28. M. N. Srinivas, *Social Change in Modern India* (Berkeley, 1966); Milton Singer, 'Tradition' in *Comparative Studies in Society and History*, Vol. XIII (1971), pp. 160–95; also *Structure and Change in Indian Society*, edited by Milton Singer and Bernard Cohn, Viking Fund Publications in Anthropology (Chicago, 1968); Edward Shils, *Tradition and Modernity: The Case of Indian Society and History*, Comparative Studies in Society and History Supplement 1 (1961).
29. Ashis Nandy argues in his classic work on the psychology of colonialism, *The Intimate Enemy: Loss and Recovery Under Colonialism* (Delhi, 1983) that Gandhi's political genius lay in transcending the bipolar political structure framed by the British for the politics of the pre-Gandhian era. Nandy employs the metaphor of man-woman bipolarity to explain colonial psychology.
30. For the essays by G. S. Amur, Krishna Rayan, R. B. Patankar, see *Critical Thought*, edited by S. K. Desai and G. N. Devy (Delhi, 1986); for Kantak's essay, *New Quest* 44 (March-April 1984), pp. 70–82.
31. V. Y. Kantak (1984), p. 70 and p. 82.
32. S. S. Prawer, *Comparative Literary Studies* (London, 1973), p. 1.
33. Edward Said, *Orientalism* (London, 1978) is an invaluable essay for students of European attitudes to India.
34. Arthur Mayhew, *The Education of India: A Survey of British Educational Policy in India, 1835–1920, and its Bearing on National Life and Problems in India Today* (London, 1926); J. P. Naik and Syed Nurullah, *A History of British Education in India during the British Period* (Bombay, 1951).
35. Sudhir Kakar, The *Inner World: A Psycho-analytic Study of Childhood and Society in India*, second edition (Delhi, 1981).
36. Ibid., p. 6.
37. Ibid., p. 6.
38. *Kavyadarsha of Dandin*, edited by C. Sankara Raima Sastri (Madras, 1959); *Shrngaraprakasha*, edited by V. Raghavan (Madras, 1963).
39. J. S. Mill, *The History of British India* in six volumes, third edition (London, 1826), Vol. II, pp. 46–7.
40. Susan Langer, *Feeling and Form* (London, 1953), p. 323.
41. Ashis Nandy, *The Intimate Enemy: Loss and Recovery Under Colonialism* (Delhi, 1983).

42. Madhav Deshpande, 'History, Change and Permanence: A Classical Indian Perspective', in *Contributions to South Asian Studies,* Vol. I, edited by Gopal Krishna (Delhi, 1979), pp. 1–28 (pp. 10–11).
43. Sir William Jones, *Works,* Vol. I, pp. 19–34, reproduced in *A Reader in Nineteenth Century Historical Indo-European Linguistics,* edited by Winfred P. Lehmann (Bloomington & London, 1967), pp. 7–20.
44. A. K. Warder writes in 1975 that "Sanskrit is the only truly national language India has ever had . . . If it disappears, with its cultural heritage, India will never be a nation. . .". A. K. Warder, 'Classical Literature', in *A Cultural History of India,* edited by A. L. Basham (Oxford, 1975), pp. 171–96 (p. 196).
45. Edward Said (1978); V. G. Kiernan, *The Lords of Humankind: Black Man, Yellow Man and White Man in the Age of Empire* (Boston, 1969).
46. *Selections from Macaulay: Letters, Prose, Speeches and Poetry,* edited by E. V. Downs and G. L. Davies (London, 1932), p. 59.
One execrable effect the climate produces. It destroys all the works of man with scarcely one exception. Steel rusts; razors lose their edge; thread decays; clothes fall to pieces; books moulder away, and drop out of their bindings; plaster cracks; timber rots; matting is in shreds.
47. Michel Hulin, *Samkhya Literature, A History of Indian Literature,* edited by Jan Gonda, Vol. VI, Fasc. 3, pp. 128–62 (Wiesbaden, 1978).
48. M. N. Srinivas (1966).
49. The study of Indian influence on English literature has so far concentrated merely on the outer features of this influence as in the work of Robert Sencourt (1923) and John Drew (1986). It would be interesting to explore whether the movement of European consciousness from Romanticism to Modernism has any dependence on and correspondence with the history of European colonialism
50. M. D. Hatkananglekar, *'Marathi Vangmayavaril Parakiy Prabhav', Marathi Sahitya: Prerana va Svarup,* edited by G. M. Powar and M. D. Hatkananglekar (Bombay, 1986), pp. 308–21.
51. A well footnoted comment on Macaulay's view is S. Nagarajan's essay, 'Children of Macaulay, *New Quest* 46 (July–August 1984), pp. 207–20.
52. Mayhew (London, 1926); Naik and Nurullah (Bombay, 1951); R. K. Mookherjee, *Ancient Indian Education* (London, 1947).
53. H. V. Hampton, *Biographical Studies in Modem Indian Education* (Madras, 1947), p. 135.
54. For an analytical history of the emergence of *bhadralok,* see J. H. Broomfield, *Elite Conflict in a Plural Society: Twentieth Century Bengal* (Berkeley and Los Angeles, 1968), pp. 1–41.
55. Hampton (1947), p. 79.
56. M. N. Srinivas (1966) suggests a comparable, but I think a reverse, analysis of the mobility in traditional Indian society, which permits an individual the freedom of upward caste mobility.
57. Percival Spear, *A History of India,* Vol. II (Penguin, 1965/82), p. 13.
58. Ibid.

59. Gallagher (1982); Seal (1968).
60. I have used several sources for collecting the dates in the table. Chief among them are: 1. Sir George Grierson, *Linguistic Survey of India* (Calcutta, 1902–28), 2. *The Cultural Heritage of India,* 3 volumes, Ramakrishna Mission Institute (Calcutta, 1937), second edition (1962/69), 3. *A History of Indian Literature,* edited by Jan Gonda (Weisbaden).
61. Manasukhalal Jhaveri (1965), p. *77.*
62. *Gujarati Sahityano Itihasa,* Vol.II (1450-1850), edited by Umashankar Joshi, Anantrai Raval and Yashawant Shukla (Ahmedabad, 1976), p. 16. [Quotation translated by G. N. Devy.]
63. Dattatraya Punde (Pune, 1986).
64. Ibid., appendix, pp. 3–23.
65. Ibid., pp. 31–33.
66. Ibid., pp. 92 101.
67. M. N. Srinivas (1966), p. 76.
68. 'Recollection: Indian and Platonic', *Coomaraswamy: Selected Papers,* Vol. II, edited by Roger Lipsey, Bollingen series LXXXIX, Princeton University Press (Princeton, 1977), pp. 49–65.
69. Ibid., pp. 51–53.
70. Ibid., pp. 56–57.
71. *The Basic Writings of Sigmund Freud,* translated and edited by A. A. Brill (New York, 1938), pp. 62–3.
72. Ronald Stuart McGregor, *Hindi Literature of the Nineteenth and Early Twentieth Centuries, A History of Indian Literature,* Vol. VIII, Fasc.2 (Wiesbaden, 1974), pp. 66–7.
73. For a detailed discussion of Ravivarma's contribution, see Partha Mitter, 'Indian Artist, Western Art and Tradition', in *Changing South Asia: City and Culture,* edited by Kenneth Ballhatchet and David Taylor (London, 1984), pp. 77–90.
74. M. N. Srinivas (1966), p. 55.

A Never-ending Transition

1. R. B. Patankar, 'The Three Alternatives', in *Towards a Common Indian Poetics,* edited by C. D. Narasimhaiah (Mysore, 1984), pp. 51–63.
2. Ibid., p. 51.
3. Edward Said (1978); V. G. Kiernan (1969).
4. R. Sencourt (1923).
5. James Forbes, *Oriental Memoirs: A Narrative of Seven Years Residence in India,* second edition revised by Countess de Montalembert, Vol. I (London, 1834), p. 330.
6. A. K. Forbes (1821–65) was appointed Assistant Judge at Ahmedabad in Gujarat, studied Gujarati language, literature and history. He established the Andrews Library at Surat in 1850. With the help of Dalpatram (1820–98), he collected old manuscripts, historical and archaeological materials. He founded, in 1848, the Gujarat Vernacular Society at Ahmedabad, and published the two volumes of his *Rasmala* (1856) describing the vanishing glories of

Gujarat. He also encouraged the launching of *Vartaman,* the first Gujarati newspaper, in 1849. He was appointed Vice-Chancellor of the Bombay University (1864), where he founded the *Gujarati Sabha* (Literary Academy of Gujarati) to carry out research. The *Sabha* was named after him on his death the same year (August 1865).

7. G. A. Grierson, *Linguistic Survey of India,* Vol. IX, part two (Calcutta, 1908), p. 333.
8. *Travels in Mogul Empire, AD 1656–68,* by Francois Bernier, translated from the French and edited by Archibald Constable (1891), re-edited by Vincent Smith (London, 1934), pp. 228–9.
9. Romila Thapar, *A History of India,* Vol. I (Penguin, 1966/83), pp. 15–27.
10. R.B. Patankar (1984) suggests a hypothesis relating 'living' tradition and 'great' problems in a society.
11. For biographical details of Jagannatha, see P. V. Kane (1971), pp. 322–25.
12. R. C. Nigam, *Language Handbook on Mother Tongues in Census,* Census of India 1971, Census Centenary Monograph No. 10 (Delhi, 1972).
13. Kamil Veith Zvelebil, *Tamil Literature* (1974), pp. 31–42; George Luzerne Hart, *The Relation Between Tamil and Classical Sanskrit Literature* (1976), both forming Vol. X, 1&2, *A History of Indian Literature,* edited by Jan Gonda (Wiesbaden).
14. K. R. Norman, *Pali Literature Including the Canonical Literature in Prakrit and Sanskrit of All the Hinayana Schools of Buddhism, A History of Indian Literature,* Vol. VII, Fasc.2, edited by Jan Gonda (Wiesbaden, 1983), pp. 167-8.
15. K. Krishnamoorthy, 'Literary Criticism: Kannada' in *Writing in India* (Bombay, 1965), pp. 102–10 (p. 102).
16. Dusan Zbavitel, *Bengali Literature, A History of Indian Literature,* Vol. IX: 3 (Wiesbaden, 1976), p. 22.
17. Annemarie Schimmel, *Islamic Literatures of India, A History of Indian Literature,* part of Vol. II (Wiesbaden, 1973), p. 22.
18. Ibid., p. 44.
19. Ibid., p. 26.
20. Ibid., pp. 18–9.
21. Romila Thapar (1983), pp. 241–88.
22. R. K. Mookherjee (1947).
23. *"Karambhakantu bhashabhirvividhabhirvinirmimatama yatha mama sodasha-bhashamayi Prashastiramavali"* Visvanatha, *Sahitya Darpana,* VI, 571, edited by J. V. Bhattacharya (Calcutta, 1874), p. 154.
24. Translation by S. G. Malshe and S. A. Gavaskar, *The History and Culture of the Indian People,* Vol. VII, Bharatiya Vidya Bhavan (Bombay, 1974), p. 579.
25. Ashok Kelkar, *Towards a Common Indian Poetics,* edited by C. D. Narasimhaiah (Mysore, 1984), pp. 18–29.
26. *Orthodoxy, Heterodoxy and Dissent in India,* edited by S. N. Eisenstadt, R. Kahane and D. Shulman (Berlin, 1984).
27. For biographical details of Abhinavagupta, see P. V. Kane (1971), pp. 161–208.

28. Detlef Kantowsky, 'Max Weber on India, and Indian Interpretation of Weber', in *Changing South Asia: Religion and Society*, edited by Kenneth Ballhatchet and David Taylor (London, 1984), pp. 11–35.
29. *Orthodoxy, Heterodoxy and Dissent in India,* p. 4.
30. P. V. Kane (1923/71); S. K. De (1923/60); Edwin Gerow (1977).
31. Visvanatha, *Sahitya Darpana,* I, 3.
32. *Kavyadarsha,* C. Sankara Rama Sastri (1959); *Srngaraprakasha,* V. Raghavan (1963).
33. Ibid.
34. P. V. Kane (1923/71), pp. 208–18.
35. Bharat L. Bhatt, 'India and Indian Regions: A Critical Overview', in *An Exploration of India: Geographical Perspectives on Society and Culture,* edited by David E. Sopher (London, 1980), pp. 35–64.
36. *A Source Book of Advaita Vedanta,* edited by Eliot Deutsch and J. A. V. van Buitenen (Honolulu, 1971), pp. 112–222.
37. Abhinavagupta's important work on poetics was a commentary on Bharata's *Natyashastra,* i.e. *Abhinavabharati*
38. S. A. A. Rizvi, 'India and the Medieval Islamic World', *A Cultural History of India,* edited by A. L. Basham (Oxford, 1975), p. 465.
39. For an analysis of the interplay of the 'vertical' and the 'horizontal' elements in Indian history, see B. Subbarao, *The Personality of India* (Baroda, 1956).
40. M. Monier-Williams's *Dictionary* offers the following meaning of *marga:* "seeking, search, tracing out, hunting, the track of a wild animal, any track, road, path, way to, course (also of wind and stars), to give way to, allow to pass, to suffer the same fate, in order to make way to any one, walk, journey, reach, range, a scar, mark, a passage, channel, a way, manner, method, custom, usage, a way of speaking, or writing, diction, style, a high style of acting, dancing or singing."
41. N. A. Jiarazbhoy, 'Music', in *A Cultural History of India,* edited by A. L. Basham (Oxford, 1975), pp. 218–9.
42. Ibid., p. 219.
43. Visvanatha, *Sahitya Darpana, IX,* 1–5.
44. Claus Vogel, *Indian Lexicography, A History of Indian Literature,* Vol. V, Fasc. 4, edited by Jan Gonda (Wiesbaden, 1979), p. 344.
45. Thomas Wilbanks, 'Accessibility and Social Change in Northern India', in *An Exploration of India,* edited by David E. Sopher (London, 1980), p. 269.
46. Romila Thapar (1966/83), pp. 241–50.
47. S. S. Narula, *Social Roots of Indian Linguistics* (Delhi, 1979), p. 102.
48. Ananda Coomaraswamy, *The Dance of Shiva* (Bombay, 1948); Sri Aurobindo, 'The National Value of Art', in *Collected Works,* Vol. XVII, Birth Centenary Library (Pondicherry, 1972), pp. 23–54.
49. Eliot Deutsch and J. A. B. van Buitenen (1972), p. 10.
50. Ibid., p. 166.
51. *A Reader on the Sanskrit Grammarians,* edited by J. F. Staal (Cambridge, Massachusetts & London, 1972), pp. 432–525.

52. *Sources of Indian Tradition,* compiled by William Theodore de Bary and others (New York, 1958/60), p. *77.*
53. *Al Beruni's India: An Account of the Religion, Philosophy, Literature, Geography, Chronology, Astronomy, Customs, Laws and Astrology of India about AD 1030,* edited by C. Sachau (London, 1888), Vol. II, Chapter LXI, pp. 118–22 (p. 118).
54. Michel Hulin (1978).
55. Romila Thapar (1966/83), p. 241.
56. Sudhir Kakar (1981), p. 142.
57. P. V. Kane (1971), p. 107.
58. R. B. Patankar, 'Three Alternatives' (1984), p. 57.
59. This translation is by Ramachandra Gopal Bhandarkar, in *A Reader to Sanskrit Grammarians* (1972), pp. 99–100.
60. Samartha Ramdas, *Sri Dasabodha,* Sabdaranjana edition, with introduction by Tarkatirtha Laxmansastri Joshi (Bombay, 1962/68). p. 45.
61. This translation is by A. K. Ramanujan, *Speaking of Siva* (Penguin, 1973/79), p. 75.
62. James Stuart Mill (1826), pp. 50-51.
63. Karl de Schweinitz, Jr., *The Rise and Fall of British India, Imperialism as Inequality* (New York, 1983) offers a good account of the sociology of colonialism in India.
64. *Oxford Advanced Learner's Dictionary of Current English* by A. S. Hornby (Oxford, 1974), p. 124, defines the term as "permanent military station, place where soldiers live (especially in India and Pakistan)."
65. James Mill (1826), Vol. II, p. 1. Quoted by Mill from Sir Thomas Roe's letter to the Archbishop of Canterbury, Churchill.
66. Francois Bernier (1891), p. 298. For a detailed study of Mughal architecture and the Italian influence on it see Ebba Koch, 'Pietre Dure and Other Artistic Contacts Between the Court of the Mughals and that of the Medici' in *A Mirror of Princes,* edited by Dalu Jones, Marga Publications (date not mentioned), pp. 29–56.
67. James Mill (1826), p. 1.
68. For a discussion of John Ruskin's response to India, see R. Sencourt (1923).
69. Kennedi Ballhatchet, *Race, Sex and Class under the Raj: Imperial Attitudes and Politics and Their Critics* (London, 1980) discusses the entire case of Fanny Epstein in its chapter, 'Low Life and Racial Prestige', pp. 123–43.
70. Ibid., p. 123.
71. Arthur Mayhew (1926), pp. 180–81.
72. E. M. Forster, *A Passage To India* (Penguin 1936/69), p. 10.
73. L. S. S. O'Malley (1941), p. 568.
74. Karl de Schweinitz (1983), p. 79.
75. L.S.S. O'Malley (1941), p. 579.
76. Ashis Nandy (1983), pp. 52–53.
77. For an elaborate account of Halhed's work in this respect, see Rosane Rocher, *Orientalism, Poetry and the Millennium: The Checkered Life of Nathaniel Brassey-Halhed, 1751–1830* (Delhi, 1983).

78. Ibid., p. 48.
79. Phanindra Nath Banerjee, 'Impact of British Policy on the Judicial Administration in Bengal in the Eighteenth Century', in *Western Colonial Policy*, Vol. I, edited by N. R. Ray, Institute of Historical Studies (Calcutta, 1981), p. 312.
80. Oliver Mendelsohn, 'The Pathology of Indian Legal System', *Modem Asian Studies*, Vol. XV, No. 4 (1981), pp. 823–63.
81. Bernard S. Cohn, 'Some Notes on Law and Change in North India', *Economic Development and Cultural Change*, No. 8 (1959).
82. Robert L. Kidder, 'Courts and Conflict in an Indian City: A Study in Legal Impact', *Journal of Commonwealth Political Studies*, Vol. XI, No. 2 (1973), pp. 121–39.
83. Oliver Mendelsohn (1981), p. 826.
84. Ibid., p. 857.

After Amnesia

1. S. K. Nandi, *Studies in Modem Indian Aesthetics*, Indian Institute of Advanced Study (Simla, 1975).
2. Ibid., pp. 291–93.
3. Joan Simon, *The Social Origins of English Education* (London, 1970).
4. Terry Eagleton, *The Function of Criticism from the Spectator to Post-structuralism* (London, 1987).
5. Terry Eagleton, *Literary Theory: An Introduction* (Oxford, 1983), p. 27.
6. M. H. Abrams, *The Mirror and the Lamp* (New York & London, 1953).
7. For a good account of the changing world view of Western philosophy and science the best book I have come across is Arthur Koestler's *The Sleepwalkers* (London, 1939).
8. G. N. Devy, 'Comparative Literature in India', *New Quest* 63 & 64, May–June and July–August 1987.
9. G. S. Amur, 'Laughter in Sanskrit Poetics', in *A Critical Spectrum* (Aurangabad, 1975), p. 154.
10. Krishna Rayan, '*Rasa* and the Objective Correlative', *The British Journal of Aesthetics*, Vol. V, No. 3, July 1965, p. 247.
11. V. K. Gokak, *An Integral View of Poetry: An Indian Perspective* (Delhi, 1975), p. 99.
12. B. S. Mardhekar, *Arts and Man: Lectures and Essays* (Bombay, 1960), p. 185.
13. William S. Willis, Jr., 'Skeletons in the Anthropological Closet', in *Reinventing Anthropology*, edited by Dell Hymes (Random House, 1969), reprinted as a Vintage Book (1974), pp. 122–3.
14. Yogendra Singh, *Modernization of Indian Tradition* (Rawat, Jaipur, 1986), p. 120.
15. Fred W. Riggs, *Administration in Developing Countries*, cited by Yogendra Singh, p. 120.

16. From here on, till the end of the section, I have used parts of my article, 'Colonial Experience and the Indian Critical Tradition'; in *The Colonial and the Neo-Colonial Encounters in Commonwealth Literature,* edited by H.H. Annaiah Gowda (Mysore, 1983), pp. 135–48.
17. Sri Aurobindo, 'The Sources of Poetry', *The Harmony of Virtue,* Birth Centenary Library Edition, Vol. III (Pondicherry, 1972), p. 105ff.
18. The next two paragraphs are adapted from my article, 'Sri Aurobindo's "Sources of Poetry" and Indian Poetry in English', in *A Common Poetic for Indian Literatures,* edited by C. D. Narasimhaiah and C. N. Srinath (Mysore, 1984), pp. 104–116.
19. Sri Aurobindo, 'The National Value of Art', *The Hour of God,* Birth Centenary Library, Vol. XVII (Pondicherry, 1972), pp. 231–54.
20. 'To My Brother' (Letter), Centenary Library, Vol. XXVII, pp. 148–62.
21. Sri Aurobindo, *The Future Poetry,* Centenary Library, Vol. IX (1972).
22. Ibid., p. 9.
23. 'Ahana', *Collected Poems,* Centenary Library, Vol. V, pp. 523–36.
24. B. S. Mardhekar, *Arts and Man: Lectures and Essays* (Popular, Bombay, 1960) and *Soundarya ani Sahitya* (Mauj, Bombay, 1955).
25. R. B. Patankar (1984). In this extended and thought-provoking article, previously referred to in the present work, Patankar presents an account of Mardhekar's influence on Marathi criticism.
26. Bhalchandra Nemade, 'Marathi Novel—1950–75', translated from the Marathi by G. N. Devy, *Setu: Journal of Indian Literature in Translation,* Vol. II, No. 1, 1986, pp. 29–70.
27. Ibid., p. 29.
28. Ibid., pp. 59–60.
29. A special issue of *New Quest* (May 1983) included papers presented at a seminar on nativism in Marathi and Kannada literatures. Many of these papers had a theoretical orientation, and nativism was treated at the seminar as a doctrine rather than as a style of critical thinking.
30. Bhalchandra Nemade, translated by G. N. Devy, *Setu,* Vol. II, No. 1, 1986, p. 68.

Epilogue

1. Sham Lal, 'A Cure For Amnesia', *The Times of India* (Ahmedabad edition), 19 May 1990, p. 6.
2. Immanuel Velikovsky, *Mankind in Amnesia* (Abacus, London, 1982/3).
3. Ibid., p. 9.

Index

'OF MANY HEROES'

An Indian Essay in Literary Historiography

For Sujit Mukherjee and Meenakshi Mukherjee,
pathfinders

We are unaware of the beginning and the end of the world:
The first and last pages of this old book have fallen away…

—*Shahjahan-nama* by Abu Talib Kalim,
seventeenth century historian and poet

Acknowledgments

I would like to thank the Forbes Gujarat Sabha of Bombay and Dr. Prabodh Parikh for inviting me to lecture in June 1988 on 'Literary History'; The Gujarat Sahitya Parishad, Ahmedabad and Dr. Chandrakant Topiwala for asking me to give the Gujarat University Lecture for 1989 on 'Literary History'; and the Commonwealth Centre for Literary and Cultural Change at The University of Virginia and Prof. Ralph Cohen for inviting me to lecture on 'Indian Literary History: Colonialism and Amnesia'.

I thank the Department of English at the Maharaja Sayajirao University of Baroda for allowing me to teach courses in Comparative Literature and Literary History and students in these courses for shaping my approach to Comparative Literature.

I also thank Prof. Dieter Riemenschneider of Goethe University, Frankfurt, Prof. Sisir Kumar Das of Delhi University, Prof. Vilas Sarang of Bombay University, Prof. Wolfgang Zach of the University at Graz, Prof. Manavendra Bandopadhya of Jadavpur University for inviting me to seminars on literary history, comparative literature, literary translation, para-literature, and related topics.

New Quest, Etad, Bombay Literary Review, Critical Practice, Litcrit have published sections of this book in previous versions. Mrs. Niyati Derasari Pandya and Dr. Shirish Panchal have translated some sections into Gujarati. I thank them.

I thank the British Council for a grant-in-aid to consult library resources in Britain in summer 1988, and the Association of Commonwealth Universities at London for the THB Symons Fellowship award, 1991; also the School of English at the University of Leeds, and its Head, Prof. Inga-Stina Ewbank, and the Department of English, Media and Theatre Studies at the University of Ulster at Coleraine, and its Head, Prof. Robert Welch for providing excellent academic facilities.

I would also like to thank the Staff at the Brotherton Library in Leeds, the University Library at Coleraine and the Sterling Library at Yale; Mr. S. K. Rana and Ms. Deepa Hari for helping me in preparing the final draft and Ms. Alphy J. Plakkoottam for preparing the press copy.

Though this book has been long in preparation, a substantial part of it was composed during my affiliation with the University of Ulster at Coleraine in August–September 1991. During my entire stay Prof. Robert Welch and Mrs. Angela Welch looked after me with utmost generosity and affection. I do not know how to thank them.

The draft I prepared at the University of Ulster at Coleraine was revised and extended during my tenure as a Fulbright Fellow at the University of Yale, New Haven. I have had the benefit of several discussions with Prof. Geoffrey Hartman during my stay there between April and October 1992.1 am also thankful to him for introducing me to Prof. Rene Wellek, the most important scholar of literary historiography in our time.

The main inspiration for this book comes from the historiographical work by Dr. Sujit Mukherjee. As a modest token of the acknowledgement of that debt, I dedicate this book to him and to Prof. Meenakshi Mukherjee, whose scholarship I have admired over the last three decades.

G. N. Devy
Baroda/Leeds/Coleraine/New Haven, 1991–97

Contents

1

Some Indian Questions

Indian literature is a historian's despair. The three thousand years of its past, within which there is an amazing recurrence of trends, styles and themes, makes a mockery of periodization. The profound interdependence between religion, philosophy and literature in India defies assessment in terms of the aesthetic categories evolved in the modern West; and the healthy acceptance of certain kinds of re-renderings (particularly those originating in the epics) as 'original' works, raises important philosophical questions about the nature of literature as a form of creativity. The multiplicity of cultures, sects and languages in India poses an incredibly difficult challenge to literary comparatism. All modern literary languages in India, of the Dravidian family as well as of the Indo-Aryan family, have had intimate literary exchanges with the ancient Sanskrit, Pali and Prakrit languages, the medieval Apabhramsa languages as well as Persian and Arabic, and modern European languages (primarily English, but also, in some cases, Portuguese and French). Besides, there have been similar exchanges between the Dravidian languages and the modern Indo-Aryan languages, and, inevitably, within the Dravidian and Indo-Aryan languages. Altogether, the cultural history of literatures in Indian languages is far more complex than one imagines.

The oldest among the living literary languages in India, Tamil, has a continuous history of three thousand years. The youngest among the literary languages in India, English, has a history, within the Indian context, of not more than two hundred years. Histories of other literatures stretch in between these two outer limits. Kannada has a literary history of fifteen hundred years, Marathi about eight hundred years, and Oriya five hundred years. Obviously, a single historiographic formula cannot prove adequate to describe each and every literature in India. The appropriateness of a common approach is further called to question by the fact that there is a vast variation of sociology, culture and political history from language to language. Some languages such as Sanskrit, Persian and English have been the languages of political domination; other languages have been for most part of their history the dominated languages. Some languages have had the sociology of trade, industry and a general economic prosperity. Others have had a sociology of combative survival. These variations are naturally reflected in the respective literatures. In addition to these native differences in the contexts of Indian literature, there were differences added to them by a large variety of interactions with the two experiences of prolonged political domination by foreign cultures. Of these, the Islamic domination affected the northern languages and literatures more profoundly, and gave India a new literary language, Urdu. The British colonial domination affected the upper layers of Indian society, mainly in the urban areas, giving another literary language to India, the Indo-English. A literary historiography not sensitive to the range and complexity of differences in Indian literary traditions stands the risk of distorting its subject.

Literary history as practised in India in the twentieth century has been greatly interested in devising critical labels for periods, genres, styles and schools of literary writing. It has certainly made impressive achievements in locating documentary sources and textual evidences towards constructing narratives of literary practices in India. The beginning of this difficult task of constructing historical narratives about India was made by European Indologists during the nineteenth century; and, in the course of time, when they left, Indian scholars took over. Thus the sense of history, institutionalized in modern literary historiography in India, is mainly of Western origin. Since the context for this development was that of colonialism, the Western sense of history came to be considered in India as the universally valid sense of history. This practice has two damaging consequences for the field of literary study in India: one, the question whether India ever had any sense of literary history of its own before the contact with the modern West became a permanently sealed question; and two, there exists an inevitable gap between the nature of histories of various Indian literatures and the master narrative employed to construct these histories. In recent years there has been a movement towards re-defining the goals of literary historiography in India. This movement comes mainly from the advocates of comparative literary study; but much of its brilliance and energy are devoted to postulating a non-existent pan-Indian field of literary study, an 'Indian literature' though it is composed in several dozen languages.

Since the question of alterity is implicit in colonialism, the cognitive exchanges between the confronting cultures take place necessarily in terms of closed concepts. The rituals of cultural exchange, cautiously guarded by the rules of domination, render an equal exchange impossible. During the colonial period a static image of India was circulated in the West, and a static image of the West was circulated in India. The Western sense of literature, and the Western sense of history of literature, which in fact have been fields of cultural thought full of cross-currents and radical disagreements, are seen by Indian literary scholars as relatively stable structures of unified thought which can be transplanted in India. It would be interesting to enquire whether the discourse of literary history, which was in the making precisely during the period of high colonialism, was not in any way influenced by Europe's colonial encounter with the rest of the world, and what, if any, is the relationship of 'knowledge' to 'power' in that discourse. One of the aims of this essay is to discuss, in relation to the major issues briefly outlined above, the gap between Indian literature and the current practices in literary historiography.

An attempt is made here to reconstruct the conventions of literary history in India prior to India's colonial encounter with the modern West. The area of traditional historiography in India is indeed very vast, and within the scope of the present essay no more than a bare outline can be offered. My attempt is not to prove that the discipline of historiography existed in ancient and medieval India in the form acceptable to contemporary fashions in literary study. I have merely tried to point out that a certain amount of textual evidence is available in Sanskrit, the bhashas and Persian to indicate the nature of historiographical consciousness in ancient and medieval India. I have further tried to explore the dependence of Western literary historiography on the experience of colonizing other cultures. That exploration, it is hoped, will provide the proper context to understand the shift in Indian literary historiography from the precolonial conventions of history to postcolonial approaches to literary history. A brief account of some major twentieth century theories of literary history in the West is presented in order to indicate how the contemporary Indian approaches are substantially different in orientation. Since the history of literature in Indian languages is governed by their specific cultural features, it becomes necessary to bring in a discussion of these features. The concluding sections of this essay, therefore, move in the direction of a theoretical discussion of issues pertaining to some unique aspects of Indian literary culture.

The primary aim of this essay is not to refute Western literary historiography. The aim is also not to substitute in place of the current historiographical practices some new or more appropriate practice. This essay is not an attempt at fresh theorizing. Its simple aim is to understand and review the conventions of literary historiography in ancient, medieval, colonial and contemporary India. If, in the process, my explorations are found to have any theoretical substance, it should be seen as an entirely unintended effect.

2

History and Literary History

History did not emerge as a discipline until it became the basis for ideological rhetoric. Whether it was initiated by the revolutionary intellectual or Napoleon Bonaparte himself, the striking worker in the British factories or the white colonizers, every procedure of power-acquisition commenced in the West with the claim of being on the right side of history. Similarly, the emergence of literary history as a 'subject' is intimately linked with the rise of literature as a means of social domination.[1] As is the case in Europe, so too in India. When literature gets institutionalized, it gets into classrooms and, in turn, becomes an instrument of class-division. That is when a given literature generates the rhetoric of its history.

Literary history is basically an apparatus of canon formation, which is a process of drawing and re-drawing the boundaries of fields of literary production in terms of what is socially acceptable or unacceptable. Literary history reflects the values of the society in which the historian lives, or for which he writes. A history of literature without these values and the judgements implicit in them is as impossible as a state without power-structures. Justification of the authority wielding power is in fact the main purpose of canons.

Panini, the ancient Indian linguist, had a good insight into the procedures of canon formation. Commenting on canonical language, the *updishtha,* he says, it is the community of the learned, the *shishtha,* that decides what is good in language.[2] And it is their language ability that decides who are learned. So the learned decide what is learning, which decides who is learned. But when it was pointed out to him that this is a circuitous argument, he confessed that it is the social consent that ultimately puts the stamp of recognition on the learned, vesting in them the authority and the function of legitimizing language. Canon formation is thus the process of translating the rules of social domination to the field of aesthetic creation.

What the exact relationship between the growth of colonialism and the development of literary historiography has been in Europe has not been studied so far. However, it is worth noting that the earliest literary history in English, Thomas Warton's *History of English Poetry* (1774),[3] came about the same time as the earliest translations of Oriental literary texts by European scholars. The earliest historians and historiographers of literature in Germany were themselves scholars of Oriental languages. Wilhelm von Humboldt published *On the Task of the Historian* (1821), which influenced the *History of the Poetic National Literature of the Germans* (1835–42) of Gervinus, who also authored *Fundamentals of the Theory of Historiography.*[4] All through the nineteenth century history, historiography and literary history developed rapidly in the world of European scholarship. Colonialism and nationalism provided the appropriate background for this development.

Primarily, canon and nation were the two goals of European literary historiography.[5] However, histories have also been written keeping in view forms of literature, genres and sub-genres, style-epochs; single author, influence and reception; gender, class and race; philosophic, political and social contexts; and periods of literature. At the same time literary history has received attention from philosophers and literary theorists. Thus during the last two centuries literary history has been a dynamic field of literary study.

Though the expression 'literary history' does not accurately reflect the major themes and concerns of this field, the designation has acquired stability. The main problem that the expression poses is that if a narrative is literary, it ceases to be history. On the other hand, if it is historical, it ceases to be literary. One would have liked to replace the expression with a more suitable one. However, critical expressions come to acquire their privileges through long historical processes which are better left uncontested. What is more important here is to note that, whether it is the organic vision of history or the analytical vision of history within which a historian works, literary history has to negotiate a highly problematic relationship between the objective and the subjective. It is so for the obvious reason that 'literary history' at once refers to two different, if interdependent, systems of signs: (a) the past of a literary tradition as *it was,* the system of signs that literary texts form, and (b) a narration *about* the past of a literary tradition, the system of signs that represents the past.

Whatever be one's vision of history, literary history cannot escape the fate of being a narrative, a kind of fiction which represents an order of signs in past existence. The narrative gets further complicated because literary signs are no less complex than events in human existence, whereas the degree of freedom with which a historian can narrate them is relatively restricted. The discourse of literary history is required to operate within the conditions imposed upon it by the nature of language, logic and reality that literary history deals with.[6]

Historical narratives not only order events to be represented, but also select them; and quite often these events are invented by historians. The process of exclusion and inclusion of events in historical narratives is tacitly guided by the general principles of inclusion and exclusion sanctioned by the community for which, and within which, the narrative is being constructed. It is these principles, which remain almost entirely unarticulated, that constitute a community's sense of self. In fact, the same sense of self, in relation to the associated sense of the other, becomes the community's sense of tradition when projected onto a vaster temporal scale. Literary history, like other forms of historical narrative, can but represent through symbolic selection of texts this unconscious sense of tradition formed collectively and unconsciously by a community of readers. Yet, the sense of self itself is considerably influenced by works of literature in its oral and written forms. The historiographical community is not a community tightly sealed off from literary practice and participation. If literary history is moulded by a community's sense of the self-other relationship, this sense itself originates, to some extent, in literature and language. Literature, and the historical consciousness of literature in fact form a continuity, which literary history intercepts temporarily, and, thus, creates a fiction.

As in other forms of narration, in literary history too the narrator does not have unconditional and uncontroverted space to construct the narrative. The historian has to be involved in the narration not as a disinterested analyst but as a politically pre-constituted subject. The narration is conditioned, therefore, by the conscious or the unconscious ideology of race, class and gender within which the historian's intellectual sympathies are engaged. It can be said that every historical narrative was written in the ideological space within the consciousness of the historian much before it was written in language.

Histories may be fiction; yet, the temporal sequencing in history does not have the same degree of freedom as the temporal sequencing in fiction. For instance, one cannot begin a historical narrative in the present and lead it backward in time. This binding is accepted by history because the discourse of history is required to have consistency with the dominant concepts of space and time that the community of its readers puts into circulation as meaningful concepts. Fiction has the verbal space and a fictional time to allow it a greater freedom of temporal movement. The concept of time and the temporal scale employed by literary history have to have a sanction from what the community of its users believes to be rational.

Literary events differ from other historical events in that literary events do not affect the material world in the same way as the 'real' historical events affect it. Literary events are 'virtual' events. On the other hand, literary events, such as plays or poems, have the capacity to survive over long periods of time; and every time they are encountered, they may take on a fresh life. Clearly, literary events belong to a different order of events. Besides, history deals clearly with past events, whereas literary history has to deal with events which seem to belong to the past but also belong to the present. History mediates between the readers of the narrative and the past that is narrated; but in the case of literary history this mediation is superfluous because the readers of literary history have direct personal access to the past literary events.

If the superfluity of literary history stems from its being language about indestructible language, it also faces a limitation on account of being a narrative about a discourse of language, a tradition or convention of literature. Literary history may be a narrative; but the exact form it will or should take depends on the nature of the events to be narrated. Not all narratives are good enough for each and every kind of literary tradition. In fact, it is always the literary events themselves that guide the discourse and mode of literary history.

At the same time, like fiction, history of literature depends on a prior existence of conventions of historical writings for its own survival and growth. History and so also literary history are not inventions that can be suddenly made by a genius of great imagination in any given period. Both disciplines acquire identity and visibility through slow progressions during which these disciplines acquire the ability to represent happenings. In other words, literary history initially has to develop its system of symbolic representation—in which gradation, classification, designation become symbolic modes—simultaneously as it orders and selects literary events. All subsequent developments in the field try to systematize the symbolic system of representation.

If literary history, like other forms of history, is indeed a form of fiction, it cannot take birth unless a community has invented fiction as a medium of encountering life and the universe. The development of history in any given society will correspond to the development of fiction and its status as a mode of organizing perceptions in that society. The forms of history too will correspond to the forms of fiction. Besides, since literary history is expected to account for the aesthetic fluctuations within a literary tradition, it has to employ standards of excellence, criteria of assessment, categories of description and other apparatus developed by literary criticism, theory and aesthetics. Hence any historical narrative depends for its cognitive ability on the status of criticism and theory backing it up. In turn, criticism and theory depend on developments in other disciplines such as philosophy, linguistics, anthropology, political thought and psychology. On the other hand, literary criticism itself depends on developments in literature, and, therefore, on the cognitive store of literary history. Thus, literary history is an involved interdisciplinary enterprise.

Conceding that the discourse of literary history is severely restricted, does it have any space of its own to form an interpretative discipline, with what R. S. Crane calls, "the critical and historical principles" of its own? The answer to this polemical question lies in pointing out not the theoretical viability but the historical necessity of its existence. The answer is that it *is* there, that it has come to stay in modern intellectual pursuits.

In fact, literary history has been at the very heart of academic study and research of literature all over the world during the last two centuries, and, even if in a different form, much longer in India. What is taught as literature in schools and universities all over the world is some form of historical representation of literature rather than the process of literary creativity itself. Institutionalized study of literature turns literary history into the means of raising powerful and persuasive myths about literature, privileging some areas of creativity and repressing or concealing others. No literature, recognized as literature, escapes the fate of being represented by literary historiographers.

3

Time and Territory

Structures of historical narratives invariably depend on the sense of time shared by the community for which the narratives are produced. Concepts of time, in turn, are interlocked with other cultural constructs. Western discourses of knowledge about non-Western societies assume that the concept of time operative in traditional societies is 'cyclical'. This other sense of time is opposed to the 'linear' sense of time in Western societies. Often, the imitative scholarship in non-Western nations tends to accept this facile distinction as a valid philosophic observation.

'Cyclical' and 'linear' are in fact only historiographical notions and not attributes either of time or of the perceiving human consciousness. The distinction, whatever its source, accurately reflects the unequal power positions of the cultures having a 'linear' sense of time (the colonizing cultures) and those with a 'cyclical' sense of time (the cultures that were colonized). Similarly, it is claimed that the communities that have not mastered their immediate natural environment, live in some kind of 'mythical' or 'magical' time. In mythologies all over the world one comes across the notion of a supernatural keeper of time. Similarly, most schools of metaphysics accept the idea of eternity, time beyond human grasp, as an objective fact. The origin of a community's sense of time can be traced to its perception of the geographical space which it inhabits.

Ancient Indian iconography recognized the interdependence

between notions of Time and Space by depicting Time as a coiled serpent, *Ananta,* who forms the seat or bed of Vishnu, the supporter of Space. Heinrich Zimmer comments on the representation of the *sheshashayi* posture of Vishnu:

> Vishnu sleeps. Like a spider that has climbed up the thread that once issued from its own organism, drawing it back into itself, the god has consumed again the web of the universe. Alone upon the immortal substance of the ocean, a giant figure, submerged partly, partly afloat, he takes delight in slumber. There is no one to behold him, no one to comprehend him; there is no knowledge of him, except within himself.
>
> This giant, "Lord of Maya", and the cosmic ocean on which he is recumbent, are dual manifestations of a single essence; for the ocean, as well as the human form, is Vishnu. Furthermore, since in Hindu mythology the symbol for water is the serpent *(naga),* Vishnu is presented, normally, as reposing on the coils of a prodigious snake, his favourite symbolic animal, the serpent Ananta, "Endless". So that, not only the gigantic anthropomorphic form and the boundless element, but the reptile too is Vishnu. It is on a serpent ocean of his own immortal substance that the Cosmic Man passes the universal night.[1]

The interdependence of the notions of space and the notions of time, their essential unity, is depicted in Hindu myth as much as in Hindu art. Ananta, the symbol for time, is endless and yet potentially a figure that moves forward, one of its motions is cyclical and the other linear. In Hindu iconography, Vishnu is the mythological figure in whose person Time and Space unite.

Myths compress vast temporal spans within the brief moment of narration probably because they are created in communities which imagine themselves to be living at the centre of the vast space engulfing them. Myth is thus the earliest science that reduces space to humanly perceptible measures.

The quest for creating historical narratives originates in communities that have acquired the intellectual means of arriving at complex spatial abstractions, or alternately have political control of vast territories. The great Indian epic *Mahabharata* was called in its earlier and simpler form *Jaya,* which was *itihasa,* history of a king's triumph in a war. Thus, the intimate relationship between territorial conquest and creation of historical narrative is owned in the initial title of the *Mahabharata.* The Homeric epics in the Greek language show a comparable intimacy between the sense of time and the sense of territorial possession. Virgil's *Aeneid* can be cited as the third great illustration of this correspondence.

At an abstract level the modern discipline of psychology provides a fascinating story of history replacing myth in correspondence with the associated sense of mental space. In Greek mythology, Psyche was believed to be a beautiful young princess, so beautiful that she caused much jealousy among other princesses. Not only were her two older sisters jealous of her, but also the goddess Aphrodite. The jealous goddess ordered Cupid, or Eros, to inspire Psyche with love for the vilest among men; but, as it always happens in myths, Cupid himself fell in love with her and started visiting her secretly every night. The jealous sisters of Psyche told her that the person she embraced in the darkness every night was a hideous monster. So, Psyche lighted her lamp while Cupid slept, and she saw the most beautiful of the gods. However, as she stared at him, a drop of hot oil fell on his shoulder. It woke him up, and he fled. She then wandered in search of him, till, at last, she found him; and the two entered into an immortal union.[2] This myth, contained most of the central concerns of Freudian psychoanalysis: jealousy, desire, sex, fear, guilt, nostalgia, quest for pleasure, and the revolt of the youngest sister (the Ego) against the two older sisters (the Super Ego and the Reality Principle). The atmosphere in the traditional story, full of darkness, desire and deception is in consonance with Freud's conception of the working of the mind. Freud's achievement was that he turned this myth into a historical narrative by introducing temporality in terms of a sequence of the stages through which the mind is formed: the subconscious associated with childhood or the primitive followed by the more accessible parts of the consciousness associated with the adult and the civilized aspects of life. Thus the mapping of the territory of consciousness resulted in the case of Freudian psychoanalysis in turning a myth into a neat historical narrative. When the initial mapping of the inner space acquired more empirical evidence, the history of human consciousness was further extended beyond the province of the individual's psyche into the collective unconscious and racial memory.

Communities confined to relatively small geographical areas are content with the local folklore for their history and mythology. On the other hand, communities poised for vast territorial explorations or occupation tend to project aggressive historical images. The *Ramayana* describes the entire genealogy of Rama, giving this character an immense historical proportion; on the other hand the vanquished Ravana is given a relatively compressed historical representation. When spatially dispossessed societies involve themselves in attempts to regain their territorial autonomy, they often tend to create fresh and alluring images of their past. The Celtic Revival in Ireland at the beginning of the twentieth century, or the so called Indian Renaissance with its revival of tradition, are some important examples of this tendency.

If, as conjectured so far, the human attitude to time is so closely intertwined with the human attitude to space, perhaps then, the rise of history as an academic and political project towards the end of the eighteenth century in Europe, its subsequent growth during the nineteenth century, and the attendant development of historiography during the last two hundred years may have had a corresponding sequence of attitudes towards territorial control. Of course, such interdependence cannot be proved through any mechanical and uniform formula. Nor can one expect this initial correspondence to guide the disciplines of history and historiography beyond the most elementary stages of their birth and spread. Nevertheless, it will not be amiss to assume that the European colonial aspiration of establishing political and administrative order over unimaginably vast geographical areas directly affected Europe's desire to create an intellectual order within its own history. There is another dimension to this hypothesis, one of greater importance to us in India.

If colonization gives a boost to historiography in the colonizing cultures, it also creates serious historiographical inversions for the colonized cultures. Colonization adds to the history of the colonizers; it also takes away some history of the colonized. As examples of this process of dehistoriation one can think of the disciplines of anthropology and Orientalism. Anthropology, a science of the study of 'primitive' cultures, a science created in Europe, places its subject out of the flow of history first, before analysing it. Orientalism, another science thus created for the study of the 'once civilized' cultures, freezes parts of the historical flow to which its subject belongs. In it, the ancient Orient is given precedence over the contemporary Orient. Repression or reversal of history of other societies is an attribute of colonialism because it seeks to make comparable territorial ingression.

As the structuralist view goes, history is never controlled in isolation and exclusively by some master devices: it is being made and unmade by every single relationship among the constituents of the whole process. To go by this argument, colonialism has had an extremely important role to play in shaping the discourse of history in Europe. E. H. Carr, eminent British historian, admits as much in his comments on recent changes in history:

> What I have called the expansion of reason in our twentieth century revolution has particular consequences for the historian; for the expansion of reason means, in essence, the emergence into history of groups and classes, of people and continents, that hitherto lay outside it...Modern history begins when more and more people emerge into social and political consciousness, become aware of their respective groups as historical entities having a past and a future, and enter fully into history.[3]

Certainly, the history of History (and of literary history) in Europe cannot at all be thought of in isolation from the history of colonization. If one were to try, one could perhaps identify in the story of colonialism the shadows of Ranke, Hegel, Marx, Nietzsche, Collingwood and others.

Given that history as an academic discipline does not dwell on neutral ground, it becomes necessary to re-examine two popular assertions about Indian history: the first is that the Indian sense of time is cyclical, the second, that consciousness about history is a unique gift of the West to India, and that such a sense did not exist in India to the same degree as it did in Europe. Any Indian intellectual interested in history is invariably faced with the following two posers: Was there a native historiography in India? And what, if any, is the Indian sense of time? Both these are very large questions. And in the context of general history and historiography some contemporary Indian scholars have tried to face at least one of the two questions. Thanks to their efforts we know much about history in ancient and medieval India. However, literary scholars have not made much progress in understanding the native traditions of literary historiography in India. Sujit Mukherjee makes a tentative beginning towards founding a truly Indian literary historiography, but does not go far enough as he considers literary history to be a discipline entirely of European origin.[4] Probably, the most significant work on literary historiography published in India in recent times is Ram Vilas Sharma's *Bharatiya Sahitya Itihasa ke Samasyaen.* He analyses the linguistic complexity of Indian literature.[5] Similarly, the question of Indian philosophies of time has not attracted adequate scholarly attention within India so far. Anindita Niyogi Balslev's study of time in Indian philosophy points to an area of scholarship that Indian scholars will do well to develop.[6] The recent work by Romila Thapar, *Time as a Metaphor of History: Early India* provides a fascinating example of how explorations in this direction can enrich our understanding not only of history but also of culture and creativity.[7]

The result of not exploring the native conventions of literary history is the failure to understand the native processes of canon formation and, therefore, the aesthetics of literature. Indian tradition is rich in literary theory. Most of these theories are available to modern Indian scholars as texts to which they cannot relate intellectually. Nor do they understand why the theories disappeared suddenly and mysteriously. These problems come from the general failure to internalize tradition, and from not knowing the means to do so. Again, contemporary histories of literature may generally leave Indian readers unsatisfied; not all that one values in literature is included in these histories.

During the twentieth century, Indian literary scholars have paid much attention to criticism and theory. In comparison, literary history and historiography have remained perilously neglected. If in modern India there *seems* to have occurred a radical break with the Indian literary past, it has nevertheless occurred without a continuous intellectual battling with that past. The break shows no signs of being a historiographical rebellion; it is just a case of simple amnesia that colonization inevitably causes. In order that the intellectual energy expended in the sphere of abstract criticism by modern literary scholars in India should bear the desired fruits, it is first necessary to re-examine Indian literary historiography on its own terms.

4

Two Paradigms of History

"History is of two types," writes Rajashekhara, "of a single hero, and of many heroes."[1] The terms employed by the tenth century poet-critic to represent the two types are *parakriya* and *purakalpa,* and his respective illustrations for them, the *Ramayana* and the *Mahabhharata.* Rajashekhara, the first Indian critic to propose sociology of literature as a distinct field of study, is so completely forgotten now that this remark of his is likely to be brushed aside as a stray intellectual accident by modern literary scholars. However, it is neither stray nor accidental, for it is integrated with the typology of knowledge as presented in his *Kavyamimansa.* Anticipating the modern term 'humanities', Rajashekhara calls the fields of knowledge described by him *paurusheya vidya,* human sciences. According to him, history is one of the fourteen human sciences. And he does not forget to caution his readers against the popular confusion between *purana* and *itihasa,* myth and history, while pointing out that they have distinct narrative styles.

The semantic range covered by the four terms put to service by Rajashekhara—*purana, itihasa, purakalpa* and *parakriya*—is vast. According to V. V. Apte's dictionary,[2] *pura* means 'in former times', 'up to the present time', 'the east', 'a castle'; *purakalpa* means 'a former creation', 'a story of the past', 'a former age'; and *itihasa* means 'legend' as well as 'tradition recognised as a proof'. The awareness that history is a narrative about the past, as well as the past itself, brings Rajashekhara to modern historiographical concerns. Yet, 'tradition recognised as a proof', the acceptance of tradition as the source of legitimation of new experiences, is an aspect of his historiography which sets him off from postcolonial historians of literature.

The typology of knowledge presented by Rajashekhara, and the conceptualizing of history within it, enable us to locate a paradigm of history handed down the generations in Indian intellectual tradition. If this vision of history as a source of intellectual authority and legitimation can at all be placed in opposition to another view of history, perhaps, the terms 'organic' and 'analytical' should be used to designate the two visions. The most crucial difference between the two visions would be that the relationship between the past and the perceiving consciousness is more of mutual accommodation in the organic vision of history, while it is more of mutual appropriation in the analytical vision.

Where does one find an expression of the analytical mode? One is not only tempted to turn immediately to Western discourses of history, but, indeed, the temptation is enhanced by the etymology of 'history' in English. Initially, the Greek *histor* meant 'judge' both a noun and a verb, before it gave rise to *historein,* 'to narrate'. When it was accepted by Latin, it became *historia* and acquired the meaning of 'enquiry'. The English term 'history' combines all these meanings: 'to judge, to narrate, to enquire' as well as 'judgement, narration, enquiry in the past'. Besides, English has given history, as have the other modern European languages derived from Latin, the dignity of being a human science. The judgemental tone of historical inquiries in the West points to the analytical vision implicit in them.

Tempting though it is to contrast Rajashekhara's view of history with the views of Western philosophers of history, such a juxtaposition is not really necessary. It is possible to seek the historiographical counter-point to the *Kavyamimansa* within the Indian intellectual tradition itself. Rajashekhara's criticism was written in times of great political turbulence in the subcontinent. In his century, the tenth, institutions of political authority had been declining rapidly; and with them the concept of authority in religious and metaphysical practices. It was this radical shift in the sense of authority that triggered off the philosophic clash between the *acharyas* and the *bhaktas* during the next four centuries. Rajashekhara himself was acutely aware of the changes taking place in his times, as his play *Karpuramanjiri*[3], written in the *Shataka* style, shows. The play was written in the Maharashtri Apabhramsa dialect and not in Sanskrit, indicating that Sanskrit as the language of literature was soon to be a thing of the past. The play depicts moral chaos as the ruling passion of his times. Other changes too were taking place, in linguistics and semantics, in the theory of *sphota* in particular, and in the sense of Time proposed by the Sankhya eschatology. It was inevitable then that the community of scholars and critics for whom the *Kavyamimansa* was composed received Rajashekhara's historiography in relation to the profound changes that distinguished their century. As a result, we find that the organic model of history is quietly dropped by Bhoja of the next generation. *Atitartha pradhanyad itihasa:* history must produce meaning, it must have a logical sequence, was the pronouncement of Bhoja.[4]

The *Shringaraprakasha* of Bhoja is a compendium of critical concepts, with information about their historical evolution and the debates surrounding the more important concepts. This work amply displays the love for hair-splitting classification that Sanskrit scholarship valued. Bhoja's classification of literary plots provides an instance of his analytical zeal. Narrative plots had been classified into two broad types by Bharata,[5] who preceded Bhoja by seven or eight centuries. The two types were plots based on already known stories and those invented by poets. Dhananjaya, a commentator of Bharata who preceded Bhoja by a century, had added one more type, the cross-breed of Bharata's two types.[6] Bhoja, on the other hand, speaks of five types of narratives. Two of those should interest us here: one is purely history, *itihasa,* the other history-based, *itihasashraya.*[7] He does not accept the view that the *Mahabharata* and the *Ramayana* are the best examples of history. For him history-plays must depict historically known personalities and not mythological persons. Historical narratives must be organized within rational temporal schemes. He opines that poetry can improve upon history by combining fact with imagination so as to produce well structured narratives. He calls this class of story the history-based plot, illustrated by the play *Kumarasambhava.* On the other hand, the plots using history in its 'pure' form should have a *prabandhasharira,* a structural order. The narrative structure which the history writer employs to construct his story is described by Bhoja by using the concept *of pratisamskara.* It is his comprehensive term for the analytical and imaginative investment by the narrator in his narrative. *Pratisamskara* corresponds to 'representation'. Clearly, then, Bhoja's view of history is substantially different from the view Rajashekhara had taken. In one view the present judges the past; in another view the past valorizes the present.

It must immediately be stated that neither Rajashekhara nor Bhoja were greatly original when it came to literary classification. They both allude to a number of predecessors and contemporaries from whom they borrowed ideas freely. One imagines therefore that they represent the general trends in philosophic and critical thinking prevalent during their times. The versions of history presented by Rajashekhara and Bhoja had been shaped through philosophical and cultural movements during the initial phases of the classical period. A large variety of theories of time, theories of meaning and theories of cognition had gone into the making of the discourses of history current in classical India, from the third century to the tenth century. An awareness of some of the more important of those theories can be useful in reconstructing traditional literary historiography in India.

5

Bhartrihari's Metaphors

Though historiography was not his primary concern, Bhartrihari was interested in the dialectical relation between Time and human consciousness. His enquiry into the philosophical status of Time, and into the linguistic devices employed to represent abstractions of Time, forms the subject of *Kalasamuddesha,*[1] a section of hundred and fourteen verses *(karikas)* in his *Vakyapadiya.* Because he was primarily a poet, it is easier to get into the spirit of his argument through his metaphors.

The metaphors in the *Kalasamuddesha* are pastoral, and they reflect a metaphysics affected by the ease and quietude of agrarian life. One of the metaphors for Time used in the early part of Bhartrhari's thesis is that of a bird-catcher who uses captive birds to allure other birds. As he describes it, the birds captured are tied to an invisible string which the bird-catcher releases to let the birds fly, only to pull it back to get the flying birds home, and with them more birds.[2] Time is the bird catcher, and all human actions are like birds tied to it by an invisible string. Thus, for Bhartrihari, Time is one of the permanent limits of human existence. On the other hand, Time cannot be perceived independent of human actions. Time is eternity, but it is also duration. If human existence is entrapped within eternity, duration is entrapped within human action. To bring out this mutual confinement, Bhartrihari likens Time to the air entering the human body.[3] Air by itself has no 'before' and 'after', no temporal sequence;

but once inside the body, it performs all the actions that the body performs and, thereby, acquires a temporal sequence. In the philosopher's view, duration and temporal sequence are caused by the cognition. Time is eternal and transcends durations created by the human consciousness, for durations vanish but Time does not vanish.

According to Bhartrihari, Time is like a road on which durations walk. He asserts, "There is no difference in the length of the road because of the difference of wayfarers and their goings."[4] The image of the solid steady road is likely to create the impression that in Bhartrihari's abstraction Time is static, even if it is imperishable. However, this philosopher-linguist was not interested merely in conceptualizing an abstract time. His interest was to study the cognition of Time in relation to its impersonal pre-cognition form. Hence, in another metaphor, which he uses repeatedly, he speaks of Time as a current or a stream. Occasionally he also speaks of it as a fountain. Given a current of water, says Bhartrihari, and two openings of different width filtering the current, we may have two different speeds for the outflowing currents.[5] The speeds are caused by the recipients of the current which has its own speed. Durations, sequence and temporality are caused by the perceiving consciousness.

Hydraulic imagery is used by Bhartrihari once again in explaining the etymology of the Sanskrit word for Time, *kala;* and it must be understood in the context of the ancient Indian concept of *dravya,* indestructible substances which constitute the universe. He writes:

> *Jalayantrabramaveshasadrishibhih pravrittibhih*
> *Sa kalahkalayan sarvah kalakhyam labhate vibhuh.*[6]

In the words of his translator, "With motions similar to the turnings and agitations of a water wheel, it [that is, Time] all-pervading, driving all parts [*kala,* of the material world], obtains the name 'Time' *[kala].*"[7]

At the beginning of his discourse on Time, Bhartrihari refers to the dispute existing among other schools of philosophy regarding whether *kala* is *shakti, atman or devta*—a force, spirit or godhead. He then states that whatever *kala* may be, it turns the metaphorical water wheel driving the individual containers of water in an endless cycle. It is this image of the water wheel, or windmill, taken quite literally and out of its philosophic context that gives rise to the vulgar idea that the sense of Time in India is 'cyclical'. We should not overlook Bhartrihari's image of a road—a linear image—for Time. Besides, the purpose in using the water wheel or windmill image is not to show the circularity of Time but to show the origin of temporality and durations caused by the cognitive process of fragmentary perceptions. Sequentiality, whether of events taking place in durations or of phonemes culminating in words, was of abiding interest to Bhartrihari. If Time is eternal, transcendent and essentially indivisible, what is it in human perception that causes the cognition of temporal sequentiality of events ? This is the major philosophic anxiety in Bhartrihari's thesis on Time. To explain the duality of Time (and time), he postulates the principle of "suspension and permission": *pratibandhabhyanujnabhyam.* "It [that is, time] is called the operator [literally, string holder] of this mechanical contrivance 'world'. It ... divides the universe by suspension and permission".[8] In this particular formulation, Time is the puppeteer bringing about events which have beginnings and endings. Events are 'permitted' by Time to take place, then they are 'suspended' from the game of existence. Here, once again, we are in danger of overlooking the fact that Bhartrihari is employing a metaphor with which he seeks to reconcile the duality of Time. It is not a metaphor commenting on human destiny as such. It is indeed necessary to be patient with Bhartrihari. His primary interest in *Kalasamuddesha* is not the human life but the inevitable fragmentation of Time in human cognition. So, immediately after employing the metaphor of a puppeteer,[9] he hastens to add: "Its [that is Time's] self is manifoldly divided by differences resting on alien activities. For, there exists no elementary substance that could be either divided or undivided."[10]

If Bhartrihari was interested in the philosophy of Time and its cognition, it is in his linguistics that the interest originated. Appropriately, the *Kalasamuddesha* is a constituent of the

Vakyapadiya and not an independent treatise. All his metaphors for time, therefore, finally point to the behaviour of language in relation to time. Having asserted that Time is single and indivisible in essence, and having explained the apparent divisions of Time through the principle of suspension and permission, he goes on to comment:

> [Time], having activity as its superimposition, becomes past, future and present, [which are] divided by eleven forms. Amongst these, past [time] is of five kinds; future [time] is of four kinds; present [time] is of two kinds; thus (altogether) there are eleven fabrications....[11]

The five forms of the past tense, or the five varieties of cognition related to the past that Bhartrihari mentions, are drawn from Panini's grammar—the general past *(samanya)*, the past related to the current day *(adyatan)*, that related not to the current day *(anadyatan)*, that which combines the *adyatan* and the *anadyatan*, and finally the unknown past *(paroksha)*. These are cognitive possibilities that language opens up in the context of human relation to the past. In order to get closer to the spirit of Bhartrihari's philosophic speculations on Time it is useful to refer to the semantic theory of *sphota*. Bhartrihari himself was the leading figure among the grammarian-philosophers of his time who subscribed to one variety of the *sphota* theory in opposition to another variety of the theory propounded by the Vaisesika school of philosophers. The doctrine of *sphota* in the grammarians' version argued that words are not merely a collection or sequence of phonemes. They are signs which help us identify meaning. However, meaning has a pre-phonetic existence; and thus, meaning is at once identical with the sequence of phonemes and, at the same time, transcends the phonetic representation. *Sphota* is the term used by the grammarians, the *vaiyakaranas*, to denote meaning which exists in pre-verbal and, therefore, eternal form. We can now see how close Bhartrihari's concept of *kala* is to his concept *of sphota*. In his thesis, they both appear fragmented in language, and are seemingly dependent on duration and sequence, but have in their essential form a non-fragmented and, therefore, eternal existence. Just as meaning in the human cognition has its source in *sphota,* time and tense in the human cognition have their origin in *kala.* And, again, just as *sphota* endows cognitive structures to material episodes of verbal articulation, *kala* endows cognitive structures to the temporal fragments perceived in the sequential events of human life. Clearly then Time is completely analogous to Meaning for Bhartrihari; and to that extent, the *Vakyapadiya* is as much a philosophy of language as it is of history. Once we get to see the analogy between semantics and the philosophy of Time in ancient India, we are no longer surprised to find that the thinkers who opposed Bhartrihari's semantics are also those who opposed his view of Time.

The most significant critiques of Bhartrihari's theory of cognition and semantics were presented by the Buddhist thinker Dignaga and the *mimansaka* Kumarila Bhatta, both of whom were Bhartrihari's near contemporaries. The entire debate between Bhartrihari and Kumarila is splendidly summed up in Mandana Misra's *Sphotasiddhi,* an illuminating treatise on the history of the *sphota* theory.[12] Mandana Misra was a senior contemporary of Sankara in the ninth century. It is important to take into account these details, because Sankara put Bhartrihari's *sphota* theory to the most central use in propounding his theory of the *brahman,* turning the theory of linguistic cognition into the theory of knowledge of the self.[13] But to catch up with Kumarila we must travel four centuries back in time.

The Mimansaka view of meaning was that the phonetic sequence and structure of words have absolute ontological status. Sequences of phonemes do indeed reveal the meaning of words, but the sequentiality by itself is no proof to say that meaning, or *sphota,* transcends and precedes the phonemic expression. Kumarila Bhatta, who is the chief spokesman of this view, maintains in his *Slokavarttika* that even if meaning is not entirely contingent as a linguistic category, there is no need to postulate an independent entity of *sphota* over and above the phonetic expression of meaning. "The word, whether it be the sentence or the individual word, is nothing more than a collection or group of phonemes and it is with this collection that meaning is associated."[14] And, in this thesis on cognition, as in Bhartrihari's, meaning is seen as being completely analogous to Time. In fact, at the height of his polemics, Kumarila almost starts speaking of Time instead of meaning. For instance, he writes:

> The reaching of the preceding point of space become the cause of the reaching of the next point of space... [because] Moments of the act of going, succeed in bringing one to the desired place...[15]

If Kumarila provides the critique of Bhartrihari's theory of meaning, Dignaga provides the critique of the theory of cognition. Dignaga's major philosophical work, *Pramanasamuccaya,* comes to us filtered through the *Pramanavarttika* of Dharmakirti, who was the main commentator on Dignaga.[16] However, recent scholarly interest in his work has led to remarkable achievements in recovering his thought. His objection to Bhartrihari's semantics was that meaning does not exist outside the carriers of meaning. Reviving the debate about the place of names in language initially started by Katyayana, Dignaga says that "names are given to things on the basis of a quality which properly belongs to them".[17]

That is, Dignaga denies the need to posit a transcendental sphere of *sphota* for language to be able to transact meaning. Dignaga further extends his logic to assert that language is not eternal, "nor is it an independent source of truth."[18] His view of language is that it functions by virtue of being logically structured, by sharing structures with *anumana.* Inference is, therefore, the primary mode of cognition in Dignaga's theory.

Kumarila's linguistics and Dignaga's theory of inference have a corresponding philosophy of Time. There is a lively debate among the philosophers of their time about whether Time is perceived or whether it is inferred. Several philosophers from the Mimansaka school and the Nyaya-Vaisesika school join the debate, carried out through texts, such as the *Sastadipika* of Parthasarathi Misra, *Manameyodaya* of Narayana Bhatta, the *Kalaprakaranam* section in *Nyaya-Kandali* of Sridhara, and the *Nyaya-Manjari* of Jayanta Bhatta.[19] These are, perhaps, textual records of scholarly debates that took place among assemblies of scholars. In this debate we find these two points of view contending with each other: 'Time is perception' and 'Time is inference'.

Apart from this debate there were other philosophical positions on the question of Time and change in other schools of Indian thought. Among the Brahminical schools, the Sankhya and Yoga schools of philosophy had valuable things to say about the philosophy of Time. The non-Brahminical schools, namely, Buddhism and Jainism had even more important things to say about the issue, and they said them in even more sophisticated ways. In the *Yogasutra* Patanjali had argued that "just as the atom is the minimal limit of matter, so the moment is the minimal duration taken by an atom to change its position."[20] The Yoga school considers the minimal duration, the moment, as absolute reality. Change is inherent in the nature of things; and, therefore, the universe will not be alike at any two given moments. In other words no two moments are alike. Thus this school distinguishes the present from the past. The Sankhya school has a different method of approaching the problem of change. K. C. Bhattacharya presents a contrasting picture of the two approaches:

> Neither system admits time as a separate *tattva:* time is to both concrete becoming or *parinama,* which is not conceived as an event in time. *Parinama* may be undestood as the cause turning up its own limitation or as the limited effect having got manifested. In the former conception, the real objective fact is the act of cause, its act of turning up or the reproduction, the succession of cause and effect being only a retrospective construction as in the Bergsonian view. In the latter conception, the real fact is the antecedence of the cause to the effect, the prior becoming of the effect, but the causal act as the initial moment of this becoming is but an abstraction. Hence to Yoga, which represents the former conception, time is real as the causal act, the initiation or the initial moment of becoming *(kshana)*.... To the latter or Sankhya conception of becoming, the effect being pre-existent in the cause is never turned up, so that the time-relation of sequence alone—the prior process of manifestation constitutive of the manifestness of the effect—is real time.[21]

Indeed, the Yoga concept of Time is at the very heart of its philosophy of salvation, through concentration or *ekagrata* on a single point of time, the present. The concepts of Time in Jainism and Buddhism made radical departures from the concepts in the Brahminical school of thought. The Jain philosophers—and a large multitude of them wrote on Time—propose that Time exists as atoms. Time was considered as one of the basic substances constituting the universe. The definition of Time offered by Kundakunda, about a century before Bhartrihari, sums up the Jaina view:

> The quality of space is to give room, of *dharma* to cause motion, of *adharma* to cause rest. The quality of time is to roll on, of the self, awareness. You should know, in short, that all these qualities are formless. Souls, aggregates of matter, *dharma, adharma,* and the space contain innumerable dimensional points. Space is both in the universe and in that which is beyond it. *Dharma* and *adharma* extend throughout the universe only; likewise time, because it depends on the other two substances, these other substances being soul and matter. As the dimensional points of space, so are the dimensional points of other substances, except time. The atom has no dimensional point, but hence is explained the development of dimensional points. But a moment has no dimensional point. It occurs when a substance with a single dimension crosses a dimensional point of space.[22]

The Jaina thinkers made a broad distinction between Time as it *exists,* and Time as it *is measured,* between the ontological and the epistemological abstractions about time. Time exists by itself in the form of the *kalanus,* atoms of Time, whereas Time as measured by human intelligence is seen as *vyavahara kala.* The Jaina view lists nearly twenty-five such measures beginning with *samaya,* the minutest, to *Samvatsara,* a year's measure.[23]

The depth and the variety of the philosophy of Time in India cannot be brought out in a sketchy account such as the present one. There is no reason to believe that once a certain view was propounded it remained unmodified throughout the centuries of Indian tradition. There was a continuous exchange and confrontation between different views, each of which was enriched further by continuous cross-fertilization with views originating in other schools of philosophy and theology.

In her study of cognitions of time in ancient India, Romila Thapar observes:

> the characterizing of societies as using either cyclic or linear time is an inadequate explanation for the centrality or otherwise of history...It seems more appropriate to enquire into how a society uses a particular category and what is being intended by that use.[24]

Therefore, it will be profitable to examine the ways in which various theories of time in classical India were put to use by literary scholars while reconstructing literary traditions.

6

The Conventions of Literary History

Was there any literary history in India prior to India's contact with the modern West? And if there was, what was the nature of that consciousness of history? In attempting to answer these large questions, one must first move from the singular 'history' to the plural 'histories'. Plurality of relations with the literary past was a distinguishing mark of ancient Indian literature. The nature of each of the several relations with the past depended on the type of literature in question and its social function. In order to understand the polyvalence of literary historiography in ancient India it is necessary to step out of the concepts of genre and period. Literary works apparently belonging together by virtue of a common genre were often accorded greatly dissimilar status in Indian literary canon; and vastly different aesthetic expectations were brought to bear on stylistically comparable works belonging to one given period. This was so because in ancient India literature was classified in terms of several canons existing simultaneously. To a student of Sanskrit literature in the tenth century it was acceptable to classify literature into the following five categories: (1) *Suta* literature, (2) *Mantra* literature, (3) *Shastra,* (4) *Akshara* literature, and (5) Prakrit. And if this student knew Tamil, there would be the sixth category of *Sangam* literature.

Suta Literature

The distinction between *suta* literature and *mantra* literature was proposed by S. V. Ketkar, and was approvingly accepted by scholars like Irawati Karve and V. S. Sukhtankar.[1] According to Ketkar, *suta* (or *sauta)* literature is "literature belonging to the *sutas,* preserved and sung by the *sutas* and perhaps largely composed by the *sutas.* This literature embodied the secular political tradition of Sanskrit literature..."[2] According to Irawati Karve:

> A class of people called *sutas,* representing the illegitimate progeny of the *Kshatriyas,* performed various functions at the court. They were counsellors and friends of kings, charioteers, and also bards. Some of these moved from place to place, wherever they knew that people were likely to assemble, and told their stories which consisted mainly of exploits of love and adventure of ancient and ruling kings and princes. A book in many respects like the *Mahabharata* was the *Ramayana,* a narrative sung from place to place. Out of these grew a later type of literature called the *Puranas...*[3]

Thus, *suta* literature was largely an oral tradition of literature, though it was not a non-lexical tradition. Almost every work in this tradition of Indian literature was initially a written work, which was handed down to subsequent generations in the form of public recitation. In the process of oral transmission the text was changed, enlarged, and to it was also added the history of recitations. Since the *suta* texts were treated as essential parts of collective memory and collective inheritance, the particulars about their specific historical moments of origin and individual authorships were not considered important in the *suta* literary canon.

The *Mahabharata,* which is easily the most complex of the *suta* literary works, offers us glimpses into the history of its making and transmission. Vyasa, to whom the initial authorship of the poem is ascribed and who was an eyewitness to the war composed it, perhaps under the title *Jaya* or *Itihasa.* At that stage it is believed to have been much shorter in length. The original had perhaps not more than 24,000 verses. Vyasa seems to have taught the epic to five of his pupils who made their own recensions. One of the pupils was Vaishampayana. He recited the epic on the occasion of the serpent-sacrifice ritual performed by King Janmejaya. Lomharshana, who was present on this occasion, heard it, and recited it again in the hermitage of the sage Saunaka in the Naimisha forest. By this time, probably, the 24,000 verses of *Jaya* had already turned into the 60,000 verses of the *Mahabharata.*[4] But even after this, generations of poets kept adding verses to it. The result is the present version comprising 100,000 verses.

The *Ramayana* is another important *suta* text; and the *puranas* too are *suta* texts. Not only scholars, but even common people knew that the *Mahabharata* was composed first, the *Ramayana* later, and the *Puranas* last; but the cultural centrality of these texts was such that they were, or are, rarely thought of as merely linguistic compositions. As a result, they were never allowed to belong to the past, or to have an existence that was detached from the collective consciousness. Hence, their historical status as texts was of marginal interest to scholars involved in their transmission.

In India people are rarely self-conscious about the intimate inter-textuality of the *suta* texts and life as it is lived. This phenomenon strikes an outsider as uniquely Indian. Milton Singer, for instance, comments:

> Before I went to India, I knew these stories as occurring in printed books called the *Ramayana,* the *Mahabharata* and the *Bhagvatapurana,* parts of which I had read in translation. This knowledge gave me a welcome sense of recognition when I heard some of the stories, but it did not prepare me for the rich variety of ways in which they are told and retold. Seldom did I come across an Indian who had read these stories as I did, simply in a book. This is not how they learn them and it is not how they think of them. There is a sense of intimate familiarity with the characters and incidents in references made to Harishchandra, Rama and Sita, Krishna, Arjuna, and Prahlada as if the world of the stories were also the everyday world... The cultural and physical landscapes are literally and imaginatively printed with them.[5]

Thus, the Indian attitude to the *suta* texts involves the sense of 'the presence of the past' but not of 'the pastness of the past'. The principle subject of *suta* literature was history itself. Even the *puranas,* which have a greatly rambling style of narration, were basically 'historical' records providing information about dynasties and genealogies, and also contain within themselves some historical information about their composition and transmission; but to think of them as 'books' will not be appropriate to their purpose and history. It is only during the last hundred years or so that *suta* texts have been subjected to textual research and scholarship; the first critical edition of the *Mahabharata* was published by the Bhandarkar Oriental Institute in Pune;[6] the first critical edition of the *Ramayana* was published by the Oriental Institute in Baroda;[7] and in Varanasi, V. Raghavan started issuing editions of various *Puranas* through the Kashiraj Trust. Traditionally, however, *suta* texts were seen as constituting the continuous collective memory and were not considered as literary events. That is why Naimisharanya, the location of every recitation of the *Mahabharata* and the *Puranas,* became an essential part of people's unconscious personality, and Vyasa, the original author of these texts, came to be considered a *Chiranjiva,* an ever-living mortal.

It is, however, necessary to first distinguish the *suta* literary tradition from other traditions of folk literature or oral literature. The linguistic structures, narrative strategies and aesthetic devices such as characterization and plot-structure in *suta* literature are as sophisticated and imaginatively varied as in any tradition of 'written' literature. Besides, this tradition continues to survive even in the age of printing and electronic mass communication. An interesting example of a *suta* text in contemporary use on a wide scale is the *Satya Narayan Katha.* This *katha* has a definite textual source; and in fact the story itself is about a certain text and its several recitations. Thus it is a text about a text; and the person who recites it usually reads it out from a printed text. Yet, no one who knows the story has ever read it as a book. It is to be heard by people, as it is recited by a Brahmin. The practice has nothing to do whatsoever with literacy and education.

The *suta* narratology, whether in the epics, the *puranas* or the *kathas,* has some recurring features. One of them is the opening which seeks to combine myth and history. Ludo Rocher comments, "The *Mahabharata* begins like most *puranas,* with the arrival of the *suta* in the Naimisha forest.... And the seers ask Ugrashravas: 'Tell us that ancient lore....'"[8] The fictional time created in the narrative, time which seeks to combine myth and history, conceptually corresponds to the cognitive possibility recognized in the grammar of Panini and Bhartrihari when they describe the past tense which combines the *adyatan* and the *anadyatan.* The historiographical attitude to *suta* literature in Indian tradition allowed for the recitation's simultaneous existence in the *adyatan* past and the *anadyatan* past. Traditionally, Indian audiences were brought up to believe that the recitation by a known *suta* within their hearing was essentially no different from one that was heard in Saunaka's hermitage in the Naimisha forest from Lomaharshana or Romaharshana in some remote and unspecified past.

Mantra Literature

The historiographical attitude towards the *mantra* literature— the Vedic hymns, the *Brahmanas, Upanishads,* and in extreme cases some *Vedangas*—corresponded to the cognitive possibility offered by the grammatical category of *paroksha* past tense. Once Panini, Katyayana and Patanjali had constructed the enormous *vyakarana*-machinery to prohibit 'vulgarization' of the bhasha, the Vedic verses began to be treated as if they were divinely and not humanly, composed. Vedic literature forms an excellent instance of linguistic creativity fully integrated with the life of the community surrounding it; it is an eloquent commentary on the history of the people who wrote it. Yet scholars in the post-Panini period were encouraged to believe that the *Vedas* were gospel, literally heard by the *rishis* from a divine source. The *Vedas* became *shruti,* the *Upanishads, smriti.* And both were removed from the historical sphere altogether.

During the nineteenth century many European scholars took an interest in ancient Indian literature. Some of them determined 1500 BC as the possible date for the earliest of the Vedic compositions. On the other hand, Indian scholars, more particularly B. G. Tilak and his followers, argued that the Vedas were composed much earlier—around 4500 BC.[9] It is claimed however, by every scholar of Vedic literature that it is the most ancient body of literary expression anywhere in the world. The history of transmission of this literature through a period of four thousand years, or perhaps more, shows that unparalleled scholarly care and editorial precision have been lavished on it by the generations involved in the process of its transmission. Indeed, the historiographical attitude claimed and enjoyed by the Vedic literary tradition has been simply unique. The transmission of Vedic literature cannot be compared to the transmission by the *sutas* of the epics and the *puranas.* The *sutas* were free to make marginal changes in the metres, accents and, occasionally, whole sections of verses. They were at liberty to add new verses to the body of poetry they handed down to the next generations. The transmission of Vedic literature permitted not the slightest linguistic freedom to the individual involved in the process. Max Muller has observed that, unlike the Homeric epics, the *Vedas* make no reference to the art of writing.[10] But no written text, reproduced by different Scholiasts and reprinted in different lexical styles, would have succeeded in preserving the original poetic speech in the exact original form to the last and the finest phonetic detail. The mind-boggling achievement in continuous memorization of the Vedic verses for four thousand years can only be imagined when we have some idea of the stylistic features of Vedic texts.

The Vedic metre depends on the number of syllables, but not on the length of the syllable. The *Gayatri* metre has twenty-four syllables. *Ushnik* has twenty-eight syllables. *Anushtup* has thirty-two syllables. And, in this manner of change in the metre with the addition of every four syllables, the Vedic metres range from the *Gayatri* with twenty-four syllables to the *Atidhriti* with seventy-six syllables, adding up to fourteen metres. The total number of *riks* or verses in the *Rigveda* is 10580 1/4, divided into ten chapters or *mandalas.*[11] These are composed by twenty-three different *rishis,* and over an extended period of several centuries. Thus the style of composition, the level of semantic complexity, registers of poetic diction and thematic concerns vary considerably from one *mandala* to another. To commit to memory all the verses without the slightest variation of accent and change even of a syllable must have required long years of disciplined training. That this training formed an essential part of school education in ancient India is evident from the fact that specialist text books, companion volumes and classified indexes were prepared to assist this training. Katyayana, for instance had prepared a Vedic *sarvanukramani,* a general index giving the names of the *rishis* credited with having contributed to *Rigveda,* the exact number of verses composed by each, the chapter and section division of the verses, the metres and also the names of gods in whose praise the verses were composed.[12] In terms of historical scholarship in literature, such *anukramanis*—and there were many—are of pioneering importance. However, the aim of these scholarly exercises was not to enable other scholars to place the *shrutis* in a historical context and to see them critically. The aim was the exact opposite; it was to abstract the *shrutis* from the flow of time altogether so that they became timeless and ahistorical. What happened to the *Vedas,* happened also to the *Upanishads* and the associated Vedic texts. And, though Indians made impressive progress in certain sciences, agriculture, philosophy and linguistics continuously for a thousand years after the *Vedas* were composed, the ancient literary scholarship persisted in its belief that the *Vedas* held literally all knowledge in them, and that no knowledge could surpass that contained in the *Vedas.* Traces of this historical fallacy survive in India even today. The logical result of making Vedic literature the ultimate authority in the sphere of knowledge was the emergence of a rhetoric of knowledge which made *authority* a fundamental source of knowledge. This view then was institutionalized through the Nyaya school of philosophy.

The profound impact of this faith in Authority as knowledge on historiography can be seen in works like Kshemaraja's *Pratyabhijnahrdayam.*[13] An eleventh century Kashmir philosopher and a disciple of Abhinavagupta, Kshemaraja draws an imaginary topography of spiritual fulfilment by describing the descent of the divine into the human world, which in his opinion is necessarily followed by a corresponding human ascent. This doctrine of' 'recognition' postulates perception as recollection of what was always known: the greater the capacity to 'remember', the higher the human consciousness can ascend in the realm of the spirit. His argument that all new knowledge has always been present in the human consciousness, even if momentarily clouded, derived support from the notion of authority vested with sovereignty in the *Vedas.* And, hence, even if the Vedic texts are supremely historical as documents, and even if the very history of these texts is eloquently inscribed in them, these texts were removed from the sphere of history by a jealously guarded tradition of scholarship. If the attitude to the *suta* literature was non-historical, the attitude to the *mantra* literature was trans-historical. It did belong to the past, but that past was *beyond* the grasp of students of literature.

Shastra Literature

As against the two traditions of literary transmission discussed above, the *shastra* tradition and the *akshara* literary traditions were given greater historiographical attention in ancient India. The *shastras* were numerous; and the ancient Indian scholars were prolific writers. Though generally speaking a *shastra* text was a text dealing with any subject systematically, *shastra* and imaginative literature were not thought of as mutually exclusive categories. Rather, *shastra* was the ethical and cognitive aspect of a text. An illuminating example of actual usage of the term *shastra* by ancient Indian writers is to be found in Anandavardhana's *Dhvanyaloka.* In chapter four *(Uddyota IV),* he is discussing the aesthetic complexity of the *Mahabharata* in terms of the *rasa* aesthetics, when he writes:

> And so... it is revealed that everything different from the blessed one is ephemeral, and thereby it is well established that looking at the *Mahabharata* as a *shastra,* the highest goal of man, namely *moksha,* is alone intended as the most important of the goals of life, and looking at it as poetry, *shantarasa,* which is characterized by the nourishing of

> the happiness that succeeds the destruction of desire, is intended as the most important of all the *rasas*.[14]

The fact that the canonical status of texts did not depend on the genre in which they were composed but rather on the function they were expected to perform in the sphere of their reception needs to be stressed again and again when we consider the history of ancient Indian literature. Both the *shastras* and the *akshara* texts were composed in verse, prose, or a combination of the two. Both were seen as products of known human authorship. And, as against the *suta* literature and the *mantra* literature which remained in 'fashion' for ever, the *shastras* and the *akshara* literature were freely subjected to the vagaries of literary taste, shifts in critical views and the climate of philosophical opinion. Philosophical debate and literary disagreement were the common features of the scholarly community that developed these two branches of ancient Indian literature. In other words, these two types had the benefit of belonging to critical traditions with clear historical perspectives.

Linguistics and poetics were considered *shastras*. Between the fourth century BC and the seventeenth century AD—a period of about two thousand years—every linguist in India knew about all linguistics scholarship preceding him. He knew the major *sutras* or theoretical formulations as well as the *bhashyas* or the related commentaries. Between Bhamaha and Dandin, critics of the sixth and seventh centuries, and Bhoja, who belonged to the eleventh century, there was a gap of half a millennium; and yet, Bhoja knew their exact critical positions in relation to narrative poetry, *sargabandha*, or poetic styles, *riti*. Between Bharata and Abhinavagupta the gap was of more than six centuries; but Abhinavagupta knew Bharata's formulations on aesthetic emotion to the last letter.

It was not just the relationship with his predecessors within the same *shastra* about which a given thinker was aware; invariably, he was also aware of the relationship between his intellectual or philosophical position and the other related sciences. It is very clear from the text of Abhinava's comments on the *shantarasa* that he was fully aware that his theoretical position related in various ways to the literary criticism of Ashvagosha, Bharata,

Anandavardhana, Bhattatauta, Bhattanayaka, as well as the philosophic positions in *Vedanta, Vijnanabhairava, Yogavasishtha* and Kashmir Saivism. On the other hand, Abhinavagupta, in *Gitarthasangraha,* his commentary on the *Gita*[15] leaves us in no doubt regarding the line of philosophers and critics to whom he alludes, and who included Katyayana, Saushuka, Bhutiraja, Bhattenduraja, Kallata, Mukula, Somananda, Utpaldeva, Lakshamanagupta and many other scholars.

In the ancient Indian style of philosophic or critical commentary textual evidence was considered of very great importance. Even when critics made some very original point or observation, they tried to establish its validity by quoting a multitude of verses in support from the available literature, written by predecessors as well as their contemporaries. Modern scholarship of Sanskrit texts has often found that whereas the verses quoted were accurate there was usually no mention of the name of the author quoted. In any text on poetics, for instance, one finds citations from other poets running into hundreds; but the acknowledgment of authorship is rare. This was so not because the writers and critics were plagiarists but because the verses quoted, and their sources, formed a vast collective fund of literature to which the community of readers had an active access. It would have been superfluous, therefore, for an ancient Indian critic to mention the names of each and every author and text to which he alluded. The *shastras* were generally taught in schools and universities. Scholars were required to defend their philosophical positions in assemblies of scholars; and, therefore, exacting knowledge of the *shastras* was essential for every aspiring scholar. Similarly, a knowledge of poetry and drama was considered a social asset. The ability to talk about literature was considered the mark of intellectual and social nobility. There was thus a sense of community among the people who wrote and those for whom they wrote.

Akshara Literature

The *akshara* literature, composed primarily for aesthetic pleasure, used a variety of genres and forms. It included works written in verse, prose and narrative or dramatic forms. The *akshara* canon was fairly well defined during the later centuries of classical Indian literature. It included works by Sudraka, Harsha, Kalidasa, Vishakhadatta, Bhattanayaka, Bhavabhuti, Bhartrihari, Bharavi, Bhatti, Kumaradasa, Magha, Dandin, Subandhu and Banabhatta. After the eighth century, the volume of compositions expanded. They became stylistically more rigid and thematically less complex. The community of literates declined, giving rise to excessive and often pointless advancement in theoretical literature. And the canon lost its purpose as well as real social importance. But, till such a time as there was a relatively unified literary community— perhaps till the end of the eighth century— the *akshara* literature was preserved very systematically; and its historicity was never overlooked.

Between the fifth century BC and the tenth century AD literary and philosophical works were preserved by reproducing manuscript copies from time to time. These copies were made by teachers in schools and universities, more particularly those living in residential institutions.[16] Rajashekhara describes a normal day in the life of an *acharya*-poet. In this description, Rajashekhara records that poets wrote every day for a certain number of hours.'[17] Poetry, or linguistic compositions in other forms, were perceived during the post-Vedic period of Sanskrit (as well as Prakrit) literature as essentially written forms. The manuscript copies at schools and centres of learning were used by scholars being trained in the *shastras* and *kavyas.* Often scholars from other centres visited these institutions as part of their nationwide pilgrimage and brought information with them about new compositions or older, lesser known works. Thus through the networks of places of pilgrimage and the residential schools literary manuscripts were replicated and preserved. This method was in use till the beginning of the thirteenth century when paper replaced the traditional materials used for writing manuscripts.

The major difference between the *shastras* and the *akshara* literature, however, was that the *shastras,* which required explanation and comment from learned teachers, formed a part of the school syllabus. The *akshara* literature, on the other hand, was self-explanatory. Initially, the *shastras* made no claim to authority. But their place in the education system inevitably brought an association of authority with them in the course of time. When we compare the texts of philosophic treatises from the time of Panini with those in the age of Sankara, periods separated by about eleven centuries, we find that the later texts have no hesitation in claiming direct lineage from the *Vedas.* The later *shastras* share with the *Vedas* their authority, a consequence of the institutionalized teaching of the *shastras.* On the other hand, the works of *akshara* literature, the plays, stories and poems, were perceived and experienced with a sense of immediacy. The readers were expected to be *sahridaya,* on the same mental plane as the author himself. And, even if a certain mythological characterization was associated with poetry in the figure of *Kavyapurusba,* its metaphoric nature was never entirely overlooked.[18] This variation in attitudes towards the *shastras* and the *akshara* literature, as reflected in the historiographical status of the two types, corresponded roughly to the cognitive difference between the two categories of the *anadyatan* past and the *adyatan* past.

Bharata, the earliest literary critic gives us the impression that he comes at the end of a long line of theorists, and that he is presenting a mere summary of their work, but there appears to be no textual evidence to support his statement. That is exactly what happens with Panini's grammar. That is also the case with Chanakya's *Arthashastra.* As a matter of historical fact, there is no major literary or philosophical 'lost' period between the composition of the Vedic anthologies (*samhitas*) and a settled text of the *Mahabbharata,* on the one hand, and Panini, Patanjali and Bharata, on the other hand. One has to conclude, therefore, that the cultural practice of assigning an older date of origin to the *shastra* texts than their actual date of composition was aimed at enhancing their authority.[19] This was possible because the organizing criterion for the *shastras* was not 'period' but 'school of thought.' Every text was given a very definite place in terms of the school of philosophy or thought it postulated or explained. The chronological placement of a text was given secondary importance, and it was subsumed within the category of' 'school'.

In contrast, the *akshara* literature was accorded the status of 'undiminishing youth'. The mythological *Kavyapurusha* was but a youthful child. There are numerous references to the capacity of poetry to remain 'ever-charming' in discussions of *alamkara* and *vakrokti,* poetic language. *Akshara* meant undiminishing, just as it meant 'letters'. When Bhavabhuti hoped that perhaps his poetry would be appreciated by the right kind of readers a thousand years later,[20] he was voicing the received notions of the everlasting immediacy of *akshara* literature. For ancient Indian readers, all *akshara* literature belonged to the *adyatan* past.

Prakrit Literature

Perhaps the only area of literature in ancient India which received the kind of historiographical care that would find modern approval was the area of Prakrit literature. It needs to be added at once that it is not a body of literature in a single language or a single language variety. Traditionally, Prakrit literature would include the works in Pali; the Buddhist canonical works; dramatic literature in regional deviations of Sanskrit such as Sauraseni, Magadhi, and Maharashtri which had dramatic as well as lyrical literature; and finally, the Jaina canonical works in Maharashtri and Sauraseni. Prakrit is perhaps a negative description, being a comprehensive term applied to languages and literature without social support and cultural sanction. In other words, Prakrit literature includes all para-literatures in ancient India. And, precisely for this reason, Prakrit languages and styles have been more experimental. This experimental nature of Prakrit styles is reflected in the reactions of the Sanskrit writers to them. Practically every Sanskrit writer or thinker has had to come to terms with the changes taking place in Sanskrit in the course of its history. Bharata makes a mention of dramatic literature in Prakrit. Some writers like Kalidasa, Bhavabhuti, Vishakhadutta and Bana made use of Prakrit registers of diction to make their characters life-like. Dandin even went to the extent of building a theory of poetic diction—the *riti* theory—by legitimizing the influence of Prakrit on Sanskrit vocabulary. And, as the Prakrits became stronger, and as they were about to branch off as independent languages, writers like Hemachandra, Rajashekhara and Jayadeva, though scholars of Sanskrit, employed Prakrit as the language for expressing new ideas. Throughout the history of classical Indian literature, Sanskrit kept declining in its power of expression, whereas the Prakrits kept gaining greater expressive power. As such, in the linguistic texture of every work in Prakrit is inscribed the history of social tensions and conflicts in India. Thanks to its non-canonical status, it is the only literature in India in ancient times, the history of which has not been distorted by the conventions of scholarship.

Ashoka's inscriptions are among the earliest samples of recorded Prakrit. There has been no doubt about their historic value and their own historicity. But some of the Buddhist scriptures were written even before these inscriptions. The Pali *Tripitika* on the more philosophical side and the *Jataka* stories on the more popular side, have a very clearly defined historical place in Buddhist literature. The *Mahavamsa* offers a good example of versified history written by monks in Sri Lanka. The Jaina history of literature is even more properly preserved. The Jaina canons, with forty-five *agamas,* eleven *angas* and twelve *upangas,* were arranged by Devadhi Ganin in the year 454.[21]

It was about the same time that *Setubandha,* an epic narrative of exquisite beauty was composed, in the fifth century AD to commemorate the building of a bridge by Pravarasena, a Kashmiri prince. Similarly, *Gaudavaho* was composed by Vakpatiraja, under the pseudonym Bappairaa to celebrate the conquest of Bengal by Yashovarman of Kanauj in the eighth century. So did Hemachandra write in the thirteenth century about the deeds of Kumarapala. All these narratives show a preference for historical themes. Most of the Prakrit works were forgotten quickly or neglected by literary culture dominated by Sanskrit. An anthology of lyrics, most of them composed in the Maharashtri Prakrit, and put together by Hala, usually identified with Satavahana or Salivahana, was known up to the times of Rajashekhara, who mentions it in his Prakrit play *Karpuramanjiri.* Many of the lyrics included in this anthology—it was called *Sattasai*— were lost in the following centuries. However, it is clear that some of the stylistic features of the lyrics included, particularly their extraordinary musicality, were assimilated by Sanskrit versification. This was true of Sanskrit dramatic literature too. Prakrit became, through fifteen hundred years of its coexistence with Sanskrit, an unfailing source of linguistic and literary enrichment for Sanskrit. Thanks, however, to the social stratification, Sanskrit scholarship kept Prakrit literature out of its institutions of learning. Whether it was written in Pali, or in the regional varieties branching off from Sanskrit itself, Prakrit was left to itself to form its own canon. This canon (or canons, perhaps) was taught and preserved in the Jaina and Buddhist monasteries. As these religions began with human teachers, Mahavir and Gautama, whose historical existence was never in doubt, the literary canons in Prakrit were not anxious to deny or transcend historicity. Prakrit literature in ancient India existed in the normal past tense, the *samanya;* and the dominant tradition of scholarship felt no need to change that status till the generation of Hemachandra and Jnaneshwara.

Sangam Literature

It is difficult to speculate about the attitude of the Sanskrit scholars of Rajashekhara's generation to the ancient Tamil literature, at least some of which they would have surely known. Not only that, but even the attitude of the Tamil scholars of Rajashekhara's generation to their own past is difficult to imagine. Tamil literature itself has left few clues to its medieval historiography and its attitude towards the ancient literary past implicit in it. Perhaps, the influence of Sanskrit literary culture was all too captivating;[22] perhaps, the transition from ancient Tamil to modern Tamil involved a total historical break with tradition. In order to stress how complete the break was, let us quote from a well-researched history of Tamil literature:

> The classical bardic poetry of the literary Academies *(cankam,* Sangam) ceased to be a living literature and became part of an 'extinct' classical heritage sometime in the 6th-8th century AD. It gave way to the religious hymnody of the Saiva and Vaishnava *bhakti* movement. In that period, everything changed: in the evolution of

> language, this was the time of the transition from old Tamil to middle Tamil; in prosody, this was the period of the first strong impact of Sanskritic *aksara-matra* oriented metres on indigenous Tamil structures; secular, anonymous love and war poems gave way to religious, highly individual hymns; the itinerant bard moving from court to court quitted the scene and his place was taken by a Saiva or Vaisnava poet-saint, visiting shrine after shrine and singing the mercy of Siva and Visnu. The classical heritage was preserved almost exclusively by learned poets, commentators and scholiasts. After ca. 1450 AD even the scholiast ceased to be interested, and with the exception of a few anthologies which still contained ancient matter, militant brahminical Hinduism apparently branded as taboo and irreligious all secular texts of the ancient era and the study of Jaina and Buddhist literature was forbidden. Even great scholars were unaware of the existence of the earliest and greatest of Tamil literary texts.[23]

Prior to this breakdown in the cultural memory of the Tamil people, literary compositions were preserved through anthologies edited with carefully conceived thematic and metrical plans. Every anthology contained several hundred poetic compositions belonging to two or three centuries. Most of the poems included in these anthologies are ascribed to human authorship, and the names of the author were clearly known. For example, *Purananuru,* the last of the anthologies, which contained four hundred compositions, indicated the names of one hundred and fifty-seven poets who contributed to it. Similarly, the conventions of writing were handed down from generation to generation; and the anthologies show a remarkable consistency of the 'grammar of poetry'. The conventions were all set up by the *Tolkappiyam,* the founding book of Tamil grammar, linguistics and aesthetics. The poems included in the anthologies show that a 'school' or 'schools' of poetry existed in Tamil in the pre-Christian centuries; and this school literally grew round an academy of scholars in Madurai.[24] The compositions by the poets' collective, working in and around the academy, were traditionally known as Sangam poetry; and the anthologies of these compositions received patronage from successive kings who ruled the Tamil people. Many of the compositions, therefore, are devoted to the patron princes. After the eighth century, Sangam poetry declined as the patronage to it diminished.

The chart of historiographical conventions in ancient India which classified literature into the six categories discussed above was not based exclusively on linguistic, literary or aesthetic principles. It did not classify literary works in terms of primary and secondary, simple and complex, or natural and aesthetic works. The *Mahabharata* is as complex as any works of *akshara* literature. The *prakrit* works are philosophically as competent as some of the *shastra* works. And many of the Tamil lyrics are as spontaneous as the songs in the Vedic anthologies. This classification was not based on any formal principles, for certain identical verse and prose forms of literature can be found in all six categories practiced. It was not based entirely on difference in language, for, though the *prakrit* literatures and Tamil literature were seen as different from literature in Sanskrit, there were also clear distinctions within Sanskrit—*mantra* and *suta, shastra* and *kavya*. Similarly, literatures were not categorized on the basis of religious difference alone.

The classification combined the differences in race, religion and social status as the three criteria for literary historiography. Thus, Tamil literature was seen as being different from Sanskrit literature on the grounds of linguistic difference, which, however, can be further traced to racial difference. The *prakrit* literatures were differentiated from the Sanskrit tradition of literature on the basis of religious differences. Prakrit languages were used for literary composition primarily by the Buddhist and Jaina writers. The *suta* literature was differentiated from the *mantra, shastra* and *akshara* literature on the basis of the social status of the composers, those who transmitted the works, and the audiences. The *mantra* literature was treated as the preserve of the brahmins; the *suta* literature was open to those who were considered socially 'inferior' to the brahmins.

The six categories discussed in the foregoing pages can be placed in three broad categories using contemporary critical diction: (a) Oral literature, which would include *suta* literature and *mantra* literature; (b) Textual literature, which would include *shastra* and *akshara* literature; and, (c) Para-literature, which would include Prakrit and Tamil literature. This classification had no 'aesthetic' justification; but, in the classical period of ancient Indian literature it had received a general social sanction.

The perception of the relationship between literature and society changed radically from the eleventh to the fourteenth centuries. The ideological content of the category 'literature' too underwent profound changes. The sociology of oppression sanctioned by ancient literary historiography was sought to be challenged by the writers and thinkers of the new era. And, consequently, the attitude to the literary past too changed fundamentally. The agenda for the new literary history was written all over the Bhakti poetry which flourished in all parts of India during the first half of the second millennium; but nowhere else does it find a clearer articulation than in the poetry of the Marathi saint Jnanadeva.

7

Jnanadeva's Agenda

The *Bhavarthadipika*, popularly called *Jnaneswari*,[1] has greatly influenced Marathi literature and the speakers of the Marathi language during the last seven centuries. Written as a popular commentary on the *Gita*, it pioneered a new literary aesthetic and founded a new literary language. The discourse of Jnanadeva in this seminal text abandons the conventional historiography of stratification and announces to the world the arrival of a new literary epoch in which the *suta*, *shastra* and *prakrit* registers were to melt together into one luminous *bhakta* speech. Throughout the *Bhavarthadipika*, its young revolutionary writer offers explicit comments on his literary politics. And it is this 'meta' commentary that reveals Jnanadeva's agenda for the 'new' literary history.

There had been a long and illustrious tradition of writing commentaries on the *Gita* before Jnanadeva's times and, as mentioned in passing earlier, even Abhinavagupta had composed an innovative commentary.[2] Jnanadeva was almost certainly familiar with the entire tradition, particularly since a part of his mysticism came from the Kashmir-school of Saivism, of which Abhinavagupta was the greatest exponent. But Jnanadeva's aim was to integrate the yoga of the Nathas with the bhakti of the, Bhagwats.[3] Therefore, while working within the framework of traditional discourse of commentaries, Jnanadeva seeks to transform the tradition by adding a complex intertextuality to the established discourse.

The *Gita,* as a text, contains two levels of communication. At one level, Sanjaya, with his envisioning capacity, narrates the happenings on the war-field to Dhritarashtra, the blind prince and the father of the Kuru warriors. Often, the impatient listener urges the commentator to hold back his sense of sheer amazement at what he sees and hears. Thus, there is one level of the *Gita*'s dialogic discourse within which the other, and philosophically the more important, dialogue is set. This second dialogue is that between Arjuna, the despairing hero, and Krishna, the philosophising charioteer. To these two levels of discourse, Jnanadeva adds his own dialogues with his guru, Nivrittinath on the one hand, and, on the other, with his raptly attentive audience, Sacchittananda, the scholiast who committed the text to writing. The Saiva commentaries on the *Gita* had interpreted it as a dialogue between *Jiva* and Shiva. To this interpretation, Jnanadeva adds another originating in his devotionalism and construes the conversation between Krishna and Arjuna as a dialogue between God and the *bhakta,* his human lover. The *Bhavarthadipika* operates at various levels of communication; and because its composer can simultaneously play upon and control all these levels, the poem never fails to charm the reader. During the course of his narrative, Jnanadeva often identifies himself with Arjuna or Krishna, and, occasionally, he asserts that it is in fact his guru who is writing the narrative through the disciple. The simultaneity of his communication strategies is also the soul of Jnanadeva's literary historiography.

The *Bhavarthadipika* begins in the traditional manner, by offering propitiating invocations to all the necessary gods and literary muses; and its author presents himself as a modest disciple to his guru: "I will say what you inspire in me, just as a puppet dances when moved by a string."[4] But, by the time he enters the third chapter, the *adhyaya* that presents the *Karmayoga,* the yoga of action, the narrator has become politically more active. Taking a cue from Arjuna's critique of Krishna's advocacy of knowledge over action in the preceeding chapter, Jnanadeva introduces the question of language. Arjuna says to Krishna: "with speech that seems equivocal you confuse my intelligence." *(vyamisreneva vakyena buddhim mohayasiva me)*[5]

To this Jnanadeva's Arjuna adds, "say it all in Marathi", and with metaphors so persuasive that they would outdo Krishna's childhood implorings to his foster mother Yashoda. Arjuna says in Jnanadeva's words, or perhaps Jnanadeva says in Arjuna's words: "Are you deceiving me, or does your teaching have hidden implications? ... O Lord, do not speak of such deep meaning. Tell me those things in Marathi."[6] And then follows the logic:

> If a disease is to be cured, medicine must be given, but it should be sweet and palatable. These truths, which are so full of meaning, should be properly told, but in a way that will enlighten my mind. O Lord! You are my own teacher! Then why shouldn't you grant my desire? Why should I stand in awe of anyone? You are our mother! ... If a person were to reach the ocean of nectar and then suffer from thirst, why should he have taken the trouble to reach it?[7]

Thus, Arjuna is presented as the advocate of Marathi in quest of the ocean of nectar that is Krishna's teaching. Later in the poem, Jnanadeva repeatedly claims that the Marathi discourse he has invented far surpasses the Sanskrit nectar.

By the time Jnanadeva's commentary comes to the *atmasaiyam yoga,* the sixth *adhyaya* of the *Gita,* the advocacy of the cause of Marathi acquires a moral urgency. It is at the beginning of this chapter that Jnanadeva utters his famous pronouncement, "My language is Marathi, but I will compose this work with such beautiful words and style that it will easily surpass nectar."[8] It is worth noting that he uses the same image twice before in the preceding thirteen *ovis,* involving, in the process, Sanjaya in favour of his argument. In the third *ovi,* Sanjaya says to Dhritarashtra: "I cannot express how great our good fortune is. It is as though a thirsty man, when drinking water, discovered that it was nectar."[9] And, in *ovi* 11, Jnanadeva says, probably, to his guru that his commentary on the *Gita* is like the mythological churning of the ocean of milk from which arose nectar. Clearly, then, the Sanskrit *Gita* is the ocean of milk, from which the nectar of Jnanadeva's Marathi is drawn; and both Jnanadeva and his Sanjaya are delighted at this prospect. But not so Dhritarashtra, the blind king, about whom Sanjaya muses: "How can a blind person see the light of the day?"[10] From this point onward in the poem, the narrative assumes the self-conscious moral responsibility to deny the hierarchic distinction between Sanskrit and the Marathi Prakrit, and to play the Marathi nectar to the milk of the original Sanskrit.

Together with his rejection of the Sanskrit-Prakrit discrimination, Jnanadeva also starts rejecting the distinction between the spoken and the written, between the orality of literature and its graphicality. In defiance of the conventional Sanskrit segregation between the *shastra* literature and the *suta* literature, Jnanadeva asserts that in listening to his Marathi composition, "tongues will spring up in the ears."

> Although listening to speech is the function of the ears, the sense of taste will say, "This joy is mine. My words will be the fragrance enjoyed by the sense of smell." Marvelling at the flowing style, the eyes will be filled with satisfaction and exclaim, "What a wonder! The treasure house of beauty has been opened for us here!" When the sentences have been arranged, the mind will rush forward with outstretched arms to embrace the words.[11]

In defence of this integration between speech and writing in his Marathi commentary, Jnanadeva further says, "Just as crows cannot recognize the moon, ordinary people will never be able to understand this work. Just as the *chakora* bird feeds on moonbeams, similarly, this writing is meant only for the wise."[12] And, in the same chapter, Jnanadeva in fact states that this promise is fulfilled as, when he praises Krishna's love for Arjuna in some domestic images, his listeners exclaim, "Oh what good fortune! What beautiful language! Doesn't its excellence surpass even that of the *Vedas*?[13] Jnanadeva's response is predictably, "There is nothing strange about this. When I speak in my mother tongue, Marathi, literary excellence will appear in it like the different colours in the sky."[14]

As the poem progresses, Jnanadeva's claims for the beauty of the Marathi language increase in frequency and insistence. Marathi is not only the language which can integrate speech with writing, but, in Jnanadeva's conception, the language which will allow the audiences to perceive the deeper truths hidden in Krishna's message.

> The eye will perceive the meaning before the ears hear it. And the senses will be revived by the beauty of the words, even before the tongue of reason has tasted the inner meaning. The nose enjoys the fragrance of *malati* buds, but doesn't their beauty also please the eye? Similarly, after the senses have enjoyed the beauty of the Marathi language, they will be ready to approach the deeper truths.[15]

When Jnanadeva composed his commentary, the Marathi language had hardly had any literary past. However, there was a community of listeners and readers for Jnanadeva's poem for whom Marathi was the language of everyday life. When, in an apostrophe he claims that he was going to utter "words that will surpass all other speech,"[16] he was, in fact, thinking of the community of his listeners that would provide legitimation to his literary aesthetics:

> So listen to me, for when my power of speech is fed by attention, a wealth of exposition will come forth in my words. The meaning waits on the words, meaning calls forth further meaning, and there is a full blossoming of feeling in the mind. Therefore, when the favourable wind of dialogue begins to blow, clouds of learning gather in the sky of the heart. But if listeners are inattentive, the essence of the explanation will melt away. The moonstone melts, but it is due to the action of the moon. In the same way, a speaker cannot be a speaker without listeners.[17]

This insistence on calling the listeners' attention is much more than a rhetorical strategy of the poet's discourse. There is a clear perception in Jnanadeva's meta commentary that literature is not mere composition in language, but also a living circulation of it within the community of the speakers of the language. Therefore, his image for founding a literary canon is that of founding a city. In the twelfth chapter of the *dipika,* he makes a passionate appeal to his guru to give him the power to establish the 'city' of the

Marathi language:

> I beg of you, open up in the soil of the Marathi language, a gold mine of literary composition, and cultivate in it vines of discernment. Jnaneswar says, plant in it dense gardens ever full of abundant fruit of the discussion of philosophic problems. Break up the ravines of heresy, destroy the bypaths of controversy, and slay the evil beasts of false reasoning. Make me always remain seated at the feet of Lord Krishna, and set the listeners on the throne of learning. Let the blessed day of the knowledge of the Absolute come to the city of the Marathi language....[18]

Literature was performance, in Jnanadeva's agenda. It was not just graceful language stored by scholars in obscure texts. Literature was, for him, the simultaneity of speech and writing, Sanskrit and Prakrit, orality and textuality. Literature, and the community within which it circulates, were inseparable in Jnanadeva's conception of creativity. His programme for literature as integration and performance, so ably demonstrated in his own poetry, received immediate and spontaneous response. His spiritual companion and disciple, Namadeva, travelled in northern India and composed devotional songs in Hindi. His teaching and poetry subsequently influenced Kabir and Nanak, through the saint Ramananda. Namadeva, who wrote a biographical account of Jnanadeva, also became the leader of a community of saints, all of whom composed songs in Marathi following Jnanadeva's agenda. The community of saints that gathered round Namadeva included persons of all castes and having different social standing. In the subsequent centuries, the practice of composing and singing the kind of integrative and performable poems as envisioned by Jnanadeva came to be one of the most important cultural traditions in Maharashtra. Nearly three hundred years after the *Jnaneswari* was completed, Ekanatha, a poet—with versatility in many forms of composition, undertook the first major piece of historical research in the tradition of Marathi literature by preparing a scholarly edition of the *Jnaneswari.* As a critic rightly comments, "Ekanatha produced it with such meticulous care and close study of the various manuscripts available to him that it is still regarded as the standard text."[19] Ekanatha lived during the sixteenth century. During the first half of the seventeenth century Tukarama, the greatest poet in the entire history of Marathi literature, continued the work initiated by Jnanadeva in the thirteenth century. The entire movement that grew around the *bhakti* poetry written by the four major Marathi saint-poets mentioned here, made Vitthala, the god in Pandharpur, its favourite figure for worship. Vitthala was not just an idol, he was primarily the symbol for social equality and liberation. This cult of liberation, which came to be known as the Varakari cult, continues to exist in Maharashtra as an immensely popular movement even today.

The Varakari movement was but one manifestation of the bhakti-spirit. Jnanadeva was but one of the saints to initiate it. Marathi was just one of the languages invigorated by it. What has been described in the foregoing pages as Jnanadeva's agenda, through close reading of a single text, was, in fact, the literary and cultural agenda of the entire subcontinent; and its authors were numerous ranging from the Alvars and the Lingayat poets in the south, the Saivaites and the Tantrik poets in Kashmir, Hemachandra and other Jaina writers in Gujarat, Chaitanya and the other Krishna worshippers in Bengal, Tulsidas and the followers of Rama in central India, the Sufi mystics and their exquisite poetry of symbolism in Persian, and many others. The new languages of their writing ranged from Bangla, Assamiya, Oriya, Kashmiri, Punjabi, Sindhi, Hindi, Rajasthani and Gujarati to Marathi, Kannada, Telugu, Tamil, Malayalam, Urdu, Persian and Arabic. Various forms of creativity were invented and used in the movements: while poets like Amir Khusrau in Persian and Thyagaraja in Telugu integrated poetry with music, the Mahanubhava writers in Marathi employed history and biography; poets like Akkama in Kannada and Mira in Hindi invented an enigmatic confessional mode, and Ekanatha put the folk forms like *bharud* and *johar* to use. The variety was breathtaking; the heterogeneity was immense. In this rich harvest of great literary creativity which vehemently denied class monopoly as the basis for forming literary canons, the formation of sects became the historiographical strategy.

The dynamics of Indian society during the last ten centuries has been characterised by the process of sect-formation. Sects in India are not a matter just of theological dissension; though some theological totems are the rallying points in them, they originate in social and economic differences. It is worth noting that if there is one feature common to the hundreds of Indian sects, it is their attack on the institution of social castes. Implied in this attack is also the critique of the 'establishment', which included, among other things, the monopoly of a small minority on the institutions of learning. Sects have helped the Indian masses in seeking legitimation of diverse forms of 'knowledge' and life-experiences through collective dissension. Sects therefore always have a spiritual solace for the collectivity. Their forms of knowledge easily merge into activities of one kind or another, rather than evolving into refined theories. The process of sect formation in Indian society dates back to the eighth century, a time when sects were formed around Shiva, Shakti, Vishnu, etc. This process was then appropriated by the vast-communities that were trying to give literary dignity to the languages they used in day-to-day life. That is why, invariably, every new language that emerges as a literary language in India revolves around one or more prominent sects. Thus, the modern Kannada language came into being together with the Virashaiva Lingayata sect; the modern Punjabi originated with Nanak's Sikh panth; modern Hindi emerged along with Kabir's sect known as the Kabirpanth. Modern Marathi dates back to the period of the emergence of the Mahanubhava and Varakari sects. In other words, sect-formation has been the central process of maintaining the progressive dynamics of society in India.

However, the procedure of sect-formation involves a self-limiting act, for though sects are formed in order to raise new questions, they are not formed around these questions but rather some totems that symbolize these questions. Totems involve rules of exclusion and inclusion; and they tend to exert a hypnotic influence on the thinking capacity of the devotee. Through this hypnosis is released a tremendous unconscious power, anarchic, equalising and restless; but it also diminishes the ability to reason. Jnanadeva raised several radical questions for Indian society. But his text was adopted by the Varakari sect as the most sacred totem; and after that, his text ceased to appeal to the rational side of the Varakaris. Some of the later saints participating in this sect, perhaps, saw with clarity the sect's appeal to the unconscious. Their knowledge of the power of the sect's impact was effectively translated in the metres they used. The metres are necessarily easy, incantatory, soothing to the ear. The attendant diction is simple, repetitive, and full of 'non-sense' phrases which directly appeal to the primeval side of the listener. Ekanatha's *bharuds*, Tukarama's *abhangas*, and the *bhajanas* eclectically adopted by the Varakaris immediately acquired totemic value in their sect. Each of the millions of Varakaris knew the songs, the poems, the texts, with greater intimacy and passion than modern printing technology would enable the ordinary reader to have. Hence, for generation after generation, the Varakari literature retained its audience, kept it spellbound, and managed to remain alive and vital. In fact, the history of this literature was indistinct from the history of the sect.

These sects always flourished in the countryside and away from the cities and centres of government. During the colonial period, the sects did not undergo as much transformation as the urban communities did. The result is that the innumerable sects in India, through which and around which literature in modern Indian languages flourished, continue to inherit and carry in themselves innumerable 'texts' and versions of literary history that the modern literary scholarship has as yet barely examined.

The 'sectarian' literary history in medieval India—and also as it continues to exist in modern India—is strikingly different from what modern scholarship would label 'oral history'. Oral history is based on memory and not on rigorous memorization. Oral history makes allowance for distortions of events remembered; and the persons who are used as the 'source' for collecting oral history are rarely aware that they are 'carriers' of any history. The followers of sects are, on the other hand, conscious about their knowledge of the literature and the past of their sects. They are encouraged to stick as close to the original texts as possible. Four hundred years after the death of Kabir, hundreds of his followers gather on a tiny island in the Narmada river in Gujarat on the anniversary of his death, and sing his poems in the same rhythm and *raga* as he would have sung them. They sing certain songs while going towards the island, and certain other songs while returning, in the same sequence year after year and century after century. This phenomenon is clearly very different from what is understood as oral history,

A unique feature of literary traditions in India, a feature entirely unknown in the literatures of the Western world, is that in India literary texts may be accorded divine status, and literally treated as being at par with God. A set of literary texts, mostly poetic but occasionally prose biographies as in the case of the Mahanubhava sect, is treated as divinely ordained; and the sect considers it a bounden duty to preserve the texts. Thus, literature and worship become overlapping: all forms of literature are worshipped and all forms of worship are literary. Owing to this feature of Indian sects, they continuously keep the texts of their worship alive. New copies of the texts are made from time to time. Poems and songs are memorized and recited with ritual discipline. Occasionally, special scripts or codes are invented to keep the texts from any defilement. Biographies of the saints— poets or writers—are composed and circulated in the communities of their followers. Sect formation thus gives rise to a strategy in literary history.

As sociological processes, sect-formation and canon-formation are analogous processes. In India, they are not only analogous but even identical. It may be said that the history of the Sikh *panth* is inextricably woven together with the history of the *Granthsaheb* or that the history of the Lingayat sect is almost the same as the history of the *Vachanas* of the Lingayat saints. With regard to the Varakari *panth*, Ekanatha's edition of *Jnaneswari,* completed in AD 1584 (the *Shaka* year 1506), which forbade any interpolation in the text as taboo, is the high watermark of the formation of the sect. At this time several canons of literature existed in India side by side. Those who learnt Sanskrit had access to the *mantra* canon, the *shastras* and *akshara* literature. Those who did not learn Sanskrit had access to the *suta* literature and the *pantha* literature. In addition to these, there were forms of literature which exploited the performative possibility of literary arts to their utmost, forms flourishing in the centres of political authority and the military camps. These gave rise in course of time to written histories of literature.

8

Pre-colonial Historiography

Between the *Rajatarangini* of Kalhana[1] composed in the eleventh century and the *Peshavyanchi Bakhar* composed by Krishnaji Sohoni [2] in the nineteenth century, several forms of history writing emerged in India. Some of these forms were practised widely enough to form traditions of history writing. The royal chronicles in Kashmir, the hagiography practised in all parts of India, the *burunji* in Assamiya, the *bhat-poetry* in Rajasthani, the *bakhar* and *ajnapatra* in Marathi, the diaries and autobiographies in Persian, the travelogues in Arabic, official records, gazettes and histories, and many more lines of the development of history and historiography can be traced down the span of the eight centuries. Initially the histories were composed in verse; but, after paper became available to Indian writers in the thirteenth century, histories began to be written in prose form. In the beginning, there was little distinction between literature and history. Kalhana and Amir Khusrau, whose writing is used as history, were primarily creative writers. Gradually, however, history acquired a more specific purpose and method. By the time the accounts of the 1761 battle of Panipat were written, history had become an independent science with its own methods of recording facts and examining the causes of important events.

In any society, the emergence of history as a discipline distinct from literature also brings the awareness of alterity on the part of literature, an awareness that it is not history. In the process evolves the awareness of the historicity of literature, of literary history. This process took place in Europe from the middle of the eighteenth century to the middle of the nineteenth century as convincingly argued by Linda Orr in her brilliant essay, 'The Revenge of Literature: A History of History.'[3] This process took place in India about a century before it took place in Europe; and, in the seventeenth century, India started producing 'literary histories' that would be acceptable to modern scholars as being 'proper' literary history. This is not surprising considering that the use of paper for writing, the development of the prose form used for history writing, a general discourse of history, and traditions of literature about which to write, existed in India in the seventeenth century. Besides, a native variety of modern nationalism was emerging in India at this time.

In the Mogul court of Shahjahan and Jahangir there were many poets who had migrated from far off places to gain patronage from the emperor. Abu'l-Barakat Munir Lahari (1609–54) was one of them. He travelled extensively, and wrote copiously. One of his works, the *matnawi* on Bengal resulted from such travels. It records several literary and cultural details about seventeenth century Bengal. Munir also composed a commentary on Urfi's *Quasidas*. Such commentaries were common among the scholars of that period. A modern history of Islamic literature in India observes:

> Munir was also a man of his time in writing a *tadkira* of poets, for the 17th century was the time when *hommes-de-letters* began to collect every conceivable bit of information about classical and contemporary poets and compiled biographical dictionaries. One of those famous for their *tadkiras* is the prolific Taqu Aubadi (died in 1630) who came to India in 1606. His production includes *quasidas* and *matnawis* as well as a Persian dictionary (*Surma-yi-sulaimani*) and a *tadkira* called, *Arafat al- asiqin*, 'The mountain Arafat of the Lovers', a title which gives the date of its completion, i.e. 1024/1615. The book deals with 3168 Persian poets, and one of Taqu's numerous versions of this compilation, an extract called *Ka'ba-yi' irfan*, 'The ka 'ba of Gnosis' was often used by later writers...

> Another specialist on poets' biographies was Amin Razi, a first cousin of Shah Jihan's father-in-law, I'timad ad-daula. He had compiled, in 1594, the *Haft iqlim,* 'Seven Climata', a work dealing with about 1560 poets, saints and scholars arranged according to their towns and countries, so that not only the historians of literature but the geographers as well can draw upon it.[4]

The *tawarikhs* and *tadkiras* were exercises in biographical criticism and history. They contained encyclopaediac information, made interesting through their anecdotal style, about scholars, schools, poets, saints and men of letters. These histories often had a moral and theological argument. However, the material they contained used to be reliable as history due to the extreme care taken to maintain accuracy in chronology and dates. Besides, they were generously illustrated with quotations from poems and scholarly debates. In her histories of Turkish, Arabic, Persian and Urdu literature in medieval India, Annemarie Schimmel refers to a number of literary histories written during the Islamic period in India, most of them composed mainly during the seventeenth century. Their geographical sources ranged from Lahore, Meerut and Delhi in the north to Golconda, Aurangabad and Bijapur in the south. They were also composed in Gujarat and Bengal. The tradition was continued till the establishment of a Persian printing press at the British factory in Calcutta in the early nineteenth century. Most of the historians were able poets themselves, and most of them taught in Islamic *madrasas.* The purpose in writing these histories was, clearly, to use them as text books. Since these writers came from a variety of geographical areas in India, and since they were invariably bilingual, it can be assumed that scholars in Bengal, Gujarat, Sindh, Maharashtra, Karnataka, Andhra, central India and Rajasthan—to use contemporary geographic labels—had a definite idea of what literary history is and what it ought to be.

Schimmel mentions the following histories of literature in her survey of medieval Islamic Indian writings:[5]

(a) Sayyid Ali wrote a biographical compendium on Arabic poets and scholars. It was called *Sulafat al-'asr,* 'The Best Wine of the Century', and was a history of contemporary literature. He also wrote a biographical work describing his journey from Mecca to Golconda, *Salwat al-garib.* 'Consolation of the Stranger', which is of interest from the viewpoint of literary historiography.

(b) Al Badaoni (or Badauni) wrote in his *Muntakhab ut tawarikh* an account of native and expatriate poets and writers at the court of Akbar covering a period of half a century (1556–1605). His work was written in Persian; but it covered Muslim poets writing in various languages.

(c) Isma'il Binis wrote several 'romantic' *matnawis* depicting the literary scenes in Lahore and Kashmir.

(d) Muhammad Aslah wrote an encyclopaedic work related to literary history and criticism. It was called *Tadkira-yisu 'ara-yi Kasmir'.*

(e) A similar work was produced a little later, that is in the mid-17th century, by Nasib. It was called *Risinama,* and was mainly a biographical dictionary of Kashmiri saint-poets.

(f) This had been preceded by a comparable work in Gujarat: Gauti Sattari's *Gulzar-i abrar,* a dictionary of biographies.

(g) Of interest to literary historians should be an early seventeenth century composition by Muhammad Tahir Nisyani, *Ta'rih-i tahiri,* a history of Sind, complemented by Yusuf Mirak Sindi's *Mazhar-i sahgihani.*

(h) Mirza Bedil, the great eighteenth century Persian poet who lived in Delhi, wrote a *Cahar 'unsur,* 'The Four Elements' completed in 1704. A mixture of prose and poetry, this work offers a wealth of biographical data.

(i) Mir Gulam Ali Azad, who spent the later part of his life in Aurangabad, wrote two books of literary history. He had complete mastery over poetry in Arabic, Turkish, Hindi and Urdu. The *Ma'atir al-kiram* gives biographies of 150 scholars from his home town, and *Sarw-i azad,* 'The Free Cypress', a biographical dictionary of 143 poets from all parts of Asia.

(j) Lakshmi Narayan Safiq, a Hindu pupil of Azad, who lived in the early part of the eighteenth century composed two literary histories. *Gul-i ra'na,* 'Lovely Rose' is a widely used *tadkira* of Indian poets who wrote in Persian. On the other hand, the *Sam-i gariban,* 'The Evening of the Strangers', gives an account of Persian poets who visited India.

(k) Ali Hazin, who died in Benaras in 1766, wrote a critical account of his contemporary poets in *Tadkirat al-mu'asirin.*

(l) Sher Khan Lodi's *Mirat al-hayal,* Binraban Das Hosgu's *Safina-yi Hosgu,* and Walih Dadistani's *Riyad as-su'ara,* etc., are among the *tadkiras* written during the eighteenth century.

(m) A poet called Sirajuddin of Aurangabad (1714–63) put together an anthology of Persian poems which contains examples from some 680 poets.

(n) Mir Taqi Mir, an eighteenth century poet and scholar, who composed a *tadkira* called *Nikat as-su-ara,* 'The Fine Points of the Poets', deals with poets in Urdu from the Deccan and Gujarat up to his times.

(o) Gulam Hamadani 'Mushafi '(1750–1824) completed his most important *tadkira,* the *Tadkira-y-Hindigoyan* in 1794. It contained information about some 350 Urdu poets.

(p) Nawab Ali Ibrahim Khan's *Gulzar-i Ibrahim* (1784) contained notices about 320 Urdu poets.

(q) Nawwab Ali Khan 'Mubtala Lakhnawi' composed *Gulsan-i suhan* 'Rose Garden of the Word' in 1780.

(r) The *tadkira* by Mir Qudratullah Qadiri, *Magmu' a-i nagz,* 'Elegant Collection', which brought together the poetry of 800 Urdu poets, was completed in 1806.

(s) Nawab Azimuddaula Mustafa Khan 'Sefta', more famous as a friend and patron of Ghalib, put together a biographical dictionary of 600 Urdu poets in northern India under the title *Gulsan-i be-har* (in 1845).

Not all of these biographical dictionaries, autobiographies, anthologies and histories are of equally high standard. However, the chronological data provided in them is invariably accurate. The names of the places with which the poets discussed were associated, are also generally correct. The titles of their works, wherever mentioned, are dependable. The problem of inaccuracies comes up when we start examining the verses ascribed to each poet. Since printing was not used for the production of Urdu,

Persian and Arabic books until the beginning of the eighteenth century, the historians had to depend on handmade copies. This is one reason why Islamic calligraphy was so well-developed. But, often, the historians recorded the source of the verses quoted by them, whether they were from the poets themselves, or reproduced from memory. In order to examine more critically the nature of literary historiography during the pre-colonial centuries in India as found in Islamic scholarship, let us turn to Al Badaoni's *Muntakhab ut-tawarikh*.

Badaoni who worked as a historian in the court of Akbar, is counted as being among the more important historians of medieval India. However, as Muhammad Mujeeb observes, he was more passionately interested in literary history than in political history.

> Badaoni had no taste for investigation and research, no desire to add to existing historical knowledge. He states quite ingenuously that for the period beginning with the establishment of the Delhi Sultanate to his own time his account is just a selection from *Tarikh-i-Mubarakshahi*. . . . But he has added 'something of his own'. . . . The 'something more' which Badaoni has added to his selection of events from his two sources includes also continuous references to *sufis* and poets.[6]

The third part of Badaoni's *Tawarikh*[7] deals with poetry, language and literature. It is divided into four chapters. The first chapter describes thirty-eight learned men "who were regularly employed in the Imperial service until their fame reached such a pitch that it was as manifest as the sun at midday." The second chapter describes seventy other scholars whom the author had met at one or the other time in his life. The third and the shortest chapter presents an account of fifteen men of medicine who had acquired the power of performing miracles through their spiritual powers. These three chapters give an account of the Sufi movement, their leaders, and the religious establishment in Mogul India and the sociology of Islamic literature in Badaoni's days.

The fourth and the last chapter of the *Tawarikh* offers an anthology of a hundred and sixty-eight poets in combination with a biographical dictionary. Badaoni asserts that he has known most of the poets discussed; those he has not known are so famous that he has reliable knowledge about their work. Besides, he makes it clear that he has used the previously written historical material. In his introductory remarks, Badaoni states:

> A full account of the poets of the reign of the Emperor Akbar is given in the *Nafa'isu-l-Ma'asir,* well known as the *Tazkirah* of Mir 'Ala'- ud-daula, which is the source from which the materials for this brief account are extracted. Some of these poets have composed *divans.* I have written of those with whom I was acquainted, whom I have seen, whether near or from afar, or who have acquired fame.[8]

Badaoni's method in his history is to offer the essential outline of the poet's biography followed by samples of some of his best poems. There are, then, remarks on any special features of the poet's work. For example, the use of music to accompany the recitation is mentioned in the case of some poets. In some cases, Badaoni mentions the ideological peculiarities of the poets. And finally, he gives a critical assessment of the stylistic features of the poets he discusses. There is also plenty of information about their financial and social condition. There is a sense of proportion in Badaoni's comments. He gives far more space to the major poets, while the minor poets are given no more than a paragraph or two each. For instance, writing about a poet known as Sipahi, the historian comments:

> He was the grandson of the famous Khwaja Kalan Beg. This quatrain is by him: 'Alas, that the season of the rose has passed so quickly, Alas, that it has passed in the twinkling of an eye! Without thy eyes and the dawn on thy cheek the violet and the hyacinth pass their days in blindness and in mourning.' He died in Agra in the year H. 978 (AD 1570–71).[9]

But when he discusses major poets, he offers elaborate comments on their styles, with reasons for his liking or disliking them; his meetings with them; the more important events in their lives. There are, occasionally, bits of gossip that Badaoni introduces in his narrative to make it interesting. It is because of his habit of making personal remarks that we get very valuable information about the social, sexual and cultural life of the men of letters in Badaoni's times.

The history of poetry written by Badaoni can be described as a 'contemporary history', for it does not describe the entire development of Islamic literature in India from its very beginning to Badaoni's age. But, given his method of using only personally verified material as historical material and not accepting written material as authoritative, it was not possible for the historian to go beyond his own generation and period. However, in the histories of literature written after Badaoni, the span of the narrative is generally much larger. Badaoni himself was conscious of the limitation of his narrative; but he did not aim at writing any 'conclusive' history of poetry. In his opinion, history writing should be an ongoing process:

> This is the account of some of those poets, most of whom were contemporary with the author and writing during the time in which he was writing, and whose *divans* are current in this age and are circulated as examples. As for those who have leapt from the net of this memoir and are here neither described nor indicated by casual mention, I make them over to those who shall hereafter set foot in the plain of existence, for this series of poets is as endless as *Burhan-i-Tatbiq,* and to comprehend them all within the limits of one age, or one short space of time is beyond the limits...[10]

In other words, Badaoni does not accept the responsibility of introducing periodization in his history. This is not to say that he was not sensitive to historical changes in literary style and the function of literature. On the contrary, he was so acutely conscious of the changes taking place during the period of his narrative that he made *that* awareness his chief justification for writing the history:

> I shall now explain what it was that originally led me to collect these fragments. Since a complete revolution, both in legislation and manners, greater than any of which there is any record for the past thousand years, has taken place in these days.... [11]

The great literary change that Badaoni then points out as having taken place is that poets had moved away from the love of language to the love of political patronage, power and worldly gains. Implicit in this passion is Badaoni's main historiographical principle.

In Badaoni's opinion, the love for language is identical with the love for God and religion, in this case Islam. The criterion for judging poetry, therefore, should be the saintly quality in the life of the poet and in his verses. This, of course, is a subjective judgement. To avoid the risks implied, Badaoni avoids making a distinction between 'literature' and 'para-literature'. Thus, he assumes no responsibility towards canon-making. Similarly, he avoids the division of literature into 'written' and 'recited'. As quoted above, he considers the 'circulation' of a work as the distinguishing feature of literature. His view is that the purpose of literature is to keep the grace and beauty of language alive as well as to enhance social morality. Hence, in his history, there is scope for discussion of the orality as well as the lexicality of poetry, of mainstream literature as well as 'para' literature, of poetry by native Indians as well as that by expatriates. But there is no scope for the poems written by non-Muslims, even if they are written in Arabic, Persian, Turkish, Urdu or Hindi. Again, there is severe criticism in Badaoni for those who had any Turkish connection, an aspect of his historiography that can be explained only in terms of his religious views.

Thus, Badaoni's history does not use 'period', 'genre', 'canon' or 'language' as principles of literary history. It uses, on the other hand, 'sect' as the central principle. Within it are subsumed such categories as 'oral' and 'written', 'marginal' and 'central', etc. These principles are not entirely different from the principles of historiography employed by the Hindu and other non-Muslim *panths* in medieval India.

An exact replica of Badaoni's biographical anthology of poetry within contemporary Hindu cults can be found in the anthology of songs prepared by the Dadupanth saints. Thanks to German scholarship of Indian literature, this anthology, known as the *Panchvani,* is now available in a critical (and computer-analysed) edition.[12] It includes songs by Dadu, Namadeva, Raidas and

Hardas. The inclusion of the songs in this conventional collection avoids 'period', 'language', 'canon' and 'genre' as the criteria. The collection attempts a total integration between the written and the spoken, for even the *ragas* to which each of the songs is ascribed are fully recorded. The historiography in medieval India follows, as was logical, the actual literary practice. In this respect the comments by W. M. Callewaert, one of the two editors of the *Panchvani,* are worth quoting:

> Studying the songs of a poet like Namdev or Kabir is quite different from studying Shakespeare or Kalidasa. It is the ambition of a text-critic studying Shakespeare to bring out the text 'written' by the author, by looking at the various versions available in manuscripts. The text-critic soon realizes that this is impossible in the case of a Namdev or Kabir. There is no way by which we can reach beyond the oral tradition to the poets themselves. This oral tradition, unlike that of the *Vedas,* did not shun variety and creativity. . . Fortunately, the manuscript tradition allows us to reach the threshold of this oral tradition, or the moment when it started to be written down, some time before 1600 AD (while the oral tradition continued).[13]

The separation between the oral and the written seems to have started occurring some time in the seventeenth century. It is significant that Badaoni too felt worried about the 'gap' between writing and speech. Literary historiography in India during the seventeenth and eighteenth centuries seems to have been guided by the anxiety about the disintegration of the literary communities created by the emergence of the new languages at the beginning of the millennium.

In recent years scholars of Indian history have suggested that the 'modern' period in Indian history begins with Akbar. Whether that is true in political history or not, in literary history that indeed seems to be the case. During the seventeenth century, literatures in modern Indian languages showed signs of becoming more literate, urbane, highbrow and to some extent institutionalized or patronized. This change introduced in Indian literature, once again, the gap that Jnanadeva had sought to bridge, the gap between the 'spoken' and the 'written'.

In tune with the emergence of new canons of literature, the sense of literary history too changed, as did the anxiety and the rhetoric of literary historiography. The split between the spoken and the written was dramatically enhanced and quickened by the introduction of printing technology in India, initially and accidentally in Goa in the seventeenth century, and in all parts of India subsequently during the nineteenth century. In its turn, the technology of printing was linked with the British colonization of India. Therefore, in order to continue our narrative of historiography we must allow other beings to step in.

9

Warton's Imaginative Savages

In the story of the rise of English literary history,[1] the publication of Thomas Warton's *History of English Poetry* in four volumes (1774–90)[2] marks a crucial turning point. Before its publication there existed a vast body of raw material for literary history such as biographical dictionaries, reviews, genre studies, historical researches related to single authors and verse anthologies. After Warton's compilation of the available body of researches in the form of an argument, all subsequent narratives about the literary past acquired the distinctive features of literary history.

Like so much else that happened in England during the last quarter of the eighteenth century in various fields of knowledge—biology, economics, psychology and linguistics,[3] Warton's historiography was not only a pioneering achievement but it also defined, for the future, the ground rules for the discourse of literary history. As Wellek points out,

> Warton was not satisfied merely to collect materials for a history of poetry, but wanted to present them in a scheme of historical and literary values, based on 'fundamental principles . . .' largely the conception of a progress from 'rudeness to elegance,' the idea of a uniform advance from barbarism to refinement.[4]

Warton's evolutionary concept of literary history was in tune with the spirit of optimism that pervaded English sciences and literature in his generation, and which was expressed in a poem like

Thompson's *The Castle of Indolence.* However, this evolutionary optimism was not just the ruling sentiment in Warton's history, it was the very backbone of his argument. In employing the opposition between rudeness and elegance as a theoretical argument, Warton was no doubt following a long established controversy about the nature of the poetic imagination.

About a century before Warton, the English philosopher Thomas Hobbes had taken up the issue in his famous *Leviathan,* in which he had carefully differentiated between imagination aided by reason and imagination not so aided.[5] Similarly, John Milton had written his twin poems, *L'Allegro* and *Il Penseroso,* precisely to make a similar distinction. Poetic and philosophic speculation about creativity and imagination occupied an important place in all intellectual activity during the eighteenth century. Invariably, the English philosophers and poets perceived imagination in terms of an opposition between the simple, untainted and barbaric imagination and the sophisticated, urbane and 'reasonable' imagination. The culmination of this aesthetics came through Edmund Burke's distinction between the sublime and the beautiful.[6] Hence, when Warton employed this opposition as his argument in the *History,* he was drawing upon a vast fund of philosophical speculation about primitivism.

In Milton's poetry the opposition between forms of imagination was presented through myth, in the form of the opposition between the mental activity of Satan and God. Half a century later, the same opposition found expression in Pope's poetry through a pair of human characters, Belinda of *The Rape of the Lock* and Eloisa of *Eloisa and Abelard.* Less than half a century later, landscape had replaced human interest; and in Thompson's *Seasons,* geography provided the metaphors for the mind. This was not surprising considering that at this time England had explored vast geographical areas and had encountered several 'primitive' races. The in-flow of information from the colonies fed the established English epistemology and aesthetics, consequently, creating a discourse that can be termed 'savageology'.

Orientalism was one of the branches of savageology. It was guided by the existing British ideas of what primitive people ought to be. At the same time it strengthened these ideas by its discoveries of ancient languages and polytheistic people. This curious interlocking of Orientalism and the British ideas of primitive imagination had a profound impact on Warton's historiography. And, in order to appreciate this relationship, which in turn has great significance for literary historiography in India, it is necessary to look closely at Warton's 'savageology'.

While it would be a slight exaggeration to say that there was a cult of primitivism in England during the mid-eighteenth century, it would be an understatement to say that there was only a nominal interest among intellectuals in primitivism. The truth is that this interest ran very strong in a variety of intellectual areas.[7] First, there were poetical works such as the *Death Song of a Cherokee Indian* by Mrs. John Hunter and the *American Love-Ode* by Lady Winchelsea. The father of Thomas Warton, the elder Thomas Warton, attempted an imitation of this poem, and Joseph Warton, the brother of the historian, wrote *Dying Indian.* Next, there were the translations of literary works that had started pouring in through the work of the Orientalists. Sir William Jones, who later translated *Sakuntala,* had published *Poems Consisting Chiefly of Translations from the Asiatic Languages* as early as 1772. In this book, Jones argued that the poetry of Hafiz was 'naturally' excellent, that poets in warmer climates had a more active imagination. Then, there was a current of opinion in literary criticism which considered an opulence of imagination a natural prerogative of 'primitive' poetry. In his history of literary history, Rene Wellek offers a careful account of this element of English literary criticism:

> The most common approach was through the theory of climate, popularized by Temple... The mild climate of the South was contrasted with the rigours of the North, while extreme heat was considered detrimental to the growth of literature. Or sometimes East and West were contrasted, in which case the East was identified with the South and considered favourable to the 'warmth of imagination'... Addison assigned 'extravagant imagery' to the 'warmer climates'. Husbands in 1731 spoke of the 'Genius of the east' which 'soars upon stronger wings,

> and takes a loftier flight than the Muse of Greece or Rome' ... Sir William Jones praised the climate of Yemen in recommending Arabian poetry and spoke of the immoderate heat of the East as disposing the Eastern people to a life of indolence, which gives them full leisure to cultivate their talents. He made the alternative suggestion that the sun has a direct, physical influence on the imagination. [8]

This crude 'climate theory' of 'warm imagination' gradually came to be transformed into a critical label that could be applied to all primitive poetry. Hugh Blair, himself a poet who composed some memorable poetry on the theme of imagination during the years of the 'Sensibility School' of English poetry, used 'primitive poetry', or as he called it the "Oriental vein of poetry", as a descriptive critical label rather than a geographic designation. The Oriental vein was, according to Blair, "characteristic of an age rather than a century."[9]

Implicit in the Oriental/primitive thesis about active poetic imagination was a view of the development and decay of languages. This view held that in the earlier phases of the growth of a language it has greater concrete character by virtue of the immediacy between objects and words. In later stages this immediacy is lost and replaced by a greater degree of abstraction. In other words, according to this view, the primitive languages were more spontaneous and metaphoric than the synthetic and developed languages. These considerations, first applied to the evolution of languages, later attracted the attention of literary critics. When this 'organic theory of language' with its fantasy about the great emotional force of a language in its early stage was applied to the field of poetry, it followed that a sharp distinction between the primitive and the sophisticated styles of poetry had to be made. As Wellek points out:

> This emotional theory of the origin of language explained the supposed characteristic of all primitive languages (and thus all primitive poetry), its figurativeness. 'From this deduction it is plain,' said Blackwell, 'that any language formed as described above, must be full of metaphor. We

> must imagine the speech of savages to be broken, unequal and boisterous.' The Turks, Arabs and Indians are described as taciturn people, who, when they open their mouths and 'give loose to a fiery imagination, are poetical and full of metaphors'.[10]

The theories about the primitive imagination, those about the early stages of languages development, and the in-flow of literary information about the Oriental and other exotic cultures combined in Thomas Warton's literary historiography to form an argument. The argument was that initially the romantic fictions, folklore and myths were imported to Europe from the Oriental nations. Gradually, however, these synthesized with reason, logic, religious wisdom and stylistic good manners to produce 'literature'.

Thomas Warton's *History of English Poetry* runs into more than two thousand pages, each of the four volumes of which has an impressive length of five hundred or more pages. Its aim was to tell the story of the rise and development of English poetry from its beginning towards the close of the eleventh century to the commencement of the eighteenth century. However, when the fourth volume was published, the story had not reached even up to Spenser. As it was going to be a history of poetry, and as Shakespeare was considered more a dramatist than a poet, Warton's plan had excluded Shakespeare from his narrative. Thus, in effect, the four volumes of Warton's history offer us no comments on any really major English poet except Chaucer. The section on Chaucer runs into several chapters, most of which repeatedly show that the sources of his plots and characters are in Arabic, Turkish or other Oriental poetry. For instance, alluding to Milton's praise of the *Squires Tale* of Chaucer, Warton says: "The imagination of this story consists in Arabian fiction engrafted on Gothic chivalry. Nor is this Arabian fiction purely the sport of arbitrary fancy : it is in great measure founded on Arabian learning."[11] And after explaining in great detail the Arabic elements of Chaucer's poetic motifs, he adds,

> To trace the matter home to its true source, these fictions have their origin in a science which professedly made a considerable part of the Arabian learning. In the twelfth

> century the number of magical and astrological Arabic books translated into Latin was prodigious.[12]

The last two volumes of the *History of English Poetry* are anthologies of obscure poems rather than a history of the poets or texts.

The first volume of the history has three lengthy 'Dissertations' forming a length of almost 300 pages. They are, respectively, (i) *Of the Origin of Romantic Fiction in Europe,* (ii) *On the Introduction of Learning into England,* and (iii) *On the Gesta Romanorum.* The first of these three dissertations is devoted to showing that romance fiction in Europe is solely of Oriental origin. At the very outset, Warton states his aim:

> That peculiar and arbitrary species of Fiction which we commonly call Romantic, was entirely unknown to the writers of Greece and Rome. It appears to have been imported into Europe by a people, whose modes of thinking, and habits of invention, are not natural to that country. It is generally supposed to have been borrowed from the Arabians.[13]

The second dissertation describes at length the decline in learning after the fall of the Roman empire, and the recovery of knowledge at the beginning of the present millennium. Warton considers the Arabic contribution to this recovery of the greatest importance. He writes:

> After the calamities which the state of literature sustained in consequence of the incursions of the northern nations, the first restorers of the ancient philosophical sciences in Europe, the study of which, by opening the faculties and extending the views of mankind, gradually led the way to other parts of learning were the Arabians. In the beginning of the eighth century, this wonderful people, equally famous for their conquests and their love of letters, in ravaging Asiatic provinces found many Greek books, which they read with infinite avidity: and such was the gratification they received from the fortunate acquisition, and so powerfully their curiosity was excited to make further discoveries in this new field of knowledge, that they requested their caliphs to procure from the emperor

> at Constantinople the best Greek writers. These they carefully translated into Arabic.[14]

Of course, Warton does not forget to add that the Arabs translated only those Greek and Latin works which 'their extravagant and romantic' imagination approved.

The third dissertation prefixed to the first volume of Warton's history is on the *Gesta Romanorum,* a form of story-telling more popularly known as the mirror stories, which were moralising stories for rulers and administrators. Warton traces the textual histories of such mirror sequences in English and French, and argues that the origin of these stories was in Arabic philosophy and literature.

The question one likes to ask is: Why did Warton spend nearly three hundred pages at the very beginning of his history to show the Oriental beginnings of English literature? One starts getting some ideas of his intention when one looks at his language a little more closely. In the dissertation on the *Monks' Tales,* he describes the age that produced such prolific imagination as "the age of ignorance and imagination".[15] At the very outset of his 'brief' Preface', Warton states:

> In an age advanced to the highest degree of refinement, that species of curiosity commences, which is busied in contemplating the progress of social life, in displaying the gradations of science, and in tracing their translation from barbarism to civility.[16]

Again a little later, he stresses that the purpose of a literary history is to show its readers the *"progress* of our *national* poetry, from a *rude origin* and obscure beginnings, to its *perfection* in a *polished age."*[17] Spenser's poetry was, in Warton's opinion, that perfection and polish which the English nation had brought to the obscure imaginative tales of an ignorant age in the Orient. However, he does not lavish praise on 'progress' without simultaneously lamenting the decline in 'imagination'. Wellek points out the ambivalence in Warton's vision of history:

> This curious double point of view—acknowledgement of the progress of modern civilization and even of modern

> taste, and yet regret for the 'world of fine fabling'—had an interesting, logical consequence. The period of English literature which combined the advantages of both early and later poetry must have seemed to Warton the natural summit and the real ideal...

Ultimately, a conception of the development of English poetry in three stages emerges: a primitive, imaginative stage; a condition of synthesis between imagination and reason, realized by the Elizabethans; and a period of judgment and correctness which seemed final to Warton and ideal from the point of view of the social advance of humanity, even though it might spell death to imagination and poetry.... To a certain extent Warton anticipates Hegel's brief that the owl of Minerva flies in the dusk of a creative civilization, or—in agreement with his own metaphors—that the bright daylight of reason has dispelled the foul mists of superstition together with the golden haze of imagination.[18]

Thus the central historiographical principle in Warton's account of English literature was the dichotomy between imagination and reason.

As stated earlier, the dichotomy between imagination and reason had been a major theme in English poetic and philosophical traditions. Warton's unique and phenomenal contribution to this theme was to provide it a space-and-time framework. Space as a metaphor for the imagination was in use in English poetry during the mid-eighteenth century. More particularly, the school of poets known as the 'Graveyard School', which included poets like Young, Gray, Akenside and Blair, had been using the dark and the bright aspects of a given landscape to depict the dark and the bright sides of the human mind, and to show the opposition between imagination and reason. The Warton brothers themselves had a part to play in this poetic movement. However, in his history, Thomas Warton extended the metaphor to include global space. In this new form, the South and the East represented imagination, the North and the West represented reason. This new reading of the problematic of imagination was further enriched by Warton by giving it a vast temporal dimension too. The primitive ages and the remote past were the times for spontaneity and imaginative outbursts. The modern periods were the times for restraint and a cultivated sensibility. In other words, in writing his history of English poetry, Warton effectively historicized what so far had been considered a conflict within an individual's consciousness.

The spatial and temporal distribution of the creative faculties of the mind in Warton's historiography had drawn substance and scholarly support from 'savageology'. There were other forms of this savage-imagery in circulation during Warton's age. There was, for instance, Shakespeare's Caliban; and there already was Defoe's Man Friday. In France, Rousseau had floated the philosophy of noble savagery. Drawing on all these, Warton transformed the savage-imagery to accommodate the historicised process of creativity in it. His achievement was that he provided English literature with a sense of selfhood defined in terms of the alterity between the primitive and the modern, imagination and reason, and the Eastern and the Western.[19] Implicit in this self-definition was the possibility of a rhetoric of -literature as civilizing force. Less than half a century after Warton proposed his historiography, this possibility found its full realisation in the works of the British Utilitarians. However, during Warton's own time and in the years that followed, it was his savageology that exerted a stronger influence among English intellectuals. one branch of savageology to flourish with abundance was Indology.

10

Jones and the Gentoos

Images of India were formed in ancient Europe; and they had been handed down through isolated strands of folklore as well as through the writing of Plotinus and Pythagoras. These images were more fantasy than knowledge; and in modern Europe's intellectual discourse, India as a constituent part of the Orient, had come to represent a certain kind of impious imagination. It was for this reason that during the British renaissance the dichotomy between imagination and reason acquired importance as part of the process of Britain's cultural self-definition. And if, subsequently, Warton employed the antithesis between imagination and reason as his historiographical logic, it was also used by the early historians of India to establish India's otherness from Britain's selfhood. One of the earliest histories of India written by British historians was Alexander Dow's The *History of Hindostan* (1770).[1] It provides the context within which we can appreciate the work and contribution of Sir William Jones, who turned Indology from a hobby to an academic discipline.

The History of Hindustan, which was published as a translation of Ferishta's history of India, was, in fact, a combination of translations from several historical works. Its main bulk was from Ferishta's history; but it also drew upon Abul Fazl's *Ain-i-Akbari,* Matimad Khan's *Jehangirnama,* Mirza Kasim's *Shahjahan-nama* and such other works available in Persian. Dow's English vision of India and the Hindus was thus coloured by the vision of India in Islamic-Persian historiography.

Dow's rendering of Indian history made no secret of his censorious attitude to Indian historiography. This attitude rejoiced in the discovery of India's antiquity but lamented the utter lack of historical sense among Indian scholars and historiographers. It asserted that India had an abundance of history (as the past) but little history (as the narrative about the past). This attitude was not peculiar to Dow's response to Indian scholarship alone; it was generally shared by other British scholars engaged in interpreting Indian culture during the last quarter of the eighteenth century.

An excellent account of the early phase of British Indological studies is presented in Bernard Cohn's essay 'The Command of Language and the Language of Command'.[2] Among the more important works of this period, Cohn lists the following: *The History of Hindostan* (1770) by Dow, *A Grammar of the Persian Language* (1771) by Sir William Jones, *The Practical and Vulgar Dialects of the Indostan Language Commonly called Moors* (1772) by George Hadley, *A Code of Gentoo Laws* (1776) by Nathaniel Brassey Halhed, *A Dictionary of English, Persian* and *Arabic* (1780) by John Richardson, *Institutes Political and Military of Timour* (1783) by William Davy, *The Forms of the Herkern* (1781) by Francis Balfour, *The Bhagvet Geeta* (1785) by Charles Wilkins, *A Vocabulary, Persian, Arabic and English* (1785) by William Kirkpatric, *Ayeen-i-Akberry or the Institutes of the Emperor Akbar* (1783–6) by Francis Gladwin, and *A Dictionary of English and Hindustani, Part I* (1787) by John A. Gilchrist. Cohn comments:

> ... the production of these texts and others which followed them began the establishment of discursive formations, defined an epistemological space, created a discourse (of Orientalism), and had the effect of converting Indian forms of knowledge into European objects. The subjects of these texts were first and foremost the Indian languages themselves, represented in European terms as grammars, dictionaries and teaching aids in a project to make the acquisition of a working knowledge of the languages available to those British who were to be part of the ruling groups in India.[3]

This discourse of Indology created in Bengal during the last quarter of the eighteenth century subsequently became the preamble to the cultural relationship between Britain and India. The relationship was full of ambivalent spaces thus allowing a modern day historian like A. L. Basham to defend William Jones ("When Jones translated *Sakuntala* are we to believe that he consciously thought, I am doing this in order that my country may dominate a subject people?"[4]), as well as provoking a fierce tirade against him by Edward Said ("To rule and to learn, then to compare Orient with Occident: these were Jones' goals..."[5]). The important question for us is not what William Jones's intentions were, but what effects his scholarly procedures and literary products had on literary historiography in Britain and, as a result, in India.

When Sir William Jones arrived in India, the image of the Gentoo that had been circulating in British scholarship had two main sources: the Greek legends and histories which had depicted India as an exotic and intractable culture, and the travel books written by Europeans during the seventeenth century and the early part of the eighteenth century which depicted India as a land ruled by despots. This imagery thus combined allurement with fear in the contemporary British attitudes to India. Jones's scholarly project aimed at making sense of the confused imagery and in examining if those images corresponded to the reality of India.

There is no doubt that Jones's fascination with Indian culture, religions and literature never subsided during his years in Calcutta. During these years, he went about exploring as much as he could from as many sources as were at his disposal in areas as diverse as music, law, grammar, languages, philosophy, poetry, drama, myths and religion. He did not stop there: he wanted his contemporary scholars in Britain to share his excitement about the India he had discovered; and so he kept publishing the results of his researches in British periodicals and journals. The measure of his success in communicating to the British world of learning his delight in Indian literature and culture was indicated by the continuous demand for his publications in Britain. Commenting on the extent of diffusion of Jones's work in Britain, John Drew records:

> Jones's own work and that he inspired among members of the Asiatic Society was diffused most widely in the early 1790s through the *Asiatic Researches*... Neither Journal (that is the *Researches* and the short lived *Miscellany)* was readily available in England and the shortage of copies gave rise in the 1790s to a series of reprints, mainly of Jones's work and mainly from *Asiatic Researches,* entitled *Dissertations and Miscellaneous Pieces Relating to ... Asia.* At least partly on account of their scarcity, if more particularly because of their merit, periodicals like the *Monthly Review* and the *British Critic* especially, and to a lesser extent the *Critical Review,* reprinted considerable extracts from Jones's articles.[6]

Jones was a pioneer in several areas: historical linguistics, comparative etymology, comparative musicology, myth-study, the Western discourse of Sanskrit scholarship and the study of Hinduism. These aspects of his work have been discussed and evaluated by critics. But one more area of study inaugurated by Sir William Jones has not received adequate attention. He was the first British scholar to perceive India in terms of a literary culture. Prior to him, others had translated or mentioned Indian source books as 'texts' of interest in law, grammar, religion, etc. But it was Jones who for the first time firmly established in the British consciousness India's image as a country with rich literature. His hymns and the translation of *Abhijnanasakuntalam*—which attracted serious literary attention in Britain and Germany—effectively made the point that the land of Gentoos (the term used by Halhed for Hindus) is not only the land of antiquity but also a literary nation. He likened Indian literary works to Greek works while speaking of their literary merit:

> Suppose Greek literature to be known in modern Greece only, and there to be in the hands of priests and philosophers; and suppose them to be still worshippers of Jupiter and Apollo; suppose Greece to have been conquered successively by Goths, Huns, Vandals, Tartars, and lastly by the English; then suppose a court of judicature to be established by the British Parliament at Athens, and an inquisitive Englishman to be one of the

> judges; suppose him to learn Greek there, which none of his countrymen know, and to read Homer, Pindar, Plato, which no other Europeans had ever heard of. Such am I in this country.[7]

Jones's discovery of India as a nation with literature, and literature extending to remote antiquity, enthused his readers in Britain to look at India for literary inspiration. Jones himself believed that his discovery of the richness of Indian literature would infuse English literature with a new and powerful imagery. He was not wrong in anticipating the change: a generation of English poets—Coleridge, Shelley, Robert Southey—and the immensely popular Irish poet, Thomas Moore, derived poetic strength from the new image of India that Jones tried to popularise. The new movement, Romanticism, while in no way entirely fuelled by Indology was nonetheless, one in which Jones's literary Gentoo was one of the motivating factors.

Romanticism in English literature was in profound disagreement with the historiographical premises underlying Warton's presentation of English poetry. For Warton, the movement from imagination to reason was the hallmark of literary progress. For the Romantics it was a literary decline. Both Wordsworth and Shelley lavished praise on the primitive and the socially unhindered poetic expression in their critical writings. Warton had acknowledged the contribution of the warmer South at the inception of England's poetic tradition, but had praised the cold reasonableness of the English genius. Byron turned against this aesthetic geography and pushed the heroes of his narrative poetry southward and eastward in search of warmer climates and a more fertile imagination. Warton, who belonged to the Sensibility school of poetry, valued moral restraint, adulthood and social order in conceptualising his history. The Romantics believed on the other hand, in the primacy of innocence, freedom, childhood and the unconscious. Sir William Jones's depiction of Indian literature as comparable to Greek literature in range and richness found its place in the historiographical reversals taking place in Britain at that time but not without a certain distortion of truth which marks all cross-cultural transactions of imagery.

Jones's enthusiasm in proving to his English contemporaries the antiquity of Indian culture and literature made him and his audience forget that Indian literature was a continuously flowing cultural current and that its development in the second millennium was as important as the developments prior to the tenth century. When he compared Indian literature with Greek literature, he did not emphasize the crucial difference between the two, namely, that while Greek culture was a thing of the past, Indian culture was still surviving. In outlining the aims of his researches, Jones had very clearly put down the eleventh century as the historical limit for his enquiries. Having shared the savageology as a component of Indology during his formative years in Britain, Jones could not bring himself to think of India after the eleventh century as a country with a living literary culture. Perhaps, the decline of Sanskrit literary traditions in the Indian *bhashas* failed to win Jones's approval because the library resources and oral information on *bhasha* literatures at his disposal were not adequate to enthuse him about them. The result was that in spite of Jones's pioneering work in establishing India as a literary culture in British literary discourse, the image of Indian literature created by him could never escape the state of being chained to antiquity, almost like Shelley's Prometheus or Blake's Albion in *Jerusalem*.

In India, Jones had a phenomenal following. Partly owing to his success in British literary circles and partly owing to the demands of the colonial situation, practically every British civil servant working in India throughout the nineteenth century took an interest in Indian learning and culture. One wrote at least travel books adding to the available information about India in Britain; but none crossed the line of historical demarcation that Jones had drawn. The result was that by the end of the nineteenth century British, German and French scholars came to believe firmly that the only literature in India fit for cross-cultural dissemination and worth comparing with Greek, Latin, English, French or German literature was the canon of texts in Sanskrit, or occasionally in Persian. The rest was all decline and degradation. This image provided the narcissistic structure of European—and in particular English—literature with an image of the 'other' literature. If the history of English literature was—as laid down in the historiography initiated by Warton—progress, the history of Indian literature was, as perceived from Jones's *Asiatic Researches*, a continuous decline. Jones focused his attention on the past of Indian literature and, by the same token, diminished in great proportion the image of literature in the bhashas. There was an unintended agreement between Warton's savageology and Jones's Indology, namely, savages may be opulent in their imagination but they do not know how to cultivate it so that it receives the blessings of reason. The two pioneers shared the view that savages rest content with their past, they need no present.

About half a century after Sir William Jones began his exploration of the Indian literary past, the British opinion of India's literary wealth had gone through a radical reversal. In Britain, the Romantic revolution had come to a dead-end, the Utilitarians had taken over the task of forming public opinion, the signs of social unrest had started gaining momentum, gathering themselves towards the 'sinister' Chartist Movement, and the British government had become politically more alert to the affairs of the expanding empire. It was in this context of social rift at home and political assertion abroad that Lord Macaulay denied the imagery of Indian literature circulated by Jones' researches. In fact, Macaulay was not alone in this distrust of Jones's imagery of India. James Mill, his contemporary, had no hesitation in raising doubts about Jones's Sanskrit scholarship. Mill was convinced that though Jones had praised the *Ramayana* so lavishly, he had never read it.[8] The Macaulay generation was doing to the past of Indian literature what Jones had done to its present, namely, attempting to wipe it out of India's cultural memory. Though Indologists following Jones kept working at their researches throughout the nineteenth century, the process of reducing the history of Indian literature went on unhindered. Occasionally, someone like Friedrich Max Muller succeeded in temporarily averting the process; but in the colonial situation the odds against such solitary attempts were heavy.

The British image of Indian literature had taken such a beating during colonial rule in the nineteenth century, and the sense of British superiority over India in the domain of artistic culture and the notion that Indians had no sense of history were so fully consolidated, that, in the first quarter of the twentieth century, a patriotic poet like Sri Aurobindo had to launch a crusade against these biases. He wrote a passionate defence of Indian culture in his *Foundations of Indian Culture.* Though the immediate reason prompting Sri Aurobindo to write his monumental book, first serialised through the *Arya,* was to counter William Archer's attack on Indian culture, he was at the same time responding to the colonial imagery of Indian literature and culture.

William Archer's negative criticism had enraged even some British Indologists, one of whom, Sir John Woodroffe, wrote a rejoinder under the title 'Is India Civilised?' Sri Aurobindo entered the debate through the columns of his journal *Arya* and proposed that Archer's criticism of Indian literature and culture was nothing if not politically motivated. "But hostile criticism to be of any sound value must be criticism," retorts Aurobindo, "not slander and false witness, not vitriol-throwing."[10] He pointed out that Archer's book, "had an ulterior, a political object; it started with the underlying idea that India must be proved barbarous in order to damage or destroy her case of self-government."[11] Yet Aurobindo did not overlook the benefits of facing a rationalist critique of Indian culture. He fully examines the grounds on which such a critique could be raised. While undertaking an elaborate defence of Indian literature and culture he did not forget to offer his own critique both of Indian tradition and European modernity. In the process he offers an original historiography for Indian literature, a historiography which avoided Jones's lop-sided appreciation of the past and Macaulay's thoughtless negation of the tradition of Indian literature. In this sense, Sri Aurobindo was the first original historiographer of Indian literature during the twentieth century.

Sri Aurobindo argued in his passionate defence of Indian culture that though temporarily occluded, it was not an entirely atrophied culture. "The greatness of the ideals of the past is a promise of the greater ideals of the future." He pointed out that 'civilization' and 'barbarism' are relative terms, and to 'civilize' India on the lines offered by European models would go against the central principle of cultural evolution in India. He added that in order to understand

and fully appreciate the principle of evolution it is necessary to have an indigenous perspective:

> Certainly we must repel with vigour every disintegrating or injurious attack; but it is more important to form our own true and independent view of our own past achievement, present position and future possibilities,—what we were, what we are and what we may be. In our past we must distinguish all that was great, essential, elevating, vitalising, illuminating, victorious, effective. And in that again we must distinguish what was close to the permanent, essential spirit and the persistent law of our cultural being and separate from it what was temporary and transiently formulative. For all that was great in the past cannot be preserved as it was or repeated for ever; there are new needs, there are other vistas before us.[12]

The last sentence alludes to the pervasive debate between the advocates of 'tradition' *(sanatana* or *purana)* and the advocates of 'modernity' *(nutana* or *adhunika)* carried out in India throughout the nineteenth century. If William Jones's work gave rise to a new discourse about the literary past, the debate during the so-called Indian Renaissance gave rise to the concept of a radical break between the past and the present. Though Sri Aurobindo sought to reconcile the past and the present, the social history of India during the century preceding Aurobindo's historiography had made such a happy reconciliation almost impossible. Through a series of collaborative attempts from the times of Raja Rammohan Roy to the beginning of the twentieth century, the British administrators in India and Indians seeking Anglicisation had made the knowledge of English language and English literature synonymous with progress and modernization.

The single most important factor influencing historiography in India after the Asiatic researches of Jones was the creation of the classroom for literary appreciation. Jones had highlighted Indian literary tradition in a fragmented manner; the literary classroom further eroded the authority of that tradition by validating a new and alien canon of literature. It may be of interest to us to investigate this link between the canon and the classroom.

11

Formation and Transformation of a Canon

Conventionally, the history of a literature is viewed as the history of the formation of canon and its subsequent transformations. The process of canon formation implies acts of inclusion and exclusion of literary texts, trends and traditions. One of the prime factors motivating these acts is the dominant ideological position within a given culture. When this position changes, there is a corresponding change in the literary canon. Thus formations of literary canons reflect the formation and transformation of ideological positions and power relations. When a power relation involving the domination of one culture by another involves a collision between the respective literary canons, both canons undergo a radical change. On the one hand, even minor texts, trends and traditions within the literary canon of the dominating culture are given high aesthetic value. On the other hand, even major texts, trends and traditions within the dominated culture are given a relatively low aesthetic value. The literary history of politically dominating culture swells; the literary history of politically dominated culture shrinks. Subsequently, the 'low' value literary aesthetics starts making attempts to internalise the 'high' literary aesthetics. Thus, the 'high' value literary aesthetics starts influencing the 'low' value literary aesthetics. It is when cultural ingression follows colonial formations of literary aesthetics that literary canons of the dominating society become the literary *kanuns* for the dominated society.

The English term 'canon' has several meanings; but most of them relate to religion and legal authority. The term originates in the Greek *kanon*, where it meant 'rule', 'rod for measuring', 'standard', etc. In Latin, it came to acquire religious meaning: 'church decree', 'a church office', etc. During the Middle Ages the term was used to designate a body of religious Christian laws. This meaning is still current. Gradually, the term came to be applied to music, to indicate a ground rule in musical composition, and to literature, to indicate a given set of ancient and modern 'classics'. There are other meanings of the term which need not interest us here. One would have thought that the term *kanun* used in most Indian languages to indicate a set of moral or legal conventions has been accepted from one of the modern European languages. However, the case seems to be different, for we find this term in other Eastern languages such as Arabic and Persian. Possibly, it has a close link with the Islamic concept of *ka* indicating spiritual purity. Or, perhaps, the Arabic and Greek *kanun/kanon* have their origin in the mysterious past of the Indo-European family of languages. However, what is important here for us is that the concept of a canon existed, as the linguistic evidence shows, in the Indian languages and in English independently from the pre-colonial times. Since the concept was already available in the Indian languages, it may not have been difficult for Indian literatures to grasp the notion of English literary canon when the colonial encounter took place. Moreover, it may not have been a difficult passage for English literary canons to become the Indian literary *kanun*. This particular process occupies a centrally important place in history and historiography of modern Indian literatures. The institutional teaching of English literature has been the chief agent in its becoming a canon. Introduction of English literature in Indian education has been the more visible consequence of the literary-historical process in England; and the impoverishment of critical sensibility in India has been its less obvious but more damaging consequence.

If the history of English literature, that is literature to which the modern reader can relate, extends back to the fourteenth century, the history of institutionalized teaching of literature, has, in contrast, had a brief run of not more than a century. Introduction of the study of English in higher education in England was a result of the pressure to keep the British hold over its Indian empire, and was historically subsequent to the introduction of English study in India. The teaching of English in British schools was a result of the social and class tensions within British society during the nineteenth century. On the whole, one sees a general neglect of literary education throughout British history. If one compares the place given to literature in British social life and in some of its former colonies such as Ireland and India, the British neglect of literature becomes strikingly evident.

For centuries in its initial history, England did not have any civilized forms of education. Children were allowed to receive rudimentary private instruction till the age of seven, and then they were handed over to a guardian for vocational apprenticeship which continued till the age of fourteen. In *Beowulf*, the hero recounts that he was sent at the age of seven to the court of king Herthel, his grandfather. In such a system there was no possibility of literary education. The vestiges of this system can be found in the general upbringing of English children even today. In comparison to an Indian child, or an African child, an average English child receives far less literary input from its parents in its upbringing in early childhood. English society depends for literary education either on self-study or institutional education. This is also reflected, perhaps, in the discourse of criticism that English society has developed. No literary critic in England—except the ostracized generation of English Romantic critics—ever displays a childlike sense of wonder towards creativity and language. The critical attitudes reflect highly institutionalized, conventional observations which can be empirically verified. This is so, perhaps because an average English literary scholar gets to know his literature at a slightly more advanced age than literary scholars in India.

Organized education, not only literary education but any education at all, is of twelfth century origin in England. The medieval world , in the Orient as well as in Christian Europe, had evolved indigenous systems of higher learning. There were well developed universities in Italy, China, Persia and India around the beginning of the present millennium; and these offered systematic education in classical literature. The concept of a university in medieval England was very different from that in contemporary Italy, China or India. Joan Simon, a historian of medieval British education who has studied the social roots of education, comments:

> The medieval universities were not centres of higher education as the term is now understood, or of research at the expense of teaching as is sometimes held against universities today. Their primary concerns, which shaped not only curriculum and methods but scholarship itself, was the teaching of intending teachers. To examine the tradition established from this point of view casts light on various problems which are still actual.[1]

In medieval English universities the least important faculty was, we are told, the Arts faculty. This faculty was seen as a place for preparatory education leading to higher courses, though teaching in schools was geared towards training students to take up an Arts education. Thus the Arts faculty was somewhat like a 'junior college'. It was concerned with the seven liberal arts: grammar, rhetoric and logic (the trivium) and arithmetic, geometry, music, astronomy (the quadrivium). The aim of this education was primarily utilitarian:

> The surest sign of a learned and wise man is his ability to teach what he knows, said Aristotle. Medieval universities inherited from the ancient world, and the fathers of the church, the idea that knowledge is for teaching. Indeed the church itself rested on the idea that, after God first taught man, it remained for a chosen body... to continue this teaching to see the world to its end...[2]

Pragmatism has been a strength of English education all through its history. However, subjects like literature and the arts do not find much favour in utilitarian educational systems. To turn back to our narrative, English education stood, at the beginning of this millennium, in sharp contrast to the more lively education on the Continent, not to mention the extremely sophisticated Oriental education. In the Continental universities it was a common practice to employ complex philosophical and poetic texts for the purpose of refining the intellectual abilities of students.

The text used was known as *littera* which was analysed through dialogues between the teacher and the taught. Here is an instance:

> *Teacher:* You should know that when the ancients were about to expound a text they asked seven questions: author, the title of the work, its nature, the purpose of the author, the number and sequence of the books and then the interpretation of the text itself. Nowadays we are satisfied if four things are established about a work: its subject matter, its aim, its underlaying purpose and what branch of philosophy it belongs to.
>
> *Pupil:* Tell me what matter, aim and underlaying purpose are.[3]

Historians of medieval education such as Anders Piltz tell us that the *littera* was not only an item in the curriculum, but an interpretative strategy too. Contemporary English education was totally innocent of such interpretative strategies.

The Renaissance saw major and radical developments in English education. These were collectively initiated by John Foxe's *Book of Martyrs* (1563), which was a radical history of Christianity, the *Thirty-nine Articles,* and the *Oath of Supremacy* (both in 1563), which defined the relation between the Crown and the Church.[4] The oath imposed on 'all schoolmasters and public and private teachers of children' ensured that they recognised the supremacy of the Queen in Church matters before receiving their Episcopal licences to teach. In addition, a scheme of inspection of schools was provided for, to ensure that 'lewd schoolmasters' were not 'corrupting religion'.

Sir William Cecil, Queen Elizabeth's principal Secretary of State, was appointed in 1561 Master of the Court Wards, an office he held for thirty-seven years. At Cecil House in the Strand he set up what has been called 'the best school for statesmen in Elizabethan England, perhaps in all Europe' [5] The curriculum of this school included subjects like mathematics, geography, physics, surgery, philosophy, Greek, Latin, Hebrew, logic, rhetoric, Spanish, Italian, French and High Dutch. It did not include English as a subject. The literary education included a study of the classics, elements of style and language. The Elizabethans did not think English works fit to be included in school syllabuses. Education was firmly wedded to priorities set by the Crown and the Church. Robert Browne, who ran a school in London without licence, tried to escape this extra-academic domination, and was saved from being punished for it, thanks only to his kinship with Cecil.

In India, in any given age, literary education quickly assimilated new works of literature into established canons. This happened to the literary texts in Pali during the advent of Buddhism, to Lingayata and other *bhakti* texts during the early centuries of the present millennium, and more recently, to English literary texts during the so-called Renaissance. Such assimilation of new or alien literary texts into the realms of knowledge becomes possible in cultures which think of language in terms of a divine presence, *shakti* or power. The attitude to language inherited by the Elizabethans was anatomical, one which perceived language as a body to be dissected. The results of this metaphysics of language were reflected in the pedagogic rituals of the classroom, and literary education had to occupy the back benches there.

Throughout the last four centuries of English educational history, the main emphasis has been on education of materially useful subjects such as science and technology, medicine, law and economics. Until the beginning of the high Romantic cultural revolt, there was practically no spokesman for the cause of English literary education; and till the generation of I. A. Richards and F. R. Leavis the spokesmen have been either feeble or ambivalent in their persuasions regarding the need to introduce English literature in the British education system.

Many ideas relating to education developed through the institution of the coffee house in eighteenth century England. It was through coffee houses that the British Society for Encouragement of Arts originated. Among the members of this society, two chemists, William Shipley and Robert Dossie, impressed Dr. Johnson so much that he proposed to help them set up a centre for dissemination of scientific ideas. The literary study that enjoyed high reputation in the eighteenth century was that of the classics; and as a poor substitute for those who were in no position to undertake it, many writers, including John Dryden and Alexander Pope, produced English translations of classical works.

The Romantic Age produced a strong reaction to the advocacy of exclusively scientific learning. Growth in literary criticism and the interest in institutionalizing literary education are closely interrelated, as argued by Chris Baldick in *The Social Mission of English Criticism: 1848–1932.*[6] It is possible, therefore, to connect the growing body of literary criticism during the Romantic Age with the emergent awareness of English as a subject. However, it should not be forgotten that during the last decade of the eighteenth century and the first two decades of the nineteenth century a tremendously valuable treasure of Arabic, Persian and Sanskrit literature was being made available to the more serious reading public in England through the Indological translations. Moreover, those who started using English texts in schools were persons who had some exposure to other cultures, as in the case of Hannah More. She borrowed ideas on education from France, and started using English literary texts enthusiastically in her classroom. A certain Reverend Leigh Richmond brought out his *Dairyman's Daughter* (1809), about the same time as Mrs. Sherwood, wife of a colonial servant in the 53rd regiment in India, sent home a best-selling story called *Little Henry and His Bearer.* A historian of British education comments:

> Sold to a Shropshire publisher for £5, it inaugurated Mrs. Sherwood's career just as that of her old schoolfellow, Jane Austen, was closing. What Jane Austen became for Victorian adults, Mrs. Sherwood became for their children. *Little Henry* marked the first impact of her work on a society where the nursery and governess were soon to flourish.[7]

These and other such popular texts were used for English study in British schools for the lower classes during the early part of the nineteenth century. At the same time, a few 'higher' books in this field such as Hugh Blair's *Lectures on Rhetorics and Belles Letters* (1784) started becoming influential. The first Chair of English was established in 1828 at the University College of London University. To this Chair was appointed a person who was a philologist rather than a literary scholar. These isolated facts correctly reflect the tensions within the newly emergent field: the antagonism between philology and literary study which subsequently gave two distinct models of English to Oxford and Cambridge, respectively; the class-monopoly of higher knowledge related to literature, with English as the poor man's field, and the growing need of culture-control in the colonies. These were to become the three central themes of the history of English throughout the nineteenth century. Matthew Arnold must have found himself caught in these conflicts, which in turn formed the greater conflict between 'culture' and 'anarchy'. He wrote, therefore

> Why no effective remedy is applied to this serious evil... [is]... because the upper class amongst us do not want to be disturbed in their preponderance, or the middle class in their vulgarity. Even though these prejudices are unconscious, the result is the same.[8]

The nineteenth century had much to say about intuition, inspiration and imagination; it generated some of the most hostile critiques of science; yet, its educational philosophy was always in favour of science education. Cardinal Newman as well as Matthew Arnold felt that a knowledge of poetry was necessary to bring refinement to minds rendered unimaginative by too much science education. Poetry was to be the finishing touch. The nineteenth century English ideology of education was freely borrowed from Germany. Here again, true to its utilitarian and pragmatic grain the English mind felt more easily attracted to German education in the sciences than that in literature. England's most distinguished inspector of schools, an Oxford Professor of Poetry, and a great poet himself, said in 1872 that

> it is in science that we must need to borrow from the German universities. The French university has no liberty, and the English universities have no science; the German universities have both.[9]

The study of English, as against that of the classics, took a considerably low priority in Arnold's vision of culture.

British progress in institutionalizing literary study during the nineteenth century was very slow. The Indological scholars had brought to Britain a fund of knowledge about ancient traditions of Oriental literature kept alive through their systematic transmission from generation to generation. The German philosophers had given British intellectuals a new branch of knowledge called Aesthetics. Ever since the Napoleonic wars and the unification of Italy, the growing spirit of nationalism had created a national bias in other areas of human study. And above all, there was a sufficiently large number of English literary texts which compared well with the classics. Yet, none of these reasons for initiating the study of English appealed to the English mind. The reasons that did appeal were of extreme pragmatic expediency. The two hallmarks of the nineteenth century British attitude to literary study were insularity and utilitarianism. No literary texts from the colonial world were ever accepted as being of any literary value; and no policy decisions were made unless they were impelled by economic or political considerations.

All through the century, several regulations about the kind and quality of British education were passed by the British government. It is interesting to see the more central concerns of some of those regulations. The 1839 document about the creation of the Committee of Council for Education stated[10] that the aim of education was to save British society from the menace of crime. School children from the poorer classes are described in this document as "pauper orphans, children deserted by their parents, offspring of criminals and their associates. It is from this class that the thieves and housebreakers of society are continually recruited."[11] Naturally, literature had no place in the plans of educators whose perception of poverty was so hidebound. In fact, the Wales Education Inquiry Report of 1847[12] records that "an opulent proprietor (of a private school) had withdrawn his annual subscription of £1 because writing had, against his judgement, been added to the subjects of instruction."[13]

The standards of school education in Britain during the

nineteenth century were very low. The aims of school education, reflecting the literary expectations from children, as recorded in the Minutes of 1846 Committee on Education[14] were: "To read with fluency, ease and expression; To write in a neat hand with correct spelling and punctuation, a simple prose narrative slowly read to them; To point out parts of speech in a simple sentence", and so on.[15] These objectives did not change until 1861, when the Newcastle Report was compiled. That report gave English literary texts a place in the school curriculum for the first time in the history of British education. This provision was finally consolidated in 1904 by the Regulation of Secondary Schools, which stipulated that a certain minimum number of teaching hours be given to English and allied subjects.[16] These changes were closely connected with the economic history of industrial Britain, and the political history of its colonial empire.

Britain's overseas interests were one of the primary motivations for the growth of English studies in Britain during the nineteenth century. Chris Baldick records three primary causes for it:

> We can isolate three factors which ensured literary study, in particular of English literature, a permanent place in higher education. These are first, the specific needs of the British empire expressed in the regulations for admission to the Indian Civil Service; second, the various movements for adult education including Mechanics Institutes, Working Men's Colleges, and extension lecturing; third, within this general movement, the specific provisions made for women's education.[17]

The introduction of English literature in the syllabus for the Civil Services examination was soon followed by its introduction into other competitive examinations in Britain. Thus knowledge of English literature became a passport to easy success and affluence. Many British scholars made use of this opportunity by starting private tuition and coaching classes. One of the great pioneers of English study, and a candidate for the Oxford English chair, John Churton Collins, was involved in engaging tuitions for some time for Civil Services aspirants; and scholars took pride in their being appointed as examiners for the Civil Services. Matthew Arnold was an ICS examiner, and he was proud to be one. Walter Raleigh was another such scholar.[18]

The reasons for introducing English as a major component of Indian Civil Services examination were far from being literary. Macaulay, who institutionalized English studies in India, had expressed his fear in an address to the British House of Commons that if the British did not learn their literature, the day was not far off when the Indian subjects of the Crown would surpass Britain in literary scholarship. His own words were:

> Consider too, Sir, how rapidly the public mind of India is advancing, how much attention is already paid by the higher classes of the natives to those intellectual pursuits on the cultivation of which the superiority of the European race principally depends. Surely, in such circumstances, from motives of selfish policy, if from no higher motive, we ought to fill the magistracies of our Eastern Empire with men who may do honour to our country, with men who may present the best part of the English nation.[19]

It should be noted that the moral calibre of the Company administrators during the three-quarters of a century from 1757 to Macaulay's mission in India had been consistently low. The British government would probably not have bothered much to cure this malaise had it not been for its immediate effects on the political and public life in Britain itself. The flow of money from Bengal, through the Company administrators and investors, towards British elections, had created unprecedented corruption there. All through the first half of the nineteenth century the situation had been worsening. Besides, the signs of native resistance to colonization meant that the colonial administration had to be improved. Thus the question of colonial success got tagged on to the moral quality of the British administration. It was felt, therefore, that it would be desirable to select prospective administrators from among those who had received literary education. In recognition of this pressing need of the day, the Civil Service of the East India Company Report of 1855 stipulated that a maximum of 1000 marks be allotted to the sections on

English literature and history. The report said:

> Foremost among these subjects we place our own language and literature... to (enable them to) show the extent of the knowledge of our poets, wits and philosophers.... (In imparting) a taste for pleasures not sensual, literature would help the young administrators to resist the dangers of corruption and 'scandalous immorality' to which their power might expose them.[20]

The needs abroad—to keep literate administrators in good supply, and to keep ahead of the Indian educated class in literary scholarship—were matched at home by the need to contain the growing sections of literate women and tradesmen. The Chartist Movement had given the British upper classes a taste of the social consequences of industrialization. Therefore, a movement like Christian Socialism, which dreamt of uniting classes through common sympathies, found English literature a useful political tool to ward off social discontent. English thus became, in England and in the colonies, a civilizing subject.[21]

In Warton's historiography the genius of the English people lay in civilizing the barbarous imagination of the 'rude' nations. In the colonial institutionalization of English literature as a canon for the classroom was implicit the faith that English literature could civilize the rude nations colonized by the British. Such a perspective of literature invariably surfaces through literary criticism and literary history. Critical texts and literary histories are essentially the tools of literary pedagogy. Therefore, when literature becomes an institutionalized practice and a classroom subject, there inevitably occurs a proliferation of histories and digests of literature. All histories of English written after Warton's pioneering work followed one general guiding principle, namely, they divided the course of English literature into three broad periods, the old, the middle and the modern. Where exactly to place the lines of demarcation between these periods was a matter of the individual historian's freedom and choice, but to place these lines of demarcation was the general practice. Two more subsidiary principles were used by literary historians in England. The first was to make a historical classification of literary production in terms of the political history of England by using categories such as the Elizabethan Age and the Victorian Age. The second was to categorize it in terms of style-periods or theme-periods such as Romanticism and Modernism. When 'civilizing' becomes the central purpose and concern of literature, 'periodization' becomes the central historiographical principle. How can one prove the civilizing effects of literature if one did not divide it in terms of a dark period and a luminous period?

The impact of this historiography was profound. Jones had already spoken of a luminous ancient period of Indian literature. The advocates of *nutana* and the educated classes of colonial Indians held forth the promise of a new vibrant era in literature that India would produce by following the British models and modernizing native traditions. Naturally, therefore, the Middle Ages, the centuries from the eleventh to the eighteenth were designated the dark period. Jones had given his tacit consent to the concept of the darkness of the intervening centuries. The influence of English literature on Indian literary education strengthened the assumption. That it had no real historical support and that the so-called dark age had, in fact, given rise to several vibrant and highly experimental literary traditions in the bhashas was a matter easily overlooked and pushed into the twilight region of cultural amnesia.

After all, Jones had not only discovered Indian literature, he had also inaugurated a style of writing about it. The institutionalized literary education enhanced the importance of writing about literature. Thus history as the story of the past became more important than history as the past itself. Since Westernisation or Anglicisation was seen as a mark of progress in thought and vision, it became necessary for those with a vested interest in the literary classroom to make their writing about the literary past as similar as possible to that prevalent in England.

The influence of the notion of canon and period on the Indian sense of literary tradition resulted in the denial of literary status to all non-secular and sectarian literary works. Traditionally, the links between the canonical and the non-canonical had been intimate and strong in India. The written and the oral were not distinct in qualitative terms. The high-brow and the low-brow had been mutually interdependent, and the *marg* and the *deshi* had a fascinating history of fruitful exchanges. But these relationships were ignored, suppressed and erased by historiography hedged in by the notions of progress, period and canon. Warton, Jones and the literary classroom, between them, brought about this unintended result and turned what the web of literary traditions had held as sacred into vulgar and rude. If, as Warton maintained, the rude nations of the Orient had provided imaginative sources to English literature, Warton's historiography —which was one of the products of colonialism—deprived India of its right to designate a large part of its imaginative products as 'literature'. If the image of the Orient as the barbaric Other had given English poetry a sense of its historical vitality, the view of Indian literature through the colonial British perspective deprived it of just that sense of historic vitality.

It may be appropriate to conclude this brief account of the impact of colonialism on literary historiography in India by quoting from a well-researched account of various histories of Indian literature by Sujit Mukherjee:

> English literature was a major subject in our higher education, and through it we received our most abiding concept of literary history—namely, that the history of a language ought to be studied in order to appreciate the literature in that language, from where it seemed to follow that the history of a literature is the extension or elaboration of the history of that language. As the study of modern Indian languages entered our universities, courses were designed on the pattern of English literature courses. If the English language could look back to Anglo-Saxon and Teutonic speeches for parentage, so could most Indian languages to Sanskrit. On the Grimm-given analogy of Old English/Middle English/Modern English, each regional language that earned university-level study was fitted into a similar sequence even if the ancestry of each language did not lend itself comfortably to such treatment. Uncertainty about dates of composition made it possible for literary works to be assigned to arbitrary

> chronological periods, while western terms were freely borrowed to describe forms and trends in Indian writing. By planting a 'Romantic Movement' in the virgin soil of our literary historiography, we hopefully tried to ensure the sprouting of a healthy crop of modern literature in all our languages. That this entire strategy belongs to a unilanguage literary culture like that of England's has never deterred our literary historians from applying it wholesale to our multi-lingual literary culture.[22]

Any further comment is unnecessary!

However, it is well worth recording that the 'Grimm-given' model seems to have limited the influence on literary historiography to the classroom only. It is necessary to differentiate between the histories produced as intended textbooks and the approaches to the literary past implicit in the writings of thinkers, writers and critics. It is more profitable, therefore, to examine some of the major approaches to the history of Indian literature implicit in the writings of significant thinkers and creative writers while determining the extent of the colonial influence in literary historiography. In the following two sections an attempt is made to review the dominant philosophies of literary history in the West and some contemporary approaches to literary history in India. These outlines, though by no means comprehensive, should help us to determine the extent to which the allegedly nonexistent sense of a literary past in pre-colonial India was affected by the influence of Western literary historiography.

12

Some Western Approaches to Literary History

Hans Robert Jauss, one of the chief figures, along with Wolfgang Iser in the Constanz Group,[1] has done writing of significance on the question of literary history. At the beginning of one of his celebrated essays, he writes:

> In our time literary history has increasingly fallen into disrepute, and not at all without reason. The history of this worthy discipline in the last one hundred and fifty years unmistakably describes the path of a steady decline. Its greatest achievements all belong to the nineteenth century. To write the history of national literature counted, in the times of Gervinus and Scherer, De Sanctis and Lanson, as the crowning life work of the philologist. The patriarchs of the discipline saw their highest goal therein, to represent in the history of literary works *(dichtwerke)* the idea of national individuality on its way to itself. This high point is already a distant memory. The received form of literary history scarcely scratches out a living for itself in the intellectual life of our own time.[2]

Had Jauss paused after mentioning that nationalism provided the breeding climate for literary historicism, he would have, perhaps, chanced upon the other factor responsible for its growth, namely, colonialism. Naturally, with the decline in nationalism and colonialism, there has been a corresponding decline in literary historicism in Europe. However, during the two centuries of its history, Europe has made a remarkably impressive contribution to the field. It is impossible to present even a brief outline of all major European thinkers in the field of general and literary historiography. Almost every major European thinker from Hegel to Foucault has made some contribution to this field. Of these, we will examine some major strands by taking up three specific theoretical texts.[3] They are: R. S. Crane's *Critical and Historical Principles of Literary History* (1967); Gyorgy Lukacs's *Notes on the Theory of Literary History* (1910); and Hans Robert Jauss's *Literary History as a Challenge to Literary Theory* (1970). These texts have been widely acclaimed as major texts on literary historiography. Besides, literary historiography is the main and professed subject of these three texts. Therefore, they are less ambiguous in their historiographic attitudes than texts not primarily about historiography. The main reason for selecting these three texts is that they are representative of the historical discourses to which they belong, and taken together, cover the entire ground of Western discourse of literary historiography. Crane's aesthetic argument represents the established line of historiography; Lukacs's text, with its Marxist leanings, represents the counter discourse of European historiography; and Jauss's text, propounding the reception aesthetics represents both a cross between Crane and Lukacs, as well as the more recent theoretical trends in literary thought. Jauss's historiography is a discourse resulting from the clash between the two other discourses—a second generation and a second order discourse.

Crane's literary historiography comes from the literary and critical concerns of what is referred to by its adherents as liberal humanism. Though extremely ennobling, the critical concerns of this branch of literary study stem from the belief that literature is a civilizing subject. Firmly rooted in the historical necessity to create a mystique around literature, the liberal humanistic criticism culminated in the Anglo-American Formalism through various branches: Richards's Practical Criticism, Leavis's Traditionalism, New Criticism and Neo-Aristotelianism in the USA. In all these branches of Anglo-American Formalism, a work of art is considered a kind of mystery, an aesthetic structure, the beauty of which can be explained only in its own terms. Hence all critical attention is to be focused on the construction of a literary work.

Crane's essay on the principles of literary history begins by observing that literary criticism often follows two misleading modes of interpretation, the philological or grammatical mode, and the dialectical mode. The first mode merely connects parts of a work with comparable parts of other works. The second mode employs a bipolar scheme of perception in which the form and the content are treated separately, and, worse still, are profoundly misrepresented. Crane offers minute descriptions of the formal aspects of literature, and concludes that forms, materials, techniques, and individual achievements are "the major variables which must be combined somehow in any adequate narrative history of literary forms."[4] If literary histories are expected to explain the chronological changes taking place in these elements, then histories tend to be insufficiently 'literary' or critical in orientation when the principle of change alone becomes operative. Crane names the predominantly 'historical' history of literature "atomistic history". To this type, Crane finds opposition in the type he calls "organic history". Organic history does, unlike the atomistic history, explain causation and succession of literary events. However, its drive is towards reconciling historical antitheses. A third type of history described by Crane is "narrative causal history", which has a greater capacity to disengage the complexities of historical changes. In his own words, the differences between the organic history and narrative history are:

> In the first place, the continuity achieved in narrative history is the continuity not of a dialectical integration of historical differences in terms of a single analogy or scheme. Rather it is the continuity of a sequence of distinct events connected causally by whatever individual men or groups of men, through a period of time, happened to do with respect to the element constituting the continuum of the change. Accordingly, the degree of integration attainable in such a history depends upon the possibility of discovering causal connections, in materials,

> techniques, forms, or ends, among the different sequences with which it deals. The particular contrarities in a narrative history, therefore, cannot be deduced from any unified scheme of common terms.[5]

In Crane's view the difficulty in writing a literary history which offers a 'systematic' causal explanation for literary phenomena, is that causal connections between the preconstruction stage and the construction stages of literature never really explain the aesthetic form of a literary work. This difficulty has its source in Crane's literary philosophy which views literary structures as self-sufficient and autonomous entities. In other words, the formal structure of literature can be explained more effectively by using the principles of literary criticism rather than the principles of historical criticism. Thus, Crane's historiography is an attempt to establish the primacy of practical criticism over philological criticism even in the sphere of literary history. In his view, history is not all historical criticism; it is, in fact, more of a practical formal analysis of forms, techniques, and materials of art. Here is the focal statement of Crane's historiography:

> In any history founded on the principle of artistic synthesis the central though by no means exclusive emphasis would be on the constructional aspects of literary works considered from the point of view of the problems faced by writers in the process of making poems, dramas, or narratives of different kinds. The collective enterprise of historians in this mode would consequently have as its ultimate purpose the writing of a narrative-causal history of the various literary arts in terms of four things.[6]

These four things are: formal ends, materials, new devices and techniques, and actualisation of these formal elements in literary production.

It should be clear that Crane considers the aesthetic aspects of literary art to be of supreme importance. The events to be dealt with by the literary historian are, to follow Crane, only aesthetic events such as the invention of new techniques, art materials, devices, formal modes, and so on. This kind of literary historiography overlooks, if it does not deny altogether, the pre-constructional condition of literature. The assumption behind such a position is that there are critical standards and procedures of literary assessment that have a universal standing and validity. One can indeed think of critical standards and procedures of evalution in terms of universality within the limited sphere of Western or European literatures. But when those standards or procedures are applied to literary works outside Western or European cultures, their universality seems to shrink.

Critical standards, values, procedures originate within specific cultural and historical contexts, and are relevant and useful for those specific traditions and contexts. The European canons of criticism acquired universal currency during the coercive cultural context of colonialism.[7] If one were to use those canons for constructing the history of Indian literature, a large bulk of good Indian literature will have to be left out and a large bulk of imitative, and therefore weak, literature will have to be given an important place in the narrative. Thus the critical concepts to be used as tools of literary history need to be culture-specific. Once this argument is accepted, it will follow that the discourse of literature cannot be autonomous; it is created and acquires meaning within a culture where it is circulated as a system of meaning. And, if literature is not an autonomous system, Crane's historiography needs to be radically altered before putting it to use in postcolonial literary cultures.

The fact that history precedes criticism is accepted by the Marxist-literary historiography, of which George (Gyorgy) Lukacs is an extremely important spokesman. His *Notes on the Theory of Literary History* was first published in 1910 in Hungarian, and has become available in English through Ian Fairley's translation. It is a work from Lukacs's early phase, known generally as his pre-Marxist phase. This particular work forms a fine balance *vis-a-vis* Crane's text belonging to the post-New Criticism phase. Thus, here we are not dealing with extremes of historiographical positions, but rather more balanced and nuanced positions on it.

Any reader of Lukacs's literary history, with a pre-determined idea of Lukacs as a hardcore Marxist theorist, is likely to be surprised by his energetic advocacy of the formal elements of a literary work. Lukacs's theory does not dispense with poetics and criticism at all. On the contrary, it stresses that "without poetics, literary history would lack all perspective other than that of pure sociology." [8] It is logical then to expect in Lukacs's theory an idea of form which has some legitimacy as a 'purely aesthetic construct'. The notion of form in this theory is highly intriguing, and it is central to his argument. Lukacs considers form as a psychic reality; and art exists only through form. "Within the field of literature the concept of form has no mutually exclusive opposite; there are only ever degrees of form. That which literary history and criticism in practice call 'formless' is, at most, only badly or unsuccessfully formed."[9] However, one must carefully distinguish between the idea of form in Lukacs and that in the Formalists and New Critics. For the Formalists, form is an essential hypothesis related to the inter-relationship among constituents of art. For Lukacs, form is a means of communication, and without form there can be no aesthetic communication. "Literature is therefore the communication of lived experience, and the medium of this communication is form. Form is the truly social constituent of literature..."[10]

The sociological nature of form has two important aspects: it is sociological because it mediates between the creator and the recipient; and it is sociological also because the material (such as language) that it forms is socially determined.[11] Or to represent Lukacs's views precisely, form is aesthetic in its non-temporal aspect, and sociological in its historical aspect. To combine these two aspects in literary enquiry is the main function of literary history. That is the keynote in his theory of literary history.

> The synthesis of literary history is the combination, in a new, organic unity of sociology and aesthetics. Aesthetics pursues only what is constant within those phenomena that we are accustomed to call literary; sociology attempts to describe and account for change within these phenomena. Literary history is faced with the paradoxical task of uniting these two viewpoints, of pursuing the constant within the variable and the variable within the

> constant. It must seek the developmental possibilities, paths and tendencies of forms conceived within the abstractions of aesthetics, while also pursuing what is constant, regular and recurrent within the highly complex mesh of the literary work, its influence and effects.[12]

The programme proposed here is to legitimize the subjective moment within the historical flow of literature as an institution of cultural production. The legitimation of the subjective within the overall sociological flow is offered by the unity of the aesthetic and the sociological, the non-temporal and the temporal, within the form. Crane's essay, on the other hand, legitimizes the historic dimension of formal, aesthetic structures, by visualizing for history the possibilities of forming a narrative. Thus, though leaning towards opposite ends of the spectrum spanning the private and the public, present and past, aesthetic and social, the later-Crane and the early-Lukacs have a relationship of close collaboration. Within this relationship, disagreements are possible, but within a common context of argument. The *literary* history and literary *history* in the West form a connected discourse and counter-discourse. They co-exist, and continuously define each other.

Writing in 1910, sixty years before the publication of Jauss's *Literary History as a Challenge to Literary Theory,* Lukacs anticipates Jauss's position in a passing flash of vision:

> One can certainly envisage a history of psychical culture (unfortunately, none as yet exists) which endeavouring simply to establish the facts, would describe without any evaluative commentary what people—and, if possible, particular groups and classes of people—read most and liked best in different periods. This type of study is perfectly conceivable—but it would not be literary history.[13]

It is precisely this aspect of literature, which Crane called the post-constructional aspect, that forms the heart of Jauss's literary historiography. Of course, Jauss offers elaborate critiques of Formalistic as well as Marxist concepts of literary historiography, before proposing his own alternative. The critiques offered are, however, based on the hard-line views on both sides. In fact, in his enthusiasm to found a new style of literary historiography,

Jauss even picks up an argument with the Positivistic school of literary history, a school which does not have even the remotest chance of revival. In spite of the strongly articulated disagreement with the three schools of literary historiography, Jauss actually builds upon the foundation laid by them. The central argument of his theory is related to the importance of the process of 'reception' of literature, which completes the process of its becoming 'literature':

> Literature and art only obtain a history that has the character of a process when the succession of works is mediated not only through the producing subject but also through the consuming subject—through the interaction of author and public.[14]

It is in the interchange of the producing subject and the consuming subject that Jauss's theory deviates from Lukacs's. But through this vital shift, Jauss creates a whole new poetics of reception, or what he calls reception-aesthetics. Towards that end, Jauss proposes (true to his German tradition) seven theses. They are, in abridged form:

a) Literary reception should be given priority over literary production.
b) Literary works can be judged advantageously within the context of an "objectifiable system of expectations".
c) Objectively reconstructed horizons of expectations help judge the degree of literary influence and quality of reception.
d) Reference to the past and present horizons of expectations brings in view the hermeneutic difference between the past and the present understanding of a work.
e) Reception aesthetics unfolds the meaning of a single work in its historical sequence, as well as the meaning of the 'literary series'.
f) Reception aesthetics can be strengthened by help from diachronic linguistics so as to create a new reception-historiography.
g) The social function of literature manifests itself in its genuine possibility only where the literary experience of the reader enters into the horizons of expectations.

The essay, formulated in an extremely systematic way through the introductory section and the seven theses, is highly programmatic. It is philosophically sophisticated in the sense that it alludes to numerous European thinkers dealing with aesthetic and historiographic problems, and draws substance from a multitude of philosophers.[15] It is possible, of course, to question the practical viability of Jauss's project. Would it ever be possible to write a history of any literature with reception aesthetics at its centre? However it is not that question that should concern us here. What is of immediate relevance here is that Jauss follows the path of European historiography to its only open frontier. The liberal humanistic and formalistic notions of literary history have concentrated mainly on the idea of literature as a language put in forms, a 'play with signs'. The Marxists, Freudians, structuralists, and others have concentrated on the notion of literature as a web of meaning, a 'represented structure of signifieds'. Reception aesthetics looks at literature as a process of reception, a 'posibility and practice of signification'. Thus the historiographic triangle is complete. It is on some point of this triangle that any given western historiographer stands and argues; it is *this* triangle of concepts of literature which forms the basis of the European discourse of literary historiography. As indicated earlier, the discourse was initiated by the history of colonialism and nationalism. Europe produced its counter-discourse in the Marxist view of history; and the two apparently antithetical positions—liberal humanism and Marxism—though constanly collaborating within a general area of disagreement, are reconciled by the reception theory, a second-order discourse.[16]

The postcolonial understanding of the Western discourse of literary historiography cannot be easily abstracted from the context of the political history within which it emerged, without rendering it mere abstraction. What use is Crane's historiography to literatures that, on perfectly justifiable grounds, have not developed externalized concepts of critical evaluation and classification? Would it be possible to use Lukacs's concept of sociological form in cultures that have been forced to accept literary forms developed in alien sociological conditions as universal and ideal forms of literature? How far can Jauss's theory of reception aesthetics go in communities that have thought of literature as an expression of a supernatural agency, and therefore have not preserved any records of the creators, creations and receptions of literary works?

There are many communities in our postcolonial era that are forced to think of their own literature in terms of myth while they think of the rulers' literature in terms of history. There are other societies, as in India, whose sense of literary history has been badly fractured and amputated during the colonial cultural encounter. All these cultures have to think of literary historiography in terms of their own history and culture. The sophisticated Western discourse of literary history is well developed, indeed. But it cannot be easily extricated from its particular history. It would, however, be very useful to pose for ourselves some of the central problems that were repeatedly posed by Western literary historiography for itself. Jauss has formulated the central one: "[T]oward what end and with what right can one today still—or again—study literary history?" This in itself is a necessary twentieth century replication of the historiographical question raised by Schiller:

> Citations customarily call upon an authority to sanction a step in the process of scholarly reflection. But they can also remind us of a former way of posing a question, to prove that an answer that has become classic is no longer satisfactory, that it has itself become historical again and demands of us a renewal of the process of question and answer.
>
> Schiller's answer to the question of his inaugural lecture at Jena on 26 May 1789, "What is and Toward What End Does One Study Universal History?", is not only representative of historical understanding of German idealism; it is also illuminating for a critical survey of the history of our discipline.[17]

In reviving that question, in posing it afresh for ourselves at this juncture in India, we may try to examine some of the contemporary Indian approaches to literary history.

13

Postcolonial Indian Approaches

It should be stated at the very outset that these are not 'theories' of literary history. They are, rather, positions taken by historiographers, historians, critics and writers with reference to their encounter with literary culture in modern India. These positions can be placed within a broad system of classification in terms of their central concerns. The eight positions are:

1. Literature as a universal entity
2. Literature as a strictly regional entity
3. Literature as a web of divergent trends, styles, etc.
4. Literature as national convergence of trends, styles, etc.
5. Heterodox modernity as a new literary tradition.
6. Modernity as a manifestation of preconditioning tradition.
7. Literature as a perennial recurrence.
8. Literature as a specific temporal occurrence.

Position '1' differs from position '2' on the question of a single language as the basis of a given or postulated literary tradition. Position '3' differs from position '4' on the question of sociology and ideology. Position '5' is different from position '6' in terms of its vision of the native tradition. Position '7' and position '8' hold opposite views on characterization of literary periods and styles. This classification may provide us a tentative framework of historiographical themes in India during the twentieth century. It may also bring out the nature of the problems faced by the discourse of literary history in contemporary India. The discussion of these eight positions does not aim at providing an exhaustive review of literary history in contemporary India. Rather it discusses representative trends and tendencies in the field. A tabular presentation of the dominant themes in the modern Indian discourse of literary history is as follows:

Twentieth Century Indian Styles of Literary Historiography

Dominant view	Universal	Convergence	Heterodox modernity	Recurrence
Perspective	Language	Sociology/ Ideology	Culture	Philosophy
Counter view	Regional	Divergence	Foreclosed tradition	Singular occurrence

The Universal and the Regional

Our illustrations for these two historiographical arguments will be, respectively, Sri Aurobindo's *Future Poetry*[1] and a collection of essays in Marathi *Vangmayetihasaci Sankalpana.*[2]

Aurobindo's *Future Poetry* is an extremely fascinating colonial text within which many battles are fought. It is a book that battles against the coercive influence of the English sensibility on Indian literature. At the same time it defies the restrictive heritage of Sanskrit metre, style and diction. It embodies too a fierce conflict between political nationalism and aesthetic universalism. Sri Aurobindo had rehearsed the argument of *Future Poetry* several times before he actually got down to writing his critical opus: one can see several previews in fragments in his *Harmony of Virtue* (1891), 'The Source of Poetry' (1905), *The National Value of Art* (1907), and in a long letter to his poet brother, Monomohan, written in 1898.[3]

The heart of the argument in all these is that the history of poetry is not a story of its steady decline. In fact, the really great poetry has not yet been written. There have been some prefatory attempts in that direction: but great poetry, which comes from the home of Truth, can be written only by divinely inspired sages, for poetry is nothing short of the aphoristic essence of the truth of all existence, presented in rhythmic language. Perfect poetry is backed by perfect inspiration. Perfect inspiration, in its turn, is possible only for perfect yogis. Once this view of literary aesthetics is proposed, the seed of a new historiography is sown. All those poets who do not appeal to Sri Aurobindo's sensibility are then described as the poets farthest from the source of divinity. All those poets against whose influence he is fighting are described as 'yogis'—but not quite perfect. Pope and Dryden are sent by Aurobindo to the aesthetic inferno he has envisioned. Shelley, Keats and Coleridge are allowed to enter the aesthetic purgatory. So is Kalidasa, who has a largeness of soul and sweetness of rhythm. The aesthetic heaven is reserved for Vyasa, Valmiki, Homer, Virgil, Dante and Shakespeare. *Future Poetry* is essentially a statement about this aesthetic heaven which will be populated by yogi-poets in future, if they succeed in combining the genius of the English language and the genius of Sanskrit poetry, particularly that of Vedic poetry. It is then that poetry will become *mantra.*

This theory is fascinating for its visionary zeal. It is an adventurous theory, for it challenges the English canon during the heyday of English colonialism. Perhaps, *Future Poetry* is the only independent history of English literature written in India. It is also the first major book of criticism that thinks of the possibility of an international English literature (now called 'New Literature'). It is also a text which has a close integral relationship with the philosophy of spiritual evolution propounded by Sri Aurobindo through his *Life Divine* and the epic *Savitri.*[4] Sri Aurobindo's history of English poetry is harmoniously blended with his history of Sanskrit poetry, as well as that of 'Indian' poetry within the scope of *Future Poetry.* His book, which is a major critical statement of this century in India, was initially published as a series of essays, and later compiled in a book form. The essays were written when the First World War was just about coming to an end, and Gandhi's influence in Indian politics was to replace Aurobindo's Bangla nationalism of extreme intensity. Since Sri Aurobindo was at the centre of political events in the first decade of this century, one cannot say that he was not involved in the contemporary social and political context. However, he could not have used that context for formulating a universalist historiography. It is therefore to his philosophy of the inner world that he has to turn while discussing the past and the future of poetry.

It is quite logical that any universalist historiography must cease to refer to the specific social, political or cultural context in order to be able to build a sustained vision of literary history. While a universalist literary history is likely to leave any of its readers cold, it must be acknowledged that this kind of history can be produced only in a colonized culture, which has bottomless inner cultural resources to fall back upon as dream-world compensation. Appropriately, therefore, the historiographer proposes poetry as *mantra* to be the ideal for the *future.*

Vangmayetihasaci Sankalpana (edited by Dattatraya Punde, 1986) is an anthology of historiographical essays in Marathi, including some essays translated from English to Marathi. The translated essays are by Srinivas Pradhan, Motilal Raina and Sujit Mukherjee. Of the Marathi essays, some were written specially for this volume, and some reprinted. Five appendices are added to the main body, in which various plan-proposals for a history of Marathi literature are reproduced, and bibliographical information is compiled. It is a volume that students of Marathi literature should find useful as a textbook. There may be similar volumes in existence in other Indian languages. The main aim of this volume is "to create a conceptual understanding about literary history in Marathi."[5] The editorial perspective is unambiguously monolingual. The volume is prepared so as to bring together important essays on literary history, to create a field of literary historiography in Marathi, to think afresh about the existing histories of Marathi literature, and to help the students of Marathi literature. These aims are not accidental in nature; they represent a well defined line of historical thought within which Marathi culture and community operate.

When modern historiography made its initial dent in India during colonial times, British historians were greatly interested in the history of the Marathi empire. Fortunately, the documentary sources for Maratha history were in plenty. As Indian scholars of history took over historical research from the British, they found the field of Maratha history very attractive for a different reason: the Maratha history of resistance and nationalism provided modern India with some ideals to look up to. The result of this concentration on one branch of Indian history by several non-Indian and pan-Indian historians was to activate history and historiography in Marathi.

When the discourse of Marathi history was being enriched, literature too had a place of significance in the cultural life of Maharashtra. As such, occasionally, some important historians have given thought to literary historiography. Since their training in history was based on the view of Maratha history as a unit, their literary historiography is closely akin to their general historiography. The best examples of this tendency are V. K. Rajwade and T. S. Shejwalkar. The volume on Marathi literary history edited by Punde owes much to the intellectual background created by these historians, though not explicitly acknowledged by the editor.

It would be very interesting to compare the two historians and their literary perspectives. Rajwade, in his essay, 'History of Prakritic Language and Literature in Maharashtra'[6] insists that the history of literature is at once the history of its language as well as the history of its sociology. In his view, "the history of creative writings is only one aspect of literary history." Rajwade thinks of literary history in terms of a science, the purpose of which is to arrange literary works chronologically, causally, and generically. If Rajwade's views on literary history can be thought of as the mainstream discourse of Marathi literary historiography, Shejwalkar's views form the counter-discourse of Marathi literary historiography. In an essay, 'Literature, Writing and Life',[7] Shejwalkar argues that literature cannot be allowed to become an end in itself without causing damaging effects on life itself. For him praxis is more important than intellection. "At present, there is a custom of spending the whole life in reading, writing and thinking. There are many who do so. But it is a social perversion." He then presents a Utopian picture of an egalitarian society, in which each will contribute as much physical labour as everyone else. Literature has its place in that society, but not at the cost of everything else. The history of literature for him is the history of its relation to labour in a given society. It is not exactly a Marxist vision. It is inspired by Marxist thinking but worked out through the local history. What is common between Rajwade and Shejwalkar is that they both look at Marathi literature as a single tradition; and, whatever their differences on the nature of historical narrative, they both envisage a single and exclusive history for Marathi literature.

The route through which other Indian languages have come to think of a single language literary identity may have been somewhat different from the one through which Marathi arrived at that position. Perhaps the historical studies of Indian languages, which subsequently culminated in Grierson's monumental *Linguistic Survey of India,*[8] have created the convention of thinking of literature in each language as a self-sufficient entity. The most common trend in literary historiography in modern India, and also the most dominant one at present, is the trend of regionalism. The political context which sanctions legitimacy to this trend is that of the formation of linguistic states. This approach is obviously restrictive in a country where bilingualism (particularly among people along state boundaries), translation, literary eclecticism and wide-ranging influences are common traits of literary traditions. Often, the linguistic regions and literary histories are seen as identical areas, with the result that literary productions in a language outside the territorial region of that language are left out of the historical account. It needs to be stressed that literary regionalism is a recent phenomenon in India, and it coincides with the colonial and postcolonial perceptions of India's nationhood.

Convergence and Divergence

Our illustrations for these two types of historiographical models will be, respectively, Sujit Mukherjee's two valuable books on literary history, Sisir Kumar Das's *A History of Indian Literature'*[9] and several essays by Gayatri Chakravorty Spivak, Daya Pawar, Kumkum Sangari and Salman Rushdie.

Sujit Mukherjee's two books, *Towards a Literary History of India* (1975) and *Some Positions on a Literary History of India* (1981)[10] have been among the few works on literary historiography published in English in India. In both these works, he makes an extremely systematic presentation of the concept of Indian literature as visualized by him. In the Preface to the first volume, he writes:

> What has been argued here is a concept. Its validity will be proved or disproved when the project outlined in the final section is actually put into practice. To those who may reject the concept altogether and can find no interest in the project, I should like to quote Bhavabhuti:
> *Utpasyate mama to koapi samanadharma*
> *kalohyaya nirahadhir vipula cha prithvi*[11]

The idea in the immortal verses of Bhavabhuti is that since Time has eternity and Space has infinity, some day, somewhere a like-minded person will appreciate a good poem (or concept). Sujit Mukherjee's concept is indeed worth appreciating, especially for the form in which it is presented. His book is a kind of copybook for a future historian of Indian literature. It has a chapter each on literary criticism, institutional teaching of literature, history of literary history, and the concept of Indian literature itself. In addition there are several useful appendices compiling information about common themes in Indian literary history such as translations, renderings of national classics, etc. And to top it all, there is an elaborate plan for the writing of a common history of Indian literature. The working plan covers, with great meticulousness, various aspects of history writing such as planning, research, compilation, coordination and editorial tasks (even these are arranged in a chronological sequence). Further the plan offers a ten-point-programme for those who are likely to take up the task of preparing a history of Indian literature.

The fact that such histories have appeared in the past as discussed in Mukherjee's chapter on the history of literary history in India, and are also appearing now through works like Sisir Kumar Das's recent history, shows that the position argued by

Sujit Mukherjee is no mere fancy. It represents a strong strand in India's cultural life, past or present. Let us use the term conventionally employed to describe this particular strand *marg*, the mainstream or the dominant. The *marg* view of culture and history always highlights convergence of constituents rather than the opposite.

Mukherjee refined his historiographical position and restated it in 1981 at a seminar in Pune, as well as in *Some Positions on a Literary History of India* (1981).[12] His presentation at Pune was later published as a Marathi translation in 1982, and reprinted in 1986. In that presentation, the thesis of his book is neatly reduced to five points. These five points, according to him, are the basic principles of Indian literary historiography:

(a) Though India does not have, for its ancient period, a sustained historical record, there is a wealth of literary sources, (available through references and cross references to other works), which can be used to reconstruct the narrative of remote historical periods in Indian literature.

(b) Indian literary historiography demands that the concepts of literary history need to emerge from other Indian fields of knowledge and social sciences. At present there is a lack of correspondence between the conceptual framework and the surrounding reality.

(c) Literary historiography in India has to have a keen social awareness of the context which produces works of literature. Particularly in the history of those periods of literature which are rich in contextual information, literary historiography has to have a clear social orientation.

(d) It is necessary to create a general framework of critical standards which will enable historians to evaluate any work from any given Indian literature.

(e) The principles of literary historiography for the ancient period, and the principles for the medieval and modern period, have had no mutual correspondence so far. The reason for this lack of correspondence is that literary historiography for Indian literature was developed by Western scholars. It is necessary to have a consistent historiographical strategy.

Thus, in Mukherjee's formulation of literary historiography, it is necessary to have: (i) an indigenous definition of history, (ii) an indigenous critical framework, (iii) an indigenous historiographical perspective. His view of literary history is, therefore, decidedly different from Sri Aurobindo's. But at the same time it is different from regional historiography. Mukherjee's view lies between these two views. For him, literary historiography ought to be culture--specific; but the specificity should not be narrowed to the level of a single language or region. At the same time, literary history should highlight similarities between various literatures; but the comparison should stop at the national boundary. Of course, Mukherjee looks at India as a cultural unit rather than a political unit. In his account of the history of Indian literary historiography, he presents a brief account of the origin and growth of historiography in the bhashas in India.

> Early models for such undertakings were supplied by the potted histories of regional literatures prepared by well meaning Englishmen for the *Heritage of India* series planned by J. N. Farquhar and published by the Association Press (YMCA) of Calcutta in collaboration with the Oxford University Press, London.[13]

The need for such histories had been more particularly felt ever since Indian languages were given a place of honour in Indian universities after India's independence. Inevitably, the imitative historiography created its opposite in historiography of cultural chauvinism, which treats all sacred literature in a given language as world class literature. Thus the material considered changes, but the perspective does not. Mukherjee comments:

> Perspective is what has been steadily eroded in our literary historiography. From one extreme of trying to measure our writers and writings only in terms of English (or, at time, European) literature, our literary critics have taught our literary historians to swing to the other extreme of confining literary history only to consideration of literary evidence available in that particular language. In their anxiety to prove the authenticity of a particular regional literature, its historians tend to stress its autonomy by

> overlooking the stimulus received from neighbouring languages and literature.[14]

The kind of integrative national history of Indian literature that Mukherjee conceptualizes is to be found in the two volumes by Sisir Kumar Das prepared for the Sahitya Akademi's proposed ten volume series. These two volumes treat India as a single and relatively unified literary field. Though the data presented in them is immensely useful for comparative literary research, these volumes treat the movements and trends covered with a minimum of critical evaluation. Almost exactly opposite in orientation and method is the work of the Subaltern Studies group.

Subaltern Studies is a new movement in political and cultural historiography launched by a group of scholars, most of whom are Bangla or are interested in Bangla history and culture. Collectively, these scholars (Shahid Amin, David Arnold, Gautam Bhadra, Dipesh Chakrabarty, Partha Chatterjee, Ranajit Guha, David Hardiman, Gyan Pandey and Sumit Sarkar) have produced a series of volumes entitled *Subaltern Studies* during the 1980s.[15] Each of the volumes includes long and informative essays about the processes of formation of colonial historiography and its inadequacy to narrate the micro-processes of history. The ideology of subaltern historiography is derived from Antonio Gramsci, who thinks of history in terms of "multiple elements of conscious leadership".[16] Gayatri Chakravorty Spivak, who acquired fame with her translation of Jacques Derrida's *Of Grammatology*, has contributed to the *Subaltern Studies*, two 'interventions', a long essay on a provocative Bangla story *Stan-dayini* by Mahasvetadevi, and a review, 'Subaltern Studies: Deconstructing Historiography'. She has also co-edited with Ranajit Guha the selected subaltern works.[17] Thus, though she is not a member of the subaltern 'collective' she is closely associated with the group.

The term 'subaltern', which is a creation of the British colonial contact with India, means 'subordinate' or 'inferior', and by implication, 'inferior modes of knowledge'. The subaltern historiography seeks to re-establish the balance of knowledge by demonstrating that the 'inferior' is made so through discourses of power and politics. Bernard S. Cohn's essay[18] on British attitudes to Indian languages—Persian, Arabic, Hindi, Sanskrit, Bangla, Telugu, etc.—is a fine example of deconstruction of the power structures shaping the forms of native knowledge. In this essay, Cohn's intellectual sympathies are with Persian against English, with Sanskrit against Persian, with Hindi against Sanskrit, and finally with Bangla against Hindi. Thus, he looks at the colonial hierarchy of languages from the perspective of the oppressed and the marginalized. Subaltern historiography is thus the perspective of the marginalized, of many against the dominant one. The approach is closer to Marxist historiography; but it does not poeticize peasants, and it does not undervalue the individual consciousness.

Gayatri Chakravorty's theoretical comments make a systematic statement of the aims and methods of the subaltern historiography. According to her, "The work of the Subaltern Studies group offers a theory of change." The theory of change relates to the functional changes in systems of social signs within the broader text of history. However, the change has to be defined in terms of a previously existent manner of perception of signs. Hence, subaltern studies "perceive their task as making a theory of consciousness or culture rather than specifically a theory of change."[19] The implication here is that subaltern historiography views history as a continuous chain of changing signs, the changes being continuous in times of insurgency as well as in times apparently stagnant. This historiography differs from elite historiography, and from the bourgeois nationalist perspective, in that the parameter for the change for the subaltern historiography is the consciousness of relatively small groups having marginal social importance. The studies published by Ranajit Guha and his collective of scholars show an obsessive interest in the colonial period, giving the concept of 'subaltern' a specific historic grounding. Gayatri Chakravorty records her response to *Subaltern Studies* thus:

> I am progressively inclined, then, to read the retrieval of subaltern consciousness as the charting of what in post-structuralist language would be called the subaltern subject-effect. A subject-effect can be briefly plotted as

> follows: that which seems to operate as a subject may be part of an immense discontinuous network ('text' in the general sense) of strands that may be termed politics, ideology, economics, history, sexuality, language, and so on. (Each of these strands, if they are isolated, can also be seen as woven of many strands.) Different knottings and configurations of these strands, dependent upon myriad circumstances, produce the effect of an operating subject.[20]

It should be clear by now that subaltern historiography fights the tendency to essentialize India. In the subaltern system of significance 'India' is a changing concept, signifying a variety of social formations, power-structures, linguistic histories to a variety of social and cultural groupings of consciousness. Therefore, when extended to cover literary history, the subaltern strategy tends to deny a common identity, and a continuous diachronic self-cognition of all literatures in India, which then can be collapsed into the larger category of 'Indian literature'. In fact, the subaltern perspective likes to look at all literature as parasitical. In any case, it looks at the question of the subaltern consciousness in terms of systems of signs, a writing of sorts, with its own phonocentrism. The metaphor reverses itself when writing is the subject of subaltern historiography. Gayatri Chakravorty writes :

> The cross-hatching of the revolutionary non-possessive possibilities in the structure of writing in general and its control by subaltern phonocentrism gives us access to the micrology or minute-scale functioning of the subaltern's philosophic world.[21]

Her own essay on Mahasvetadevi's *The Breast-giver* (*Stan-dayini*) is intended to be a reading of the system of 'writing-in-general' within which the novelist articulates the marginal, tribal consciousness as its own but authentic history.

The attitude that history, and history of literature in particular, has been a long and untold tale of deprivation has its origin in several regional, national, postcolonial and international literary movements. One may specify the following three of them here, all of which are new and progressive movements: (a) Dalit writings;

(b) 'New' literatures in English; and (c) Feminist writing and criticism.

Among the most distinguished thinkers in India during the twentieth century, Ambedkar has a prominent place. Apart from his part in drafting the Constitution of free India, he played a crucial and pioneering role in organizing 'lower caste' Indians into a community seeking emancipation and equality. By combining the teachings of the Buddha and Karl Marx in his message to the deprived classes in Indian society, he provided a sense of self-hood to the 'untouchables'. As a result of his teachings, and the new self-consciousness flowing so powerfully from it, a new school of creative writing has emerged in Marathi, Kannada, Gujarati, Telugu and Hindi literatures in the last twenty-five years. This new writing on the assertion of self-hood is extremely appealing, disturbing and challenging. Dalit literature, however, is not just texts or documents. The writers, in this movement show a clear awareness of belonging to a distinct literary culture and history. The origin of dalit literary historiography can be traced back to Ambedkar's history of dalithood. In an extremely well-argued and well-researched history of untouchability, *Untouchables: Who Were They*?[22] he discusses the anthropological and linguistic aspects of the problem, and presents a wealth of historical evidence to prove that untouchability has its roots in internal social discrimination in India and not in racial difference as had been previously argued by the sociologist Stanley Rice.

> If anthropometry is a science which can be depended upon to determine the race of a people, then the results obtained by the application of anthropometry to the various strata of Hindu society disprove that the untouchables belong to a race different from the Aryans and the Dravidians. The measurements establish that the Brahmins and the Untouchables belong to the same race. From this it follows that if the Brahmins are Aryans the Untouchables are also Aryans. If the Brahmins are Dravidians the Untouchables are also Dravidians. If the Brahmins are Nagas, the Untouchables are also Nagas.[23]

The literary historiography of dalit literature derives from this principle of racial equality of Indian society. It focuses on the questions of otherness, difference, marginality, canon and the categories of aesthetics. In order to voice the protest of the marginalized, dalit literature often follows the subversive historiographic path of personalizing history. It is therefore, perhaps, that autobiography is the most potent and often exercised form of fiction produced in dalit literature.[24] If long entrenched social discrimination separates history from its original twin, fiction, dalit literature seeks to revert to the primal unity between fiction and history.

One of the poignant statements of dalit aesthetics and literary historiography comes through the preface to *Kondwada,* the first verse collection of the Marathi poet Daya Pawar. The term *kondwada* refers to restricted cultural and social space. Its literal meaning is cattle-camp/prison. In this preface, Pawar offers us a personalized history of dalit literature. "No star shone in my direction when I was born. Nor did the sun appear like a red fruit to me".[25] Beginning with his birth in deprived social circumstances, Pawar graduated to various levels of social violence and discrimination. His growth as a poet was also his growth as a self-conscious *dalit.* Thus, *dalithood* is something which gets into the consciousness of writers like him along with language. Pawar is acutely aware that his poetry is a class/caste poetry:

> I have had the opportunity to read my poems to audiences at various forums. Because of that I can make some surmises. In rural areas, a new educated class is coming up. There in the high school and college setting my poems are being appreciated. There is the unforgettable experience of the poetry reading at the literary conference at Mahad (the place associated with Ambedkar's social protest). The audience took poems such as 'First Night' and 'Sabha' to their hearts. Alongside are some discouraging experiences. The Marathi academic class is turning up its nose at the poems; so also there is the cold reception at the poetry reading at the Indian Institute of Technology, at Powai, Bombay. It was like cutting ice with a knife.

Once again I am sharply reminded of the cleavage in Indian cultural life. If my poems fall a victim in the attempt to close this divide, I shall not mind. I have come to perform that role. In my poem 'Maran' [Death] I have written:

> Like elephants crushed
> Against sharp spiked doorways
> One should die laughing[26]

Women's emancipation has been as powerful and as debated a theme in recent Indian literature as the dalit question. Literary feminism in India, native as well as derivative, is too vast a subject to be discussed even sketchily in the present work. However, the literary historiography proposed by gender equality activists needs to be paid special attention in our discussion of the historiography of deprivation. Most of the concerns of literary gender equality activists in India—and they do not have much use of the category 'nation'—get sharply focused in a valuable essay by Kumkum Sangari, 'Of Ladies, Gentlemen, and "the Short-Cut"', which appeared in *New Literary History.* The central argument of the essay is stated by her with characteristic clarity at the outset:

> Modes of consciousness and self-consciousness, identity and experience, personality and subjectivity are constructed in response and reaction to the pressure of a given historical moment and are neither self-sustaining nor perennially 'male' or 'female'. Femaleness is neither the 'natural' property of women, nor an eternally subversive Other, nor even, beyond a point, the product of a special experience. It is not an essential, homogenous quality at the *core* of all women waiting to be discovered once social oppression and repression are removed. Like maleness, femaleness is not a fixed inalienable quantity: it is rather a mode of *social* being and so a historically specific value which can be redistributed and reformulated.[27]

The argument about the nature of difference between femaleness and maleness presented here is comparable to Ambedkar's argument about the difference between the 'touchables' and the 'untouchables'. Similarly, both protests seek for removal of the social conditions that determine the difference; they do not seek to accentuate the difference so as to establish a doctrinaire antagonism and autonomous identity. The protests are to be seen as a corrective shift in literary history rather than as revolutions.

It is a similar assertion of equality between all writers in English that we see in Salman Rushdie's essay, '"Commonwealth Literature" Does Not Exist'. He has been grouped together with other non-British, Irish and American writers writing in English in a category called 'Commonwealth Literature'. His argument is that the differences between various units of the Commonwealth are more substantial than the similarities. Rushdie vehemently explodes the artificial historical category:

> The dangers of unleashing such a phantom into the groves of literature are, it seems to me, manifold...there is the effect of creating a ghetto, and that, in turn, leads to a ghetto mentality amongst some of its occupants. Also the creation of a false category can and does lead to excessively narrow, and sometimes misleading readings of some of the artists it is held to include; and again, the existence—or putative existence—of the best distracts attention from what is actually worth looking at, what is actually going on.[28]

It should be noted that Rushdie is not criticizing merely the use of the term 'Commonwealth', or the category of Commonwealth literature. He is in fact, like the dalit writers and the feminist critics, challenging the patronizing attitude behind it:

> The term is not used simply to describe, or even misdescribe, but also to *divine*. It permits, academic institutions, publishers, critics and even readers to dump a large segment of English literature into a box and then more or less ignore it. At best, what is called 'Commonwealth literature' is positioned *below* English literature... or it places Eng. lit. at the centre and the rest of the world at the periphery.[29]

The sense of outrage is caused by what Rushdie himself calls the creation of the Commonwealth 'ghetto'. This ghetto can be no less oppressive to writers who wish to relate themselves to the entire English canon and the totality of the English language than the caste ghetto created for the *dalit* writers, or the gender ghetto created for women writers.

The three forms of protest, their explicit plea for equality, their desire to reconstitute the category of the aesthetic, go into their revisions of history. Their literary historiography seeks to recast literary histories based on colonial, cultural and caste discriminations and deprivations; and in their own fashion, they emphasize the texts of such deprivations against established historical narratives.

Heterodox Modernity and Foreclosed Tradition

Our illustrations for the two antithetical views on literary traditions come from the writings of two extremely significant novelists, both profoundly similar and yet greatly dissimilar. They are U. R. Ananthamurthy and Bhalchandra Nemade. They are both known as trend-setting novelists in their respective languages, Kannada and Marathi. Both have left their respective fiction traditions significantly altered since the sixties. They have been in the forefront of the little magazine movements in their languages. Though teachers of English, both have been committed to their own languages. Both have a tremendous sympathy for medieval Indian literature. Here the similarity ends. The differences will be clear when we analyse their texts: Ananthamurthy's long essay, 'Why Not Worship In The Nude?'[30] and Nemade's long essay,'The Marathi Novel: 1950–75'.[31] Both these have by now become celebrated texts, mainly because each is a comprehensive revaluation of a major tradition of fiction.

Ananthamurthy's essay, with its anecdotal style and self-dramatization, makes delightful reading. Within the scope of this essay he presents the whole range of his response to Kannada fiction written by some major writers of this century: Shivaram Karanth, K. V. Puttappa, Masti Venkatesh Iyengar, Yashwant Chittal, Lankesh, Shantinath Desai, Poornachandra Tejaswi, Devanuru Mahadeva, and others. In reflecting on their contribution to the growth of the Kannada consciousness, Ananthamurthy examines the phenomenon of modernism in India. The central question as he raises it is: Can a novelist be progressive in his rational sphere of thought and at the same time engage sympathetically in his novelistic creation? To this question, there are unambiguous ideological answers. There are also unambiguous attitudes available in the given discourses of anthropology, journalism, politics and social work. However, these unambiguous answers prove reductive and fail to understand the complexity of Indian society and culture, as Ananthamurthy argues.

The more significant fiction in Kannada is that which tries to get to the centre of the complexity in Indian culture. It is a culture, or rather a set of cultures, which brings every rational act in confrontation with an incredibly humane transcendence, every act of escape from tradition comes face-to-face with surprising discoveries of modernity in the backwaters. Making a choice between tradition and modernity in any exclusive way is, in Ananthamurthy's view, to falsify and to deny India:

> The reality of novelists in India, I am speaking from my Kannada experience, is so complex as to disallow the comforts of either status-quoist acceptance or of revolutionary ruthlessness. R. K. Narayan can afford to say 'India will go on' only as a comic realist, in his inimitable low mimetic mode. But when his insightful Indian experience is translated into ideas in a polemical indictment of Indian reality, he can afford to speak angrily and ruthlessly and plead for a thoroughgoing modernization in India—only in a polemical context. I wonder if he can maintain his position unambiguously in a novel where his imaginative sympathies are fully engaged.[32]

From this position, Ananthamurthy then analyses the works of major Kannada novelists to show that at the heart of each of the major Kannada novels is the ambiguity about modernization. It is so, because the major writers have understood the issues involved in the transition from tradition to modernity. They cannot have clear affiliations either with tradition or with modernity. All they can have is a heterodox acceptance of things as they have been, uneasily combined with the desire to change them:

> Yes—all of us are modernizers in one way or the other, but with an uneasy conscience, if we are sensitive. The great writers among us see it as inevitable and search for ways to preserve what is best and unique in Indian civilization.[33]

The reflections of the novelist in his time, as Ananthamurthy calls them, are all set in the disturbing social context of a tragic struggle between the forces of modernization and a group of devotees that goes through the ritual of worshipping at a temple in the nude. The conflict between the two is, in essence, the conflict between India of the past and India of the present. Ananthamurthy understands both, and therefore cannot take any one side. His is an ambivalence which desires to preserve the past and wishes it radically changed. Translated into the terms of literary historiography, this attitude articulates an intimate enemity with the literary past as well as the literary present. And, in fact, a closer look at Ananthamurthy's responses to other Kannada novelists does reveal this sense of uneasy intimacy. He likes them, and at the same time he disapproves of them. Given such a vision of one's literary tradition, and its relation to the social reality surrounding it, the only viable attitude to literary history has to be based in a poetics of heterodoxy. For Ananthamurthy, modern Kannada fiction is a combination of traditional Indian wisdom, ignorant but faithful religious rituals, rational and scientific progress, fragmented modern emotional life, and an uneasy involvement in all these on the part of the novelists. Ultimately, the essence of being a great modern Kannada novelist lies in coping with a range of heterodoxy.

In contrast to Ananthamurthy, Bhalchandra Nemade believes in an active moral engagement in the social context on the part of the novelist. This social engagement is described by Nemade by using a pair of terms, one aesthetic and the other ethical *kriti* and *navaniti*. *Kriti* is, in his exposition of it, the linguistic action that a novelist performs in a given novelistic context dealing with social reality. *Navaniti* is the writer's ethical commitment to his medium as a means of progressive (not in the Marxist sense) critique of the society to which he belongs, for the language which he uses is social material. Nemade's aesthetic demands on fiction writers originate in his larger critical perspective of *desivad.* Nemade's *desivad* believes that literature is a subsystem of culture and the society that produces it; and, therefore, it acquires serious meaning only when it reflects social reality in all aspects and areas of life. This may be a highly debatable assumption. However, what interests us here is the historiographical expectations raised by *desivad.*

The Nemade style of *desivad* combines ethics and aesthetics, in effect, to create a gradation in fiction. The fiction that depicts social reality from a progressive, ethical point of view is judged the best kind. The others which either do not reflect social reality or do not show the ethical awareness expected of fiction are thought of as inferior varieties. Thus, there is a hierarchy of fiction. In Nemade's own terminology the classification, in descending order of importance, is: (i) *Kriti*-oriented novel of social realism and linguistic action; (ii) *Riti*-oriented novel of formalistic interest and linguistic self-centredness; (iii) *Pratikriti*-oriented novel of illusions, fantasy and day-dreams.

Once this hierarchy of fiction is conceptualized as a framework for critical evaluation, it implies also a historiographical strategy. Using the three-fold classification of fiction—within which one can devise further sub-classes when necessary—one can show literary history as a continuous pattern of exchanges between the three trends. Since Nemade privileges the *kriti*-oriented forms of fiction as progressive forms, he reads the history of Marathi fiction as a clash and competition between *kriti*-fiction, on the one hand, and *riti*- and *prakriti*-fiction, on the other. In his survey of Marathi fiction since 1950, he first sets out to show the history of this conflict during the preceding century of Marathi fiction, and then presents *that* history as the precondition for reading the subsequent periods of history. Thus, the concept of tradition in Nemade's historiography is that of a foreclosed tradition, which can acquire further complexity but never face complete displacement. Tradition always guides any subsequent period of literary history. Again, it is tradition which provides the grounds for literary criticism, by suggesting appropriate criteria to judge new developments. In justifying his method of historical assessment, Nemade states that if one wishes to understand literary culture in a given period, it is necessary to trace the dominant trends back to their origin, that is, to the very moment of the commencement of that particular literary tradition, so as to see them in their pure form. The rest of the history is nothing but a many-stranded narrative of the interplay of these strands. He calls this historiography, the "nativistic method of historical reconstruction".

The literary historiography proposed by Nemade offers a challenging perspective in the context of fiction criticism, since it alters the established method of considering prose-fiction as a purely imported literary form. According to Nemade's historiography, the ground rules of literary development are established at the inception of a given literary tradition. Literary history involves the gradual unfolding of those rules, the ingrained tendencies, which pass through processes of fluctuation, interplay, occasional mutations or cross-fertilization. These changes can be explained in terms of the material of social reality reflected in literature. Thus literary traditions are essentially foreclosed systems. They are open to manipulation by writers, but not so open as to be completely wiped out. Literary trends which seem eliminated, survive underground. All of Nemade's critical writing is suffused with this faith in the predictable creativity of traditions.

If Ananthamurthy constructs modernity as a condition of knowledgeable ambivalence, the inability to decide which of the cultural pressures demanding his novelistic attention should be privileged, Nemade implies that tradition leaves very little for the writer to choose. For Ananthamurthy, tradition is freedom, for Nemade tradition is a nesessity. For Ananthamurthy, tradition in pluralistic societies is heterodox. For Nemade, tradition in postcolonial societies is a means of recovering the nativistic self-awareness so as to be able to perform linguistic *kriti,* creation which is also action.

Eternal Recurrence and Specific Occurrence

The critic whose work illustrates the view of history as a perennial recurrence is Ananda K. Coomaraswamy. To illustrate this view of history I will refer to some of his major essays.[34] The text illustrating the opposite view, history as a temporally conditioned and specific occurrence is a recent essay by Rajeev Patke[35] providing a historiographical model in the context of Indian-English poetry.

Coomaraswamy's works are far too well known to require an account of his critical contribution. Here, we are concerned with the implications of his criticism for literary historiography. Obviously, we cannot benefit in that direction from his popularly known essays on Hindu aesthetics that one encounters in *The Dance of Shiva.* It is necessary to examine some of his other major essays, particularly 'Recollection: Indian and Platonic', 'The One and the Only Transmigrant', and '*Kha* and Other Words Denoting "Zero" in Connection with the Indian Metaphysics of Space'.[36]

In his discussion of the concept of zero in relation to space, Coomaraswamy reproduces the definition of infinity given by Bhaskara in his *Bijaganita,* with an English translation:

> *ayam ananto rasih khahara ity uchyate. Asmin vikarab khahare na rasavapi pravistesvapi nihsrtesu babusvapi syal layasrstikale 'nante' 'cyute bhutaganesu yadvat',* that is, This fraction of which the denominator is Zero, is called an infinite quantity. In this quantity consisting of that which has cipher for its divisor, there is no alteration, though many be added or subtracted; just as there is no alteration in the Infinite Immovable (*anante acyute*) at the time of the emanation or resolution of worlds, though hosts of beings are emanated or withdrawn.[37]

It is interesting to note that what was used by Bhaskara, the ancient mathematician as a metaphor is treated by Coomaraswamy as literal description. The mention of 'Infinite Immovable' in the original is not as emphatic as in Coomaraswamy's translation. The reason why Coomaraswamy attempts this peculiar foregrounding of metaphysical infinity in his discussion of mathematical infinity is, perhaps, that he seeks a legitimation of his own concept of perennial philosophy in the definition he discusses. The belief in perennially present wisdom or philosophy was the most central of his persuasions.

To Coomaraswamy, the fund of wisdom to which human societies have access is *anant,* infinite. What appears as new discoveries, inventions, original contributions, revolutions in thought, are nothing but fresh manifestations of knowledge that was already in existence. Hence, in the essay 'The One and the Only Transmigrant' he tries to show that the idea of transmigration in Sankaracharya, Plato, Plotinus and a host of other Indian and Western thinkers is essentially the same idea. Of course, in pointing out these similarities, he does not intend to hint at any influence of any particular philosopher on the others. The point he makes, so eruditely, is that essentially one philosophic thought can be inspired in the minds of different philosophers in different cultures and at different times. This is his perspective of perennial philosophy.

The concept of perennial philosophy has extremely important implications for historiography. And, in fact, Coomaraswamy exploits that implication to the fullest in his distinguished body of art history and literary criticism. The implication is that the history of art and literature is nothing more than a series of recurrences of some basic thought-clusters, theme-structures and styles. For a provocative articulation of his historiographical perspective we have to turn to Coomaraswamy's essay on memory, 'Recollection: Indian and Platonic'.The preamble to 'Recollection' lays bare the very heart of the entire work of Coomaraswamy:

> In the following article, the doctrine that what we call 'learning' is really a 'remembering' and that our 'knowledge' is by participation in the Omniscience of an immanent spiritual principle will be traced in Indian and Platonic texts. This corresponds, in same Perennial Philosophy, to the doctrine that the beautiful is such by a participation in Beauty, and all being a participation of Being absolutely.[38]

By drawing on a plethora of evidence from ancient scriptural sources, Coomaraswamy does indeed build a case for the view that memory is not the storehouse of new experiences, but an outlet for knowledge belonging to an order of existence prior or superior to human existence. Memory is from the Self, and "the Self knows everything." Thus what we remember is really what we recollect; and to remember becomes the dominant mode of Becoming. All knowledge is in this sense a mere reminding. "Memory is a kind of latent knowledge." And again, "the ultimate source on which all memory draws"[39] is the Self or Spirit.

Given Coomaraswamy's metaphysical approach to memory, history—which persists in its attempt to recollect—becomes a highly privileged subject. At the same time, the events of history become only virtual events, being reproductions of events that have happened many times in the past. Thus, Coomaraswamy's historiography undercuts the importance of history as the past, forcing it into the realm of an ever-present, at the same time inflating the importance of history as a discourse which he makes the source of all knowledge including spiritual knowledge.

The view of literary history as a pattern of recurrences is not peculiar to Coomaraswamy's philosophy alone. Some variants of this philosophy can be traced to some nineteenth century philosophers. Friedrich Nietzsche was the most important of its exponents. In a sense, works of literature, which survive their own chronological time, come into existence repeatedly in every subsequent period when new generations of readers encounter them. However, it is not in any metaphorical sense that Coomaraswamy thinks of philosophy, knowledge and literature as eternally recurrent phenomena. He thinks of history as a recurrence in the literal as well as philosophical sense.

> The providential principle, in other words, is the immanent Spirit, the Knower of the field, apart from whom, on the one hand, no birth could take place... and apart from whom, as only seer, hearer, thinker, etc. in us..., neither experience nor memory could be conceived.[40]

The historian becomes, then, a prophet who must keep looking for immanence of the Self in all recurrences seen outwardly as history.

Rajeev Patke's essay, published recently in *Kavya Bharati* is an attempt to make sense of the large crop of anthologies of Indian poetry in English, and to provide a historical perspective to the process of canon formation in this new branch of Indian literature. He rests his argument on Frank Kermode's observation about canons being trans-historical in some sense but which also have to be set within the framework of historical periods.[41] By following closely the changes in the patterns of imitation in Indian English poetry during the last hundred years, Patke splits it into periods, that match respectively with the two criteria (which Lionel Trilling devises for a different purpose) of sincerity and authenticity. Thus in his reading of the history of Indian poetry in English, there is a period of sincerity followed by another period of authenticity. What is worth appreciating in Patke's historiography is that he divides the poets into periods without any strained attempt to show them totally different from one another. Thus there is a continuity between the two periods as well as a difference. Therefore, Patke can speak of the canon as well as periods in Indian English poetry. He states this aim with clarity at the outset of his essay:

> The usual way of making sense of any such body of writing is to treat it not as a mere sequence in time but as an historical process. The notion of process recognises change as the effect of a cause which may be located in the literary sensibility of a culture. When a change in literary sensibility is shared by a number of authors, the literary historian can nominalize it as literary period. The concept of period may be open to abuse as mere convenience or as a bed of Procrustean simplification. But when properly used, it defines the recognition that literary changes of a substantive and irreversible kind have occurred in the process that is literary history.
>
> The authors and texts who reflect these changes constitute the canon for that period. Canons are necessarily plural. They are also thoroughly historical, and contingent on the values of specific periods.[42]

The need to periodize rests on the recognition that large scale changes in literary tastes call for corresponding shifts in the perception of literature. This recognition helps historians to link all literary events in a single chronological category of literature or tradition, while enabling them to link together all literary events of a specifically common character into a single synchronic category of period. Thus each literary period is *literary* but not literary in the same way as all other periods are. Each literary period, author, text, or event is an occurrence by itself and never totally *identical* with any other period, author, text or event.

The view that literature is an occurrence in itself, only marginally linked with the literature of preceding or succeeding periods, reflects the critical values and literary historiography available in the dominant Anglo-American schools of literary thought. This view can be seen at play in those literary histories which consider periodization as an essential function of literary historiography. It can be located in the critical and philosophic perspectives dominant in the European discourse and preception of general history. The same historiographical prespective is also at the base of most of the textbook histories of literature currently produced in India.

A perceptive critic like Namvarsingh, who writes in Hindi, has given a brilliant exposition to a contrary view. In his *Itihasa aur Aalochana,* Namvarsingh points out the dangers of using periodization in constructing the history of Hindi literature. However, he does not mystify history as Coomaraswamy does. His is a culture-specific argument which in translation would read as follows:

> If periodization is to be seen as a 'methodological necessity' its appropriateness must derive justification from its practical utility. Therefore, if the concept interferes with our perceiving the past as it really was, it is desirable to abandon the method.
>
> Judging by the use of the device of periodisation in the history of Hindi literature so far, it needs to be said that it does distort the historical reality. The periods conceptualized have fragmented our literary history. The

> periods offer only fragmented images of the past not its continuous flow. The points of time demarcating the periods become not only disjointed but, in the process, one stands to miss a lot from history.[43]

The discussion of these postcolonial Indian approaches to literary history indicate the range and variety of critical responses to India's literary past. These approaches, though not fully developed philosophies of literary history, indicate the direction in which literary historiography in India has been moving during the twentieth century. Taken together, they indicate that history is open to numerous interpretations, all of which can be 'valid' interpretations, and possesses, like a literary text itself, the quality of interminable indeterminacy. They suggest that the polemics of progress along the fixed line of transition from imagination to reason will diminish the complexity and diversity of the literary past and present in India.

Considering the vast temporal scope of Indian literary creativity and the numerous social dissensions that it has drawn upon, literary historiography demands of a historian a multiple and complex mechanism of cognition with regard to India's literary past. The differences among the approaches outlined regarding the phenomenological limits of literature—ranging from the universal (Sri Aurobindo), national (Sujit Mukherjee), regional (the bhasha historiography) and the sub-linguistic/regional (dalit and subaltern historiography)—show that the concepts of selfhood operating behind them are not identical. Hence, literary historiography in India will gain by exploring the notions of *self* and *other* in Indian social practice and philosophical traditions. Besides, the question of the relationship between canon and para-literature, between literature and the non-verbal arts will have to be tackled before establishing the guiding principles of literary historiography in India. Taken together, the Indological attitude, the nationalistic attitude and the nativistic attitude suggest that any definition of tradition in Indian literature will have to take into account the micro-level cultural transactions more seriously than any history based on the concepts of progress/periods/canon has done in the past. In short, a literary history in India, if it has to be a properly ordered illumination of the literary past, will have to be a history, to allude to Rajashekhara's eloquent phrase, "Of Many Beings".

14

Para-Literature

"In every literary epoch there is," according to Russian Formalism, "not one but several literary schools. They exist in literature simultaneously, but one of them represents the canonized crest. The others are not canonized and exist obscurely..."[1] The Formalistic historiography allows an element of arbitrariness in canon formation, which it describes as "automatization-perceptibility". Once allowance is made for the mysterious arbitrariness in how some literary trends get to become the canonised crest and others exist obscurely, the creation, existence and decline of the non-canonised other trends becomes a foreclosed question. However, the question of obscure traditions, marginal styles and non-canonised texts is of utmost importance to literatures with multilingual historical contexts. The question has a great political urgency in societies that have experienced colonial domination and gender discrimination.

Let us try to conceptualise the 'other, obscure, suppressed or sub-cultural' literary phenomena by using the epithet 'para'.[2] This prefix has travelled from its Greek origin through Latin, and Middle French to Middle English, retaining most of its original sense, and it now means: 'by the side of, beside, alongside of, by past, and beyond.' Para-literature would, therefore, include all such activities as are normally considered socially parallel, linguistically parasitical, psychologically paranoid and historically parenthetical. What is common to all forms of para-literature is that they are literatures without interlocutors, taboo to literary history.

Para-literature as creative activity is analogous to comparative literature as a method of literary study in one important respect. In the initial stages of its development, European scholars of comparative literature divided the entire field of literary study into national literature, comparative literature, and general literature.[3] Whereas national literature and general literature were defined with relatively greater precision, comparative literature, being neither, was given the nebulous and vast middle space between the two. Similarly, para-literature occupies the middle space between literature and non-literature. It is not literature, because it is not accepted in literary canons. It is also not non-literature, because it has the formal attributes of literature. Para-literature is, thus, the middle space literature.

The middle space is densely populated. It contains a bewildering range of forms of linguistic creativity such as science and crime fiction, magazine stories, film and television scripts, street-plays, biographies, autobiographies, memoirs, travelogues, philosophic writings, religious discourses, popular and folk songs, folklore, proverbs, *mantra*, *tantra* and liturgical verses, lullabies, oral narratives, archaic literature, works in slang and dialect, children's literature, performed poetry (as in *mushairas),* pornography, graffiti, comics, advertisements, jokes, cartoons, translations, adaptations, abuse terms and letters. Of course this is a random list of middle space literary forms. It can accommodate other forms not listed above provided they are literary and overlooked by histories of literature.

The middle space literature can be differentiated from non-literature by virtue of its context, style and performance. For instance, abuse terms, graffiti, pornography, popular romances and love-letters have in common the theme of sex-relations; yet each of these has its proper style, context and performance. We cannot interchange the style, context and performance of any of these genres without risking disastrous consequences. In other words, the middle space literature is not without its aesthetic form, unlike non-literature. All forms of middle space literature involve a certain linguistic skill and aesthetic sensibility. They have their own distinctive discourses and conventions, standards of excellence and criteria of achievement. They all have their cultural uses. Any language would be much the poorer without these or similar forms of linguistic creativity.

It is the differentiation between literature and the middle space literature that is the more problematic. One may hastily assume that para-literature or the middle space literature is "low-brow" literature. But that is not the case. It cuts across all social classes. Who does not require, at one time or another in their lives, abuse words, graffiti, detective or pulp fiction, oral narratives, popular poetry, love-letters and religious recitations? Can we say that liturgical verses or national anthems are low brow?

One may argue that the creative imagination called in operation by para-literature is inferior to the imagination employed by the writers of classics. This claim needs to be investigated by psychologists. However, there are countless writers who work as journalists, commercial copywriters, film and television writers. For instance, one of the most creative of India's contemporary poets, Arun Kolatkar, works in the field of advertising. He writes very good poetry in two languages: Marathi and English. Can the imagination that writes poetry in Marathi be different from the imagination that writes Kolatkar's poetry in English? And is the "poetic" imagination different again from the imagination that writes advertisement copy?[4] To put this in another way, not all good poets can be good prose writers, or good journalists or commercial artists. Each kind of writing requires a specific kind of linguistic orientation, and none of these orientations is superior or inferior. The notion that poetic imagination is closer to Truth, and therefore superior to other forms of imagination, is a belief left over to us by the nineteenth century European conflict between reason and imagination, which created exaggerated and romantic claims in favour of imagination. On the other hand, if poets were traditionally expected to be prophets in India, they were also expected to quieten their mental activity, including that of imagination, in order to be able to receive large visions of life. The idea that literature employs imagination which is superior to the kind of imagination used in para-literature reflects the equation of power between the two types of literature rather than any valid aesthetic perception.

The question of power immediately brings in the question of institutionalization of literature. Rather than saying that para-literature is non-literature, it would be more appropriate to say that it is non-classroom literature, that as literature it is neither taught nor learnt. Para-literature is all literature which is excluded from literary history; and if seen grudgingly as a document it is never given the status of a monument. The difference between literature and para-literature has to be sought, therefore, with reference to the causes behind institutionalized literature teaching. Two questions need to be asked here: Why do we teach literature? And, why do we not teach all manifestations of literary creativity?

Literature teaching is a unique invention in human history. It does not pass on knowledge in the same way as the teaching of sciences and technology do. Sciences and technology face the danger of extinction if they are not transmitted through some form of teaching. Literature faces no such danger, for literature as a creative activity does not depend on the teaching of literature. Literature teaching does not aim at shaping future writers as the classroom work in fine arts aims at shaping artists. While other human sciences deal with human reality, literature teaching deals with a level of reality *created* by human beings. Closest to it come the teaching of linguistics and philosophy which handle a secondary level of reality, namely, language and thought. But they rarely glorify the aesthetic and emotive aspect of their subject to the extent literature teaching does. To generalize, literature teaching has the following two characteristics: it is a non-useful activity, and the thought content it seeks to transmit is irrational.

Perhaps the above generalization can be restated by saying that the greatest use of literature teaching is that by using ambivalent literary signs for the construction of its pedagogic narratives, it allows the irrational elements in a culture a respectable articulation. If scientific thinking keeps a society moving forward, signs of irrational impulses keep it integrated. Literature is such a system of signs. It is, in other words, a totemic system. It is a system embodied in verbal signs which continue to persist in their meaning over long periods of time, signs which are totems that articulate for successive generations of people the irrational content of their own personalities. Literature, this system of totems, keeps successive generations bound by a sense of historic flow of time, by a sense of being a community. All communities are bound together by the literary signs they value. No literature is objectively beautiful or useful in itself. Literatures are vested with these qualities by the communities that are bound together by those linguistic totems. Literature is taught as a valuable discipline because it helps us to identify the most persistent and irrational images of our ancestors in the verbal icons created by them. Totems do not possess any inherent significance. They acquire it by virtue of their situation in a given community.

It may be possible to understand the universal urge to impart literary teaching to younger generations in any given society in the light of the above comments. The reason why all kinds of literature do not receive an institutional status is that totems always create, and almost inevitably depend on, a contrary system of taboos.[5] If, literature is understood as a system of totems, para-literature can be seen as a system of taboos, which is not allowed to enter the sacred portals of a classroom. In fact, collectively and irrationally agreed upon, taboos too keep communities bound together. Totems and taboos, respectively, represent a community's desires in their sublimated or repressed forms. The relationship between the two is the relationship between the sacred and the profane. This relationship depends on how a given community distributes its cultural space. In terms of the material substance of which they are composed, their structural organizations, and their expressivity, totems and taboos may be identical; but their status in terms of the sacred and the profane may vary radically. For instance, pornography and romance, or abuse terms and proverbs, may have identical substance, structure and complexity; yet the irrational needle of a community's compass mapping the range of the sacred and the profane will show the forms in these pairs as distinct as the east and the west, or the north and the south.

It may be deduced from these anthropological observations

about the nature of canon formation in literary studies that the distinction between literature and para-literature, even if explained in terms of a science of literary criticism, is really guided by the systems of totems and taboos of the society that creates and preserves a given literary tradition. Exclusions of authors, texts, styles in a given history of literature, or inclusion of certain other authors, texts, forms and styles; are matters which, in the first instance, are determined by extra-literary considerations. It is not because the critical consensus about an author or a technique is initially wrong that after a time that author or technique is given legitimacy. These fluctuations occur because taboos can turn into totems in course of time. For example, travelling across the seas was taboo in India till the early part of this century. Today it has a totemic importance. Neither totems nor taboos have permanence of status. They may interchange their positions with appropriate shifts in the cultural history of a community. This exchange is an essential aspect of literary history, though unfortunately it has remained generally neglected.

When new literary traditions emerge, or branch off from an established literary tradition, the new literatures are initially treated as taboo/para-literatures. The history of literature in the modern Indian languages tells us that in the initial period of development of these new traditions, the period of transition from Sanskrit to these new languages was seen as a gradual vulgarization. A similar attitude was displayed in Europe towards the literatures and languages branching out of Latin in medieval times. In the early phases of English literary writing outside England and Scotland, in countries like Ireland, America and Australia, the British attitude to such literature was invariably patronizing. On the other hand, when a literary tradition acquires substance, the preceding literary trends or traditions lose their acquired status. Though it is true that not all obsolete literature gets relegated to the category of para-literature, literary history does keep agitating against literary obsolescence.

However, not all para-literature is a product of literary history's amnesia, nor is all of it the result of hesitation on the part of literary criticism to assimilate new modes of writing. Much of para-literature is downgraded to that status due to contemporary repressions guided by the hierarchic stratification within a community. In most communities a lower 'aesthetic' value is attached to literature produced by and for women and children in literary criticism and history controlled by the men and adults of those communities. Children and women form two major repressed segments of most communities. Their literary requirements, and aesthetic sensibilities are taken less seriously than they deserve. Para-literature, therefore, accurately reflects the patterns of social repression. In addition to these, there is one more conventional method of repression in India. The subcontinental and poly-linguistic country always has had a common mainstream literary tradition, whether in Sanskrit, Pali, Persian, Hindi or English. The regional literary traditions in India have to encounter the imperialism of the mainstream traditions. At present, this is the condition of about eighty-five tribal and minority languages and literary forms in these languages. Each of these languages is spoken by more than 10,000 people but not listed as languages of administration in the Eighth Schedule of the Indian Constitution.[6] The literary aesthetics of these languages is never given even the minimum passing consideration in Indian literary discourse. Their situation is like that of literatures in Indian languages in relation to the contemporary world canon of literature. Para-literature is thus the literature of linguistic communities on the periphery of political orders.

The psychological desire to castrate one's adversary often takes linguistic expression. The linguistic creativity of politically subjugated sections is then made a victim of this desire by the dominating language groups. During the nineteenth century, European anthropologists turned perfectly normal literary activity in Africa into para-literature. Orientalism did that for the Asian nations. Para-literature, in which it is the usual practice to include oral narratives and folk forms, is perceived to be closer to the region of the unconscious. If one were to follow psychoanalytic criticism with persistence, it would seem to provide an explanation of the phenomenon. However, the unconscious itself is not a category free of political conditioning, as argued by Kumkum

Sangari.[7] In a thought-provoking essay, she shows how Freud's discovery of the unconscious was an inevitable result of the political history of European colonialism during the nineteenth century:

> A significant facet of the history of designating the unconscious in Europe consists of the histories of primitivization. In the late nineteenth century the primitivization of certain categories becomes quite strident: most notably of sexuality and of women who, along with non-western societies are placed on the scale of evolution.

The scientization of the primitive is carried out side by side with its aesthetization through a series of 'revaluations'. The 'primitive' ranges from the external and measurable to the internal and immeasurable... Conversely, the 'primitive' can either be equated with or contained in the unconscious.[8]

The primitive in society, the unconscious in the psyche, and the 'para' in literature may have intrinsic attributes in a given period, but these are not absolute categories. Their attributes in a given period are gradually determined over a preceding long period through processes of repression. Therefore, what is civilized can come to be considered primitive, what belongs to accessible areas of consciousness can be relegated to the territory and terror of the unconscious, and what is literature can invite description as para-literature. Movements in the opposite direction too are possible. These movements are of crucial formative importance in the history of literature, both as a system of totems and taboos and as dynamic cultural practices.

Since there is essentially no difference between literature and para-literature, the boundaries between the two are not permanently sealed, and there is a constant mutual exchange. This exchange proceeds along certain established lines. To articulate the nature of this exchange should be one of the primary objectives of literary history. As in the history of language, so too in the history of literature, the trends and styles initially developed on the margins tend to gravitate towards the centre. Removed from the original context, sometimes the para-styles change their intended performance in the changed literary context. Conventions of comic literature often originate in the not-so-comic dialects of the socially less privileged classes. Conventions of the tragic, epic and canonical originate in the well-formed registers of the socially privileged classes. Once formulated, these languages and literatures become socially usable systems. Thus, the marginal (or *deshi:* regional) and the dominant (or *marg*: mainstream) literary traditions keep alternating their positions.[9] This continuous and inevitable mobility of literary conventions is what the term 'evolution' of literature should rightly imply.

Literature, as a social and cultural activity, is a continuous reordering of the total field of meaning available to a society through language, a continuous restructuring of various levels of received language. Literature, in order to be socially meaningful, has to reappropriate the sources of language so as to invest the language system with new possibilities of consciousness. Hence, the linguistic activity on the margins of a language community, the para-literary activity, has an important role to play in the literary enrichment of that language. For this reason it deserves attention as literary history.

It may be said that the distinction between literature and para-literature is not a distinction between two different fields, but a distinction within a single field, as the one between totems and taboos within a single culture, or as between the self and the non-self within a single field of consciousness. The political dispossession of linguistic and social margins is the root cause of the creation of such categories. The relationship between literature and para--literature is closely comparable to that between the psychologically masculine and the psychologically feminine other. It is a relationship in which the female other is seen as being closer to the unconscious, the primitive, the marginal, and yet indispensable. Ultimately, it is the need for this dialectics of self-cognition of literature that creates the category of para-literature.

If the dialectical relationship between the dominant trends and marginal trends is considered a process forming the backbone of the history of literature, it would still be necessary to specify the nature of this dialectic in a given culture, for it may vary from culture to culture. In other words, canon formation may be a common experience for all literatures in the world, but the processes through which canons are formed in a given literary culture are likely to be peculiar to that particular literary tradition. For instance, the canons of English literature have been shaped generally speaking by the conservative forces in British society. The canons of post-Sanskrit Indian literatures have, on the other hand, been formed by socially heterodox tendencies. It is not enough for literary history to describe the canons; it is also necessary, and even more important, to explain the culture-specific processes of canon formation so as to make literature a socially integrated sub-system of culture. Therefore, if the relationship between literature and para-literature is of vital importance to the self-cognition of literary canons, it would be essential for any perspicuous literary history to take into account the nature of a society's narcissistic structure.

15

Swa and Para: Self and the Other

It is at this stage that we have to introduce another term to help us conceptualize the narcissistic structure of Indian society, as understood in Indian traditions. The term we can use is *para,* which is accepted by a large majority of modern Indian languages as the term for 'other'. The original Sanskrit term, replete with meanings, indicates: "distant, further, enemy, afterwards, beyond, other, far off, etc." Its superlative form, *param* however moves into a more idealistic plane by generating sacred terms such as *parameshwar* and *parabrahman,* terms related to the discourse of the other world. The term is shared by Dravidian languages too, with revealing deviations. Tamil uses *parai* as the term for drums played by outcaste drummers of the *paraiyar* community, which, incidentally, is also the origin of a similar English term, 'pariah'. One is not sure if the Greek *para* and the Sanskrit *para* have a forgotten common source; but it is possible to deduce from the linguistic evidence we have, that in all languages in which the Greek and the Sanskrit term *para* has been assimilated, the term is used to indicate 'otherness' as a psychological phenomenon as well as a spatial term, as if the psychological space is revealed through this term as a geographical metaphor. Thus modern English has 'parish' and 'parochial' indicating restricted psychological and geographical spaces. In Indian languages the term *paradesh* is used to indicate foreign or alien land. Such peculiar usage of the term for describing space as well as otherness, indicating unarticulated wisdom inherent in human languages, is properly theorized in Lacan's formulation:

> The notion of the role of spatial symmetry in man's narcissistic structure is essential in the establishment of the basis of a psychological analysis of space... Let us consider that animal psychology has shown us that the individual's relation to a particular spatial field is, in certain species mapped socially, in a way that raises it to the category of subjective membership. I would say that it is the subjective possibility of the mirror projection of such a field into the field of the other that gives human space its originally 'geometric' structure, a structure that I would be happy to call *kaleidoscopic* ... Such, at least, is the space in which the imagery of the ego develops, and which rejoins the objective space of reality.[1]

Indian epistemology too admits the kaleidoscopic structure within the ego-space. But the kaleidoscoping it visualizes is not between the field of the self and the field of the non-self. It is rather between the field of the self and the field of the greater-self. It is a theology-bound epistemology. The *Katha Upanishad* is eloquent on this issue:

> The tree of eternity has its roots in heaven above and its branches reach down to earth. It is Brahman ... Brahman is seen in a pure soul as in a mirror clear, and also in the Creator's heaven as clear as light; but in the land of shades as reflections in trembling water. When the wise man knows that the material senses come not from the Spirit, and their waking and sleeping belong to their own nature, then he grieves no more. Beyond the senses is the Spirit of man, and beyond this is the Spirit of the universe, and evolver of all. And beyond is Purusha, all pervading, beyond definitions. [2]

Here too, as in Lacan, the key terms are 'mirror' and 'reflection' which complete the grand circle of human consciousness by inductive leaps. But the mapping of the narcissistic structure is different.

Indian texts, whether emerging from the *Vedas,* the *Upanishads,* or secular literature, see the self and the non-self as reflections of

Purusha, the greater-self, as mere passing images of a realitv beyond human perception. In that sense, the dichotomy between the self and non-self has not been conceptualized in radical terms. Buddhist psychology too did not visualize any such opposition between the self and the non-self. In fact, the entire spectrum of human existence is seen in Indian thought in terms of a complex continuum. To introduce concepts of polarities in it is considered by Indian thought as tantamount to a profoundly ignorant act of consciousness.

How can one reconcile this concept of the ego-space with the rational and sensory perceptions, which form the physical basis for the recognition of the non-self? Traditional Indian epistemology circumvents this difficulty by introducing a taxonomy of knowledge. Indian tradition divided knowledge into false knowledge, *avidya,* and authentic knowledge, *vidya.* The two are not radically different, but they can be recognized as such in terms of a polarity in the spectrum of knowledge. *Avidya* is the knowledge flowing from the senses to the soul. *Vidya,* on the contrary, is the knowledge flowing from the soul to the senses. The knower of *vidya* is a guru, a spiritual guide. These categories were neatly separated from those related to systematized perception of material phenomena, for which the terms *jnana* and *vijnana* (approximately corresponding to modern humanities and science, respectively) were employed. The knower of the latter was known as *acharya,* a teacher, a scholar. An experience of *para,* the foreign or alien, thus brings into play the knowledge of the other, which, when it is guided by *vidya* (spiritual knowledge) obscures the duality between the self and the non-self, leading to a recognition of the self within the non-self.

Sudhir Kakar, who has presented highly engaging theses on Indian psychoanalysis, comments on the sense of the self in Hindu tradition at length in his study *The Inner World.* His observations as a professional scholar of psychology would be of immense use to us in defining the priorities of Indian literary history. Discussing the concepts of 'I', 'Ego' and 'Self, he writes :

> The distinction between *vidya* and *avidya*—true and false consciousness—between reality and *maya,* illustrates a

> fundamental difference between Hindu and Western world images, as well as a discrepancy in the modes of thought and perception, which even the best intentioned movements of cultural ecumenism cannot hope to bridge satisfactorily. The maintenance of ego boundaries, between 'inside' and 'outside', and between I and 'others', and the sensory experiences of social relations based on these separations, is the stuff of reality in Western thought and yet *maya* to the Hindus. The optimal discrimination of this reality of separateness, expressed in terms of heightened ego functions such as reality sense, reality testing and adaptation to reality, is the stated goal of most Western psychotherapies, but of paltry importance in the Hindu ways of liberation. A good reality sense, according to psychoanalysis, shows itself in the absence of a conscious feeling of the self or the various selves. This, however, is precisely the situation which the Hindu ways of liberation would seek to reverse. And if in the course of development, the child learns to differentiate between himself and what is not a part of him, between 'me' and 'not-me'—a process in which the individual's sense of space, time, causality and individuality are formed, and ego boundaries are constituted—then in a certain sense the Hindu ways of liberation ... seek to undo this process of ego development.[3]

If, as modern psychoanalysis tells us, the tendency of the dominant Indian psychological type is towards establishing the non-duality of self and non-self in the narcissistic field, the tendency in the altruistic field must, therefore, be that of allowing a free interplay between the central and *para* cultural elements.

It would, however, be inaccurate to think that the Aryan epistemology of the self-other relationship remained unchanged in the long history of India. Hinduism has been an amorphous mass of ideas and practices, within which an amazing variety of dissenting viewpoints emerged and eventually merged. Besides, for about a thousand years India has produced a powerful and complex tradition of Indian Islam, and for two centuries created hybrid cultural practices out of the encounter with the modern West. Yet, the amazing capacity to assimilate alien cultural, linguistic and literary elements is a unique and essential feature of Indian history. Though the western countries too have been exposed to a very large number of alien cultures during the last two hundred years, their assimilation of alien cultural traits has been relatively restricted in correspondence with their relationship of otherness with the foreign cultures.

It is of course not true that the metaphysics of non-duality between the self and the non-self did not create social stratification in India. All the evidence in Indian history goes directly against such an assumption. No other society in the world is, has been, perhaps more fragmented, stratified and torn with strife as Indian society. It is divided linguistically, regionally, in terms of caste, income, faith, and profession. What is true, perhaps, is that the tendency of dissension is counterbalanced by the political and social organization based on consensus. It is for this reason that a careful study of the exchanges between literature and para-literature becomes all the more vital to a proper understanding of India's literary past, and through it the literary present.

16

Tradition and Transactions

European literary historiography uses the paradigm of a single dominant literary tradition. There is very little debate about the central canons of British literature. Occasional debates about particular preferences of styles and periods do take place, such as the one created by T. S. Eliot's preference for the Metaphysicals over the Romantics, but the overall range of the canon has never been in doubt. At no stage in the tradition of English literary criticism was any allowance made for the inclusion of a non-British writer in the British canon,[1] even when some very good works were produced in the language of the British isles, outside, in other continents. On the other hand, in India a writer of Greek ancestry like Ashvaghosha, or of Irish nationality like Nivedita, or with Caribbean background like Naipaul or with Arabic training like Ibn Battuta, have been accepted as *Indian* writers. Languages such as Persian, Arabic, English, French and Portuguese have been accepted in India as languages of *Indian* literature. The English canons have never thought of any translation as a *great* work of literature, the emphasis of Anglo-poetics being on the original (though perhaps aesthetically the most intricate work in English is the King James' version of the *Bible,* a translation). In India some of the most respected literary classics have originated in attempts to translate: the *Jnaneswari* in Marathi, Kamban's *Ramayana* in Tamil, Tulsidas's *Ramayana* in Hindi, Tagore's *Gitanjali* in English are some examples. Again, Indian literature has in it the peculiar phenomenon of bilingual writers. The number of bilingual writers in India is so large, and the longevity of this practice is so substantial that bilingual literature is more a norm than an exception in India. Considering these major differences between literary practices in India and Western countries, it is obvious that the concept of a single dominant literary tradition, a single and fairly well-defined literary canon and historical criticism couched in a unidirectional philology will not prove adequate to interpret the history of literature in any Indian language.

This particular problem for literary historiography can get a useful lead from developments in general historiography in India in recent years. Specifically useful in this respect is Romila Thapar's important essay on tradition in *Cultural Transaction and Early India: Tradition and Patronage.*[2] In this essay Thapar discusses the Indian views of tradition, more particularly the historical reconstruction of tradition. Through several convincing examples, she makes it clear that at any given time there may be a normative code of tradition, but at the same time there exist numerous deviations from the norm. It is therefore possible, as Thapar argues, to project a variety of traditions as dominant in Indian history and culture, none of which is more or less authentic than the rest. One of the more striking examples she selects to put her view across is that of the *Mahabharata.* The story of Shakuntala used by Kalidasa existed in *Mahabharata* previous to his rendering. The two versions have different philosophical and ideological orientations. After Kalidasa's use of the story, the two versions co-existed in Indian culture. Thapar asks: Which of the two is more authentic? Her answer is that authenticity of tradition arises out of subjective reading by historians:

> For such a diverse community to create a uniform cultural tradition for itself can become an exercise in juggling with history. Traditions are not self-created: they are consciously chosen, and the choice from the past is enormous... If we are to understand the role of religion in the Indian society of earlier times we may have to be moved away from the paradigm of Hinduism and the other religions in India as projected in the colonial

> period... Complex societies have competing value systems and attempts are made by the more established to delete ideologies of protest or of divergent values.[3]

What is true of the national history of India is also, and far more pertinently, true of its literary history, given the multilingual literary context. Western historiography of literature is based on literary histories which do not have multiple parallel traditions. The term 'parallel' can be applied to popular or folk traditions in European contexts. In India the parallel traditions are really alternative traditions rather than 'low' value traditions.

When Panini wrote his grammar in the pre-Christian centuries, he spoke of two discourses in Sanskrit, one used by the common people and another that was grammatically correct. When Bharata composed his treatise on drama, he spoke of two types of theatre, one catering to the public and the other based on dramatic conventions. Both Panini and Bharata speak of the popular and the doctrinaire as insiders, not in terms of the self and the other. Dandin, the seventh century Sanskrit theoretician, describes several competing literary styles from different regions of India. They were all styles of Sanskrit poetry; in describing these, Dandin does not arrange them in an aesthetic or sociological hierarchy. In the eleventh century, Rajashekhara could write plays in Maharashtri as well as in Sanskrit. Jayadeva in the twelfth century wrote poetry in Bengali as well as in Sanskrit. Hemachandra, in the thirteenth century, wrote in Gujarati and in Sanskrit. Namadeva wrote poems in Hindi and in Punjabi too, in addition to writing in Marathi. Thyagaraja, writing in Telugu had no hesitation in learning the diction and metre of Gujarati poetry. Ekanatha prepared a scholarly edition of Jnanadeva's *Bhavarthadipika,* using writing as the medium, and 'published' most of his own poems using the oral medium of singing. There are innumerable writers who write in Urdu and Hindi, Hindi and Punjabi, Oriya and Bangla, Gujarati and Marathi, English and some Indian language. None of them show signs of any unusual anxiety of being torn or split between traditions. An average Indian reader, if he or she is reasonably well educated, reads works in his or her own language, in one or two other Indian languages, in English translation from other languages; and yet does not feel anxiety or guilt for the loss of his linguistic, literary or cultural identity. The Indian tradition has given to every sensitive Indian the ability to internalize a multiplicity of traditions.

In India, the folk traditions can be as erudite as the dominant lexical traditions; and apparently outmoded styles and diction can find unexpected revivals. Thus it would be improper to classify the traditions either into clearly demarcated periods, or into categories with clearly demarcated class origins of literature. It would be inappropriate even to speak of literary traditions in terms of a tradition of texts in a single given language. A more appropriate approach would be to think of literary history in terms of a constant exclusion of para-literatures from the cultural centres creating a constant assimilation of para-literatures into the centres of culture, creating a complex pattern of conflict and collaboration of many minor traditions. It may have been purely a linguistic coincidence that the term for tradition in Indian languages, *parampara,* implies the historiographic view proposed by Romila Thapar, for the term is formed by combining *param* (superlative *of para*) and *para.*[4] We may interpret the term to mean, in the light of the foregoing discussion, 'consideration of all literary margins'. Such a view of *parampara,* tradition, will not be very far from the spirit of the term *sahitya,* meaning togetherness or co-existence, employed for the literary arts.

The term *sahitya,*[5] one of the several Indian terms for literature, has implicit in it a vitally important insight for literary historiography. There are other terms in Indian languages which are synonyms for *sahitya* such as *vangmaya, saraswata, kavya, lekhan,* etc. While *vangmaya* and *saraswata* indicate the literary or poetic quality of writing, *lekhan* refers to the act of writing. None of these has superseded *sahitya* so far because it accurately reflects the historical fact that all literary traditions and movements in India resulted from a togetherness, *sahitya,* of multiple traditions.

The idea of a pure state of authentic existence at the point of origin is not appropriate to view Indian literary history; probably it is not appropriate to view any literary history at all, except that of proto-Indo-European literature, if it existed at all, for at that point of history we have with us nothing but a sense of mystery and myth. So far, Western literary historiography has not come to terms with the basic fact about literary history that all traditions of literature originate in the act of translation. An act of translation holds together two, or sometimes more, different traditions momentarily, for a cross fertilization, and in that sense all translations are *sahitya.*

17

Translation as Origin

"Translation is the wandering existence in a perpetual exile," says J. Hillis Miller.[1] The statement obviously alludes to the Christian myth of the Fall, exile and wandering. In Western metaphysics translation is an exile, a fall from the origin; and the mythical exile is a metaphorical translation—a post-Babel crisis. Given this metaphysical precondition of Western aesthetics, it is not surprising that literary translations are not accorded the same status as original works. Western literary criticism provides for the guilt of translations for coming into being *after* the original; the temporal subsequentiality is held as a proof of diminution of literary authenticity of translations. The strong sense of being an individual, given to Western individuals through systematic philosophy and the logic of social history makes them view translation as an intrusion of 'the other'. This intrusion is desirable to the extent it helps define one's own identity; but not beyond that point. It is, of course, natural for the monolingual European cultures to be acutely conscious of the act of translation. The philosophy of individualism and the metaphysics of guilt, however, render European literary historiography incapable of grasping the origins of literary traditions.

One of the most revolutionary events in the history of English style has been the authorized translated version of the Bible. It was also the literary expression of Protestant Christianity. The recovery of the original spirit of Christianity was thus sought by

Protestant England through an act of translation. It is well known that Chaucer was translating the style of Boccacio into English when he created his *Canterbury Tales.* When Dryden and Pope wanted to recover a sense of order, they used the tool of translation.[2] Similar attempts were made in other European languages such as German and French.

During the last two centuries the role of translation in communicating literary movements across linguistic borders has become very important. The tradition that has given us writers like Shaw, Yeats, Joyce, Beckett, Heaney in a single century—the tradition of Anglo-Irish literature—branched out of the practice of translating Irish works into English initiated by Macpherson towards the end of the eighteenth century.[3] Indian English literature too has gathered its conventions of writing from the Indological activity of translation during the late eighteenth century and the nineteenth century. Many of the Anglo-Irish and Indian English writers have been able translators themselves. Similarly, the settler colonies such as Australia, Canada, New Zealand have impressive modern traditions of literature, which have resulted from the 'translation' of the settlers from their homeland to alien locations. Postcolonial writing in the former Spanish colonies in South America, the former colonies in Africa, and in other parts of the world have experienced the importance of translation as one of the crucial conditions for creativity. In fact modernism and postmodernism as international movements would never have come into existence without the mediation of repeated acts of translation. Those who study theory today know that if they did not have translations of theorists from a dozen different cultures, it would be impossible to think of a revolution in literary thought at all. Thus origins of literary movements and literary traditions can be traced back to various acts of translation.

Considering the fact that most literary traditions originate in translation, and gain substance through repeated acts of translation, it would be useful for a theory of literary history to seek support from a theory of literary translation. However, since translations are conventionally perceived as *unoriginal,* not much thought has been devoted to the aesthetics of translation. Most of the primary issues too have not been settled in relation to translation: issues related to the 'form' and 'meaning' of translation. No major critic has taken any well-defined position about the exact placement of translations in literary history. Do they belong to the history of target languages, or do they belong to the history of source languages? Or do they form an independent tradition all by themselves? This ontological uncertainty which haunts translations has rendered translation study a haphazard activity which devotes too much energy to discussing the problems of the original meaning and the meaning of the altered structure.[4]

Unfortunately for translation the various developments about the interdependence between meaning and structure in the field of linguistics have been based on monolingual data and situations. Even the sophisticated and revolutionary theoretical formulation proposed by structural linguistics are not sufficient to unravel the intricacies of translation activity.

Structural linguistics considers language a system of signs, arbitrarily developed, that tries to cover the entire range of significance available to the culture of that language. The signs do not mean anything by or in themselves, they acquire significance by virtue of their relation to the entire system to which they belong. This theory naturally looks down upon translation which is an attempt to rescue/abstract significance from one system of signs and to wed it to another such system. But language is an open system. It keeps admitting new signs as well as new significance in its fold. It is also open, in the socio-linguistic sense that it allows an individual speaker or writer to use as much of it as he can or likes to do. If this is the case, then how 'open' is a particular system of verbal signs when a bilingual user, such as a translator, rends it open? Assuming that, for an individual, language resides within his consciousness, we can ask whether the two systems within his consciousness can be shown as materially different, whether they retain their individual identities within the sphere of his consciousness?

Or do such systems become a single, open and extended system? If translation is defined as some kind of communication of significance, and if we accept the structuralist principle that communication becomes possible because of the nature of signs and their entire system, it follows that translation is a merger of sign systems. Such a merger is possible because systems of signs are open and vulnerable. The 'translating consciousness' exploits the potential openness of language systems; and as it shifts significance from a given verbal form to a corresponding but different verbal form it also brings closer the materially different sign systems.

If we take the lead from phenomenology and conceptualize a whole community of 'translating consciousness', it should be possible to develop a theory of inter-lingual synonymy as well as a more perceptive literary historiography. The concept of 'translating consciousness', and of communities of people possessing it, are no mere notions. In most Third World countries, where a dominating colonial language has acquired a privileged place, such communities do exist. In India several languages are simultaneously used by language communities as if these languages formed a continuous spectrum of significance. To conceptualize this situation is beyond European linguistics, which is based mostly on a monolingual view of language. The use of two or more different languages in translation activity cannot be understood properly through studies of foreign language acquisition. Such theories work round the premise that there is inevitably a chronological gap, an order or a priority scale in language learning situations. The field is stratified in terms of value based indicators L1 and L2, though in reality language learning activity may seem very natural in a country like India. In Chomsky's linguistics the concept of semantic universals plays an important role. However, his level of abstraction marks the farthest limits to which the monolingual Saussurean linguistic materialism can be stretched. In actual practice, even in Europe, the translating consciousness treats the source language and target language as parts of a larger and continuous spectrum of various intersecting systems of verbal signs.

The privileged discourse of general linguistics today is closely interlinked with developments in anthropology, particularly after Durkheim and Levi-Strauss. Colonial Europe had distributed various fields of humanistic knowledge into a threefold hierarchy: comparative studies for Europe, Orientalism for the Orient, and anthropology for the rest of the world. In its various phases of development modern western linguistics has connections with all these. After the 'discovery' of Sanskrit by Sir William Jones, historical linguistics in Europe depended heavily on Orientalism. For a long time afterwards linguists followed the path of comparative philology. And after Saussure and Levi-Strauss, linguistics started treating language with an anthropological curiosity. When linguistics branched off to its monolingual structuralist path, comparative literature still persisted in its faith in the translatability of literary texts.

Comparative literature accepts that between two related languages there are areas of significance that are shared just as there may be areas of significance that can never be shared. Translation can be seen as an attempt to bring a given language system in its entirety as close as possible to the areas of significance that it shares with other given language or languages. All translations operate within this shared area of significance. Such a notion may help us distinguish synonymy within one language and the shared significance between two related languages.

The translation problem is not just a linguistic problem. It is an aesthetic and ideological problem which has a significant bearing on the question of literary history. Literary translation is not just a replication of a text in another verbal system of signs. It is replication of an ordered sub-system of signs within a given language into another corresponding ordered sub-system of signs within a related language. Translation is not a transposition of significance or signs. After the act of translation is over, the original work still remains in its original position. Translation is rather an attempted revitalisation of the original in another verbal space and temporal span. Like literary texts that continue to belong to their original periods and styles and also continue to exist through successive chronological periods, translation at once approximates to the original and transcends it. The problems in translation study are, therefore, very much like those in literary history. They are the problems of the relationship between origins and subsequentiality. And as in translation study, so in literary history the problem of origin has not been tackled satisfactorily. The point that needs to be made is that probably the question of origins of literary traditions will have to be viewed differently by multilingual literary communities possessing a 'translating consciousness'.

18

The Course and the Discourse of History

History is a mass of facts, events and episodes, as well as a structured narrative intended for communication of attitudes, perceptions and analysis of relationships between historical events. Or more appropriately, history is not just facts, dates, events. If history is seen as being so, it will have no framework at all. The process of inclusion will be endless. If, on the other hand, history is seen merely as a narrative, a structure or framework within which all facts, dates, and events fit perfectly well, it will be unrealistic and tend to become pure fiction. History is ideally speaking, an interrelationship between facts and narratives, between the course of history and the discourse of history. It takes no great imagination to realize that not all forms of narrative are adequate for all kinds of facts. Poets use elegy when talking about death, and novelists use the stream of consciousness while revealing the working of the unconscious. Some themes find more truthful expression in some literary forms, other themes may find some other forms appropriate. Similarly, not every strategy of historical narrative may be appropriate to express the essence of each and every kind of literary culture, movement or tradition.

The relationship between the course and the discourse of history is like that between language and reality. Reality is understood, philosophically speaking, as an undistinguished and continuous stream or spectrum of existence, material as well as non-material. Language is understood as a system which imposes 'meaning' on reality through arbitrary signs and systems of signification. It is through the apparently arbitrary signs that language creates meaningful patterns out of the experience of existence. Similarly, the course of history is a continuous, inexorable flow, which the discourse of history tries to illuminate. There is another similarity between the two relationships. This similarity is that the discourse of historiography is itself not history; the discourse is merely a series of statements about history. Due to these similarities, a philosophy of language-meaning relationship can be of interest to the study of the relationship between the course and the discourse of history.

It is again to Bhartrihari that we have to turn in order to understand the language-meaning relationship in its central form of conceptualization in Indian tradition.

The central tenet of Bhartrihari's opus on semantics, the *Vakyapadiya*[1] is that meaning is not a property of an isolated word or phonetic unit; it is a property of complete sentences. A sentence, in his idea of meaning, is a single undivided utterance which conveys a single undivided meaning.[2] He maintains that the sentence-meaning is grasped as a unity. This aspect of his theory allowed Indian critics in the past to build a theory of poetic meaning, as John Brough points out:

> The important point is that the sentence-meaning is grasped as a unity. The situation is compared to our apprehension of a picture. This we perceive as in some sense a unity, and although we can analyse the field of vision...nonetheless, we are normally aware of the integrated whole...In the end the utmost that can be said of the meaning of a sentence according to Bhartrihari is that it is grasped by an instantaneous flash of insight *(pratibha)*.[3]

Brough points out that it was this theory *of vakya com*bined with the semantic concept of *sphota* that led to Anandavardhana's theory of *dhvani* in the ninth century.

If we think of the interdependence between the facts of history and the story of history in the light of this theory it can be proposed that literary facts, events, episodes, etc., have no historical meaning in themselves. This is not to say that they have no meaning at all (which they must have as texts, writing, etc.) but rather they will acquire a historical identity only when placed in an order, either as a canon formed by writers, or as a tradition formed by texts alluding to earlier texts.

Our sense of history gets blunted by descriptive labels which are over-used. Labels like 'Romanticism', 'Classicism', 'Gothic', 'Renaissance', 'Modernism', 'Post-structuralism', 'Bhakti-period', 'Indian sensibility ', 'Postcolonial literature', are without exception hopeless as indicators of any discernible literary quality or styles. The worst failure common to all labels is that they tend to be too inclusive; even if this is not intended initially so, they come to be so in the course of their career. A time comes in the life of these labels when their meanings can be clear only in opposition to some equally nebulous label: thus 'romantic' is that which is not 'classical', 'postcolonial' that which is not 'precolonial', and so on. Such labels defeat the very purpose of literary history, which is to impose a structure of meaning on the flow of literary history. If literature is seen as an activity in which hundreds of people belonging to a given culture take part, which makes a feeble faltering beginning before becoming a powerful trend or current, it follows that prior to history, in any given literature, there exist orders, discourses and traditions. For a realistic perception of literary history, it is necessary to understand these distinctions clearly.

Every history is ultimately an exercise in criticism. All historical description, by its very nature, is also critical description. Works of literature are arranged by critics, and also by historians, in order of their merit. An ordering of writers, and texts, is an extremely useful activity for writers belonging to subsequent generations. They choose their past for themselves by ordering the existing past according to their own taste. T. S. Eliot's concept of the past that is also present was of this nature. When he 'dropped' Milton and 'included' Donne and Herbert in his order, it was not an exercise in rewriting the history of literature. It was an attempt to show that multiple orders co exist within a single tradition, with which a given writer can establish his/her relationship. An order is, therefore, an intellectual abstraction, a certain projected subjective perception within a single chronological unit, or within a given tradition, or within the consciousness of a critic or writer. Several such orders can coexist simultaneously.

When critics and historians notice pronounced similarities, contrasts, or correspondence of some kind between various texts or authors within either a single language tradition, or a multilingual tradition, they can speak in terms of certain conventions of writing, style, thought, theme, treatment, and so on. When these conventions become sufficiently clear to establish relations of a certain kind among the works in question, one can speak of a discourse of literature—a new form, trend, fashion, style, wave, movement, protest, revolution, shift, and so on. The discovery of a discourse by a historian is relatively value free. That is, if locating a literary order involves great critical self-consciousness, locating a literary discourse does not involve the same degree of critical self-consciousness. A literary discourse need not be restricted to a single language. Thus if an order is predominantly a single language phenomenon, discourse need not be so. For example, one can speak of the nationalist discourse in Indian poetry, or the discourse of psychoanalysis in the short story. Every literature is made up of several concurrent discourse as well as several possible orders that co-exist simultaneously.

If orders and discourses are predominantly contemporary, that is, restricted in their temporal spans, traditions exist in an extended time span. For instance, one can speak of the Petrarchan sonnet as a tradition, or the tradition of children's writing, or the tradition of socially committed poetry. Tradition is different from discourse mainly in that tradition refers to the chronological space, discourse refers to stylistic or philosophic practices. Traditions subsume orders, and they overlap with discourses. However, traditions do not come into existence unless they are willed to come into existence. Tradition is like the command of a computer to search for a definite line of arrangement in a given data. One can speak of the tradition of saint poets in Bangla or Telugu; it is only recently that we have started speaking of the tradition of women writers in Indian languages. So far, we have not looked for a tradition of environmentally alert literature but it is possible to think of it. If and when we do so, perhaps oral poetry, which consumes no paper, will be offered a higher aesthetic position. It is possible to think of a tradition of urban or rural literature, a tradition of writers who died young, writers who were sexually liberated, writers who did not attend formal school, and so on. Within a tradition one can locate several orders of writing and several discourses of literature. The history of literature contains descriptions of literary orders, descriptions of literary discourses as well as a narration of literary traditions. It is the business of literary history to describe the emergence of various literary discourses and the decline of other discourses, the formation of new literary orders, and subsequently, over an extended temporal span, the formation of several literary traditions. The dynamic relationship between orders, discourses and traditions should be of abiding interest to literary history.

19

Nation and Narration

Literary orders, discourses and traditions are not primarily logical or ontological formations. They are phenomenological strategies which assist the celebration of a culture's self-recognition. Just as every nation with a modern state-structure likes to acquire an independent military force, every society in possession of printing technology likes to have a literary history of its own. In those societies where the creative use of language of literary merit has not been frozen in cold print, the need for a cold chronological record of literary events is not felt so strongly. In India there are about eighty-five such language communities whose literature remains non-printed, and therefore, non-historicised even now. Of course, the technology of long distance (or impersonal) literary communication is not the only condition for the emergence of literary history. There are two more, and equally important conditions: the institutionalized teaching of literature, and the emergence of a culture's self-recognition. For example, millions of people all over the world travel every day for various reasons; and often they travel through towns, territories, nations which are not their own. No one has thought of writing a history of literature by and for travellers in the world. But as soon as these people acquire a sense of sharing a common fate, the sense of being a community, there will emerge a need for the history of expatriate literature. This imaginary history, then, will appropriate the epic form of poetry which narrates long and heroic journeys, the picaresque form of fiction which depicts the moral growth of travellers, expatriate writers like James Joyce, Beckett, Conrad, Naipaul, Rushdie, and texts like *Don Quixote, The Divine Comedy, Heart of Darkness, India: A Wounded Civilisation,* etc. If some academics decide to create such a course in their university, college or polytechnic, the need for a history of this tradition of literature will be felt intensely and immediately.

Thus literary history is a phenomenological strategy the need for which is felt by communities engaged in consolidating their newly formed or perceived identities by creating systems of literary totems and taboos. On the other hand, if a community dissolves into many segments, or is swallowed up by another larger community, its need for literary history will change accordingly. The need for history will also undergo a major change when the present mode of storing knowledge, which is the printed text, changes. And, finally, it will be modified in correspondence with the changes in the courses of institutionalized literary instruction. These ideas may become clear if we examine the case of a new literary history at its very inception.

Tariq Rahman, a literary scholar from Rawalpindi, has published the first history of *Pakistani Literature in English* (1991).[1] His book is the first and the only exercise in this area and it generates several interesting questions about the nature of literary history itself. The first question is related to the antecedents of this literature: Pakistan and India were one country during the British raj, and prior to the raj from the beginning of the subcontinent's recorded history. The recorded history of the territory now called Pakistan spans about six millennia. For five out of these six millennia of its history, Islam was unknown to the people of that territory. Most of them were converted to Islam from the eleventh to the eighteenth centuries. But the people in the territory known today as Pakistan and those in the area that is now known as India had nothing to distinguish them as two very distinct units of culture. Thus there is nothing peculiarly Indian that is not in the past of Pakistan, and vice versa. In 1947, the British divided the Indian landmass in an arbitrary manner to create Pakistan, which was intended to be predominantly Islamic in culture. About twenty-five years after its creation, a part of Pakistan separated itself from the national sovereignty of the Pakistan state. Thus in effect, Pakistan has had three phases in its political history: from the earliest times to 1947 as India, then from 1947 to 1971 as East and West Pakistan; and from 1971 as Pakistan (minus East Pakistan or Bangladesh).

Tariq Rahman's problem is, how to write about the past of Pakistani English Literature. Should he include some writers in his history from the pre-Partition days? If he does, how can he explain their Pakistanness as against the Indianness which was their nationality at that time (since the two countries were not divided then)? Should he include those writers who are likely to be claimed by Bangladeshi English Literature? Should he include those writers who spent some years in Pakistan, some in India and some in an entirely different country? Should he include those Muslim writers who had left India before the Partition and settled in another country (who, had they stayed back would have, hopefully, gone over to Pakistan?) And should he include those Muslim writers who did not move over to Pakistan, but decided to stay on in India, and yet being Muslim, represent the consciousness of the pre-Partition Muslim population in India which later became the population of Pakistan? These problems are not only the problems of Pakistani literary history, or of Bangladeshi literary history. They are also the problems of Indian literary history, of the history of Hindi, Urdu and English literatures in India. The problems have to be faced by Bangla, Sindhi, Punjabi, Dogri and Gujarati literatures too, for the literary community in all these languages have been distributed between India and Pakistan. The most complicated situation, however, is that of Urdu.

Given this situation, it is interesting to watch from a theoretical perspective the reasons articulated by Tariq Rahman for writing his history and the practical strategies he employs to get round the issues raised above. In the introductory chapter of his book, Rahman stresses the need for a history of Pakistani English literature as well as the need for its institutionalized teaching: "As yet no Pakistani university offers a course in either Pakistani or even in African, West Indian and Indian literature in English."[2] He records that not much *systematic* criticism has been written in this area, and "because of this lack of criticism the history of Pakistani literature in English has yet not been written though such histories exist for other Third World literatures in English. This book is being written to fill this gap."[3] Thus the motivation is to articulate the sense of being an autonomous cultural unit, a literary community, as distinct from the community of Pakistani writers in regional languages and also, from the community of English writers in other Third World countries. This sense of community can be created by creating an order of literary taboos and totems, freshly structured:

> Some writers who have written prolifically have been given no critical attention whereas others who have produced only one slim volume of verse or collection of short stories have been commented upon. This has been done for two reasons: either the writer has not collected his separate writings in a single collection or, and here my personal judgment comes in, I have not considered the work worthy of critical attention at all.[4]

Since there is no established criticism, there cannot be any critical consensus about writers. The canon has to be created by the first historian. And it is created on the basis of aesthetic criteria as Rahman tells us. But an aesthetic cannot be defined before the tradition of literature, which is its basis, is forged. Hence, the creation of literary history, and literary canon, and institutionalized modes of its teaching, share something with the procedures for creating totems and taboos.

In the chapter devoted to the pre-Partition writers, Rahman explains the reasons for including the writers discussed in his study:

> Among the Muslims who started writing before the Partition of India in 1947, the most famous name is that of Ahmed Ali. That is why a complete chapter of this book has been devoted to his work. In this chapter I shall deal with the writings of Ahmed Ali's Muslim contemporaries, Feroze Khan Noon, Mumtaz Shahnawaz and Khwaja Ahmad Abbas. It is easy to see why the first

> two should have been included in history of Pakistani literature. Noon became a Prime Minister of Pakistan and Mumtaz's famous novel *The Heart Divided* is one of the few responses in English fiction to the creation of Pakistan from the Muslim Indian point of view. But Abbas did not emigrate to Pakistan nor is he in any political sense concerned with Pakistan. However, I have dealt with Abbas because he represents a neglected aspect of Muslim consciousness which found literary expression in English before the Partition. This is the response to the ideas of liberalism and socialism which were accepted by some Indian intellectuals before the Partition and have receded into the background in Pakistan now. Abbas's work is significant because it represents the liberal-socialist aspect of the Indian Muslim consciousness.[5]

Ahmed Ali has been claimed by histories of Indian English literature as a pioneering English fiction writer. K. A. Abbas has been claimed by the progressive movement of the 1940s, Indian Urdu writings, and Indian cinema. On the other hand, Rahman's history leaves out Salman Rushdie, though at least his *Shame* has a reason to be placed within Pakistani writing. The principle of selection and rejection is the magical formula of being an acceptable Muslim. Of course, all other methods of historical projection also stem out of this basic method. Literary history is always more of a strategy than a logically coherent order. That nation has apparently become the defining category for modern literary histories is a reflection of the fact that the European cultures show a general agreement on the identity between language, culture and nation. Otherwise the basic unit for literary history is culture which recognizes itself as distinct from other cultures.

20

The Garden and the Forest

A given culture's attitude to Language has an important bearing on its concept of literary history. In Western cultures the attitude to Language is largely anatomical—one in which Language is seen as a 'body' or a 'corpus' (which also means 'a structure of a special character in the animal body'). A 'body' can be described in terms of its birth, development and demise. It can be fitted into a meaningful historical narrative. If, on the other hand, some other culture views language as an 'ever present energy' or 'a mysterious being', it becomes difficult to speak of it in terms of a sequential historical narrative. Such energy can manifest itself at different times without decline or growth because it is beyond the laws of anatomy. Indian attitudes to Language (not language) are of this nature. Correspondingly, literature too is invested in India with supernatural powers; it is traditionally considered to have the power to control Nature and as being beyond the laws of Nature. The notion of a fixed human authorship of literary texts is relatively new in Indian literary traditions. Rather, authors are seen as vehicles of the energy that Language is.

Western literature employs the concept of 'reader'. According to the Oxford English Dictionary, 'reader' means 'an advisor, commentator,' etc. The traditional Indian term *'rasika'* for 'audience' has now been replaced by *'vachak'*. It combines the English meaning of 'commentator' as well as the conventional Indian meaning of 'someone who participates in the language act'.

Thus, the perception of literary transaction in the West is different from its perception in India. Literature, whether oral, written, translated or para-literature, is seen in India as invested with an element of the sacred. The forms of worship in India are literary, and literature too is worshipped. The literary input in a person's upbringing in Indian society is relatively far greater than that in western societies. Since Indian myths continue to circulate meaningfully and organically in Indian social practice, the distinction between myth and literature has not been established as yet in radical terms. Our most pervasive mythology, the *Mahabharata* and the *Ramayana,* are also among our greatest literary works.

In the West, literary aesthetics and literary history have been neatly separated from the aesthetics and history of the performing arts and visual arts. Many of the Indian literary practices continue till our day primarily as performances. The tribal epics and stories are never narrated without invoking gods through painting, dance and music. We cannot separate the Varakari literature in Marathi from the music and the body movements of the Varakaris. Is it possible to fully appreciate the beauty of Jayadeva's *Gitagovinda* without bringing in the innumerable sculptures and paintings inspired by the poem? Since, the arts and literature are seen as being of common origin, of a single type of imagination and aesthetic delight, the sharp and neat distinctions between them formulated by Western principles of aesthetics become inappropriate while perceiving Indian literature. In India, literature is essentially a performance, a *prayoga.*

As pointed out before, by referring to Sudhir Kakar's psychoanalysis, a dissolution in the impersonal is seen as the highest goal of a (Hindu) person's life in India. Therefore even the greatest among the artists in India resist the creation of an 'individual' or 'unique' style. Their genius lies not in initiating 'style periods' but in forging 'style communities' which defy chronological classification. Sects and not periods chapterize the Indian literary past. Sects thrive not on the rejection of the past but on a selective renewal of the past. 'Style periods' in Western literary history are distinguished by what is unique to them, but the 'style communities' in India are distinguished by their openness to influences almost to the point of self-erasure. The poetry of the medieval saints in India represents the most distinctive example of a 'style community'.

Finally, the question of imagination itself gets complicated when seen in the context of Indian literary history. The human mind has two faculties that organize the phenomenal world: the first is imagination which organizes all space through arrangements of sensory images; the second is memory which organizes time for us. Without our ability to perceive images, we would have been incapable of interpreting the physical space. Without the ability to remember, we would not have been able to link yesterday, today and tomorrow. When a civilization emerges, its first important engagement is with the physical space surrounding it. To that extent, imagination acquires importance in that culture. However, when any civilization has long been established and has had a surfeit of history, remembering the history becomes a more urgent cultural need. At this juncture, memory becomes more important than imagination. Indian literature has faced this problem for over a thousand years now. It has spent a major part of its creative energy in keeping the remembrance of things past alive. Literary forms, sects, practices, trends and styles in India indicate how important the question of memory has been to Indian culture throughout history. Western literary historiography, quite appropriately, has emphasized the primacy of imagination over memory while classifying, arranging, evaluating and representing literary events. A similar procedure, if it is to be followed in India, will fail to do justice to the creativity in Indian literary tradition. Creations are based mainly on imagination, performances are based mainly on memory. This distinction must never be taken as an absolute distinction. But it has merit when seen in relative terms.

That the literary past in India has run the course of several millennia, has seen the rise and fall of numerous languages, has assimilated influences from all over the world, is full of exceptions to every imaginable literary principle, and is being written or recited even today in more than twenty major languages and more than eighty-five tribal languages, will make the writing of any sort of history of one (or all of) Indian literature a near impossible task. Just as too little history makes historiography unnecessary, too much of it too makes historiography helpless.

It may be possible to name every tree and count every fruit and flower in a garden. But when one is left in the nowhere of a forest without a beginning and without an end in sight, the numerals fail to assist counting and measuring. Literary historiography developed in monolingual cultures and in cultures with a relatively shorter span of existence is like a rational argument about a manageable garden. Indian literary historiography is like entering the mythical Naimisharyana. In it any story will work, but no story will be the complete story. It will give rise to a thousand 'Once upon a time' but will not admit a definite conclusion. Every conclusion in it must stay perpetually tentative...

Notes and References

2. History and Literary History

1. Rene Wellek, *The Rise of English Literary History* (Chapel Hill: University of North Carolina Press, 1941), together with Chris Baldick, *The Social Mission of English Criticism, 1848–1932* (Oxford: Clarendon Press and New York: Oxford University Press, 1983).
2. See Winfred P. Lehmann, ed., A *Reader in Nineteenth Century Historical Indo-European Linguistics* (Bloomington and London: University of Indiana Press, 1967), pp. 99–100.
3. Thomas Warton, *The History of English Poetry from the Close of the Eleventh Century to the Commencement of the Eighteenth Century* (1774), reprinted in 4 volumes by Thomas Tegg (London, 1840).
4. For a detailed critical comment on nineteenth century literary historiography in Germany, see Hans Robert Jauss, *Towards an Aesthetic of Reception,* trans. Timothy Bahti (Minneapolis: University of Minnesota Press, 1982). See particularly, 'Literary History as a Challenge to Literary Theory', pp. 3–46.
5. Rene Wellek, 'Ideas On Literary History', in The *Rise of English Literary History,* pp. 47–94.
6. David Perki, 'Literary Classifications: How Have They Been Made?' in *Theoretical Issues in Literary History,* ed. David Perkins, *Harvard English Studies,* 16 (Cambridge, Massachusetts and London: Harvard University Press, 1992), pp. 248–268.
7. Rene Wellek and Austin Warren, 'Literary Theory, Criticism and History', in *Theory of Literature* (New York: Harcourt, Brace & Co., 1949), pp. 29–37.

3. Time and Territory

1. Heinrich Zimmer, *Myths and Symbols in Indian Art and Civilization,* ed. Joseph Campbell. The Bollingen Series VI (Princeton: Princeton University Press and New York: Pantheon Books, 1946), pp. 37–38.
2. *Everyman's Encyclopaedia, Vol. IX,* (London: J. M.Dent & Co., 1978). The story occurs in Apuleius's *Metamorphosis.*
3. E. H. Carr, *What is History*? (London: Pelican Books, 1964), pp. 148–49.
4. This is the view that Sujit Mukherjce presents in *Towards a Literary History of India* (Simla: Indian Institute of Advanced Study, 1975).
5. Ram Vilas Sharma, *Bharatiya Sahitya ke Itihas ki Samasyaen* (New Delhi: Vani Prakashan, 1986).

6. Anindita Niyogi Balslev, *A Study of Time in Indian Philosophy* (Wiesbaden: Otto Harrassowitz, 1983).
7. Romila Thapar, *Time as a Metaphor of History: Early India* (New Delhi: Oxford University Press, 1996).

4. Two Paradigms of History

1. Ganga Sagar Rai, *The Kavya-Mimansa of Rajasekhara edited with Prakasa* (Hindi). The Vidyabhavan Sanskrit Series, 121 (Varanasi: Chowkhamba Vidyabhavan, 1964), p. 79. The relevant verses read:
"Puranupravibhedu Evetihasah": Ityeke Yadahuh: Sa cha dvidha parakriya purakalpabhyam
"Parakriya purakalpa itihasagatidvidhu.
Syadekanayaka purva dvitiya bahunayaka".
Tatra Ramayana, Bbaratam Chodaharane.
2. Vidyadhar Vaman Apte, *A Concise Sanskrit-English Dictionary* (New Delhi: Gian Publishing House, 1926, 1989).
3. See P. V. Kane, *History of Sanskrit Poetics* (1923), 4th edition (New Delhi: Motilal Banarsidass, 1971), pp. 208–18, and G. N. Devy, *After Amnesia: Tradition and Change in Indian Literary Criticism* (Bombay: Orient Longman, 1992), pp. 72–73.
4. V. Raghavan, *Bhoja's Srngara-Prakasa* (Madras: Punarvasu, 1963), p. 109.
5. For a well-documented commentary on the *Natyashastra,* see P. V. Kane, *History of Sanskrit Poetics,* pp. 10–63.
6. Ibid., pp. 243–48.
7. V. Raghavan, *Bhoja's Srngara-Prakasa,* p. 601:
Itihasasbrayam kathashrayam utpadyetivritam
anutpadyetivritam pratisanskaryetivritam
Iti prabandhasharirani. Itihasashrayemityanen
Vrittudevadicharitashansitamab-yatha Kumarasambhave.

5. Bhartrihari's Metaphors

1. Peri Sarveswara Shrarma, *The Kalasamuddesa of Bhartrihari's Vakyapadiya (together with Helaraja's commentary translated from the Sanskrit)* (New Delhi: Motilal Banarsidass, 1972).
2. Ibid., *Karika* 15, p. 51: *Pratibaddhas ca yas tena citra visvasya vrttayah tab sa evanujanati yatha tantuh sakuntikah*
3. Ibid., *Karika 42,* p. 69.
4. Ibid., *Karika* 74, p. 99.
5. Ibid., *Karika* 70–71, pp. 96–97.
6. Ibid., *Karika* 14, p. 50.
7. Ibid.
8. Ibid., *Karika* 30, p. 61.

9. Ibid., *Karika* 3, p. 45.
10. Ibid., *Karika* 6, p. 46.
11. Ibid., *Karika* 37–38, pp. 65–67.
12. *Sphotasiddhi of Mandana Misra,* translated into English from the Sanskrit by K. A. Subramania Iyer, Deccan College Building Centenary Series, No. 25, Poona, 1966.
13. Eliot Deutsch and J. A. V. van Buitenen, eds., *A Source Book of Advaita Vedanta* (Honolulu: University of Hawaii Press, 1971), p. 50. For a comment on Sankara's use of the *sphota* theory, G. N. Dcvy, *After Amnesia* (Bombay: Orient Longman, 1992), pp. 82–83.
14. *Sphotasiddhi of Mandana Misra,* Introduction, p. 3.
15. Ibid., *Karika* 5, (Introduction), p.14.
16. For a probing discussion of the debate between Bhartrihari and Dignaga, see Radhika Herzberger, *Bhartrhari and the Buddhists* (Dorrecht, Holland: D. Reidel Publishing Company, 1986).
17. Ibid., p. 107.
18. Ibid.
19. For a cogent discussion of concepts of Time in ancient India, see Anindita Niyogi Balslev, *A Study of Time in Indian Philosophy* (Wiesbaden: Otto Harrassowitz, 1983); and Romila Thapar, *Time as a Metaphor of History,* 1996.
20. *Patanjali's Yoga Sutra III,* 52 as quoted by Niyogi Balslev, p.51.
21. Ibid., pp.52–53, quoted from K. G. Bhattacharya, *Studies in Philosophy,* Vol. 1, Calcutta, 1956, pp. 234–35.
22. Reproduced from the *Pravacanasar of Kundakunda,* in *Sources of Indian Tradition,* ed. Theodore de Barry, (New York and London: Columbia University Press, 1958), pp. 73–75.
23. "The Jaina understanding of the time-atoms *(kalanu)* as ultimate, absolute and real again points to its distinction from the conventional time *(vyavahara kala).* The conventional time periods, of which we find a long list in *Pancasitikayusara,* 25, range from the minutest moment called *samaya,* through *nimisa, kastha, kala, nali,* to *muhurta* — equal to two *nalis, divartra* — day and night, equal to thirty *muhurtas, masa* — month, *ayana*— half year (equal to three seasons), *samvastsara* — year, which is equal to two *ayanas.* These divisions and subdivisions are linked to the different units of measurement pertaining to conventional time." Niyogi Balslev, *A Study of Time,* p. 75.
24. Romila Thapar, *Time as a Metaphor of History,* p. 44.

6. The Conventions of Literary History

1. Irawati Karve, *Yuganta: The End of an Epoch* (Hyderabad: Orient Longman, 1974), 1991, pp. 2–3.
2. Ibid., pp. 2–3.
3. Ibid., p. 2.
4. C. R. Deshpande, *Transmission of the Mahabharata Tradition, Vyasa and Vyasids* (Simla: Indian Institute of Advanced Study, 1978), pp. 7–14.

5. Quoted by Ludo Rocher, *The Puranas, A History of Indian Literature,* Volume II, part 3 (Wiesbaden: Otto Harrassowitz, 1986), p.53; original source, *When a Great Tradition Modernizes* (New York: Praeger, 1972), p. 76.
6. The *Mahabharata for the First Time Critically Edited by Vishnu S. Sukhtankar and Illustrated by Shrimant Balasaheb Pant Pratinidhi* (Poona: Bhandarkar Oriental Institute, 1925–43).
7. *The Valmiki-Ramayana Critically Edited for Belvalkar the First Time by J.M. Mehta and Others, and Illustrated by the Faculty of Fine Arts, M.S. University of Baroda* (Baroda Oriental Institute, 1960).
8. Rocher, *The Puranas,* p. 81.
9. For details of the debate about the chronology of the *Vedas,* see C. V. Vaidya, *A Literary History of India,* Vol.1 - *Sruti (Vedic) Period,* published privately, (Poona, 1930), pp. 1–40.
10. Friedrich Max Muller, *A History of Ancient Sanskrit Literature* (Williams and Norgate, 1860). See, especially the introductory sections comparing the Greeks and the Hindus.
11. C. V. Vaidya, *A Literary History of India,* Vol.1, pp. 41–67.
12. For informative comments on the *Sarvanukramani,* ibid., pp. 61–67.
13. Jaideva Singh, *The Doctrine of Recognition: A Translation of Pratyabhijnahrdayam* (New York: State University of New York, 1990). This is a translation of Kshemaraja's eleventh century text composed in Sanskrit.
14. J. L. Masson and M. V. Patwardhan, *Santarasaand Abhinavagupta's Philosophy of Aesthetics,* in Bhandarkar Oriental Series, No.9 (Poona: Bhandarkar Oriental Research Institute, 1969), p. 108.
15. Abhinavagupta, *Gitarthasangraha,* trans. Arvind Sharma (Leiden: F. J. Brill, 1983).
16. R. K. Mookherjee, *Ancient Indian Education* (London, 1947).
17. Ganga Sagar Rai, *Rajashekhara's Kavyamimansa,* Chapter X, *'Kavicharya Rajacharya Ca',* pp. 129–43.
18. Ibid., pp. 14–26, in this chapter, *'Kavyapurushotpattih',* Rajashekhara narrates the story of Kavyapurusha as a widely shared myth.
19. The tendency to ascribe the awareness of all knowledge to one's ancestors is analysed by Madhav Deshpande in his essay "History, Change and Permanence: A Classical Indian Perspective", in *Contributions to South Asian Studies* Vol. I, ed. Gopal Krishna, (Delhi, 1979), pp. 1–28.
20. *"Utpasyate mama toh koapi samanadharma*
Kalobyaya nirabadhir vipula cha prithvi"
21. A. C. Woolner, *Introduction to Prakrit* (Varanasi: R. S. Panna Lal & Co., 1917, 1966), p. 83.
22. For an exhaustive discussion of the interrelation between Sanskrit and Tamil, see George Luzerne Hart, *The Relation Between Tamil and Classical Sanskrit Literature* (Wiesbaden: Otto Harrassowitz, 1976), *A History of Indian Literature,* Vol. X, part 2.
23. Kamil Veith Zvelebil, *Tamil Literature,* in Jan Gonda, ed., *A History of Indian Literature,* Vol. X, part 1 (Wiesbaden: Otto Harrassowitz, 1974), p. 7.

24. Ibid., p. 177–79.

7. Jnanadeva's Agenda

1. The oldest printed text of *Jnaneswari* was edited in 1909 by V. K. Rajwade. It has been reprinted by the Government of Maharashtra several times. Several English translations of it have been made. The Pradhan and Lambert translation (London, 1967, 1969) is available in a revised rendering as *Jnancswara's Gita* (A Rendering of the Jnaneswari by Swami Kripananda) (Albany: State University of New York Press, 1989). All citations used hereafter are from this edition.
2. Abhinavagupta, *Gitarthasangraha,* trans. Arvind Sharma (Leiden: E. J. Brill, 1983).
3. S. G. Tulpule, *Classical Marathi Literature,* in *A History of Indian Literature,* Vol. IX, part 4 (Wiesbaden: Otto Harrassowitz, 1979), pp. 329–34. These comments are reproduced in a somewhat amended form in Tulpule's introduction to the Kripananda English translation of the *Jnaneswari.*
4. *Jnaneswara's Gita,* I. 81, p. 3.
5. Ibid., III, 17 which corresponds to the *Gita* III. 2, p. 33.
6. Ibid.
7. Ibid., III, 19–24, pp. 33–34.
8. Ibid., VI, 14, p. 67.
9. Ibid., VI, 3, p. 67.
10. Ibid., VI, 7, p. 67.
11. Ibid., VI, 17–19, p. 67.
12. Ibid., VI, 29–30, p. 68.
13. Ibid., VI, 132, p. 72.
14. Ibid., VI, 133, p. 72.
15. Ibid., VII, 201–204, p. 97.
16. Ibid., VII, 205, p. 97.
17. Ibid., IX, 26–29, p. 111.
18. Ibid., XII, 12–16, p. 175.
19. Tulpule, *Classical Marathi Literature,* p. 359.

8. Pre-Colonial Historiography

1. For an excellent account of the *Rajatarangini* as history, Romila Thapar, 'The Historical Ideal of Kalhana as Expressed in the *Rajatarangini*', in *Historians of Medieval India,* ed. Mohibbul Hasan and Muhammad Mujeeb (Meerut: Meenakshi Prakashan, 1968), pp.1–10.
2. K. N. Sane, ed., *Peshavyanchi Bakhar,* 5th edition (Kalyan, 1925). For succinct comments on *bakhar* literature, see Tulpule, *Classical Marathi Literature,* pp. 442–46.
3. Linda Orr, 'The Revenge of Literature: A History of History', *New Literary*

History, Vol. 18, No.l, Autumn 1986, pp.1–22.

4 Annemarie Schimmel, *Islamic Literatures of India,* in *A History of Indian Literature,* Vol. VII, no part number (Wiesbaden: Otto Harrassowitz, 1973), pp. 32–33.

5. Ibid; and *Classical Urdu Literature from the Beginning to Iqbal,* in *A History of Indian Literature,* Vol. VIII, part 3 (Wiesbaden: Otto Harrassowitz, 1975).

6. Muhammad Mujeeb, 'Badaoni', in *Historians of Medieval India,* ed. Mohibbul Hasan and Muhammad Mujeeb, pp. 109–110.

7. *Muntakhabu-'t-Tawarikh by Abdu-'l-qadir ibn-i-mulukshah Known as Al-Badaoni,* Vol.111, translated from the Persian and edited by Sir Wolseley Haig (Calcutta: The Asiatic Society of Bengal, 1925; reprint, Karachi: Karimsons, 1978).

8. Ibid., p. 239.

9. Ibid., p. 340.

10. Ibid., p. 526.

11. Ibid., p. 529.

12. *Nirguna Bhukti Sugar: Devotional Hindi Literature: A Critical edition of the Panc-Vani or Five Works of Dadu, Kabir, Namdev, Raidas, Hardas with the Hindi Songs of Gorkhanath and Sundardas, and a Complete Word-Index* (2 volumes), ed. W. M. Callewaert and Bart Op de Beeck (New Delhi: Manohar, 1991).

13. Ibid., Vol.1, p. 9.

9. Warton's Imaginative Savages

1. For an extremely well-documented account of the emergence of literary history in England, see Rene Wellek, *The Rise of English Literary History* (Chapel Hill: University of North Carolina Press, 1941).

2. Thomas Warton, *The History of English Poetry from the Close of the Eleventh Century to the Commencement of the Eighteenth Century (1774–1790),* ed. Richard Price (1824, reprint, London: Thomas Tegg Printers, 1840).

3. For an illuminating analysis of this period in Western European history, Michel Foucault, *The Order of Things* (London: Tavistock, 1970).

4. Wellek, *The Rise of English Literary History,* p. 180.

5. Thomas Hobbes, *Leviathan* (1651), ed. Michael Oakshott (Oxford: Oxford University Press, 1946).

6. Edmund Burke, *A Philosophical Enquiry into the Sublime and Beautiful (1757),* ed. J. T. Boulton (Notre Dame: University of Notre Dame Press, 1958).

7. Wellek, *The Rise of English Literary History,* p. 180.

8. Ibid., pp. 55–56.

9. Ibid., p. 67.

10. Ibid., p. 87.

11. Warton, *The History of English Poetry,* Vol.II, p. 233.

12. Ibid., Vol. II, p. 238.

13. Ibid., Vol. I, p. i.
14. Ibid., Vol. I, p. xci.
15. Ibid., Vol. I, p. cxlii.
16. Ibid., Vol I, p. a2.
17. Ibid., Vol. I, p. a3 (Emphases mine).
18. Wellek, *The Rise of English Literary History,* pp. 192–94.
19. For an excellent account of the development of the sense of duality between Britain and India, see Sara Suleri, *The Rhetoric of English India* (Chicago and London: University of Chicago Press, 1992).

10. Jones and the Gentoos

1. Alexander Dow, *The History of Hindostan,* 3 volumes (London, 1768–72).
2. Bernard S. Colin, 'The Command of Language and the Language of Command', in *Subaltern Studies* (New Delhi: Oxford University Press, 1985), pp. 276–329.
3. Ibid., pp. 282–83.
4. Kate Teltscher, 'Sir William and the Pandits: The Legal Research, Poetry and Translation of William Jones', in *India Inscribed,* pp. 192–228. As quoted by Teltscher from O. P. Kejatiwal, *The Asiatic Society of Bengal and the Discovery of India's Past, 1784–1838* (New Delhi : 1988), Foreword, p. x.
5. Edward Said, *Orientalism* (New York : Pantheon, 1978), p. 78.
6. John Drew, *India and the Romantic Imagination* (New Delhi: Oxford University Press, 1987), pp. 70–71.
7. Garland Cannon, ed., *The Lectures of Sir William Jones, 2* volumes (Oxford: Oxford University Press, 1970), pp. 755–56, cited by Teltscher in *India Inscribed,* p. 206.
8. James Mill, *The History of British India,* 6 volumes (London: 1826), Vol. II, pp. 46–47.
9. Sri Aurobindo, *The Foundations of Indian Culture,* Birth Centenary Library Vol.XIV, Pondicherry, 1972.
10. Ibid., p. 44.
11. Ibid.
12. Ibid., p. 33.

11. Formation and Transformation of a Canon

1. Joan Simon, *The Social Origins of English Education* (London: Routledge & Kegan Paul, 1970), pp. 88–89.
2. Ibid., p. 96.
3. Anders Piltz, *The World of Medieval Learning,* trans. David Jones (Oxford: Basil Blackwcll, 1978), p. 85. Piltz has done extensive research in medieval teaching methods and has reproduced the earliest classnotes used in universities. *Littera,* any text used, helped the teacher to initiate the *lectio* or *lectura.* Ibid.,

p. 86.

4. The book popularly known as *Foxe's Book of Martyrs* was *The Acts and Monuments of Matters Happening in the Church.* W. H. G. Armytage comments: "This anecdotal treasury was bought by many clergymen for their churches where it was chained to the lectern and sifted for sermons. Almost all Puritan households turned to it as the standard authority for church history." *Four Hundred Years of English Education* (Cambridge: Cambridge University Press. 1964, 1970), p. 2.
5. Ibid., p.2. Quoted by Armytage from Joel Hurstfield, *The Queen's Wards* (1958), p. 255.
6. Chris Baldick, *The Social Mission of English Criticism: 1848–1932* (Oxford: Clarendon Press, 1983).
7. Ibid., p. 70.
8. Ibid., pp. 71–72.
9. Ibid., p. 140.
10. Ibid., p. 168–69.
11. J. Stuart Maclure, ed., *Education Documents—England and Wales: 1816 to the Present Day* (London: Methuen, 1965, 1986), pp. 42–45.
12. Ibid., p. 41.
13. Ibid., pp. 56–57.
14. Ibid., p. 57.
15. Ibid., pp. 52–55.
16. Ibid., pp. 53–54.
17. Baldick, *The Social Mission of English Criticism: 1848–1932,* p. 61.
18. Ibid.
19. Ibid., pp. 71–72.
20. Ibid., p. 70.
21. For a full discussion of the three factors leading to the establishment of English studies in Britain, see the chapter 'A Civilizing Subject' in Baldick. Also see Bernard Bergonzi, *Exploding English: Criticism, Theory, Culture* (Oxford: Clarendon Press, 1990), p. 40. Bergonzi offers an extremely readable and illuminating survey of the development of English studies at Oxford and Cambridge. His account is full of nostalgia. However, as historical document it is extremely useful
22. Sujit Mukherjee, *Towards a Literary History of India* (Simla: Indian Institute of Advanced Study, 1975), pp. 17–18.

12. Some Western Approaches to Literary History

1. For an initial introduction to the ideas of the Constanz Group, see Robert C. Holub, *Reception Theory: A Critical Introduction* (London and New York: Methuen, New Accent Series, 1984), pp. 53–106.
2. Hans Robert Jauss, *Toward an Aesthetic of Reception,* translated from the German by Timothy Bahti, Introduction by Paul de Man (Brighton: The Harvester Press, 1982), p. 1.

3. Important works in the area of literary history are listed in the Bibliography. The three works discussed in the present chapter are respectively: R. S. Crane, *Critical and Historical Principles of Literary History,* first published as a chapter in *The Idea of the Humanities and Other Essays, Critical and Historical,* ed. R. S. Crane, (Chicago: University of Chicago Press, 1967, reprinted as a single volume, with a Foreword by Sheldon Sacks in 1971). Gyorgy Lukacs, *Notes on the Literary History,* translated from the Hungarian and introduced by Ian Fairley, in *Comparative Criticism* (Cambridge: Cambridge University Press, Vol.13, 1991), pp. 195–245. Hans Robert Jauss, *Literary History as a Challenge to Literary Theory* (Brighton: The Harvester Press, 1982).
4. R. S. Crane, *Critical and Historical Principles of Literary History,* p. 50.
5. Ibid., p. 35.
6. Ibid., p. 37.
7. See Baldick, *The Social Mission,* and Terry Eagleton, *The Ideology of the Aesthetic* (Oxford: Basil Blackwcll, 1990).
8. Gyorgy Lukacs, *Notes on the Theory of Literary History,* p. 215.
9. Ibid., p. 215.
10. Ibid., p. 218.
11. Ibid., p. 219.
12. Ibid., p. 211.
13. Ibid., p. 212.
14. Jauss, *Literary History as a Challenge to Literary Theory,* p. 15. On Jauss's own admission his theory rests mainly on the hermenutics of Hans-T Georg Gadamer, who in turn bases it on Kant's critique of aesthetic experience.
15. For a commentary on Jauss's debts to other theories see Robert C. Holub, *Reception Theory* (London: Methuen, 1984), pp. 63–69. The most obvious debt, however, is the use of the expression 'ideological horizon' used by Bakhtin in P. N. Medvedev and M. M. Bakhtin, *The Formal Method in Literary Scholarship: A Critical Introduction to Sociological Poetics,* translated from the Russian by Albert J. Wehrle, The Goucher College Series, (Baltimore and London: The Johns Hopkins University Press, 1978), pp. 159–60.
16. Jauss, *Literary History as a Challenge to Literary Theory,* p. 45.
17. Ibid., p. 5–6.

13. Postcolonial Indian Approaches

1. Sri Aurobindo, *Future Poetry,* first issued as a series of essays in *Arya* (1917–1919), reprinted as a single volume in 1950. Several reprints have been made, all through Sri Aurobindo Ashram Press, Pondicherry, including an authoritative edition, *Works,* Vol.8, 1972.
2. Dattatraya Punde, ed., *Vangmayetihasaci Sankalpana* (Pune: Pratima Prakashan, no date). Also important is G. M.Kulkarni and Dattatraya Punde, *Vangamayetihasa: Sadyasthiti ani Apeksha* (Pune: Mehta Publishing House, 1995).
3. All writings of Sri Aurobindo are available in *Works,* Birth Centenary

Publication, Pondicherry, 1972. 'Source of Poetry', in *Harmony of Virtue,* Vol. V, pp. 105–08. 'National Value of Art', in *The Hour of God,* Vol. XVII, p. 231. 'Letter to Manmohan', *Supplement,* Vol. XXVII, p. 148.

4. Sri Aurobindo, *Life Divine,* in *Works,* Vols. XVII, XVIII. *Savitri,* in *Works,* Vols. XXVIII and XXIX.
5. Punde, *Vangmayetihasaci Sankalpana,* 'Preface', p.7.
6. V. K. Rajwade, 'Maharashtratil Prakritik Bhashancha va Vangmayacha *Itihas*', in *Rajwade Lekh-Sangrah,* Laxmanshastri Joshi, ed. (New Delhi: Sahitya Akademi, 1958), cited by Punde, 'Appendix 43'.
7. Tryambak Shankar Shejwalkar, *Nivadak Lekhasangrah,* ed. V. Mote, Introduction by G. D. Khanolkar (Bombay: H.V. Mote Publication, 1977), pp.437–39.
8. George Grierson, *Linguistic Survey of India* (Calcutta, 1902–1928).
9. Sisir Kumar Das, *A History of Indian Literature, 1911–1956* (New Delhi: Sahitya Akademi, 1995), and *A History of Indian Literature, 1800–1910.* (1991). The two volumes form a part of the proposed series of 10 volumes.
10. Sujit Mukhcrjee, *Towards a Literary History of India* (Simla: Indian Institute of Advanced Studies, 1975); *Some Positions on a Literary History of India* (Mysore: Central Institute of Indian Languages, 1981).
11. Mukherjee (1975), 'Preface', p. vi.
12. Sujit Mukherjee, *Some Positions on a Literary History of India, "Bharatiya Vangmayetihasalekhanachi Panch Adhartatve" (Five Principles of Indian Literary History),* translated from English by S. G. Malshe, *Alochana* (April 1982), reprinted in Punde, pp. 70–85.
13. Mukherjee, *Towards a Literary History of India,* p. 18.
14. Ibid., p. 20.
15. Ranajit Guha, ed., *Subaltern Studies* (New Delhi: Oxford University Press, 1984-87), 5 volumes.
16. Antonio Gramsci, 'The Modern Prince', in *Prison Notebooks* (New York, 1973), p.196, cited by Gautam Bhadra, in 'Four Rebels of Eighteen Fifty-Seven', *Subaltern Studies, Vol.* IV (1985), pp. 229–75 (p. 273–74).
17. For Gayatri Chakravorty Spivak's views on history expressed in works other than the *Subaltern Studies,* see her *The Post-Colonial Critic,* ed. Sarah Harasym (New York and London: Routledge, 1990).
18. Bernard S. Colin, 'The Command of Language and the Language of Command', in *Subaltern Studies,* Vol.IV, pp. 276–329.
19. Gayatri Chakravorty Spivak, *Subaltern Studies,* Vol. IV, p. 330.
20. Ibid., p. 341.
21. Ibid., p. 354.
22. B. R. Ambedkar, *The Untouchables: Who Were They* ? (New Delhi: Amrit Book Co., 1948).
23. Ibid., p.62.
24. Among the more important autobiographies in Marathi Dalit writings: 1978, Daya Pawar, *Balut;* 1980, Laxman Mane, *Upara;* 1981, Shankarrao Kharat, *Taral-Antaral;* 1987, Baby Kamble, *Jina Amuche;* 1987, Laxman Gaikwad,

Uchalya. For a perceptive account of Dalit autobiography, sec R. V. Dhongade, *Dalit Atmacharitre, Sahitya Ani Samaj* (Pune: Dilipraj Prakashan, 1992).

25. Daya Pawar, *Bombay Literary Review,* No. 2, 1990, p.5.
26. Ibid., p.17.
27. Kumkum Sangari, *New Literary History,* Vol. XIX, No.3, 1988, p. 713.
28. Salman Rushdie, *Imaginary Homelands* (London: Granta Books, 1991), pp. 63–64.
29. Ibid., p. 66.
30. U. R. Ananthamurthy, 'Why Not Worship in the Nude? Reflections of a Novelist in His Time', in *Bahuvachan: An Occasional of the Arts and Ideas* (Bhopal: Bharat Bhavan February, 1988), pp. 95–117. This paper was initially presented at the Conference on Indian Literature, Festival of India, University of Chicago, 17–20 April, 1986.
31. Bhalchandra Nemade, 'The Marathi Novel: 1950–75', translated from the Marathi by G. N. Dcvy, *Setu,* Vol.11, No.l, 1986, pp. 29–72. The essay was initially presented at the Seminar on Marathi Literature: 1950–75, Shivaji University (August 1980), and included in the proceedings, *Marathi Sahitya: Prerana va Swarup: 1950–75,* edited by G. M. Pawar and M. D. Hatkananglekar, (Bombay: Popular Prakashan, 1986), pp. 13–56.
32. Ananthamurthy, 'Why not Worship in the Nude?', p. 95.
33. Ibid., p.111.
34. Ananda K. Coomaraswamy, *Works,* 3 volumes, ed. Roger Lipsey, Bolingen Series LXXXIX, 1977, Vol.2, *Selected Papers: Metaphysics,* pp. 49–264.
35. Rajeev Patke, 'Canon and Canon-making in Indian Poetry in English', *Kavya Bharati: A Review of Indian Poetry,* No.3, 1991, pp.13–37.
36. Coomaraswamy, *Works,* Vol. II, pp. 49–65.
37. Ibid., p.226.
38. Ibid., p.49.
39. Ibid., pp. 56–57.
40. Ibid., p.58.
41. See Frank Kermode, 'Canon and Period' in *History and Value* (Oxford: Clarendon Paperbacks, 1989), p. 108.
42. Patke, 'Canon and Canon-Making in Indian Poetry in English', pp. 13–14.
43. Namvarsingh, *Itihas aur Aalochana* (New Delhi: Rajkamal, 1957 and 1986), pp. 164–65. Translation mine.

14. Para-Literature

1. Bhaktin and Medvedev, *The Formal Method in Literary Scholarship: A Critical Introduction to Sociological Poetics,* trans. Albert J. Wehrle, The Goucher College Series (Baltimore and London: The Johns Hopkins University Press, 1978), p. 160.
2. G. N. Devy, 'Para-Literature' in *Approaches to Para-Literature,* ed. Amiya Dev, (Calcutta: Jadavpur University, 1992), pp. 50–57.
3. See Rene Wellek, 'The Name and Nature of Comparative Literature', in

Discriminations: Further Concept of Criticism (New Haven and London: Yale University Press, 1970); Henry H. H. Remak, 'Comparative Literature at the Crossroads: Diagnosis, Theory and Prognosis', in *Yearbook of Comparative and General Literature,* Vol. I, IX, 1960; S. S. Prawer, *Comparative Literary Studies* (London: Duckworth, 1973).

4. For a provocative discussion of Kolatkar's bilingualism, see B. V. Nemade, 'Arun Kolatkar and Bilingual Poetry' in *Indian Readings in Commonwealth Literature,* ed. G. S. Amur, V. R. N. Prasad, B. V. Nemade and N. K. Nihalani (Delhi: Sterling, 1985), pp. 71–86.
5. See Claude Levi-Strauss, 'Social Structure', in *Structural Anthropology,* translated from the French by Claire Jacobson and Brooke Grundfest Schoepf (Harmondsworth: Penguin, 1963 and 1979), pp. 277–323.
6. The 8th Schedule lists the following languages: Assamiya, Bangla, Dogri, Gujarati, Hindi, Kashmiri, Kannada, Konkani, Manipuri, Maithili, Malayalam, Marathi, Nepali, Oriya, Punjabi, Tamil, Telugu, Sindhi, Urdu.
7. Kumkum Sangari, 'Figures for the Unconscious', *Journal of Arts and Ideas,* March 1991, Nos. 20–21, pp. 67–84.
8. Ibid., p. 75.
9. For a historical account of the two categories, *deshi* and *marg* see G. N. Devy, *After Amnesia: Tradition and Change in Indian Literary Criticism* (Bombay: Orient Longman, 1992), pp.78–82.

15. Swa and Para: Self and the Other

1. Jacques Lacan, *Ecrits* (London: Tavistock, 1977), p.27.
2. *Upanishads,* Penguin Classics, 1965, p.65.
3. Sudhir Kakar, *The Inner World: A Psychoanalytic Study of Childhood and Society in India* (New Delhi: Oxford University Press, 1981), pp. 20–21. See the critique of Kakar by D. Venkata Rao, 'The Stunting Lebensraum: Sudhir Kakar and the Subject of Psycho-coloniality', *Journal of Contemporary Thought,* No.l, 1991, pp.111–124.

16. Tradition and Transactions

1. Examples of writers of non-British origin in the history of English literature that can be cited as exceptions are Henry James, T. S. Eliot, Joseph Conrad, Arthur Koestler, etc. However, each of these had to make efforts to project himself as a conformist to English cultural values in order to be accepted. W. B. Yeats, who did not follow the trend, continued to be treated as Irish.
2. Romila Thapar, *Cultural Transaction and Early India: Tradition and Patronage* (New Delhi: Oxford University Press, 1987), pp.7–22.
3. Ibid., p.23.
4. For a discussion of the difference between 'tradition' and '*parampara*' see G. N. Devy, *After Amnesia.*

5. Though the term *Sahitya* was highlighted by Viswanatha in the fourteenth century, it was in use in the discourse of Sanskrit poetics for many centuries preceding him. For a discussion of the concept see K. Krishnamoorthy's introduction to Sanskrit literary criticism in *Comparative Indian Literature,* ed. K. M. George (Madras: Macmillan, 1984–86).

17. Translation as Origin

1. I have quoted from my notes of a lecture given by Prof. J. Hillis Miller at the ninth centenary celebration symposium at the University of Bologna, Italy, in October 1988.
2. Susan Bassnett-McGuirc, *Translation Studies* (London: Methuen, 1980), pp. 58–64.
3. Robert Welch, 'Language and Tradition', in *Changing States: Transformation in Modern Irish Writing* (London and New York: Routledge, 1993), pp. 11–34.
4. J. C. Catford, *A Linguistic Theory of Translation* (London: Oxford University Press, 1965).

18. The Course and the Discourse of History

1. J. H. Shukla, *Bhartrihari's Vakyapadiya with Gujarati Translation and Notes* (Ahmedabad: L. D. Institute of Indology), 1984.
2. Ibid., p. 34. The verses quoted are from the *Prathama Kanda:* 49–51.
3. John Brough, *in A Reader in Nineteenth Century Historical Indo-European Linguistics,* ed. Winfred P. Lehmann.

19. Nation in Narration

1. Tariq Rahman, *Pakistani Literature in English* (Rawalpindi, 1990).
2. Ibid., p. 10.
3. Ibid., p. 11.
4. Ibid.
5. Ibid., p. 15.

Annotated Bibliography

The following publications will be of interest to scholars engaged in research and teaching of literary history. It may be noted, however, that the list of publications given here is by no means a comprehensive bibliography.

AHMAD, Aijaz. *In Theory: Classes, Nations, Literatures.* London and New York: Verso, 1992.

Perhaps, the most significant critical text produced in India since Coomaraswamy's *The Dance of Shiva.* Ahmad takes up a classical Marxist position *vis-a-vis* Edward Said's *Orientalism.* The most useful part of the volume is the chapter on the concept of Indian Literature (pp. 243–285), which is written from the perspective of Commonwealth literature.

ALPERS, Svetlana, and ALPERS, Paul. 'Ut Pictura Noesis? Criticism in Literary Studies and Art History'. *New Literary History,* Vol.3, No.l, Autumn 1971, p. 437 ff.

ALTIERI, Charles. 'An Idea and Ideal of a Literary Canon'. *Critical Inquiry,* Vol.10, No.l, September 1983, pp. 37–60.

Altieri argues that "the past that canons preserve is best understood as a permanent theatre helping us shape and judge personal and social values, that our self-interest in the present consists primarily in establishing ways of employing that theatre to gain distance from our ideological commitments, and that the most plausible hope for the influence of literary study in the future lies in our ability to transmit the past as a set of challenges and models." (p.40).

ARCHIBALD, Douglas, N. 'Yeats's Encounters: Observations on Literary Influence and Literary History'. *New Literary History,* Vol.1, No.3, Spring 1970, p.439 ff.

ASHCROFT, Bill, GRIFFITHS, Gareth, and TIFFIN, Helen. *The Empire Writes Back: Theory and Practice in Post-colonial Literatures.* London and New York: New Accents, Routledge, 1989.

The authors discuss issues related to aesthetics, canon and theory in the context of Anglophone Commonwealth literature with a passionate anti-colonial bias.

BALDICK, Chris. *The Social Mission of English Criticism.* Oxford: Clarendon Press, 1983.

Well-documented discussion of the contribution of colonialism to the development of literary criticism in Victorian England.

BANFIELD, Ann. 'Where Epistemology, Style, and Grammar Meet Literary History'. *New Literary History,* Vol.9, No.3, Spring 1978, p.415ff.

BARTHES, Roland. 'History or Literature', in *On Racine,* translated by Richard Howard. New York: Octagon Books, 1964 and 1977, pp.151–72.

Barthes explores the tension between the perception of an individual author as an author and his image and place in the institutional existence of literature, that is an author as part of a tradition of writing. The comments are made in the context of Racine-scholarship in France, particularly the trends issuing from Lanson's historical criticism.

BASSNETT-MCGUIRE, Susan. *Translation Studies.* London & New York: New Accents, Methuen, 1980, pp. 145–152.
Presents an excellent beginner's bibliography on history and theory of translation studies.

BATESON, F. W. 'Literary History Non-subject Par Excellence'. *New Literary History,* Vol. 2, No.l, Autumn 1970, p.115ff.

BAXANDALL, Michael. 'The Language of Art History'. *New Literary History,* Vol. 10, No.3, Spring 1979, pp. 453–66.
A distinction is established between the articulation of history of arts and the articulation of history of verbal arts.

BENJAMIN, Walter. 'Theses on the Philosophy of History', in *Illuminations,* edited by Hannah Arendt and translated by Harry Zohn. New York, 1986.

BENNETT, Tony. *Outside Literature.* London and New York: Routledge, 1990.
Bennett looks at literature as an institution with its power-structure and power-politics. A work not as original as Terry Eagleton's, but more useful for classroom discussion.

BERCOVITCH, Sacvan. 'The Problem of Ideology in American Literary History'. *Critical Inquiry,* Vol.12, No.4, June 1986, pp.631–53.
Discusses the place of ideology in the writing of literary history with reference to the author's multi-volume undertaking on American literary history. Bercovitch advocates a "flexible, open-ended, and self-reflexive" approach to literary history.

BERGONZI, Bernard. *Exploding English: Criticism, Theory, Culture.* Oxford: Clarendon Press, 1990. Bergonzi presents a personal history of the formation of the English literary canon through institutionalized teaching of literature at Oxford and Cambridge.

BHABHA, Homi K. *Nation and Narration.* London and New York: Routledge, 1990.
The volume includes essays by Ernest Renan, Martin Thorn, Timothy Brennan, Doris Sommer, Sneja Gunew, Geoffrey Bennington, Simon During, John Barrell, David Simpson, Rachel Bowlby, Bruce Robbins, James Snead, Francis Mulhern, Gillian Beer and Homi K. Bhabha. Of particular interest is Bennington's 'Postal Politics and the Institutions of the Nation' (pp. 121–37). The volume tries to bring together a variety of case studies to form a perspective on the question of nationality and the literary identity of writers/critics.

BRUNS, Gerald L. 'What Is Tradition?'. *New Literary History,* Vol.22, No. 1, Winter 1991, pp.1–22.
"I can't produce a clear idea of what tradition is. Possibly it will be enough if I can just make it harder for people to speak of tradition in the usual way, which is to say without a second thought." (p. 1). Bruns demonstrates the inner contradictions in European tradition: Ancients vs Moderns, Petrarch vs

Descartes, Allegory vs Satire, Judaism vs Christianity, Authority of the Claim vs Authority of Rule.

BUCK, Gunther. 'The Structure of Hermeneutic Experience and the Problem of Tradition'. *New Literary History,* Vol. 10, No.l, Autumn 1978, pp.31–48.
Presents the German tradition of hermeneutics and its use in grasping the complex nature of historical understanding.

CAMEROON, J. M., 'Problems of Literary History'. *New Literary History,* Vol.1, No.l, Autumn 1969, p.7ff.

CARROLL, David. *Paraesthetics: Foucault, Lyotard, Derrida.* New York and London: Methuen, 1987.
This book discusses the contributions made by Lyotard, Foucault and Derrida for pushing the question of the aesthetic beyond the usual limits of literary enquiry. Carroll uses the term *paraesthetics,* to indicate the common elements in these three thinkers. "Paraesthetics indicates something like an aesthetics turned against itself or pushed beyond or beside itself, a faulty, irregular, disordered, improper aesthetics, one not content to remain within the area defined by the aesthetic. Paraesthetics describes a critical approach to aesthetics for which art is a question not a given, an aesthetics in which art does not have a determined place or fixed definition." (p. xiv)

CHAKRAVORTY SPIVAK, Gayatri. 'Subaltern Studies: Deconstructing. Historiography'. *Subaltern Studies,* Vol.4, New Delhi: Oxford University Press, 1985, pp. 330–363.
Other essays of interest by Spivak are: 'The Rani of Sirmur: An Essay in Reading the Archives', in *History and Theory,* Vol. 24, 1985, pp.247–72 and 'Can the Subaltern Speak?', in Larry Grossberg and Cary Nelson (eds.), *Marxist Interpretations of Literature and Culture: Limits, Frontiers, Boundaries.* Urbana: University of Illinois Press, 1987, pp. 271–313.

CHANDRA MOHAN. *Aspects of Comparative Literature: Current Approaches.* New Delhi: India Publishers & Distributors, 1989.
This volume contains essays by various Indian and non-Indian scholars, some of which present surveys of developments in Comparative literature in various parts of the world.

CHAPPELL, Fred. 'Six Positions about Literature and History'. *New Literary History,* Vol.1, No.3, Spring 1970, p.513.

COHEN, Ralph, ed. *New Directions in Literary History.* Baltimore and London: The Johns Hopkins University Press and Routledge and Kegan Paul, 1974.
In this pivotal volume edited by Cohen there are essays by Hans Robert Jauss, Robert Weimann, D. V. V. Robertson, Jr., Alastair Fowler, Geoffrey Hartman, Louis O. Mink, Wolfgang Iser, Michael Riffaterre, Barbara Herrenstein Smith, Henry Markicwicz, Svetlana and Paul Alpers, Francis R. Hart, George Garrett, and an introduction by Ralph Cohen. Cohen is also the founder and editor of *New Literary History: A Journal of Theory and Interpretation* since 1969. It is published three times a year by the Johns Hopkins University Press, Baltimore, Maryland.
Cohen's essay 'History and Genre', *New Literary History,* Vol. 17, No. 2, 1986,

pp. 203–218, shows that 'genre' is a historical category and that it changes continuously in the course of time, at the same time literary history is influenced by the category of genre. His essay should be read together with two comments in the same issue by Dominick Lacapra (pp. 219–22) and Richard Harvey Brown (pp. 223–28).

COHN, Bernard. 'The Command of Language and the Language of Command'. *Subaltern Studies,* Vol.4, New Delhi: Oxford University Press, 1985, pp. 276–329.

Cohn offers an interesting account of the initial interaction between the English language and Indian literary tradition.

COOMARASWAMY, Ananda K. *Selected Works,* 3 volumes, edited by Roger Lipsey. Bolingen Series LXXXIX, Princeton: Princeton University Press, 1977.

The three volume edition by Lipsey includes 56 of Coomaraswamy's more important essays, besides a detailed biographical sketch and a comprehensive bibliography of Coomaraswamy's publications.

CORSTIUS, Jan Brandt. *Introduction to the Comparative Study of Literature.* New York: Random House, 1968.

This volume is written to help students who "have had some training in the study of literary history and are interested in comparative literature." Chapter IV, 'Conventions and Literary History' (pp. 103–128) is of particular interest. Corstius takes up the issues related to the institutionalization of literary education and literary history in his essay, 'Literary History and the Study of Literature', *New Literary History,* Vol. 2, No. 1, Winter 1971, pp. 65 ff.

COSTA-LIMA, Luiz. 'Erich Auerbach: History and Metahistory'. *New Literary History,* Vol. 19, No. 3, Spring 1988, pp. 467–500.

An extremely readable account of Auerbach's vision of language, literature and history in comparison with that of Vico, who is presented here as the greatest influence on Auerbach. A profitable reading for students of comparative literature, which shows Auerbach's interest in realism as an influence on his interest in history.

CRANE, R. S. *Critical and Historical Principles of Literary History,* first published as a chapter in *The Idea of the Humanities and Other Essays, Critical and Historical,* 2 volumes edited by R. S. Crane. Chicago and London: University of Chicago Press, 1971.

CULLER, Jonathan. 'Structure of Ideology and Ideology of Structure'. *New Literary History,* Vol. 4. No. 3, Spring 1973, pp. 147–82.

An argument towards establishing a theoretical meeting point between Deconstruction and Marxism.

DAS, Sisir Kumar. *A History of Indian Literature: 1800–1910, Western Impact – Indian Response,* Volume 8, New Delhi: Sahitya Akademi, 1991.

———. *A History of Indian Literature: 1911–1956, Struggle for Freedom: Triumph and Tragedy.* New Delhi: Sahitya Akademi, 1995.

Includes a comprehensive bibliography of literary history in India during the modern period. Titles cited are from English as well as Indian languages. These volumes should be read together with Das's *Integrated History of Indian*

Literature: A Draft Working Paper. New Delhi: Sahitya Akademi, 1986. Also of interest are: *Comparative Literature: Theory and Practice* (co-edited with Amiya Dev), New Delhi and Shimla: Allied Publishers and Indian Institute of Advanced Study, 1989; 'Comparative Literature in India: A Historical Perspective', in *Aspects of Comparative Literature: Current Approaches,* edited by Chandra Mohan. New Delhi: India Publishers & Distributors, 1989, pp. 1–16. In the last mentioned essay, Das offers a survey of the development of comparative literature as an academic discipline in India.

DASGUPTA, R. K. 'Literary Historiography', in *Indian Literature,* edited by Arbinda Poddar. Simla: Indian Institute of Advanced Study, 1972.

DAVIDSON, Arnold I. 'How to do the History of Psycho-analysis: A Reading of Freud's Three Essays in the Theory of Sexuality'. *Critical Inquiry,* Vol. 13, No. 2, Winter 1987, pp. 252–77.
Strategies for the history of psychoanalysis.

DE BARY, Theodore. *Sources of Indian Tradition.* New York: Columbia University Press, 1958.
For students who have no access to medieval Indian thought through an Indian language, the following sections of this reference volume edited by De Bary will be instructive – Chapter XIX: 'The Importance of the Study of History,' pp. 519–28.

DE MAN, Paul. 'Literary History and Literary Modernity', in *Blindness & Insight: Essays in the Rhetoric of Contemporary Criticism,* 2nd edition. London: Methuen, 1983, pp. 142–65.
De Man establishes the 'historicity ' of 'modernity' in literature, and explores the paradoxical relationship between the two concepts.

DEV, Amiya. *The Idea of Comparative Literature in India.* Calcutta: Papyrus, 1984.
This volume traces the main themes of comparative literature in the context of modern Indian literatures with particular attention paid to the question of influence. The essay, 'Literary History and Comparative Literature' forms the most essential text for Indian literary historiography. The argument is that literary history is best understood when seen in terms of influence-impact-effect. 'Comparative Indian Literature', in *Yearbook of Comparative and General Literature,* Vol. 34, 1985, pp. 114-17. 'The Concept of "Influence" in the Indian Context', in *Sensus Communis: Contemporary Trends in Comparative Literature,* edited by Janos Riesz, Peter Borner, Bernard Scholz and Gunter Narr. Tubingen: Verlag 1986, pp. 227–35. In these articles Dev seeks to decolonize the study of literary influence. 'Literary History From Below' in *Comparative Literature: Theory and Practices,* edited by Amiya Dev and Sisir Kumar Das. Delhi and Shimla: Allied Publishers & Indian Institute of Advanced Study, 1989, pp. 319–28. 'Towards Comparative Indian Literature', in *Aspects of Comparative Literature: Current Approaches* edited by Chandra Mohan. Delhi: Indian Publishers & Distributors, 1989, pp. 35–46. Discusses the identity of Indian Literature.

EAGLETON, Terry. *The Ideology of the Aesthetic.* London: Basil Blackwell, 1990.
Discusses from a post-Communism Marxist point of view the formation of

the aesthetic canon in Europe by selective and provocative comments on Shaftesburry, Hume, Burke, Schiller, Fichte, Schelling, Hegel, Schopenhauer, Kierkegaard, Marx, Nietzsche, Freud, Heidegger, Walter Benjamin, Theodor Adorno, and some recent post-structuralists. Very interesting analysis of the processes of canon formation and canon-privileging.

EDEL, Leon, ed. *Literary History and Literary Criticism.* New York: New York University Press, 1964, 2nd impression 1966.
A collection of papers and abstracts of papers presented at the ninth Congress of the International Federation for Modern Languages and Literatures held at New York University, August 1963. This collection contains nine plenary papers, five East-West symposium papers and seventy-nine abstracts.*

ELLMANN, Richard and FEIDELSON, Charles, Jr. *The Modern Tradition: Background of Modern Literature.* Oxford and New York: Oxford University Press, 1965.
Of particular interest are pp. 453–533 forming Part IV of the volume, which includes selections from Hegel, Croce, Vico, Nietzsche, Spengler, Yeats, Malraux, Berdyaev and Darwin. Each selection is prefaced by well-informed comments by the editors.

FOGLE, Richard Harter. 'Literary History Romanticized'. *New Literary History,* Vol.1, No.2, Winter 1970, p.237ff.

FOWLER, Alastair. 'Genre and the Literary Canon'. *New Literary History,* Vol. 11, No.l, Autumn 1979, pp.97–120.
Should be read together with 'Periodization and Literary Analogies', *New Literary History,* Vol. 3, Spring 1972, p. 487ff. A systematic and sympathetic presentation of para-literature and para-canon, of the processes of formation of genres and periods. Also discusses the formation of the hierarchy of genres within a given literary period.

FOKKEMA, Douwe W. *Issues in General and Comparative Literature: Selected Essays.* Calcutta: Papyrus, 1987.
This selection contains essays on reception, literary history, cultural relativism, canon and aesthetics. Of particular interest are the following essays: 'Literary History: A Comment on Some Problems in Literary Historiography', pp. 24–42; 'A Semiotic Definition of Aesthetic Experience and the Period Code of Modernism', pp. 87–117; 'Canon as an Instrument of Problem Solving', pp. 157–74. Most of the discussion concerns itself with the methodology of literary history. One of the important works in the field of comparative literature published in India.

FROW, John. *Marxism and Literary History,* Oxford: Basil Blackwell, 1986.
This volume has a purely theoretical orientation. It employs Marxism, Foucault, discourse analysis and such other high-profile theories to discuss the nature of literature as a system. But the volume shows commitment neither to literature nor to philosophy, neither to Marxism nor to Post-Structuralism, and in its non-affiliations, it becomes an exercise in itself.

FRYE, Northrop. 'Literary History'. *New Literary History,* Vol. 12, No. 2, Winter 1981 (special number on 'Interpretation and Literary History').

Frye suggests that literary history as it exists in current practice has been unsatisfactory. By taking up the Bible as his example, and Vico as his philosopher, Frye designates three phases of language development—Hieroglyphic, Hieratic, Demotic—as the taxonomy that will provide the backbone to literary history.

GARRETT, George. 'Dreaming with Adam: Notes on Imaginary History'. *New Literary History,* Vol.1, No.3, Spring 1970, p.407ff.

GEERTZ, Clifford. 'History and Anthropology'. *New Literary History,* Vol. 21, No.2, Winter 1990, pp. 321–36.

An energetic discussion of the convergences and divergences between history and anthropology. Following this essay, there is a response to it by Renato Rosaldo, pp. 337–42.

GENETTE, Gerard. 'Introduction to Paratext'. *New Literary History,* Vol. 22, No. 2, Spring 1991, pp. 261–272.

Genette's definition of 'paratext' is: "the means by which a text makes a book of itself and proposes itself as such to its readers, and more generally to the public." (p.261); he also quotes another definition, by Philippe Lejeune, *Le Pacte Autobiographique,* Paris, 1975, p.45; "the fringe of the printed text which, in reality, controls the whole reading."

GOLDBERG, Jonathan. 'Making Sense'. *New Literary History,* Vol. 21, No.3, Spring 1990, pp. 457–62.

This is a defence of New Historicism against Levin's attack. Goldberg, an important New Historicist, problematizes the term 'Sense' invoked by Levin in his attack.

GOLDMANN, Lucien. *Towards a Sociology of the Novel,* translated by Alan Sheridan. London: Tavistock Publications, 1975. In the chapter 'The Genetic-Structuralist Method in the History of Literature' Goldmann argues that the relationship between literary works and social groups is the true subject of creation in literature.

GOLDSTEIN, Leon. 'Literary History as History'. *New Literary History,* Vol.8, No.2, Winter 1977, p.319.

GONDA, Jan, ed. *A History of Indian Literature.* Wiesbaden: Otto Harrassowitz (10 Volumes in 30 parts published between 1973 and 1987).

The distribution of the theme, chronology, geographical areas and language groupings are innovative. Many scholars from Holland, including the editor, contribute to the series. Each volume is very well-annotated, and is written with a considerable freedom from the general conventions of histories of Indian literatures.

Vol. 1, *Veda and Upanishads.*

i) Jan Gonda, *Vedic Literature,* 1975,

ii) Jan Gonda, *The Ritual Sutras,* 1977.

Vol. *2, Epics and Sanskrit Religious Literature.*

i) Jan Gonda, *Medieval Religious Literature in Sanskrit,* 1977,

ii) Jean Goudriaan and Sanjukta Gupta, *Hindu Tantric and Sukta Literature,* 1981,

iii) Ludo Rocher, *The Puranas,* 1986.

Vol. 3, *Classical Sanskrit Literature.*

i) Siegfried Lienhard, *A History of Classical Poetry: Sanskrit, Pali-Prakrit,* 1984.

Vol. 4, *Scientific and Technical Literature,* Part I.

i) Ludwik Sternback, *Subhasita, Gnomic and Didactic Literature,* 1974.

Vol. 5, *Scientific and Technical Literature,* Part II.

i) J. D. M. Derrett, *Dharmasastra and Juridical Literature,* 1973,

ii) Hartmut Scharfe, *Grammatical Literature,* 1977,

iii) Edwin Gerow, *Indian Poetics, 1911,*

iv) Claus Vogel, *Indian Lexicography,* 1979.

Vol. 6, *Scientific and Technical Literature,* Part III.

i) E. te Nijenhuis, *Musicological Literature,* 1977,

ii) B. K. Matilal, *Nyaya-Vaisesika,* 1977,

iii) Michel Hulin, *Samkhya Literature,* 1978,

iv) David Pingeree, *Jyotisasastra, Astral and Mathematical Literature,* 1981,

v) Jean-Marie Verpoorten, *Mimansa Literature,* 1987.

Vol. 7, *Buddhist and Jaina Literature.*

i) David Seyfort Ruegg, *The Literature of the Madhyamaka School of Philosophy in India,* 1981,

ii) K. R. Norman, *Pali Literature, Including the Canonical Literature in Prakrit and Sanskrit of all Hinayana Schools of Buddhism,* 1983.

Vol. 8, *Modern Indo-Aryan Literature,* Part I.

i) A. Schimmel, *Islamic Literatures of India,* 1973,

ii) Ronald Stuart-McGregor, *Hindi Literature of the Nineteenth and Early Twentieth Centuries,* 1974,

iii) A. Schimmel, *Classical Urdu Literature from the Beginning to Iqbal,* 1975,

iv) Braj B. Kachru, *Kashmiri Literature,* 1981,

v) Peter Gaeffke, *Hindi Literature in the Twentieth Century,* 1978,

vi) Ronald Stuart-McGregor, *Hindi Literature, from its Beginnings to the Nineteenth Century,* 1984.

Vol. 9, *Modern Indo-Aryan Literature,* Part II.

i) A. Schimmel, *Sindhi Literature,* 1974,

ii) Satyendra Nath Sarma, *Assamese Literature,* 1976,

iii) Dusan Zbavitel, *Bengali Literature,* 1976,

iv) Shankar Gopal Tulpule, *Classical Marathi Literature from the Beginning to A.D. 1818,* 1979.

Vol. 10, *Dravidian Literatures.*

i) Kamil Veith Zvelebil, *Tamil Literature,* 1974,

ii) George Luzerne Hart, *The Relation Between Tamil and Classical Sanskrit Literature,* 1976.

GOSSMAN, Lionel. 'History as Decipherment: Romantic Historiography and the Discovery of the Other'. *New Literary History,* Vol. 18, No. 1, Autumn 1986, pp. 23–58.

Offers a well-documented account of the rise of Romantic historiography in France and Germany as a project of modernizing the sense of self, process of individuation, which entailed the creation of the Other (the Orient). "Romantic historiography seems to have been no less deeply implicated (than anthropology) in the nineteenth century ideology of progress and the white man's burden." (p.51). Essential reading for Indian students of literary history.

GRABAR, Oleg. 'History of Art and History of Literature: Some Random Thoughts'. *New Literary History,* Vol.3, No.3, Spring 1972, p. 559ff.

GREEN, Geoffrey. *Literary Criticism and the Structure of History.* Lincoln and Nebraska: Nebraska University Press, 1983.
A conventional and polemical account of the relationship between criticism and history.

GREENLAW, Edwin. *The Province of Literary History.* New York: Kennikat Press, 1931 and 1968.
A general, conventional view that "Literary history is learning, having its own method, its own right to exist among the learning, and having, also, important reaction to the history of culture on the one hand and to literary criticism on the other...while no history worth the name has any value except as it is based on exact research into the facts, the mere collecting of facts and arrangements of them in book form does not constitute history." ('Preface', pp. ix–x).

GUGELBERGER, George M. 'Decolonizing the Canon: Considerations of Third World Literature'. *New Literary History,* Vol. 22, No.3, Summer 1991, pp. 505–24.
A passionately sympathetic discussion, of the expression *Third World Literature* in a historical perspective. The argument proposed is that no study of 'literature' is complete without the knowledge of 'third world literature'. The essay alludes to Frederic Jameson's 'Third World Literature in the Era of Multicultural Capitalism', *Social Text,* 15 (1986), pp. 65–88.

GUHA, Ranajit. *Subaltern Studies: Writings on South Asian History and Society,* (5 volumes). New Delhi: Oxford University Press, 1984–87.
These volumes initiate the 'subaltern' movement in Indian historiography.

GUILLEN, Claudio. 'Second Thought on Currents and Periods' in *The Disciplines of Criticism: Essays in Literary Theory, Interpretation and History,* edited by Peter Demetz, Thomas Green and Lowry Nelson, Jr., New Haven and London: Yale University Press, 1968, pp.477–510.
"In this essay (I have) discussed some of the difficulties raised by periodization, especially with regard to diachrony and the organization of historical time...I have tried to single out those forms of periodization that provide us not only an access to styles and values, but with a sensitive and genuine vision of history, and hence can serve as foundations for an idea of literary history" (p.507). Guillen favours "a multi-level characterization that would accommodate the realization that men apparently live in more than one 'period' at once". Also of interest is Guillen's book, *Literature as System: Essays Towards the Theory of Literary History.* Princeton: Princeton University Press, 1971.

GUILLORY, John, 'The Ideology of Canon-Formation: T. S. Eliot and Cleanth Brooks'. *Critical Inquiry,* Vol. 10, No. 1, September 1983, pp.173–98.
Presents the idea that canon-formation is a production motivated by ideology.

HACKING, Ian. 'Two Kinds of "New Historicism" for Philosophers'. *New Literary History,* Vol. 21, No.2, Winter 1990, pp. 343–64.
The essay has a specific philosophical orientation, being a discussion of the tradition of analytical philosophy in the USA and European linguistic philosophy.

HARTMAN, Geoffrey H. 'History-writing as Answerable Style', in *New Directions in Literary History,* edited by Ralph Cohen, 1974, pp. 95–105.
Problematizes the difficulties in creating a verbal discourse about art by separating the epistemological from the ontological in art: focuses attention on the nature of the discourse of historical narratives. The essay is reproduced from *New Literary History,* Vol.2, No. 1, 1970.

HARTT, Julian. 'Theology as a Hermeneutical Salvaging of History'. *New Literary History,* Vol. 17, No.2, Winter 1986, pp. 183–94.
Followed by comments from Arthur G. Danto (pp. 195–98), and also by Ham's rejoinder (pp. 199–202). Hartt's primary interest is in giving an account of theological attempts to salvage Christianity from the framework of history.

HASSAN, Ihab. 'Making Sense: The Trials of Postmodern Discourse'. *New Literary History,* Vol. 18, No. 2, Winter 1987, pp.437–59.
The essay offers a fine example of an exercise in writing the history of contemporary literature; coheres with Hassan's writings on post-modernism elsewhere.

HATZFELD, Helmut. 'Comparative Literature as a Necessary Method', in *The Disciplines of Criticism: Essays in Literary Theory, Interpretation and History,* edited by Demetz, Green and Nelson. New Haven and London: Yale University Press, 1968, pp.79–92.
Hatzfeld's argument is that it is necessary to study "epoch-styles" before thinking of literature or art in terms of "style-epochs"; in the light of this view he attempts a redefinition of Baroque, Classicism and Romanticism.

HERNADI, Paul. 'The Erotics of Retrospection: History Telling, Audience Response, and the Strategies of Desire'. *New Literary History,* Vol. 12, No. 2, Winter 1981, pp. 243–52.
An attempt to employ the generic scheme proposed by Frye in his *Anatomy of Criticism.*

HOLUB, Robert C. *Reception Theory: A Critical Introduction.* London and New York: New Accents, Methuen, 1984.
Chapter III, 'The Major Theorists' has the following two subsections: "Hans Robert Jauss" and "Textuality and the Reader's Response: Wolfgang Iser", pp. 53–106. The book offers a lucid introduction to Jauss.

HUBERT, Judd, D. 'Random Reflections on Literary History and Textual Criticism'. *New Literary History,* Vol. 2, No.l, Autumn 1970, p.163ff.

ISER, Wolfgang. 'The Reading Process: A Phenomenological Approach', in *New Directions in Literary History,* edited by Ralph Cohen, 1974, pp. 125–46.
This essay presents an early version of the Reader-Response Theory developed by the Constanz Group (Jauss, Iser, etc.) At the base of the formation of history is the reading process which is not only the discovery of the unformulated

meaning, but also the discovery of the capacity to formulate it within ourselves.

JAKOBSON, Roman. 'On Realism in Art', in *Readings in Russian Poetics: Formalist and Structuralist Views,* edited by Ladislav Matejka and Krystyna Pomorska. Cambridge, MA: Harvard University Press, 1971.

JAMESON, Frederic. 'From Criticism to History'. *New Literary History,* Vol. 12, No. 2, 1981 It is a critical review of the essays published in the same issue of the journal, which is a special issue on "Interpretation and Literary History". The argument of Jameson is that literature is a historical process, and to write history of literature is to come full circle after forgetting that literature was history in the beginning. He suggests that we (should) "forget about history as some reified phenomenon, and (should) think rather in terms of the conceptual and dialectical operations whereby we *historicize* our materials. If we see our critical mission in terms of a process rather than of an inert 'interdisciplinary' linkage, it will become clear that any kind of criticism is grist to the mill of history and that any critical insights of whatever variety (stylistic, psychoanalytical, archetypal, typological, generic, semiotic) can always be historicized." p.375.

Also of interest are Jameson's other essays in *New Literary History:* 'Demystifying Literary History,' Vol. 5, No. 3, 1974, p.605; "Marxism and Historicism", Vol. II, No. 1, p. 41.

JAUSS, Hans Robert. *Towards an Aesthetics of Reception,* translated by Timothy Bahti, Introduction by Paul de Man. Brighton: The Harvester Press, 1982.

This collection of essays is one of the source texts for the critical theory known as 'Reception-Aesthetics' or 'Reader-Response Theory'; it includes the essays 'Literary History as a Challenge to Literary Theory', 'History of Arts and Pragmatic Theory', 'Theory of Genres and Medieval Literature', etc. The first of these essays appeared in an abridged version in *New Directions in Literary History* edited by Ralph Cohen, 1974, pp. 11–42. The abridgement is effected by the exclusion of some initial sections of the essay.

JAY, Gregory S. *T.S. Eliot and the Poetics of Literary History.* Baton Rouge: Louisiana State University Press, 1983.

KELKAR, Ashok R. 'Making and Writing Literary History: The Critic's Role.' *New Quest,* No. 80, March–April 1990, pp. 89-95.

Any literary history has to be a critical history.*

KERMAN, Joseph. 'A Few Canonic Variations'. *Critical Inquiry,* Vol. 10, No. 1, September 1983, pp. 107–26.

Offers a study of the concept of canon in music. Essential reading for students of literary canon.

KIERKEGAARD, Soren. *Concluding Unscientific Postscript,* (1844), translated from the Danish by Dorothy Swenson and Walter Lowrie. Princeton: Princeton University Press, 1941, pp. 286–88.

KRIEGER, Murray. 'Literary Invention and the Impulse to Theoretical Change: Or Whether Revolution be the Same'. *New Literary History,* Vol. 18, No. 1, Autumn 1986, pp. 191–208.

Discusses in a philosophical vein the gap between the tendency to theorize and the historical inconsistency of reality. Thus Krieger explores the phenomenon of change in relation to theory.

KULKARNI, G. M. and PUNDE, Dattatraya. *Vangmayetihasa: Sadyasthiti Ani Apeksha.* Pune: Mehta Publishing House, 1995.
The volume is divided into three sections; the first section includes essays by Kulkarni, the second, essays by Punde and the third records a free dialogue between Kulkarni and Punde. The volume covers several areas of conceptual value as well as methods of historical research.

LACAPRA, Dominick. 'History and Psychoanalysis'. *Critical Inquiry,* Vol. 13, No.2, Winter 1987, pp. 222–51.
Exploration of the theoretical basis for history writing in Freud's work.

LEFEVERE, Andre. *Essays in Comparative Literature: A Systemic Approach.* Calcutta: Papyrus, 1988.
The volume proposes, as the title indicates, a systemic approach to the study of literature and literary history. The essays, 'Power and the Canon, or: How to Rewrite an Author into a Classic', and 'The Dynamics of the System: Convention and Innovation in Literary History' (pp. 57–74 and 95–114, respectively) deal directly with literary history. However, the volume is even more useful in its discussion of literary translation.

LEHAN, Richard. 'The Theoretical Limits of the New Historicism'. *New Literary History,* Vol. 21, No. 3, pp. 533–53.
A thought-provoking essay which argues that ideology is built into modes of time. Further, "Postmodern history has been most energetic in suppressing this view, has been trying to break down the belief that history involves a 'flow'of time by substituting paradigms for process. But the use of paradigm itself ... involves forms of the presentation which contain a sense of time as having direction or, equally revealing as in the case of Foucault, of history as being static, a matter of representation that is equally ideological." (p. 535)

LEVIN, Harry. 'Reflections on the Final Volume of *The Oxford History of English Literature*', in *Refractions: Essays in Comparative Literature.* New York: Oxford University Press, 1966, pp. 151–70.
Illustrated discussion of how literary history needs to combine artistic monuments with historic documents.

LEVIN, Richard. 'Unthinkable Thoughts in the New Historicizing of English Renaissance Drama'. *New Literary History,* Vol. 21, No. 3, Spring 1990, pp. 434–47.
Attacks 'New Historicism' on five grounds, the chief among which is that New Historicism denies the historical existence of ideas, as, previously, historicism asserted the existence of ideas. The result is that New Historicism is nothing more than a history of non-ideas. Richard Levin has been one of the most prominent critics of New Historicism.

LODGE, David. 'Historicism and Literary History Mapping the Modern Period'. *New Literary History,* Vol. 10, No. 3, Spring 1979, pp. 547–55.
Not very original or stimulating, but very lucid; useful for students as an introduction to the debates relating to Modernism.

LUKACS, Gyorgy. *Notes on the Theory of Literary History,* first published in Hungarian in *Papers in Modern Philosophy* (1910), a festschrift for Bernat Alexander, Budapest. Later translated into English by Ian Fairley, with a critical introduction, *Comparative Criticism* (Cambridge), Volume 13, 1991.

This long essay belongs to Lukacs's pre-Marxist period. It discusses the concept of literary form as an aesthetic as well as a social construct.

MACLEAN, Marie. 'Pretexts and Paratexts: The Art of the Peripheral'. *New Literary History,* Vol. 22, No. 2, Spring 1991, pp. 273–80.

"Paratext and text may be most clearly observed by applying the speech act theory. There are, as Genette observes, completely different illocutionary acts involved in the paratext and in the text of a work of fiction. Indeed, it is here that we see most clearly the working of the two "rules of law" which Serres posits as standing on either side of the textual threshold. The paratext involves a series of first order illocutionary acts in which the author, the editor, or the preface are frequently using direct performatives." (p. 274)

MAJUMDAR, Swapan. *Comparative Literature: Indian Dimensions.* Calcutta: Papyrus, 1987.

This volume of essays is essential reading for Indian students of comparative literature. It considers the concepts of the aesthetic, influence and reception in the context of the colonial experience. "Periodization in Indian Literature" is by far the most sensible critical statement on the question of periodization in India. This volume addresses itself to specific issues of evaluation and historical description in the context of Indian literatures.

MAKKREEL, Rudolph A. 'Traditional Historicism, Contemporary Interpretations of Historicity, and the History of Philosophy'. *New Literary History,* Vol. 21, No. 4, Autumn 1991, pp. 977–91.

Particularly useful for students, being an account of the philosophical interpretation of history by Ranke, Kant and Heidegger.

McDONALD, Christie V. 'Literary History: Interpretation Inside Out?'. *New Literary History,* Vol. 12, No. 2, Winter 1981, pp. 381–90.

This is a response to the articles in the special number. McDonald suggests that literary history and literary criticism are intricately interwoven; the response matches with Jameson's, but the point of view here is not Marxist.

McGANN, Jerome J. 'The Text, the Poem, and the Problem of Historical Method'. *New Literary History,* Vol. 12, No. 2, Winter 1981, pp. 269–88.

Discussion of the gap between extrinsic and intrinsic literary scholarship, between theory and history, and the inter-relations between these opposites.

MEDVEDEV, P. N. and BAKHTIN, M. M. *The Formal Method in Literary Scholarship: A Critical Introduction to Sociological Poetics,* translated from the Russian by Albert J. Wehrle. The Goucher College Series, Baltimore and London: The Johns Hopkins University Press, 1978.

Extremely important sourcebook for Russian Formalism: Part One—*The Object and Tasks of Marxist Literary Scholarship;* Part Two—*The Contribution to the History of the Formal Method;* Part Three—*The Formal Method in Poetics;* Part Four—*The Formal Method in Literary History.*

Part Four includes the following two chapters: 'The Work of Art as a Datum External to Consciousness' and 'The Formalist Theory of the Historical Development of Literature'.

The second chapter deals with the following topics: the formalist conception of literary-historical change; the psychological preconditions of literary development; the scheme of literary evolution; the absence of real evolution in formalist theory of literary history; the Law of Automatizatio-Perceptibility as the basis of formalism; Ideological material in literary history; the logical and analytical extremes in the formalist conception of artistic perception; the absence of the category of "historical time" in formalist literary history; history as the illustration of theory; formalism and literary criticism.

Essential reading for the students of literary history.

MILLER, Christopher L. 'Theories of Africans: The Question of Literary Anthropology', in *Race, Writing and Difference,* edited by Henry Louis Gates, Jr. Chicago and London: The University of Chicago Press, 1986, pp. 281–300.

History is a narrative which is inevitably restricted by the racial perspective of the historian.

MINK, Louis O. 'History and Fiction as Modes of Comprehension'. *New Literary History,* Vol. 1, No. 3, Spring 1970, p. 541ff. Reproduced in *New Directions in Literary History,* edited by Ralph Cohen, 1974, pp. 107–24.

An introductory account of the difference between the two modes of narration. Useful text for initiating classroom discussion on the topic.

MUKHERJEE, Sujit. 'Towards a Literary History of India'. *New Literary History,* Vol. 8, No. 2, Winter 1977, p. 225 ff. *Towards a Literary History of India,* Occasional Papers Series, Simla: Indian Institute of Advanced Study, 1975. *Some Positions on a Literary History of India.* Mysore: Central Institute of Indian Languages, 1981.

———. 'Five Principles of Indian Literary History', translated into Marathi by S. G. Malshe, *'Bharatiya Vangmayetihas lekhanachi pach adhar-tatve'. Alochana,* April 1982, reprinted in *Vangmayetihasachi Sankalpana,* edited by Dattatraya Punde. Pune: Pratima Prakashana, pp. 70–85.

Mukherjee is one of the very few Indian scholars who have explored the area of comparative literature systematically. His bibliographies are comprehensive, systematic and extremely useful for future research in the area of literary history.

NAGENDRA. 'A History of Indian Literature: Basic Concept and Approaches', in *Emotive Basis of Literature and Other Essays,* New Delhi: B. R. Publishing, 1986.

NGUGI, wa Thiong'o. *Decolonizing the Mind: The Politics of Language in African Literature.* James Currey: London, 1986.

A passionately presented appeal for postcolonial writers to use their own languages for creative writing; reads the English canon as an agent of colonization in the context of African literature.

NIETZSCHE, Friedrich. *The Birth of Tragedy,* translated from the German by Francis Golffing. New York, 1956, pp. 19–36.

ORR, Linda. 'The Revenge of Literature: A History of History'. *New Literary History,* Vol. 18, No. 1, Autumn 1986, pp. 1–22.

An extremely illuminating and absorbing presentation about the breakdown of the initial togetherness between history and literature, and a succinct graph of the rise of self-consciousness in the two disciplines.

PASSMORE, John. 'History of Art and History of Literature —A Commentary'. *New Literary History,* Vol.3, No.3, Spring 1972, p.575ff.

PATKE, Rajeev. 'Canons and Canon-Making in Indian Poetry in English'. *Kavya Bharati: A Review of Indian Poetry,* No. 3, 1991, pp. 13–37.

The essay discusses the process and the politics of canon formation in Indian English literature during the last thirty years.

PERKINS, David, ed. 'Theoretical Issues in Literary History'. *Harvard English Studies,* 16, Cambridge, Mass.: Harvard University Press, 1991.

Includes contributions specially written for this volume by Ernst Behler, Ronald Bush, Paul Cantor, Ralph Cohen, Alastair Fowler, John Frow, Ulker Gokberk, Jon Klancher, Jerome McGann, Michael Valdez Moses, Mark Perker, David Perkins and John Paul Russo.

Particularly important are 'Literary Classification' by David Perkins, 'Genre Theory' by Ralph Cohen, 'Problem of Origin' by Ernst Behler, and 'The Two Histories' by Alastair Fowler.

PORTER, Carolyn. 'History and Literature: After the New Historicism'. *New Literary History,* Vol. 21, No.2, Winter 1990, pp. 253–72.

The essay explores the potentials of New Historicism and explicates the present clash between Formalism and Historicism in critical practice. The essay is followed by a response from Rena Fraden, and a counter-response from Porter.

PRADHAN, S. V. 'The Concept of Literary History: A Marxist Critique'. *Journal of Arts and Ideas,* No. 6, January–March 1984, pp. 67–74.

A general Marxist approach.*

PRAWER, S. S. *Comparative Literary Studies: An Introduction.* London: Gerald Duckworth and Co, 1973.

Useful classroom material. The volume has the following chapters: What is Comparative Literature; National Character and National Literature; Reception and Communication; Influence, Analogy and Tradition; Translation and Adaptation; Themes and Prefiguration; Genres, Movements, Periods; Structures and Ideas, 'Placing'; Theory and Criticism.

PUNDE, Dattatraya, ed. *Vangmayetihasachi Sankalpana* (in Marathi). Pune: Pratima Prakashan, no-date.

Useful introductory bibliography of material on literary historiography in Marathi; various plans on history of Marathi literature are appended. The volume contains edited essays written in Marathi, or translated into Marathi.

RAJAN, B. 'Literary History and Historical Criticism'. *The Indian Journal of English Studies,* Vol.1, 1962, pp. 106–111.

Discusses the role of literary history *vis-a-vis* criticism.*

RAND, Nicholas and TOROK, Maria. 'The Secret of Psychoanalysis: History Reads Theory'. *Critical Inquiry,* Vol. 13, No. 2, Winter 1987, pp. 278–86.

A psychoanalysis of psychoanalysis from a historical perspective.

RANDALL, Marilyn. 'Appropriate Discourse: Plagiarism and Decolonization'. *New Literary History,* Vol. 22, No. 3, 1991, pp. 525–41.

Discusses the concepts of authorship, propriety and individuality and their deviance in the context of postcolonial literatures to investigate the aesthetics of originality. Uses as epigraph a quotation from Jean Cocteau, "The original artist is incapable of copying. Therefore, in order to be original, he only has to copy".

RIEMENSCHNEIDER, Dieter. 'The 'New' English Literatures in Historical and Political Perspective: Attempts towards a Comparative View of North/South Relationships in Commonwealth Literature'. *New Literary History,* Vol. 18, No. 2, Winter 1987, pp. 425–35.

Introduces 'Commonwealth Literature' to Western audiences and discusses the role of comparative strategies in historicizing it.

———. *The History and Historiography of Commonwealth Literature.* Tubingen: Gunter Narr Verlag, 1983.

In this volume edited by Riemenscehneider, there are essays dealing with the question of historiography of postcolonial literatures in various regions of the British commonwealth. This volume still continues to be the only serious work on the history of Commonwealth Literature.

RIFFATERRE, Michael, 'The Stylistic Approach to Literary History'. *New Literary History,* Vol. 2, No. 1, Autumn 1970, p.39ff. Reprinted in *New Directions in Literary History,* edited by Ralph Cohen, 1974, pp. 147–64.

Discusses the complementarity of the extrinsic (historical) and the intrinsic (stylistic) approach to literature.

———. 'Interpretation and Undecidability'. *New Literary History,* Vol. 12, No. 2, Winter 1981, pp. 227–42.

"History hopes to prove its validity by recovering the intention of the author. However, what the reader has in a text is a reflection of his own intentions, which stabilizes the moveable feast. Interpretation, therefore antagonizes the past while it purports to present it".

Riffaterre discusses the referential fallacy in use of language for historical narratives. His writings belong to the structuralist-stylistics school.

ROBERTSON, D. W., Jr. 'Some Observations on Method in Literary Studies'. *New Literary History,* Vol. 1, No. 1, Autumn 1969, p. 2. Reprinted in *New Directions in Literary History,* edited by Ralph Cohen, 1974, pp. 63–76.

Robertson's essay is an excellent classroom text for postgraduate students. It makes a case for the dynamics of semantic structures, which change the language functions from time to time as well as literary aesthetics, to be considered as the primary problem of historiography.

RUECKERT, William. 'Literary Criticism and History: The Endless Dialectic". *New Literary History,* Vol.6. No.3, Spring 1975, p.491 ff.

SANDERS, Wilbur. *The Dramatist and the Received Idea.* Cambridge: Cambridge University Press, 1968.

Particularly useful is the chapter, "Literature as History".

SCHEUB, Harold. "Oral Poetry and History". *New Literary History,* Vol. 18, No. 3, Spring 1987, pp. 477–496.

Exposition of historical methods in oral poetry. Useful in making sense of the past in Indian literary traditions. "Like the poet, the oral historian fashions a number of unique images in the process of recounting events in the social and historical life of his people. These result from a combination of significant cultural feelings linked to important historical events. The convergence of the two results in historical motifs that are as useful to the historian as they are to the artist. In history as in poetry, they are valued for their own sake and are frequently removed from their linear contexts, transcending the moment of history." (p. 494)

SCHMIDT, Siegfried. 'Problems of Empirical Research in Literary History'. *New Literary History,* Vol.8, No.2, Winter 1977, pp. 213ff.

SCHORSKE, Carl E. 'History and the Study of Culture'. *New Literary History,* Vol. 21, No. 2, Winter 1991, pp. 407–20.

A survey of the role history has played from Herodotus to the glasnost in analysing culture. Reading for the specialist.

SHAFFER, E. S. *Comparative Criticism: An Annual Journal* (Cambridge), Vol. 6. Special number on 'Translation Theory and Practice', pp. 347–59 provide an excellent annotated bibliography on translation studies.

SHARMA, Ram Vilas. *Bharatiya Sahitya ke Itihas ki Samasyaen* (in Hindi). New Delhi: Vani Prakashan, 1986.

An extremely well-informed critique of notions of national history from a Marxist perspective. This is useful for its research value in the area of Indian socio-linguistics.

SLAWINSKI, Janusz. 'Reading and Reader in the Literary Historical Process'. *New Literary History,* Vol. 19, No. 3, Spring 1988, pp. 521–40.

Written in Warsaw, this informative essay is a sympathetic critique of the Jauss school of literary history. Of interest for advanced students of literary history.

SPILLER, Robert E. 'Literary History', in *The Aims and Methods of Scholarship in Modern Languages and Literatures,* edited by James Thorpe (2nd edition). Hyderabad: American Studies Research Center, 1970, pp. 55–68.

The article contains explanations on Province of Literary History; Theory of Literary History; Sources of Literature; Shaping of Literary History and Methods of Literary History.*

SPITZER, Leo. *Linguistics and Literary History: Essays in Stylistics.* New York: Princeton University Press and Russell & Russell, 1948.

The introductory chapter, 'Linguistics and Literary History', offers an illustrated defence of the use of linguistics in defining style-epochs, and therefore, the use of style-study in literary history. This is one of the earliest essays on literary stylistics. For that reason it is historically important. It is important also as an essay by a major comparatist. But, apart from these considerations, the title of the volume is grossly misleading.

STIMPSON, Catherine R. 'Reading for Love: Canons, Paracanons, and Whistling Jo March'. *New Literary History,* Vol. 21, No. 4, Autumn 1990, pp. 957–76.

Introduces the concept of 'paracanon': "A paracanon recognizes our need for some cultural shelter, a tidy site. Simultaneously, a paracanon finds 'the canon' both a house of orthodoxy and a house of cards. To mediate between these two perceptions, the paracanon is a tenet that neither ranks cultural works nor travels a compromised *via media* among them. Instead, it negotiates a particular lease on the life of their commonalities and differences. How can a text join the paracanon? Texts are canonical if some people have loved and do love them." (p. 958)

STOCK, Brian. 'Language and Cultural History'. *New Literary History*, Vol. 18, No. 3, Spring 1987, pp. 657–70.

Presents a version of the reader response theory, whose central assertions are close to Jauss's but also invokes the linguistic structuralism of Saussure together with the phenomenological hermeneutics of Paul Recour. "In my view it is an error to focus on the written text alone. The essential element is the community, the living people whose minds are peopled and shared by thoughts, intentions, and potential actions. The normal hermeneutic activity is the experience of the text along with individual interpretations...." (p. 669)

STONE, Donald R. 'Role of Literary History'. *Journal of Medieval and Renaissance Studies* 15, 1985, pp. 115–124.

Views about the past and pastness, "how and why a literary historian might have approached the same text." *

STURROCK, John. 'Writing Between the Lines: The Language of Translation'. *New Literary History*, Vol.4, Autumn 1990, pp. 994–1013.

TAINE, Hippolyte. 'Introduction' in *History of English Literature* (1864), translated from the French by Henry von Laun. London, 1900, Vol. I, pp. 1–2, 5–9, 13–19.

TOMPKINS, Jane. '"Indians": Textualism, Morality, and the Problem of History'. *Critical Inquiry*, Vol. 13, No. 1, Autumn 1986, pp. 101–19.

Through a case study, this article discusses the post-structuralist perspective on historical narration.

VALDES, Mario J. 'Heuristic Models of Inquiry'. *New Literary History*, Vol. 12, No. 2, Winter 1981, pp. 253–67.

"A theory of literal classification that accepts phenomenological literary theory and the necessity of classification. In such a theory any concept of forms must be considered a heuristic device established for purposes of understanding the nature of literary expression. The main question for this theory is form change." (p. 265)

VIPPER, Yuri B. 'National Literary History in History of World Literature: Theoretical Principles of Treatment'. *New Literary History*, Vol.16, No.3, Spring 1985, p. 545ff.

WASWO, Richard. 'The History that Literature Makes'. *New Literary History*, Vol. 19, No.3, Spring 1988, pp. 541–64.

Argues that literature changes history by shaping the forces behind history: a history of the contribution of literature in shaping the general history should form an important feature of literary history.

WEIMANN, Robert. 'Past Significance and Present Meaning in Literary History', in *New Directions in Literary History*, edited by Ralph Cohen, 1974, pp. 43–62.

An extremely valuable critique of the attitude of New Criticism to literary history. Argument in favour of the dialectical approach in which literature itself is history.

———. *Structure and Society in Literary History: Studies in the History and Theory of Historical Criticism.* London: The University Press of Virginia (1976) & Lawrence and Wishart, 1977.

The central thesis of this important book is that "the structure of literature is correlated with its function in society and that this correlation deserves to be studied in terms of both 'genesis' (or *Entstehungsgeschichte)* and 'impact' *(Wirkungsgeschichte)"*. (p. 273)

———. 'History and the Issue of Authority in Representation: The Elizabethan Theatre and the Reformation'. *New Literary History*, Vol. 17, No. 3, Spring 1986, pp. 449–76.

"Views representation in terms of its changeful uses in literary history, as a function of social and textual identification, limitation, extension, affirmation, and even...disruption". (p.449) Offers a theory of authority in terms of history of literature.

WELLEK, Rene. *Concepts of Criticism,* edited by Stephen G. Nicholas, Jr. New Haven and London: Yale University Press, 1963.

This collection has several very useful and lucid essays, the more important among them being: 'Literary Theory, Criticism and History' (pp. 1–21); 'The Concept of Evolution in Literary History' (pp. 37–53); 'The Crisis of Comparative Literature' (pp. 282–95).

Also important is: *The Rise of English Literary History.* Chapel Mill: The University of North Carolina Press, 1947. So far the only account of literary history in England during the eighteenth century and the first half of the nineteenth century.

WHITE, Hayden. 'The Politics of Historical Interpretation: Discipline and De-sublimination'. *Critical Inquiry*, Vol. 9, No. 1, September 1982, pp. 113–38.

Politics is seen as a condition of the possibility of interpretation as a social activity.

———. 'Literary History: The Point of It All'. *New Literary History*, Vol. 2, No. 1, Winter 1971, pp. 173–85.

Comments on the essays included in the same volume of *New Literary History.*

———. 'Interpretation in History'. *New Literary History*, Vol. 4, No. 2, Winter 1973, pp. 281–314.

A comprehensive discussion of the status of interpretation and the place of narration in history.

———. 'The Problem of Change in Literary History'. *New Literary History*, Vol. 7, No. 1, Autumn 1975, pp. 97–111.

A structuralist argument about historical changes taking place in language and literature.

WOELFFLIN, Heinrich. *Principles of Art History: The Problem of the Development of Style in Later Art,* translated by M. D. Hottinger. New York: Dover Publications, 1950.

(Entries marked with an asterisk have been supplied by Dr. D. D. Punde.)

Index

THE BEING OF BHASHA and COUNTERING VIOLENCE

Introduction

The notes presented in the following pages do not constitute an essay or a 'book', most of them are drawn from my conversations with Adivasi 'writers' and thinkers over a period of about fifteen years. I hesitate to call them 'writers,' for they are all involved in conservation of their oral traditions, and if they write, it is to restore dignity to the speech conventions of their communities. The notes presented here do not form any systematic exposition of the positions of my Adivasi colleagues. What is presented here is not an essay in linguistics, a philosophical dissertation, or 'field notes' of an anthropologist. Perhaps these are sketches from an unfinished workbook of ideas. I must admit that I no longer have the intellectual energy and concentration required for writing a serious academic piece, particularly when that writing is to be done in English. All my serious writing during the last fifteen years has been in Gujarati or Marathi for entering into a dialogue with Adivasi children and students. Having given away my personal collection of scholarly books to the Adivasi Academy, my access to scholarly materials necessary for undertaking an intellectual essay is restricted. Moreover, the work with the Adivasis keeps me constantly travelling, making any attempt at sitting at my desk and writing a luxury.

Often groups of students, scholars and academics visit the Adivasi Academy at Tejgadh where I have been carrying out a long cultural dialogue. I should have expected that some of them would be making their own notes of the conversations; I had overlooked this obvious possibility in the initial days of my work. Gradually, reports of these dialogues started appearing in academic circles. Quite often, I was invited to comment on such reports through lectures or by contributing short essays. Taking into account these circumstances, I decided to accept some of the invitations to discuss the reports of the cultural dialogue. Among these institutions, the National Institute of Design has been my favourite stop. The students at the NID are encouraged to think out of the box, and their inwardness to the world of imagination of a culturally different community is well developed. As such, I have been to the NID several times for giving informal lectures to groups of students and artists working there. These were invariably informal lectures without any written scripts prepared by me. However, after a time gap, someone in the audience would turn up with a 'transcription' of what I had said, asking me to read and improve the text of the transcription. I found these transcriptions a faithful testimony to my stream of consciousness, but a grammarian's nightmare. The text offered here is prepared by bringing together disjointed sections of those transcriptions. As such the present work is not a scholarly text prepared after a serious study of all other books available on the themes covered in it. It is only a book based on someone's notes of my informal lectures, in turn based on disjointed conversations with my Adivasi colleagues; and those conversations too were not formulated as conversations, but are the outcome of various developmental activities in the villages and the struggle for rights.

I acknowledge my debt of gratitude to a group of students in Prof. Nina Sabnani's class at the NID for digital recording and transcription of the lecture series 'Understanding our Time'. Mrs. Rohini Mokashi-Punekar, formerly faculty at the NID and now at the IIT, Guwahati, had attended the series of lectures on violence in India. I wish to thank her for comparing her notes of my lectures delivered in English, with my own notes on the theme made in Marathi, and then translating those notes into English to produce an essay in translation. Previously, she and I had decided to have that translation published together with some of my other unpublished writings as a volume in English. Since then, the other essays have appeared in *A Nomad Called Thief* (Orient Longman, 2006), and the essay on violence has appeared in Marathi in my book *Vanaprastha* (Padmagandha Prakashan, 2006). I am happy that I have been able to use Prof. Mokashi-Punekar's translation in the present volume. I thank my colleagues at Bhasha Research Centre for handing over to me a scribble pad containing a fairly faithful record of my lectures on 'Freedom and Knowledge'. The Manuscript Mission, and Dr. Sudha Gopalkrishnan had preserved notes of my lecture on 'Spoken Manuscripts'. I thank them. In sum, the text presented here is a result of the efforts of several persons who kept the records of what I spoke and made the transcriptions available to me. I would like to add that I have no sense of unease in presenting these disjointed notes.

Having known at one time the kind of intellectual perfection that scholars are expected to bring to their dissertations and presentations, I am aware that most of the views presented in this book are likely to be found unacceptable in academic circles. Moreover, I do not imagine that the manner of the presentation employed will at all find favour with scholars of literature and social sciences. I would like to draw their attention to the peculiar nature of the discourse here; the present text does not seek to put forward any coherent argument, to be accepted or refuted, but a set of concerns born out of the existential anxieties of speech communities whose knowledge has been struggling to fight an imposed aphasia. It needs to be appreciated that speech communities facing forced aphasia are bound to have their own perspective on what it means to be dialect, an oral tradition or a class contributing labour to produce wealth for another class. Their ideas of truth, fiction, knowledge, freedom, creativity and ideologies are likely to be at divergence from the ideas, even the progressive ideas, developed within the confines of the established knowledge traditions. *The Being of Bhasha* is a collection of those concerns. Examples from the more familiar cultural history and allusions to thinkers or styles from intellectual traditions known to my audiences have been brought in so as to establish a certain minimum level of communication with the audience. Those examples and allusions were captured in the transcription and I have not tried to 'purify' my text by removing all that is non-tribal (or all that is tribal.) I do not disown my personal responsibility for the inconsistencies, logical contradictions, and factual inaccuracies that may have entered in the text here. But, beyond these inadequacies, if Indian linguists address some of the concerns reflected in these notes, and if Indian literary scholarship turns its attention to a renewed study of India's oral traditions, the disciplines, one likes to hope, stand to gain.

After Amnesia: Tradition and Change in Indian Literary Criticism was an essay about an 'imaginary crisis' in the field of literary criticism in India. *Of Many Heroes: An Indian Essay in Literary Historiography* was about the futility of drawing up historical charts of a polyphonic set of traditions marked with an amazing diversity of literary conventions. Those two essays were pleas for not undertaking activities that have gained a disproportionately high intellectual currency as a result of colonialism. *The Being of Bhasha* and *Countering Violence* are an invitation to undertake cultural and intellectual engagements that we have neglected. I hope the four texts placed together will form a single comment on India's literary and intellectual culture.

I started working on *After Amnesia* in 1986. At the time, I was aware that I had taken up a fairly unfashionable area of study. While offering *The Being of Bhasha* for publication in 2008, I am acutely aware that it is not just the area of study, but the manner adopted for it too that will not find favour with the contemporary scholars of Indian literature and society. However, if the combined volume is read as a continuous text and a single comment on the nature of knowledge consumed in India and the violence arising in our society because of the mismatch between knowledge and existence, I will have a sense of fulfillment for having spent a quarter of a century in exploring unfashionable areas of study.

The sections on 'Violence' have been translated by Ms. Rohini Mokashi-Punekar, partly from my notes in Marathi and merged with some of the notes made in English during the lecture series I gave on the theme at the National Institute of Design. A revised and extended version of the original Marathi has since then been published in my *Vanaprastha* (Pune: Padmagandha Prakashan, 2006).

The infinite patience that Deepa Krishnamurthy of Orient Blackswan showed while handling the production of this joint volume amazes me. I am grateful to her for allowing me my leisurely pace of work, and also for making the entire copy of the joint volume readable.

G. N. Devy
Baroda
April 2008

THE BEING OF BHASHA

Knowledge, Society and Aphasia

Contents

1

The Substance of Language

When *Of Many Heroes* appeared in 1997, I had already moved fairly deep within the universe of India's oral literature in Adivasi languages. I had started collecting manuscripts from various Adivasi 'scholars' towards a planned series of bilingual volumes of Adivasi literature. Besides, I had been toying with the idea of launching a 'periodical-collective' for several Adivasi languages spoken in Western India. All these were languages for which no scripts existed. Conceptualizing those scripts, collecting contributions from persons who had never used their speech in any written form, and developing an 'audience' for the material that would be printed for the purpose of being read out, were tasks that fully absorbed all my intellectual energies. The cultural discoveries entailed in the process were many. As I moved every day from village to village, and from one Adivasi community to another, I became increasingly convinced that no scholarship in the field of Indian literature or literary aesthetics would ever be complete unless the peculiarities of Adivasi literary traditions were taken into account. This realization was intellectually humbling for me.

For the initial years of these explorations, my understanding of oral traditions and the Adivasi linguistic creativity remained within the confines of the existing framework of folklore studies and anthropology. But, gradually, those frameworks started looking inadequate. For a while, I kept developing for my own understanding some crude premises for describing the languages and literature of India's Adivasis. For instance, in a meeting of Adivasi colleagues held in the Dangs in 1997, I argued that "imagination is a capitalist literary criterion developed through certain institutionalized processes of socializing, while memory is a criterion developed by communities that have not lost ability for realism." In another meeting, held in Hyderabad in 1998, I argued that "there is a direct correspondence between deforestation of a country and decline of human languages in it." These, I realized fairly soon, were untenable premises if put to the test of fact, history or reason. I concluded, therefore, that theorizing on these issues must await a lot more detailed sampling of literature in Adivasi languages. However, I had no doubt in my mind that a study of Indian literature or aesthetics would be incomplete without taking into consideration the oral creations in India. Hence, I decided to juxtapose the known sources of literary theory in India with samples of literary creativity in Adivasi languages.

At this time, the long forgotten manuscript of my anthology of Indian Literary Theory had somehow been recovered. Orient Longman published it in 2003 under the title *Indian Literary Criticism: Theory and Interpretation*. In the same year, Penguin published an anthology edited by me under the title *Painted Words: Literature of Adivasis and Denotified Communities*. These two were meant for being read together. In India literature and imaginative expression range from the ancient Prakrit and Sanskrit, medieval Persian and Arabic, the bhashas and English, to the yet unscripted languages of Adivasis and the code-languages of the nomadic communities. Indian literary aesthetics extends across all these, and has developed through their intimate convergence and conflict. In Indian traditions of creative expressions, the 'literary' includes the written as well as the oral. The two can be separated to the peril of either or both of them.

I have never found it necessary to think of the written and the oral in terms of binary cultural practices. Speech and not script is the primary domain of literature, even written literature. Scripts are useful, they can even be 'beautiful', but despite not being indispensable for linguistic creativity, they can easily cause 'internal displacement' of linguistic creativity in a given language. In India, we have not as yet developed a theoretical apparatus to gauge the importance of 'dialects' in the survival and growth of the bhashas. In many ways, the 'being' of the bhashas has been dependent on the dialects that presage their emergence. In a short essay, included in *A Nomad Called Thief: Reflections on Adivasi Voice and Silence* (Orient Longman, 2006), I have outlined the theoretical issues that deserve attention from Indian scholarship.

Language and Reality

The process of human evolution holds back many secrets from our understanding in such a manner that we may only build apparently scientific hypotheses about them: such hypotheses that even the exactly contrary positions may sound equally convincing. Language as a social institution, the nature of its exact origin and the clear sequence in its formation, are some of the mysteries in the epic text of human evolution. Was there an attendant sound when the universe came into existence? Did sound exist at all prior to the development of the animal ability to perceive it? Do the eternal sound — the *anahat dhvani* — and the sound coined by vocal chords belong to the same material type? Why did the human animal select regulation of breath by the vocal chords as the means for meaning-transaction, while with the human eye or through body movement (as honey bees do) the meaning transaction could have possibly been equally effective? Why didn't the human animal cultivate those other means of expressions with an equal degree of obsession? All these questions can be answered at the theoretical level; but the answers do not cross the level of philosophical propositions that are true but at the same time not entirely untrue. Once regulation of air by the vocal chords came to be the central mode of meaning transaction, and subsequently numerals and letters became the surrogates for sound, why was it that the script language did not entirely displace the sound language? While the theory of language acquisition inherent in the mind-structure of an infant has been formulated, why has the theory of the natural ability to perceive the correspondence between those geometrical shapes called letters and the human sounds called syllables so far not been posited? 'Meaning' consists of the meaning expressed through gesticulations, sound-regulation and script marks, as well as through the silence and stillness beyond the pale of these three. What exactly constitutes 'meaning' has not been conclusively determined. The theories of meaning have so far remained at the level of philosophical speculation. Besides, it has so far not been possible to state with any great precision as to whether meaning is language, or if meaning exists prior to language and is capable of transcending human language even when language is an experience within the range of perception of an individual. This has led us to conclude that language is a social institution. But is language 'meaning', is it some material, is it a transcendental energy or a purely social institution, or is it a mere biological function given to the human body in the process of evolution? Or is it all of these at once or in various aspects of the language phenomenon? All these questions need yet to be tackled fully despite linguistics being one of the most developed of human sciences. There is a well-established view that culture has no other expression but language, that the two are one and the same. It is maintained that cognition too would be impossible without language. A similar view on meaning too exists. In other words for practically every transaction of the intellect, 'language' has been used as a synonym that determines the outer boundaries of each transaction of the intellect. Even when the structure of dreams is not based on language content, it is conceptualized as being the same as language structure. The origin of dreams is in the ability to remember, in memory. In others words we are made to believe that memory cannot exist entirely in the absence of language. Similarly, we have come to believe that other psychic possibilities such as inspiration, imagination and reason cannot exist in the absence of language. While these hypotheses seem unexceptionable, it is true that there are experiences that the human animal shares with other animals that show a marked absence of language based on sound regulation. Vertigo, or the fear of falling, and love or sensuous attraction are the main instances of such experiences. Phenomenology, which is one of the sciences of human understanding, maintains that language develops in tune with the perpetually increasing scope of the phenomena perceived by the human mind. As against this, it has been argued that the human grasp of the phenomenal reality increases in proportion to the ever increasing ability of language to grasp complexities. It is indeed difficult to establish if a domain of experience exists independently and outside the domain of language. At the same time it is even more difficult to overrule the existence of such a domain of experience. Similarly complicated is the question whether those semi-verbal or verbal substances that scripts, grammars and cultures do not admit as language, are language or not? At best they find a place in marginal categories such as dialects and regional varieties. In fact, in the vast spectrum of meaning beginning with the mysterious origin of sound, to its pervasive spread through human space and time, human languages may at best be seen as dialects of the uninterrupted *dhvani.* Similarly, in the total range of meaning capable of being conducted through material and symbolic means, the sound-symbol based language will have to be counted as a dialect of the total range of meaning. Moreover, the process of the perpetual increase in the human experience interlocked with language will have to be thought of as a dialect of the universe of experience. And the totality of the human languages stabilized through words and scripts will have to be seen as a dialect of the totality of all experience, all meaning and all sound. Therefore to be a dialect is not being left behind, but to be the *avant-garde*, to be on the forefront. If we imagine a certain component of language (as a substance within the system that it is) whose destiny it is to be at the turbulent interface of the ever expanding reality, and if we imagine that this component is required to persist in its work without losing its identity as language—be in currency at least with the value of the counterfeit—we will have adequately imagined a dialect. To use a metaphor, dialect is like the amorphous substance surrounding a newly born planet which is yet to find its ultimate rate of revolution. That planet environment of the language is defined by its dialects. It is through them that language keeps its ceaseless contact with the universe outside it, and therefore manages to belong to it.

2

Writing and Aphasia

The term 'manuscript' signifies something written in hand. But this writing itself can be done differently in different situations. I will speak here about some forms of writing I have come across while working on oral traditions. I have been observing a 'speech-syndicate' from Maharashtra, which belongs to the Gondhali community. The ancestors of this community were employed in the past as spies in the army of Shivaji and his successors. While demonstrating its language skills, the syndicate splits into two groups that stand apart at a distance of two or three hundred feet. When I whisper a sentence in Marathi, Gujarati, English or any other language, known or unknown to them, one of them makes some gestures with his hands, and another person standing in the other team reproduces the same sentence without any flaw, no matter whether the person speaks, reads or knows that specific language. I wonder if this communication could not be called 'writing'. This is not a language of signs, images or pictographs, but a production of characters belonging to different kind of 'script'. There are many other forms of writing in our society which force us to re-examine our notions of 'writing'. An instance can be found in the folk practices of Lakshadweep. People there have a practice of carving on ships and boats their local history, poems and various aspects of their everyday life, so that they can visually perceive their life experience. These are a lot more elaborate than the graffiti signed on transport vehicles in mainland India These carvings are sacred to the inhabitants of the islands. Among the Rathwa tribals in Gujarat and some parts of Madhya Pradesh, there is a widespread practice of painting on walls. Their houses are usually larger than the 'census-average' of Indian dwellings; some of them measure as much as sixty feet by forty feet. I have seen paintings that measure as much as sixty feet in length, and eight to ten feet in height. The paintings are done collectively, but one part of the work is reserved for the master painter. The term used for the master painter is not *chitrakar,* 'the painter', but *lakhara*, 'the one who writes'.

When I started looking at the Pithora paintings, the Lakhara tradition, and the universe of narratives they create, I realized that the usage of the term *lakhara* was not merely accidental. The paintings depict not simply imagery, shapes or colours, but a kind of a map for the territories north of Narmada and south of Panchmahals. Though this view has never been examined by anthropologists and art-historians, there is enough in the history of the material culture of the area to hold that these paintings were the medieval tribal equivalent of the modern day Permanent Account Number. To have the map of the region painted on a wall earned the rights of a 'prominent-citizenship' in the Rathwa kingdom. The Rathwa 'writing' on the wall is one of the numerous manuscript traditions of India. It is not just the external surfaces of material that are used for writing by Indian manuscript traditions, the human body too has been used as a surface for writing in certain manuscript traditions. But apart from these, there are numerous other and more 'acceptable' writing practices on silk or other textiles, leaf or wood bark. There is an amazing variety of manuscript traditions in India even today though most of them do not fit within the institutions of formal knowledge and are barely surviving or have become increasingly invisible. The Mahanubhav prose, developed by the followers of the thirteenth century Chakradhara in north Maharashtra, was created and handed down from generation to generation to the initiates only in a coded manner, a kind of a manuscript tradition made consciously 'invisible'. The birth of several writing practices lies in the heterodox tradition of India. Whenever religious or social orthodoxy had to be challenged in India, new manuscript traditions and new scripts were invariably employed as a means in the struggle.

There is no logical connection between a given language and a given script. It is widely held in post-Saussurean linguistics that the process of matching verbal icons to signify semantic units by a given speech community itself is entirely arbitrary. The influence of Sausure's propositions on modern linguistic thought is so overwhelming that this view will continue to enjoy validity till a technical tool is developed to hold all human sound data together through digital and multimedia imagery and to fathom the taxonomy of all possible relations obtaining between sound and sense. There however will be a point in the cultural evolution of *Homo sapiens* when human speech will be left with no justification for its existence. At the present juncture, however, the question is why various speech communities develop methods and manners of representing speech in the form of scripts? Are these mere accidents in history, or just some expression of a speech community's aesthetic instinct?

I would like to think that development of script, which develops when leisure as an economic product enters the life of a society, is not a mere reflection of the leisure available to that society, but rather a means of *procuring and perpetuating* such leisure. Scripts primarily are related to the counting system rather than speech. When the first surplus out of pastoral or agriculture economy came, and it had to be transacted for labour, the community that undertook the negotiations needed to mark the quantity of surplus invested. Thus the initial characters in the evolution of a script are the numerals in their rudimentary forms. Numbers were inscribed on rock or wood surfaces or sand, as was the practice in India. The child was taught writing on dust in the first year of school. But some of these numbers did not subsequently qualify for getting into the range of characters counted as a script. For example, we still have the tick mark and cross, and the tick mark has not become a character in any script though it is understood quite widely as a mark that says 'yes' as against 'no', indicating a presence as against an absence.

Many such marks get into the script system, but initially they are quantifying signs, a way of numbering. Every community has a different world view, and therefore a different way of measuring the world. There are communities that do not particularly differentiate between the northeast and the northwest, the southeast and the southwest. The communities that do so, have a clear perception of the difference between the sharp sun and the mild sun, and between strong wind and a mild breeze as the terms *agneya* and *ishanya*, *vayavya* and *neiritya* indicate in most of the Indo-Aryan languages. Again there are communities that think in terms of four directions—east, west, north and south, and others in terms of eight, or in some places ten directions. The reasons could be traced to the given community's attitude to surfaces, space, recognition of images which change from place to place depending on visibility, light available in the area, or the surface textures of things that a community encounters over long spells of material-cultural history. The methods of counting will change from place to place, and so also the kind of characters a community develops to record speech. Thus Modi, which as a script was a purely counting system but not a writing system—something that can be compared to a contemporary software such as Tally which can 'write', but writes only accounts—was used by the ruling classes and the merchants. Writing as we know it today is a combination of numerals and various geometrical forms. Three or four geometrical forms are enough to make a script. These mainly acquire the place of 'vowels' when they attain the status of a script.

In our literary past, most of the linguistic creativity has been in the oral tradition. Though people knew how to write, writing was not used as a means of educating the next generation in remembering these compositions. I am not denying the fact that we had something written even in Harappan times, and a tremendous era of literary productivity in ancient Tamil and post-Vedic Sanskrit; but by and large, knowledge, literature and memory were handed down not through writing but through speech and oral media. What developed in India as oral tradition was not just 'writing' on walls and boards, but also composition of texts, documents, or what one describes as 'manuscripts'. They follow the logic of speech and not the logic of orthography. The aim here is not in any way to establish writing as redundant but only to indicate that considering what is non-written as non-manuscript would be inadequate in accounting for India's linguistic and imaginative traditions.

In India, numerous compositions have come to us from ancient and medieval times without the mediation of writing, but with a grammar of memorizing them. In the precolonial schooling systems the teacher set before the students one part of a word or a sentence and the remaining part was coined by the students as a complement or *samasya-purti.* It was a standard practice, not involving writing but with a clear evidence of document, text, style and unity. This kind of schooling changed after paper became available for use in India during the thirteenth century. However, the place of the oral was not entirely, or substantially, taken by the written. The two co-existed in an inter-dependent manner in Indian production of knowledge. It is said that Tukaram's *Gatha* was sunk in the Indrayani by the critics who opposed his humanized theology. But it is also believed by his devotees that the *Gatha* surfaced again. It is certain that Tukaram *wrote.* Eknath, before Tukaram's times, had prepared an edition of Jnaneshwar's writings. Though there existed the possibility of committing compositions to scripts, the dissemination of texts took place through oral means. Is Tukaram's *Gatha* then to be viewed as an oral text or a written text? Similarly with Kabir, Mira and many other *bhakti* saints throughout the medieval centuries writing and speech were not seen as exclusive or antithetical but rather as complementary practices. When paper became available, scholars used paper for writing. Previously when tree bark was available they had used tree bark. Manuscripts were copied meticulously by generations of students and every few hundred years they were renewed. But there were others who memorized this and continued handing down knowledge through speech. Therefore, manuscript was both writing and speech at the same time, and this continued in Indian history for centuries. When the print technology arrived in this country, it was not available to every language that had extensive literature in it, nor did it reach every language that had numerous speakers. It only reached some languages spoken by communities from which people could be drawn as bureaucrats, as those who would work in the East India Company's government or teach in government colleges. Languages were chosen for printing in India not on the basis of their literary capabilities, or their antiquity, but on the basis of administrative convenience.

After independence, linguistic states were created again for administrative convenience. However, these were not linguistic states, rather they were 'script states' created on the basis of those languages which had 'writing' practices considered exclusively from the perspective of print technology. Bringing this out in sharp relief, the Census Reports continued to point out that there had been quite a large number of other speech communities in India with a sizeable population. Out of the Indian languages, only twenty-two have been placed in the Eighth Schedule of the Constitution. These were languages with written literature in them; but nearly ninety other languages that have a population of over ten thousand have not been placed there because of the absence of 'writing' committed to the print medium in those languages.

In this context it would be useful to reflect on why the Dravidian and the Aryan family of languages did not form one single language family despite having such an intimate relationship for three thousand years. The reason lies in the existence of all these 'other' languages, and their specific geographical location in the central Indian belt. I will use the term 'Adivasi' to denote the speech communities of these 'other' languages. Most of the Adivasi languages do not have their own scripts. They have a very rich tradition of songs, stories, history and memory. They form a body of documents, which were not written by hand but conveyed by tongue. By not recognizing the personality of these languages, by not recognizing their citizenship we have imposed on them a condition of what may be described as aphasia, rendering these languages speechless. In psychology, aphasia is explained as falling into several different categories. A certain type of aphasia is caused by the damage to the motor system, in which the linguistic message is not conveyed from the brain to the speech organs or vice versa.

Next, aphasia may be caused due to damage of the organs of speech. And, finally, there is a psychic disorder in which one loses the ability to link word with sense. These known forms of aphasia can be cured by medical treatment. However, there could be a form of aphasia when nothing has gone wrong with the brain, the tongue or the psyche, but when one is just not allowed to speak! This is an 'imposed aphasia', which silences the vast population of India's dialects and the 'unscheduled' tribal languages. In fact most of the practices of oral history are facing this kind of terror from the mainstream languages that have received state patronage. It is necessary therefore to underscore that the Indian manuscript traditions are not solely traditions of writing.

The Sanskrit term *akshar* literally means, 'that which will not dissolve'. *Akshar* also means that which is perennial, eternal, without the limits of birth or death. In Indian mythology, the world in its entirety, the cosmos, is perceived as creation out of sound and *akshar* is the indestructible substance of that sound. The energy that created the world is *akshar*; so it cannot be destroyed. Now *akshar*, or characters are always essentially nomadic and migratory in character, and lexical units are like the sedentary state giving them a fixed location and a definition. That is the reason why a limited number of *akshars* can create many words, or a language. In India we have learned to look down upon nomadic people because the colonial British did not approve of nomads. The colonial state viewed these communities as 'criminal tribes'. Those who did not pay taxes to the state were worthy of suspicion, and therefore undesirable. To sedentarize the subject communities and to turn them into 'citizens' has come to be seen all over the world as the primary mission of the state. The idea behind this 'civilizing' mission of the state is to give the citizens fixed addresses so that they can not only be contracted but also be controlled. The main difference between other animal species and human beings is language, not writing. If we discount that, we also discount the human contribution, the humanness. So every time we think of literature, writing, documents, and manuscripts, it is necessary to remember that we are humans and therefore we have speech. It is our responsibility to preserve that. In other words it is necessary to respect this great linguistic variety which our historical and human experience has bestowed upon us. The dichotomy between writing and speech is unnecessary for the growth of good speech or writing. There is no room for any conflict between the two as long as writing recognizes the fact that all speech has a citizenship in the world of knowledge.

3

Silence, Insanity and Language

Silence is a communication zone which has the potency of language but no desire for verbal articulation. This is not a case of aphasia resulting from the neurological or physiological inability to speak. For instance, an intense mystical experience may contain a structured sensation or perception, capable of communicating an element of significance, but it is very difficult to articulate that experience through words. Silence therefore is not any absence of language but, like a dialect, it is a language frontier negotiating with unexplored fields of significance. One can compare, perhaps, the apparent aphasia contained in silence with the apparent euphoria explicit in a mental state of unruly excitement. It is known to psycholinguists that any kind of psychic imbalance has a direct impact on one's language behaviour. It activates language; it makes language so rapid that the listener cannot make good sense of what is being said. A small segment of the entire area described as insanity by Western psychoanalysis is hysteria. When one is hysteric the kind of language which is produced is far beyond the understanding of a grammarian. Thus insanity as well as silence has a bearing on language as a system of meaning. It is not just that an episode of insanity or a moment of silence will hamper the normal flow of language. This they certainly do, but more importantly, implicit in the being of a language are the possibility of a movement in the zones of silence or in the turbulent outbursts of hysteria. When the possibilities of a given speech community, or the speech systems employed by that community, start getting curtailed, or are pushed to the verge of exhaustion, in a manner of speaking, the language starts losing its nerve and starts entertaining suicidal tendencies.

Why is it that human beings alone have developed such an advanced kind of language with its immense complexity of structure? It is true that some animal species, like the honeybees, have a kind of language. They dance and communicate, and their communication is fairly accurate. It has its own grammar. One minimum condition of language is when you reproduce a certain verbal pattern, the meaning of the verbal pattern more or less conveys the same significance for every instance of its being articulated. Thus, honeybees dance and communicate, and the next time they want to communicate they perform more or less the similar kind of dance. Dolphins have a language of their own, and possibly ants too have a sense of language since we see them communicating. But despite all these very visible symptoms of language development in other species, it is in the human species that language has developed to a level of complexity which can accommodate euphoria, hysteria, insanity and silence as patterns of significance.

Why is it that human beings have developed language with voice and not with any other physical organ which is capable of communication? Though touch is not enough to communicate everything, human eyes are quite versatile in communicating innumerable shades of meaning. Most other animals have developed communication systems by using eyes; it is only the human animal that has chosen to develop a language which is verbal and uses voice as the medium, though voice is not really the most suitable medium for language. Eyes are far more expressive, the human eye can move and reflect sentiments. However, eyes age with the body naturally as voice does not, though it is true that the voice of human children changes when they attain adulthood. While it is not such a versatile medium, human beings have still accepted it as a medium because voice can transcend one material limitation that eyes cannot, namely the ability to address the things that are not in one's immediate sight. Otherwise none of the organs of speech—teeth, tongue, throat and nose—were really made for speaking. It must have taken thousands of years or longer to develop a coordination of those devices to produce voice; and then to make it meaningful must have taken even longer.

The human consciousness is made very much in the image of the earth. Those of us who apply Sigmund Freud to understand the human mind often overlook the intimate relationship between the human consciousness and the earth. Like the earth, the consciousness is in a perpetual motion. It has a core that its surface cannot see. The surface is continuously surprised by the strange things that spring up quite mysteriously from the core. The consciousness works like the earth because human beings like other life forms have sprung out of this earth. The earth has two motions, it rotates round itself and it revolves round the Sun. Similarly, the human consciousness has two movements: just as it engages itself in viewing the world, it also keeps looking at itself. This is something very peculiar to human beings. This is so because the evolution of the human body has arranged the brain, through the intervention of the spine, to be farthest from the surface of the earth. The verticality given to us by the human spine has removed the human brain far away from the surface-texture of the earth; and therefore our direct experience of the earth is quite reduced in the process of evolution. It is limited predominantly to a conceptual understanding of the material world. Therefore we are forced to look at our existence critically time and again.

The centuries that shaped the Western attitude to insanity, industrial progress, jurisprudence and the law based state-structures, were precisely the centuries of the colonial experience for India, when India was getting exposed to new forms of 'knowledge' and varieties of 'culture' from its contact with the West. Therefore, the ideas of criminality and the analysis of insanity as were established in England during the colonial times were accepted in India as scientific ideas. Even today our entire criminal law is based on the British jurisprudence and the treatment of mental illness is based on the Austrian psychoanalysis proposed by Sigmund Freud. The idea of insanity as criminality, a challenge to order and as anti-normalcy has been accepted by us without a question. It would be pertinent to ask if there existed at all in precolonial India a notion of insanity. Can we point to any character in the *Mahabharata* perceived to be insane? And the epic has quite a plethora of characters! Was there no notion of insanity in the Indian tradition or traditions, any instance of behaviour that Western psychology would describe as 'insanity'? Why was it that a great thinker and mystic like Ramakrishna Paramhansa could easily be passing through fits of what Freudian psychoanalysis would describe as 'abnormal' and yet be intelligible to Indian thinking?

Ramakrishna experienced a state of ecstasy which is called in the parlance of Indian mysticism *turyavastha*, preparation for the ultimate ecstasy where no separation exists between the self and the other, or the manifest nature and the supernatural. In this state of the consciousness, no polarities exist and, it is said, one becomes completely united with the rest. Ramakrishna's name is associated with that state of ecstasy, which seen from our 'normal' perspective is close to 'insanity', a mystical variety of communion. Having an abnormal personality was accepted in Indian traditions as a perfectly normal human condition, nor was such a person sent out of the normal social framework and there were no asylums created. Even today the creation of asylums in India is seen as a preserve of the state based on the colonial law, but not a common social practice. Families are prepared to keep the mentally abnormal persons as normal members of the family. Indian society had space for those who wanted to drop out and do things which were contrary to what they were trained to do. The society traditionally provided social space for those who showed morally questionable behaviour by accepting or at least tolerating them. I had the opportunity of interviewing a number of prisoners in Gujarat, and to my question as to where they would go after being released, they invariably answered that they would go back to their families where their mothers or spouses were waiting for them. Indian family and the social system had that space for the mentally abnormal. One is aware that there was an element of cruelty and neglect of such persons within the family; but at the societal level places for seclusion were not enshrined in India in precolonial times.

By following British education, Western psychology and psychiatry, certain metrics of values and knowledge constructs, we have today come to a situation where we have been rapidly eliminating the space for insanity. At the school level, we notice that children are systemically discouraged from even the slightest element of different thinking, 'of madness'. Rabindranath Tagore understood the importance of allowing children to be what they are. He spent an entire life encouraging the 'surplus of emotions' to spring up in the mental transactions of children. That is now not allowed. Similarly, our communication traditions valued silence. Traditionally, aesthetics revolved round the *shant*, the tranquility that follows fulfillment, as the ultimate. Abhinavgupta claimed that the culmination of all these *rasas* is attained by a combination of all—which could be described as *shantarasa*. Abhinavgupta proposed that if Ramayana is unique for its *karuṇarasa*, the Mahabharata is unique for its *shantarasa*, the ultimate aesthetic achievement. The *Upanishads* always concluded with the benediction invoking silence which passes all understanding. Silence had a core cultural significance in Indian society.

We are now not capable of experiencing silence or respecting it, nor are we capable of coping with insanity as an essential part of our being. It is because of the reduced cultural space for insanity and silence that the language of our understanding is affected. We are not able to see our 'being' through our 'understanding'. This is more predominantly so in relation to our understanding of the being of the bhashas today. The life of the Indian people continues the way it was, with whatever changes the Indian people in the villages, its lanes and the markets have accepted—but they continue to cope with their material life, maintain their families, handle materials, reproduce children, bring them up, worship gods and nature, more or less in the same way as they did a hundred years back. Life, which is closely linked to the specific geographic environment, has continued as it was, since the lived life does not change dramatically or drastically owing to mere intellectual influences. While our social practices and lifestyles have changed, they have not changed as drastically as our understanding of that life has changed. Hence we are not able to look at India the way we should do.

This is our collective intellectual failure and possibly the failure of the university system. There is another thing that has happened, which pervades our being not just our understanding, and it is that this reduced tolerance of insanity and silence has produced among us a mass hysteria. When we think of the Indian past of the last hundred and fifty years, what are the major visual memories that come to one's mind? One is of the thousands marching with Gandhi in this freedom march. However, when Gandhi walked from Sabarmati to Dandi, he did not have with him thousands of pilgrims. But in our imagery of the past we have added the mob to the image. We have in the recent imagery of India the mobs attacking a mosque or Muslim minorities. But do we remember the quiet death of Baba Amte as a profound visual experience? Most of our visual memory is related to some kind of mob frenzy. If one rebels against the cultural compulsion of belonging to the mob, that person will be labelled a criminal, social dropout or insane, and therefore to be sent to asylum. The interiors of the bhashas, shored in the past by silences and style abnormalities, are fast becoming desolate. Those areas are becoming populated with chants associated with communally charged popular religion, and an economy driven semi-scientifism.

4

The Story of Telling

It is possible to argue that consciousness is a fantasy of the phenomenal world. We do not know if the world exists outside there or not, but we all assume that it is there, and we live with that assumption as some truth. In our encounters with the world external to us, the most remarkable element is language. It is language alone that allows consciousness to come to terms with the world. If we did not have language as a means of mediation it would have been just impossible to name that outside, and then to look at it as if all the names that were given, were things already there as things. Language is what marks out the human animal in the entire range of animal world, a unique feature of human civilization.

Possibly it is a biological condition of having a spine that forces us to have language. It is only the human animal that stands perpendicular to the earth. All other animals crawl, fly, and swim. Because of the spine that removes us from the textures of the earth, we are forced to establish and reinvent relationships with the earth and the rest of the world.

Human beings are born within two conditions, one is space, and the other is time. It is just impossible for an individual to be out of space or out of time. A theatrical Hamlet may say "the time is out of joint, o cursed spite, that I was ever born to set it right", but we can never set fragments of time together, or get time to be disjointed. We just have to live with time just as we have to live with space. The human consciousness, which is essentially fantasy of the world, comes to terms with space and time with the help of the two mental faculties. One is memory, and the other is imagination. It is memory that allows us to come to terms with time. One remembers that one is the same person today as one was yesterday. Though philosophically this is debatable, there certainly is a continuity of identity; it is memory that makes it possible. It allows us to conceptualize time even if it may not exist really, for one does not know if time exists outside our minds or not; it is memory that allows us first to conceptualize time, and then, having conceptualized it, memory allows us to come to terms with it.

Imagination, a term which I am using in the technical sense and not in the aesthetic sense, is what Hobbes, for instance, defined in *Leviathan* as a "a stream of images". Images of objects enter the eye all the time and while they are stored in the mind they keep decaying. It is the arrangement of these decaying images that is imagination in the Hobbesian sense. It is this image-making power, thanks to light, that allows objects to be seen by the eye. We are able to see the objects reflecting light. Thanks to those objects, light and the eye, the images from the outside world enter the mind. It is impossible for a human being to feel the world with the senses, experience everything in the world directly with the senses. Images received by the mind are stored there and are later reconstructed in the subjective realm of perception. Memory helps us to interpret. Imagination helps us to negotiate the human defeat at the hands of space. We control our space through imagination, we control time through memory. Language, memory and imagination come together and allow the consciousness to function so that consciousness then can create a fantasy of the world. This is the beginning of fiction.

There is one more component in this transaction and that is, it is not enough for fiction just to emerge, it must be told. It is human beings again that have a sense of otherness. It is the human child alone that learns at a fairly early stage in growth (because human growth is very slow and we take much longer than other animals to grow properly) to look at itself through the eyes of the world. It is not that the human consciousness just creates a fantasy of Existence, but through its interlocking with that fantasy, allows itself to create the 'self' as a fantasy. That is where the sense of shame enters the psyche. This happens precisely at the time when the ability to speak starts developing. It is not just the story in its silent form that matters, for the human mind the telling of the story becomes necessary because the mind knows that there are others, 'not me', outside, who might be very much like oneself. Many other animals fail to recognize this otherness. Four elements: language, memory, imagination and otherness, they force us to tell a story. The first three create fiction, and the fourth one, alienation, otherness, forces us to tell the story. But then in the human evolution other things happen. For instance, memory is a double-edged weapon and it allows people in the initial stage of evolution to remember what was cultivated can possibly be saved for future use. Saving begins, capital formation begins, exploitation of labour begins, and transactions begin. When this happens the persons who save their own labour in order to hire others are required to mark entries and they start making marks, whether they are hieroglyphs, pictographs or water marks, and a script is created. The basic purpose of human scripts was counting. They had nothing to do with language. Perhaps, the best person to read all scripts properly is the most illiterate person because he or she can see only geometric forms, whereas others see 'meanings' that do not essentially belong to those forms. All scripts can be analyzed and reduced to four or five geometrical forms. They are nothing but increasingly complicated systems of geometric marks to remember what we had transacted. Greed is institutionalized in scripts. Speech is threatened by scripts. Scripts then allow monopoly over capital formation and the processes that will encourage and bless capital formation. That's where scripts begin. There is another component in the human psyche that threaten stories and that is blood. There is a mysterious fascination that the human mind has for blood. It is not just passing on blood from one time to another time, not just continuing the generation, but drawing blood. That attraction has not been explained sufficiently. But just as scripts are aided by memory the attraction for blood is aided by imagination. Imagination controls the space for us and the attraction for blood eventually turns into a controlled mechanism of 'securing' blood. Races are marked, states are created, and territories are imagined. The earth never knew its names as America and England and India, but this fascination for blood, which in other words is fascination for violence, gets institutionalized in the form of state. Script and state control stories. Language, assisted by memory and imagination and the desire for transcending the otherness, creates stories and scripts, and states throw out the stories. They try to silence them, to pose an authorized version of truth. Therefore, every version of truth, which is a fantasy of Existence that consciousness creates, comes to be a blasphemy. Silence is imposed on it. So while we have the language ability, this apparatus imposes on us a condition of aphasia, the loss of language. Phasia is the ability to speak; aphasia is a loss of language. Where we had the ability to remember and then convey through memory this tremendous forceful energetic oral tradition, that is taken away, and an amnesia is imposed on us. It is this sense of otherness with which the human child grows up that forces on the human consciousness a stratification between what is conscious and what is the unconscious, what is received, acceptable, decent, lawful and that which is rebellious, restless and must be pushed into the background. Social caste and classes are created when that instinct is compounded with others such as greed and violence. When in such stratified communities, the state and scripts force a condition of aphasia on speech and when the territorial rights, identity possibilities, and cultural freedom, are taken away, a new condition emerges in the human society which for the want of a better word I will describe with the term 'anesthesia'. Anesthesia is a mechanism of control of pain, when the fantasy of the world that the consciousness is, is shut off momentarily. When everybody else thinks you are alive but you know that you are dead within, a condition of that kind is created in the society which makes aesthesis impossible. Aesthesis, is in the Greek sense, the ability to perceive the world through your senses, touch, taste, sound, sight, the joy of being, and the celebration of life. Aesthesis becomes impossible when imagination is negated. But once again the human consciousness gets around this obstacle, manages to snap the bind created by the signs seeking to define it, challenges scriptures and scripts, and recovers the significance lost within the signs. A story is born...

5

Truth, Fiction, Cyberspace

If it is possible to argue that consciousness is a fantasy of the phenomenal world, it is also possible to argue that the phenomenal world is a virtual representation of the human consciousness. The world external to our consciousness is there, but not quite there; and therefore, every member of the human species has to keep constructing for oneself a new 'dictionary of objects' describing for oneself their 'significance' in terms of the images perceived. In the phenomenological entanglement of the consciousness with existence, the human ability to turn the 'real' into virtual and the 'virtual' into real provides a sense of purpose to the semantic universe prior to one's entry in it, as well as gives birth to the sensory transactions that continue to weave the phenomenal.

All forms of things come in as sensory perceptions; and one needs to know the significance of those forms, the exact interrelationship between those objects, and the purpose of those objects. At every new moment of experiencing events, objects and sensory perceptions, we need to know what they all mean; but the human body is a mechanism that is inadequate for grasping all that is present in this cosmos. There is a lot in our time as well as before our time that we cannot grasp through a direct sensory engagement. Considering this inadequacy of the mechanism provided to us for grasping the reality surrounding us, the human consciousness seems to have devised strategies that enable us to make sense of all that surrounds us. In its most direct and rudimentary form, the strategy is to fabricate imagery described in theological schools as 'Truth'.

Think of those people who lived in dense forests and did not know how to respond to light, such as those whom Plato made one of his case studies. Plato writes about the archetypal experience of a man who stands at the entrance of a cave and is amazed to see his shadow falling inside the cave. He does not know how to explain the phenomenon, and is scared. Out of such sublime fear arises faith, and out of it arises an interpretation of the world in the form of revelation. 'Truth' and 'revelation' as two intertwined categories are created by the human consciousness in order to make a sense of the things that surround us. In the case of truth, it is the sense of things that surround us and the ones that we can experience, or know that others before us have known or experienced; in the case of revelation, these are things which surround us but are never visible, are not experientially accessible for us, and the ones that constitute the 'invisible' and the 'unseen' aspects of existence. Truth tries to get at the limit of facts, revelation at the limit of fantasy. When we look at various historical versions of truth, we notice that attempts have been repeatedly made to arrive at unexceptionable statement of truth, and at the same time no single version has been accepted by the subsequent generations as the ultimate statement of truth.

In ancient India, we have a theory of truth which maintains that the substratum of every object is one and the same. It is almost as if all objects in the world are glued to *existence* and the adhesive *sat* is the same while the object may differ. The substratum, the invisible side or the under-belly of the objects, experiences or events, of phenomena is the same but is indescribable. Therefore the Vedic philosophers described it by merely using the 'pre-personified' term 'it', the Sanskrit *tat,* the glue, the substratum, the spirit that gives lifeness to life, objectness to objects, the phenomenal quality to phenomena. *Tat,* whether matter, spirit or nothingness or whatever it was, could not be described in words. The skeptics of those times questioned, they asked, "What is this *Tat*?, Why don't you tell something more about it to us?"; and the teachers of the *Upanishads* said "*Tat twam asi.*" "It is you", that which is in the outside world is no different from that which is in the inside world. It was maintained that the distinction between the consciousness and the world outside the consciousness is a false distinction. Therefore, the purpose of learning could be nothing more than to be able to appreciate that the distinction is a falsehood and the unity and the oneness of all things and beings alone is Truth.

In the *Katha Upanishad*, Nachiketa, a young lad, hears from his father that he was going to give away his entire kingdom, all his earnings. Nachiketa wanted to tease his father, so he said, "Father, you have given up everything, you have given away every thing, why do you not give me away as well?" The father gets angry and says, "All right I will give you away to death." Following his father's command, Nachiketa reaches the domain of death. But Yama is away at that moment and does not return for three days and three nights. As Yama returns, he notices Nachiketa.

"I am sorry I was away. I made you wait. As a reward for your patience, I grant you three wishes. Tell me, what do you desire?"

"Tell me the way to go back home."

"Granted."

"What is it that will make all that is liable to die deathless? What is the ritual that one has to perform?"

Yama tells him to perform a certain ritual so that those who die will become deathless. Nachiketa performs it with such perfection that Yama is pleased to have it named the Nachiketa Yajn.

"What is your third wish?"

"Reveal to me what is truth."

Nachiketa's point here is that truth is beyond life and death, beyond ritual and action, beyond the permanent (*yama*) and the transient (*niyam*). And because of its intractability, it cannot be 'known' and articulated, it can only be 'intuited' through revelation. That is the essence of the Upanishadic vision of truth.

But there were other versions of truth in India. There was the Buddha, for instance, who maintained that suffering and pain are true, that there is no elusive substratum but all that is manifest and experientially available to the senses is the truth. It is in itself, and what is in itself alone is true. The Upanishadic philosophy held that the phenomena of the world one sees are not true in themselves, but are 'true' because there is truth 'within' them, beyond words, beyond experience. Buddha maintained that truth is in experience of the world and within the grasp of the human perception. It is not outside experience. That version also changes as time passes. We have then the grammarians like Bharthrihari who said that there could be several layers of truth. There can be truth as it is, as well as truth as it is expressed; and that which is expressed can become truth in its own terms which is distinct from truth as it exists in the world. So, in this version, truth is considered to exist in several distinct orders. As we progress further in history, we come across a remarkable statement of truth in the works of the medieval saint poets. The poets like Tukaram, Mira and Kabir maintained that truth exists only where there is love, a possibility of affinity. Buddha was not talking of relationship. He was talking of experience in itself. The Vedic philosophy postulated truth which is universal but had ruled out the possibility of a relationship by denying all distinctions among beings. One needs to have 'two' of a kind at least in order to have the possibility of a relationship between them. It is not possible to conceptualize the relationship of one with the same one, except for the relationship of an egotistic self-absorption. It is necessary to have some kind of alienation, some alterity in order to create space for a relationship. The *bhakti* poets accepted this great need for otherness. They invented and dramatized an alterity in order to make truth possible, and celebrated their alienation from the source of being.

Almost by a universal consent, one tends to point to Mahatma Gandhi's autobiography as a canonical postulation of truth during the twentieth century. While, as a leading freedom fighter of his times, his autobiography should have more appropriately been titled 'My Experiments with Freedom', or 'My Experiments in Ethical Activism', it was entitled *My Experiments with Truth.* The autobiography is a history of his development as an activist, and it was neither by design nor by purport any postulation of a philosophy of truth. Gandhi maintained that a moral integrity that brings one's thoughts closest to one's action, a way of life that generates great spiritual force as a social product, is truth. In other words, Gandhi sought to establish that the consciousness and its various expressions through one's action must correspond, and that any kind of contradiction between the 'spiritual' and the 'political' leads to untruth.

During the post-Gandhi era, the discourse of truth in India has been increasingly assuming a purely imagistic character, as if truth can now be represented entirely through the visual and can no longer be kept within the confines of silence or any verbal language. Today, for anything to be true, it has to first exist in illusory images of the media. It has to be in cinema, on television and outside of the life as it is lived. It is as if things, perceptions and events become more real when they are represented in the imagistic language of media. And, if they do not get represented in the form of media images, they are perceived as less real than they are. In our time, it has become customary to attach a greater truth value to the virtual than to the real. It is as if existence acquires a greater gravity when it prepares itself to be submerged in its representation, as if the tragic reported in media becomes 'really' tragic, and loses its significance if it remains unrepresented.

Various civilizations in the world have dealt with the question of truth in various ways. Implicit in the exercise of setting up a public inquiry under the name 'Truth and Reconciliation Commission' in South Africa, was the assumption that making a 'spectacle' of a testimony was evidence of its being the truth. The Chinese schools of philosophy believe that truth acquires its truth-value by being visible, unlike the Indian school that believed that if truth becomes visible, and indeed if it is arrested in words, it ceases to be truth. Thus, what is truth according to one school of philosophy may be very different and even quite opposite to what another school of philosophy conceives as truth. Within a single civilization, the idea of truth changes from age to age; and in different civilizations, the ideas of truth get conceived in a variety of divergent ways. If in ancient India, the philosophers introduced a great linguistic rider by naming 'it' (the thing that the world is) as 'it' or *tat* (the essence of the world), in an early school of Western thought, the validity of a thing depended on its placement in a causal sequence of a beginning-middle-end. The question is not as to which of the theories of truth, Western or Indian, ancient or modern, is more or less appropriate than the others. There is nothing like a notion of truth that has a universal validity. Truth is only a matter of metaphysical speculation; it is but a notion, nothing more.

Despite the grand tone that various propositions of truth tend to acquire, any given notion of truth has little correspondence with reality. Though the quest for truth originates in the human desire to understand reality, truth and reality are from two completely different planes of sensory experiences, conceptual exercises and intellectual understandings. What is common to these two planes, however, is the 'is-ness' of things. All notions of truth revolve round the question of the 'is-ness', the phenomenal presence of the world that the human consciousness may have created as a fantasy. It is in order to effectively describe the presence of the present that the human mind has to build thought structures in the order of truth. Since truth struggles to explain the 'is-ness' of existence, such theories are mainly preoccupied with the present tense, often the present that has an awesome range covering what in the brief individual time looks like the future and the past. And the moment one switches over to a narration of experience in which there was a queen and there was a king, one knows that the transgression has taken place and that one has moved from truth to fiction.

All stories, all novels are 'presented' essentially in the past tense. They may pretend to be in the present tense, much like a representation of a representation. One moves over to this deceptive present when one narrates a work of fiction, the plot of a play or a movie. This may happen with a permissive mixture of the present and the past. This kind of story telling is linguistically possible; but the sentences in it are theoretically or philosophically in the past tense. Even when assimilated within the structure of the narrative, they may make sense in the present tense. Fictional narratives acquire their truth value by their ability to convince the subject that the events narrated in them have taken place in some kind of real or imaginary past. While we are aware that they are stories, we also like to believe that they are reporting something that actually took place, and while fiction is structured to make us believe that it is narrating an order of events that is close to truth, one 'knows' at the same time that the representation is free from the ordering principles of existence. Owing to the permissive freedom that fiction seeks from the ordering principles of existence, it becomes necessary to inquire if fiction indeed is a non-truth, or even a 'lie'. Truth, or any postulation of truth, refers to existence, the world of phenomena, world of events that is claimed by the human consciousness as reality. Truth refers to that which 'is'. Fiction does not apparently refer to this world, though this world becomes the material for use in a fictional creation. Or, perhaps, fiction refers not to the world in existence, rather it refers primarily to the world 'within', or to the flux of existence that the human imagination creates.

Generally, a fresh formulation of truth follows a long stretch of human history and comes at the end of a series of cultural experiences as a result of those experiences. Abstractions are drawn on the basis of repeated sensory experiences, and all those abstractions go to form philosophical constructs, eventually giving rise to a grand view of truth. Thus, propositions of truth are based on the collective human memory of the sense experiences related to nature and material textures which the human body has to encounter. Sensation, smell, touch, sound, pain, pleasure, speed, temperature, perceptions and such other agents of experience form the material out of which an abstract theory of truth is created, often positing a realm that remains untouched by these experiences, often talking about 'is' in terms of what is outside it. But, there is no possibility of a proposition of truth that does not take recourse to memory. Memory is of essence to any conceptualization of truth. Imagination is of essence to fiction. Fiction calls for an exercise in imagination, a construction of images drawn from a world that is known to have existed as well as the worlds that have not come into existence. Truth claims to refer to the world that *is*, fiction to the world that spills over the is-ness of existence. These two exercises are dissimilar not just in terms of the materials they handle, but, in terms of their linguistic abilities, they fall in a chronological sequence. In other words, construction of truth as a vision of the world necessarily comes prior to the creation of fiction as a way of narrating the existence. Telling truth is simply a philosophical and linguistic ability, telling a 'lie' is far more difficult, it is an art that societies have to cultivate through slow and laborious processes of learning to transcend the natural.

When Plato objected to poets in his idea of a republic on moral grounds, he was being most perceptive about the nature of imagination. Aristotle who is seen as an advocate of creative imagination, on the other hand, had to understate the power of imagination and, as if in order to satisfy Plato, ascribe the hypnotizing effect of drama to its structural unity. Fiction, at once deals with imagination and the past, a past that is not to be subjected to memory as a proposition of truth, but a virtual past as a foundation on which a virtual present can be erected. Imagination can grasp the future, but the fictional or literary imagination cannot take off unless it first generates a virtual flow of time. Hence, the earliest piece of fiction was not possible in human languages for a very long time after the languages emerged as systems of conveying significance. Creation of fiction does not become possible for any language just because events worth narrating have been taking place in the given speech community. Fiction does not become possible just because the human animal is gifted with imagination. It becomes possible only when through the medium of the past tense the human consciousness learns to invent a virtual existence. When we compare language codes devised by animals other than the human species, such as bees, birds and fish, we realize that human languages are superior not just because they can represent more complex perception of reality, but more so because the human languages can invent through the past tense a 'virtual' image of the 'as it is' of all that was and more. Human languages are primarily distinguished for the presence of the past tense in them, and for the exceptional ability of the past tense to move from existence to the virtual world. Thus in the evolutionary process of the human consciousness, language brings us from truth to fiction, and from fiction to the cyber space, from real to the imaginary, from the imaginary to the predominantly virtual.

On the basis of what has been argued so far, we can conclude that fiction is a culturally higher order performance than producing theories of truth. It is relatively simpler to postulate truth, which in any case cannot be verified, but culturally far more complex to construct fiction. In the space and time of 'There was a queen and there was a king,' neither the queen nor the king ever existed, but to conceptualize this kind of a non-truth as far more easily convincing than truth takes an awful lot of imagination. In philosophical language, the ability to create fiction that surpasses with its semiotic effects the referential range of truth is the aesthetic ability. Aesthetics today is considered a branch of philosophy. Philosophy rises first, aesthetics comes much later as a finer branch of philosophy because the job of aesthetics is to convince us that lies are far more meaningful than truth. There have been countless attempts to explain how the surplus of meaning is created by language turned into fiction; this may happen because of the structure of the discourse, ordering of symbols, form of communication, representational affinities of the style to what is represented, and so on. More importantly, fiction opens up the path of the human imagination towards the poise necessary to experience and understand the cyberspace of the human consciousness.

Human languages have long struggled to create structures that are at once true as the present and the past; at once capable of enabling memory and imagination, truth as well as fiction. Such indeed is the world, or what surrounds the human consciousness. And such also is the human consciousness itself. Therefore, a full verbal expression of the is-ness of existence and the illusion that it is, an adequate narrative combining the past and the present, requires the exploration of cyberspace. Samuel Taylor Coleridge, who tried to establish a distinction between memory and imagination, had probably perceived the great potential of cyberspace, not in his drug-induced poetry, but in a striking recollection of his childhood. In the *Biographia Literaria*, he mentions that on a wall in his father's home, there hung a painting that depicted a ship being tossed about in a stormy sea, which surely may have inspired his famous lines in 'The Ancient Mariner' about "a painted ship upon a painted sea." An ancient mariner known in Greek mythology was Kubernetes who, it is said, had mastered the art of remaining still and steering his ship clear even in the middle of a sea disturbed by storms and the tossing waves. The space from which Coleridge observed the painting in his childhood home, and the space from where Kubernetes could challenge the watery chaos is technically the cyberspace. This space is the logical end of the evolution of language from the stage when it is used only to state truth, through the stage when it learns to fabulate. In this space the human consciousness can start grappling with reality more meaningfully than memory and imagination together have so far allowed it to do. In an age when a rapid epistemic transition is experienced on all frontiers of knowledge, if the existing languages are disabled through structural interventions, they will not be able to enter the cyberspace possibilities, but rather will return to the atrophied stock of memory and get into an unjustified celebration of folk memory. The marginalized speech communities in India as well as the main bhashas are facing a situation in which their transition from memory to cyberspace has become challenged. The imposed aphasia has started spreading from the margins to the centres as well.

6

The 'Middle Term'

It is commonly believed that the life experience of animals is different from the life experience of human beings. There is a tacit agreement that the human race stands out in the entire range of living species. If we assume that it is so, it might be worthwhile asking what the difference is between the animal experience and the human experience of this world. One answer that is given is that human beings have language which other animals do not have. However, a close look reveals that this is not the case. Animal language may be limited in range, it may not be verbally prolific, but animals do communicate effectively. Hence this distinction between animals and human beings is not entirely correct. Human languages are more developed, qualified and made impersonal by introduction of scripts so that though born in the mind, language can come into existence outside the mind in the form of fixed signs, but there has to be another differential, other than language, between animals and humans. One may possibly say that the ability to think that human beings have is different from the ability that animals have for thinking. An animal's thoughts are not made impersonal in the form of philosophy or music. Of course, we do not know how animals think. It will be worth reflecting on this and see how thought is related to what it thinks about—the phenomenon that we like to call Reality. There are four established ways of recognizing the relationship between the mind and the world outside that we describe as reality.

One area of recognizing the relationship is science. Science believes in observation, and measures and records the phenomena which science believes is in existence. The second method of recognizing, identifying and marking the relationship between the mind and reality is called phenomenology. Unlike science, phenomenology admits the legitimacy of the human imagination. Science generally disowns the responsibility for imagination and its active intervention in the field of knowledge. Phenomenology believes that the mind, or rather the consciousness, is a dynamic faculty with its own autonomous energy, and this energy allows the consciousness to spread its tentacles round objects which exist outside of itself. For the phenomenologist, objects do not become objects till the observer's consciousness has engaged them. This is like having many things in a dark room, where you switch on the light—the light of consciousness—and then start scribbling the names on these objects such as a box, a trunk, a suitcase, a briefcase. What looked like a conglomeration of objects suddenly takes on individual identities. Thus the individuation of the world is possible through the dynamic faculty of consciousness. Of course within phenomenology there are disputes regarding the status of the subjective. Some philosophers maintain that, in order that consciousness becomes consciousness, objects have to be in existence first. What will the consciousness catch with its tentacles if objects did not exist? And if objects existed before consciousness started its activity how could we call consciousness dynamic? Science allows us to measure things, name them, and establish causes and laws. Phenomenology allows us to believe that consciousness has its own energy, and therefore there is a dynamic interplay between the world and the consciousness.

The third method of recognizing the world is the metaphysical method. In this method we are led to believe that because the world has been there before one is born, possibly there was an 'original' act of creation, which has preceded the act of an individual's creation as a biological being. Metaphysics maintains that there is a Creator. That Creator is then imagined in some form—often of a human being. When the imagination is subtler, the Creator takes the form of a fish, a pig, a buffalo or whatever else. This Creator has a set of dictates for the conduct of the world. Human beings have to keep themselves in consistency with those dictates, otherwise they will violate something which was, in the nature of that logic, created by an energy beyond the human comprehension. We start seeing life in inanimate objects in this kind of relationship and celebrate life in the lifeless.

There is then psychology which accepts that the mind is an empty container that gets sequentially filled with experience as one grows up. In psychology, experience is subsequent to the mind that will receive experience, and make it what it will be. Hence importance is given to what happens during an individual's childhood. Irrational behaviour and thoughts are explained with reference to the history of the mind. Each of these methods has its limitations.

There are deep flaws in Western psychology. It posits the idea of the unconscious shaped entirely by the experiences of early childhood. The unconscious is considered to be inaccessible and buried in the mental field. It is conceived as dark, aggressive, and rebellious, sexually more charged, and energetic—this is exactly how Europeans believed the Orientals to be. The unconscious, moreover, is seen to be full of jealousy and also filled with a sense of guilt for being what it is; raw and conspiring all the time. All these were also the adjectives used to describe Oriental society by European historians, travel writers and administrators. For instance, if we look at the image of an Oriental despot in European writings, we find exactly the same description. Psychology, framed in Europe during high-colonial times, claimed that the conscious mind is reasonable, admits civilization, allows a person to be disciplined, and is a friend of daylight; it supervises, controls and censors the unconscious mind from where irrational, sexually charged energy is constantly trying to escape.

One problem with metaphysics is that by postulating a pervasive energy, it easily becomes politically *status quo*ist. I am not questioning the saintliness of a saint, I am also not questioning any genuine spiritual aspiration of individuals. However, the expression of metaphysics in an institutionalized form, such as the church, and religious philosophy, has always sided with people who like to control the society in order to perpetuate the unequal distribution of wealth and power.

The problem with phenomenology is that the mind is seen as a single entity without any fissures. Psychology emphasizes the fragmentation of the mind. Phenomenology thinks of the consciousness, almost as some medieval thinkers would have seen all revelation of knowledge as one, as undivided. Whereas it is true that biologically all animals of the human species are more or less similar, it is not true that their life experience has been more or less identical. The biological similarities deceive the phenomenological thinker. Therefore, without taking recourse to science, psychology, phenomenology or metaphysics, could we possibly ask questions about the human ability to think? If we could do so, it would offer us a certain degree of freedom to think once again about what we are and how we relate to the world.

Here, once again, we have to turn to the animal experience of the world. Animals get angry and humans too get angry. Animals crave for things and humans do the same. Animals remember just as humans remember. Animals do imagine; they have dreams as well and we hear of animals crying because of disturbing dreams. What is different then between the other animal species and us? We began with the assumption that our life experience seems to be different from the life experience of the other animals. Possibly the difference that our thinking machine has from the thinking machine that animals have, is that we have introduced a 'middle term' in our thinking which animals have not, a mediation between what we perceive as an instinct or impulse and what we do as a result of that instinct or impulse.

We feel hunger and therefore we need food. While animals, when hungry, simply find or hunt for food and eat it, humans have learnt to place between the need and its fulfillment objective forms and systems. The system justifies, classifies, and certifies earnings, currencies, hierarchies and a mode of exchange. This middle term—the system—occupies most of our life. Animals have a sense of shame, but the sense of shame, which forces human beings to wear clothes, does not operate in the animal world. Owing to the middle terms that the human beings have established in every mental and cultural transaction, the human mind has created barriers between life impulses and their fulfillment. I am inclined to believe that the social system falls between what we are and the way we relate to the world outside, between what we perceive and the way we express that perception. This system entirely dictates our understanding of the world. Such a position is not acceptable to phenomenology, metaphysics or psychology.

Phenomenology approves of an autonomous existence of consciousness. Metaphysics approves of an autonomous existence of the Creator; and psychology approves of an individual interplay between the world as it is created and the world that is constituted in an individual's mind. If somebody were to tell the phenomenologist, the psychologist or the exponent of metaphysics that it is the social system that makes one what one is, including one's most private thoughts, they will agitate against such an assertion. All our responses are knowingly or unknowingly, whether we recognize them to be so or not, responses to society which is trying to examine, censor and control us. What is conscience within our mind, which we thought all along to be the presence of the invisible, the most inaccessible to the world, is really the most public place in the world. It is the place within us where the society stands. Therefore, if we have to make sense of our understanding of reality, of the relationship between our thoughts and reality, we have to accept that neither thought nor reality is entirely autonomous. One's response to the world, and one's relationship with oneself are fragmented because one fails to realize that one's understanding is not one's own but belongs to the society to which one forever belongs.

7

Faculty, Ideology, Creativity

It is commonly assumed that the apparatus of human understanding is divided into four agencies: sensation, intellect, imagination and memory. One does not know if these are distinct faculties of the mind or momentary functions of the same capability that the mind possesses, such that the mental energy at times becomes sensation, another time intellect, a third time it becomes memory and then it becomes imagination. There is, of course, a lot of speculative thinking about this, but it is virtually impossible to decide with any scientific certainty the exact relationship between these four agencies. In every animal species these agencies are present. There is no animal without intelligence, memory, imagination and sensation. However, in the human mind these agencies work differently owing to the social context which continually shapes them.

Sensation is the basic unit of understanding: heat or cold, solid or liquid, moving or steady are known through sensation. The senses bring to us so many images of the world. Yet in 'civilized' human discourse, intellect is privileged over sensation. This is so particularly where the human animal is forced to prolong its childhood beyond the limit of reasonableness. In all other animal groups a child is brought up, and trained to hunt, find food, attend to medical needs, build nests or residential shelters. But in the case of the human child, a social system called education artificially prolongs the natural experience of growing up. The human race has now come to a stage in its history where a child without education is not accepted as a normal child. We believe that it is immoral and unethical to keep children uneducated. Those who are not educated, those who refuse to be tutored and trained are treated as dropouts, as insane or given to criminal tendencies.

We believe that the intellect is crucial to carrying forward the accumulated human knowledge, the accumulated fund of human experience, from one generation to the next. In the process the wisdom or knowledge that sensation brings is discounted altogether. This does not happen among other animals. This attitude is typical of the human animal. Similarly, imagination and memory: at one time memory was enough to manage the affairs of the human society, but a time came when imagination started getting over-privileged. We have respected artists, art-works, and 'creativity;' but these notions received currency only when capital-driven economies started challenging the collective memory with legalized documents. So, we create arts, whereas other animals apparently do not. In the human society imagination is over-privileged, and memory is discounted. While everything in the world is art, absolutely everything that we do after inventing the use of past tense is art, human beings classify only certain things as art and certain other things as non-art.

Intelligence, sensation, memory and imagination, the four agencies of understanding correspond with each of those four methods of understanding that we discussed earlier. Intelligence attaches itself to the scientific method of understanding the world. Without intelligence one cannot have science; without it one cannot structure the world. Imagination attaches itself to the metaphysical method of understanding the world. One needs to imagine a creator; the creator is imagined to be present in each and every object. It is imagined that there will be a continuation of life beyond death, and a machinery of imaginary beings is created; religion is its most powerful articulation. In the phenomenological way of understanding, the universe is based on the importance of the agency of sensation. If this world had not been sensed, had there been no possibility of sensory relationship between the human body and the rest of the world, one could not have even thought of the phenomenological approach of the consciousness spreading its tentacles outward to things to constitute and define the structure of the universe. As against this, the psychological approach of looking at the human understanding attaches itself to memory. It is based on the idea that there are memories in the unconscious, which become special traits, special urges, and special aspirations. Things happen in childhood, which is contained in one's mind, and the memory of those events disturbs what is contained and activates the mind to act in a particular way. In short, whereas in the non-human animal the four agencies might be working simultaneously or evenly (simultaneously if these are distinct agencies, and evenly if they are four functions of the same entity), in the human mind there is a fragmentation of the energy, which distributes itself in the four agencies. Some of the agencies are privileged over the others.

Because of the social conditions, all the four agencies do not work evenly or simultaneously; and possibly for that reason the construction of the world in the animal consciousness is different from the construction of the world in the human consciousness. Human beings have become incapable of allowing all mental agencies to perform their full functions since they are burdened with identities, locations and histories. All histories, all social structures burden their existence, preventing the mental agencies from functioning naturally. There is an element of atrophy of nature in the human mind. However, one more possibility of thinking evenly is offered to human beings by what is known as ideology. The world has known two major ideologies in the last two hundred years: one ideology maintains that there has to be social justice through an even distribution of wealth generated by the human race. It argues that this can be achieved by the intervention of the state. Justice comes before freedom in that ideology. There is another ideology, which holds that human beings have acquired the ability of converting what is natural into what is cultural. This is possible because of creativity and inventiveness. The intellect should not be fettered. It should be free to flow so that it can make possible a greater inventiveness and create more and more wealth for the enjoyment of humanity.

Those who believe in these or allied ideologies, are able to link their lives with a consistency of responses to all events and objects. The acquisitive ideology privileges intellect and imagination over sensation and memory. The distributive ideology gives primacy to sensation and memory. It holds that if one did not understand history one would not understand the world; and history is in one sense accumulated memory. This ideology believes that if one does not understand hunger in this world, one will not understand human beings; and the experience of hunger is perceived through sensation.

Ideologies have a definite advantage over the thought transactions in an individual consciousness. They seek to bring within a single focus all or several of the faculties with which the human consciousness is gifted. They are a grade better, but not as much as the functioning of animal consciousness. Thus, one is a human being first, then a subscriber to an ideology, and finally one is an animal. It is necessary to understand how ideologies allow an individual to look at life experience with a sense of consistency. However, there is a limitation there. The human history has had a shorter spell in relation to animal history, and the history of civic society, of nationhood, of active capital, is even shorter. Therefore it can be argued that the history of ideologies is relatively short. Ideologies focus their attention excessively on the political sphere of the human existence. There are other spheres of human existence such as the aesthetic and the ethical though the taxonomy of existence in terms of these categories may not be entirely apt. One may say that the ethical is the political, or the aesthetic is nothing but the political. I do not deny that but, by the same argument, what is political is necessarily aesthetic or ethical.

The harmony of these three spheres is desirable for the totality of human existence. Thought, at the level of ideologies, seeks to bring within a single focus all or several of the human faculties. However, quite ironically, any two of them get prominence within this transaction. Therefore even if an ideologically charged person's responses to the diversity of experiences are relatively uniform, he can falter and be unsure of himself while dealing with the aesthetic and the ethical spheres of experience.

After the Russian Revolution, Arthur Koestler was asked to travel to Russia when the New Economic Policy was being formulated by Lenin (1924). Koestler was invited as a writer and intellectual, and he went there as an admirer of the Revolution. In *The God that Failed*, Koestler reports that when he went to Russia, he asked a friend a question: 'Will there be Tragedy in Communist Russia?' The reply was, 'No, there is no scope for a tragedy in a Communist State.' 'But what about an accident? A young man, newly married, is walking in a street and he dies in an accident. Is it possible to write fiction based on such a plot?' Koestler was told, 'But there will be no accident in Russia, under Communism.' This was an ethical as well as an aesthetic question. Tragedies are both an ethical experience as well as an aesthetic experience. The respondent's answer was satisfactory for the political sphere of tragedy. It asserted that the system would be so just that there was no scope for tragedy. We have to ask ourselves if this is possible; and even if it were possible, can every aspect of an individual's life be fully explained in terms of the political. Another example of this inadequacy is Hitler. He hated the so-called 'inferior' races, but he could not hate their music. Is this so because those who created ideologies, those who subscribe to them and those who live a life of ideological purity are inadequate thinkers? The answer is not to be found in their inadequacy as thinkers. This is probably so because the human mind, in addition to the four faculties, is gifted with a very mysterious power which can be called creativity. By this term I do not imply the human ability to write a story, or paint a picture, or sing a song, but the ability to act or interact with the objects in the outside world and the thoughts outside the individual mind. In the animal world a similar kind of creativity may be in existence, but it has not been active so far in any significant degree. Human beings can act with the environment and change it.

When one writes, it is not merely to express oneself. Every act of culturally significant writing is necessarily an experiment with the medium of expression. And, in the process the medium too acquires new tonalities. An actor will not only communicate a certain play or a story; he also addresses the body in such a way that the body's ability to express undergoes a radical change. This self-reflectivity allows human animals to change the world that is given to them. The aesthetic and the ethical belong to this power of creativity. Ideologies that are available to us have still not tackled the question of human creativity with sufficient inwardness. Thus if individuals have very fragmented responses to the world, ideologically charged people too have their responses similarly, if less, fragmented, since the unity between the political, aesthetic and the ethical remains unattained.

Very rarely in human history does a visionary comes along, and reminds us that politics will not be complete unless it is integrated with aesthetics and ethics. The highest kind of politics is sensitive to the aesthetic, understands creativity and therefore becomes ethical. The unity of the three makes one's perception of the world complete and unified, and brings the human language closest to a semiotic perfection that is seen in the silence of animals.

8

Knowledge and Freedom

Sensation accumulates in human experience, finds a place in human memory and becomes what is known as knowledge. Sometimes imagination excites the intellect, unites with it and becomes knowledge. It is always sensation and memory or intelligence that come together in any production of knowledge. Knowledge is of two types, or rather is two distinct entities. One is the knowledge inside the human mind. The other is knowledge as a system. A knowledge system has a certain prerequisite, and that prerequisite is script. In order to carry the knowledge produced by one generation to the next, human beings have come to use documents committed to scripts. It is through script that the collective accumulation of human experience moves forward, from one generation to the next and acquires the status of a knowledge system. Since a knowledge system requires carriers, both givers and receivers, every knowledge system tends to become a tool of giving and receiving power.

Those who can give or receive knowledge tend to acquire a certain authority in a given society, and what should really have been a means of knowing becomes a means of social control. While one likes to believe that knowledge is enlightenment, knowledge as a system becomes an object which can be owned, possessed, controlled and even manipulated. The manipulation of this object is probably the worst of human inventions.

In a given society those who are in a position of power or domination always like to make what they alone know, as knowledge. What the others not in a position of power know ceases to be knowledge. The Barbarians do not have knowledge, the Romans have it. Those who speak or recite Sanskrit have knowledge; those who speak Prakrit have no knowledge. Those who speak English have knowledge, those who do not have no knowledge worth the name. Such is the political context of every knowledge system!

Owing to this history of class possession of knowledge, knowledge becomes a means of exploitation. On the one hand knowledge is an inevitable and necessary human condition—the human mind just will not stop reacting to every new phenomenon and, therefore, acquiring knowledge—on the other, when human beings find themselves within social structures or communities, they tend to use knowledge for exploitative purposes.

The source of this paradox is in the biological peculiarities of the human animal. The human being is created as a vertebrate animal. Standing erect becomes a metaphor for being fully human, and a stigma is attached to bending. In all languages in the world many abuse words are related to the bending of the human body. To stand erect is a thing of pride. Since human beings are so reluctant to bend down, they have created a tremendous aversion for labour which other animals do not have. Other animals do all the activities that are possible for them and which they are required to perform for their survival and well-being. It is the human animal alone that has an aversion towards activities it needs to carry out.

Knowledge is used as a means to avoid labour. The emergence of the Brahmin class—initially emerging out of labour-inequality and subsequently transformed into a caste—is an example of how knowledge is used to avoid labour. The rise of the middle class in the Western world is another such example. Whereas knowledge should be the path to freedom and enlightenment, knowledge as a system has been the path towards inventing slavery and perpetuating it.

I am not trying to argue that all inventions are used to perpetuate slavery, and all technologies are created to perpetuate class discrimination and class distinction. Possibly man's discovery of fire, which is shared by all human beings equally is a discovery which did not split human society (though a lot of gender injustice has originated in associating woman with the hearth!). Perhaps the discovery of a medicine such as penicillin was useful for all human beings. But, whether we like it or not, any invention—even one that is of benefit to all of humankind—becomes an object to be manufactured at profit, allowing some people to accumulate wealth and preventing some other people from enjoying the fruits of human advancement in equal measure. When one says that knowledge as a system tends to become the monopoly of a class, a tool of exploitation, one would definitely like to exclude from this description, knowledge which is brought to us by persons who are imaginative, who have developed thoughts which contributed to the greater freedom of the entire human race.

So, while knowledge itself is not something undesirable, one would like to point to the tendency that knowledge has to allow it to be used as a means of exploitation. If this kind of simplistic bifurcation of knowledge, into the domain of the individual consciousness, and knowledge as a social institution, is accepted, it is very logical to argue that we should all strive towards reaching that condition of knowledge which is not a system but a knowledge which exists in the consciousness of individuals, exists within a small community, marginalized, thanks to its not having a share in the monopoly of the mainstream knowledge. When knowledge becomes a system, it develops a rhetoric of self-justification. This is the source of marginalization of communities. Marginal communities are not born out of economical inequality alone. They are born also, and perhaps in equal proportion, out of this strange definition that we have accepted of knowledge as a system. Think of medicine: if one accepts a given system of medicine, then another system of medicine becomes non-knowledge, though it could be an equally effective system. Since some system of medicine comes to the centre stage, all communities who subscribe to other systems of medicine automatically become marginalized. This is true of technology as well. Now, if this be the human situation and if we want to move forward in history rather than just drift along, we will have to think of how knowledge can be freed from the monopoly of a class, from the confines of a system, from the operation of the demand of logical consistency with the rest of the knowledge, and how it can once again be linked with what is knowledge inside the mind of individuals.

Human beings have made themselves supposedly superior to other animals, since human beings alone claim to have superior knowledge. In reality the superiority is not in knowledge that human beings have but merely of script. It is in the creation of script that we have come to think that we are superior to other animals. If we really have to become superior to other animals we will have to think of a way of acquiring and preserving knowledge in which social discrimination will be absent.

It is generally assumed that knowledge will bring freedom to everybody. A paradox inherent in the concept of knowledge is that the experiential truth may have very little to do with what exists in the knowledge systems as a universal truth. As against this, with regard to freedom, it exists only in the mind and not outside. It is a relatively more subjective notion, and that is its strength. The objective and impersonal knowledge, the so-called timeless knowledge, has been unduly privileged in the evolution of the human race. As against this, freedom which is often seen as a comparable ideal, and at times even mutually linked as in the Sanskrit expression, '*sa vidya-ya vimuktaye*', has not been similarly institutionalized. It has still remained closer to Nature than to Culture. While knowledge has come to be seen as an exclusively human prerogative, freedom is still seen in association with the more natural and, therefore, akin to all animal species. For example, democracy is a reflection of our collective desire for freedom; but fortunately democracies are bound to the idea of nations, of different geographical locations, and there is no universal idea of democracy.

One may say that rather than pursuing paths of knowledge it is better to pursue the path of freedom, so that an individual can have his perfect place as a creative thinker and a creative actor in the human race. Reality is much larger than human thought. The human mind has not yet found a way of grasping reality. Today, in order to be civilized, a person has to be enlightened, rational; such a norm came up through the economic domination of Western societies over other cultures. This norm spread over the world and was accepted out of a sense of fear of annihilation of culture and society. We have taken to thinking that knowledge brings freedom to people, that if we spread literacy, exploitation will stop. We do not think even for a moment, that this is a questionable idea. What one should have asserted is that it is freedom, which brings knowledge to people, not the other way round.

It is not the metaphysical freedom of *moksha*, or the freedom of scientific progress, or the idea of freedom, which will make the body painless. It is the freedom of experiencing reality. By reality one may simply mean an aggregate of all objects surrounding us, all that happens around us, in a completely neutral sense. This use of the term 'reality' has nothing to do with truth and untruth. Reality surrounding an individual brings knowledge. In order that knowledge becomes knowledge, two individuals should have the freedom to say 'this is blue', 'this is green' without anybody trying to prove one of them wrong, maintaining that the notion of blue and the notion of green are objective and can co-exist.

That will bring knowledge; and it is through such interpersonal communication that knowledge will exist, momentarily, between two persons or within a small community but not beyond that. In our developmental logic we believe that people should be made literate, so that they will become free and happiness will come to them. We believe that thought has to progress further, so that we will know more, and what we know out of thought should be taught to people so that they become free. This will not happen. It is not at all logical. What should happen is that people must start believing in their own knowledge traditions and start acting in their own situation. Institutions that are building knowledge blocks must be loosened up, shaken up, and we must learn to recognize many knowledges rather than a single knowledge. Knowledge becomes possible because its plurality is acknowledged. It is then that the human race will attain the concentrated and unified experience of life that has so far been possible only for animals. Then the human being will become the equal of animals and know what freedom is. It is then that the knowledge stock in the threatened languages will start contributing to the stock of creative ideas that knowledge is supposed to explore.

Index

COUNTERING VIOLENCE

Contents

1

Violence

The concepts of race, region, language and religion are the foremost factors behind the conflicts and massacres in the history of humankind. The pages of history have time after time been coloured by the destruction of other communities in the effort to retain the continuity and purity of a race. Numerous examples in history show that individuals who make tremendous sacrifices for the sake of their people are also able, without qualms, to strangulate and put to extinction entire communities belonging to other races. Many tricks and ploys are necessary to acquire land, either a tiny piece or a large area. One trick is to produce weapons, initially to kill other species of animals, and then develop sophisticated weapons so as to destroy other weapon-bearing communities of people. A second is to enforce such rules and laws that restrict the freedom of individuals. An extreme variation of such rules is the construction of systems, especially the political system, which century by century tighten the noose on individual cultural independence. The main factor behind violence is the inversely proportioned ratio of limited land resource against multiplying human populations.

Though languages have come into being as a means to conduct our affairs and communicate feelings and though it is possible to express not only physical sensations but also mental processes beyond these, yet it is language that sometimes severs communication. As geographical conditions change and mutate, the fertility of the soil dips or increases, hills, rivers and forests define the distribution of land, language too changes in its nuances and shades of meaning, and from one language emerge several secondary (ancillary) languages and dialects. Because of economic, political and cultural factors so many upheavals and changes take place between one language and another, that it becomes completely impossible to have only one language in the world. Human communities speaking numerous varieties of thousands of languages weld completely the language they speak to the identity of the community. Inevitably, the struggle for their identity gives rise to linguistic misunderstandings.

But over and above the three factors of race, land and language, the highest proportion of conflict and war is contributed by religion. Communities that keep alive conceptions of Gods and the modes of their worship do not hesitate to massacre other traditions, destroy their places of worship, uproot all other conceptions of the divine that seem to limit their own concept of God. Such acts have been performed with great regularity and dedication through human history.

It is not very difficult to discern that nation, religion, language and race—these causes of violence, also give rise to the most generous and noble sentiments. Men and women, who love their country and religion, take pride in their language and are in intimate connection with their race become in every culture and society the subject for praise and appreciation by their fellow men and women. In short, the inspiration to love and sacrifice and all emotions noble and ideal, and as opposed to these, the impulse of anger, hatred, prejudice, a desire to smash and break, emotions producing violence, both spring forth from a common source.

The twentieth century will go down as the most violent in the history of mankind. The invention of destructive arms and weapons, their actual use for human destruction, the production of chemicals for the annihilation of entire races, the use of medical means to kill countless people in concentration camps, the engineering of world wars, the kindling and inciting of battles, the banishing of communities to foreign lands and their massacre, the scheming of murder and mayhem within a country, the inciting of riots, political assassinations, plunder and arson: the narrative of violence is filled to an unprecedented degree with the paradoxes of individual criminal tendencies, murder, suicide and continual imbalances in peace of mind.

Why it is that so much violence has sprung up in the twentieth century? The same century has seen unsurpassed attempts to make human life happier, easier. Cures for many diseases, the invention of amazingly varied means of transportation, the freedom from much manual labour, the spread of education and the broadening of knowledge, the end of dictatorial regimes in many nations and the establishment of democracies therein, the ousting of monarchies, wonderful inventions in agriculture, the setting up of factories capable of enormous production, the creation of innumerable devices of entertainment; such admirable and historically incomparable milestones too have been achieved in infinitely greater proportions in the twentieth century than in any other century.

How can these almost miraculous accomplishments and the unbearable pain brought about by violence be linked? Between these two scripts of happiness and suffering which is the more authentic script in which the history of the twentieth century can be written? Several books of translation have the convention of publishing poems of the original language on the left page and the translated version on the right page. If the history of the twentieth century—in fact the history of all centuries—is structured in this composite narrative of construction and destruction then the transition from the constructive to the destructive becomes impossible to understand. It becomes necessary therefore to examine the chemistry of violence. It is essential to impartially observe the mutual relationship between the two worlds of violence: the world of reality and the world of fantasy.

Moral philosophy and ethics regard brutality as an innate tendency constituting a permanent threat to the balance of the mind. Jurisprudence, basing itself on ethics, considers violent deeds abhorrent and institutes state punishment as a deterrent. Medical science believes the propensity for violent acts is a result of a genetic disorder. Violence is considered a perverse tendency in sociology and is examined independently by criminology, a related field of study. Criminology, besides studying the forms of crimes and their sources, also explores the possible solutions to lessening crime in society. Scholars believe,

> The scholarly objective of criminology is the development of a body of knowledge regarding this process of law, crime and reaction to crime...The practical objective of criminology, supplementing the scientific or theoretical objective, is to reduce the amount of pain and suffering in the world.[1]

Since the prime purpose of criminology is to root out pain and suffering in human society, it considers criminal tendencies to be anti-social. It also lays down certain principles proposing that the structure of the body, the jaws, the shape of the lips and the colour of the eyes of such anti-social individuals differ from those of other individuals. If the sociologist Eysenck[2] formulated the theory that individuals with criminal tendencies are either extremely gregarious or extremely whimsical and inhibited, Karl A. Menninger thinks that criminals are psychotic patients with psychological disorders.[3]

The study of criminal tendencies from the perspective of the shape and proportions of the brain, parts of which may show unexpected growth, as well as of the genetic history of individuals, has been under progress in the crime-riddled USA. That the eruption of violent tendencies is dependent on secretions in the brain and their chemical action and reaction are some of the conclusions reached by these studies. In the February 1994 issue of the *New Scientist*, the following comment was made on 'Positive Aggression',

> Except for a few extreme cases nobody has yet proved that damage to a specific part of the brain can be linked to a violent personality. But there is plenty of other evidence linking violence to changes within the brain. Levels of serotonin appear to be lower in the brains of people with violent histories, just as they are in overly pugnacious animals...Serotonin, the theory goes,

> might act to suppress impulsive behaviour, and those with less of it in key parts of their brains might be more aggressive as a result.[4]

Neurology notes some instances of aggression of violent emotions due to any unusual fluctuation of substances such as dopamine and serotonin. Though from these sciences it is possible to come to some general conclusions about individual propensity to violence, yet to assume that the overflow of certain chemicals produces violence, or those persons with a large head, eyes or lips or those talkative persons all perform violent deeds are conclusions that cannot be held.

It is true that violence is socially destructive, that violence and crime have to be curbed; but it is equally true that it is still not possible even to diagnose, however superficially, the condition of the mind in which the roots of violence have deeply entrenched themselves.

In the Second World War, the Nazi government of Germany reduced the Jews to unimaginably dire conditions. The attempt was to stamp them out by terrible, brutal means. Many historians and thinkers have since written and debated copiously about the violence in the World War. Hannah Arendt is one of the foremost amongst them.[5] According to her, the Jews had been ill treated in Europe even before the Second World War. In the nineteenth century an ideal example of this would be the Dreyfus case. Though in fact innocent, Dreyfus, a Jewish army official was accused of spying against France and sentenced to death by hanging. Emile Zola ran a protest campaign against this for years on end and forced the government to annul the sentence, yet the French citizens continued to look upon Jews as murderers and traitors. In Russia too the campaign to annihilate Jews had been in practice from very early times and perhaps gained greater strength during the communist political regime of Stalin.

It is against this background that Hitler achieved political power with his anti-Jewish propaganda. Putting the propaganda into practice, he mercilessly murdered millions of Jews. According to Hannah Arendt, the Jews in Europe had prosperity but no political power, and when in any society there is a wide disparity in a section between its economic power and the political power there are bound to be violent attacks on that section. There can be an opposite theory made for India: there are continuous violent attacks on the section of society that has a share in political power but absolutely no place in economic power. Though both these theories seem apparently convincing, they cannot hold true for all societies and all epochs of history. During the French Revolution, even when both economic prosperity and political power were combined in the hands of one class of society, that class had to confront tremendous social aggression. As opposed to this, in medieval India the untouchable caste that had no political power and no economic prosperity was the victim of a terrible violent oppression. From the above it can be said that Hannah Arendt's conclusions are true for a particular period in the history of Germany but cannot be accepted as universally true for all violent transactions.

Sociology generally uses economic reasons to explain individual instances of violence and criminal tendencies. In a very important volume, *Deviant Behaviour,* Robert Merton traces the two-way process behind antisocial deeds: poverty and the stifling of opportunities in individual economic development:

> This theoretical analysis may go far toward explaining the varying correlation between crime and poverty. Poverty is not an isolated variable. It is one in a complex of interdependent social and cultural variables... only insofar as poverty and associated disadvantages in competition for the cultural values approved for all members of the society are linked with the assimilation of cultural emphasis on monetary accumulation as a symbol of success is antisocial conduct a 'normal' outcome...It is only when the full configuration is considered, poverty, limited opportunity and a commonly shared system of success symbols that we can explain the higher association between poverty and crime in our country.[6]

In Merton's view it is not poverty alone that is the reason for crime; when economic prosperity and social success are linked together, it is at that point that crime takes birth in poverty. That is, Merton has an economic perspective in his analysis of criminal violence. However, it is quite clear that though the economic angle cannot be kept away from an analysis of violence, the predisposition to kick out at cats and dogs when simply walking past, to crush insects underfoot, to pluck away branches and leaves without any reason—such violence upon natural flora and fauna, innocent of any economic interest does not figure in Merton's theories. When two countries are at war with each other, though the cause behind the colossal destructive activity may be economic, it is hardly possible that the feelings of violence in the minds of the soldiers engaged in warfare arises from an ongoing examination of the economic condition of their country.

Emile Durkheim argues that in every period and every form of economic and historical system, violence and crime appear continuously:

> Crime is present not only in the majority of societies of one particular species but also in all societies of all type. There is no society that is not confronted with the problem of criminality. Its form changes; the acts thus characterized are not the same everywhere; but everywhere and always, there have been men who have behaved in such a way as to draw upon themselves penal repression.[7]

As a particular society achieves economic development, the violent aggressions too increase in that society. According to Durkheim, crime had increased by three hundred per cent in nineteenth century France. As such, instead of understanding criminality as a social perversity, it may be better to consider it as an indivisible part of social living. It is perhaps the inevitable result of the innate cunning in the human species. Yet, deciding what crimes should be deemed punishable changes in every age in a society. The deed, which is sentenced with retribution in a particular age, may be considered innocent in a succeeding age; or conversely, blameless acts in one age are declared criminal in another. Obviously, the scales evaluating crime and violence change continually. In the perspective of the time-bound nature of criminal law and punitive measures, it may be observed that it is impossible to define violence or crime in the absence of a time framework. Human sacrifices made for the appeasement of the gods in a specific period are understood to be the handiwork of Satan in another epoch. It cannot, therefore, be concluded that human sacrifice has been universally condemned. Furthermore, it is possible that there exist different rules for punishment in different societies in the same time period. If, in a given society, the severing of limbs as a punishment for crime is unanimously agreed upon, another society of the same time may consider this inhuman. It can be said, therefore, that though punishing criminal acts is a universal custom, a universal matrix for crime and punishment is not available, nor is it easy to understand what really crime and punishment are. In the opinion of Durkheim, even if at some point of time there should be a society of exemplary individuals, perhaps the most trivial of mistakes would still shock such a society and thus even nominal faults would be punished,

> Imagine a society of saints, a perfect cloister of exemplary individuals. Crimes, properly so-called, will there be unknown; but faults, which appear venial to the layman, will create there the same scandal that the ordinary offence does in ordinary consciousness. If, then, this society has the power to judge and punish, it will define these acts as criminal and will treat them as such.[8]

One can only conclude from the above that notions of crime and violence exist in every society; however, the interpretation and definition of these notions are embedded within the framework of culture and time. It is not possible for every individual within a society to don all the identical expressions and gestures of the common collective mask of that society. There will be at least a few individuals who see differently, and who hold different opinions from the apparently common mask that a social structure engenders. As a result, such individuals are perceived as anti-social or perverse by that society. This implies that in the indistinguishable relationship between the individual and society, the dark animal instinct for violence is a permanent by-lane which every society forever tries from within itself, to block and stifle.

But any society, in the interest of progress, is always unquestioningly in need of anti-social persons who forge ever-new by-lanes in this relation between the individual and society.

Every social reformer opposes established social norms and brings forward new thoughts and new ways of conducting life. The scientist Galileo, or the saint Tukaram were treated by their contemporaries almost as if they were criminals. Human societies seem to progress on the principle embodied in the words of Durkheim, "Nothing is good indefinitely and to an unlimited extent". Socrates was declared a criminal by the laws of Athens. Jesus Christ was crucified for his criminality and beside him was nailed on a second cross, a thief, one whom we would still consider a criminal. Every individual who has been declared a criminal by his or her society has attempted to transgress established rules of conduct and to that extent is an 'original thinker'. Obviously radical thinkers and social reformers on the one hand and criminals and persons of violent tendencies on the other cannot both be measured on the same scale. Even so, in order to produce thoughts that modify and change the shape and contour of society, it is necessary to have an unlimited harvest of what might at any given moment be considered to be anti-social acts. According to the theories of Durkheim, in the lush undergrowth of anti-social ideas and deeds, somewhere the huge trees of visionaries take root and vigour:

> To make progress, individual originality must be able to express itself. In order that the originality of the idealist whose dreams transcend his century may find expression, it is necessary that the originality of the criminal, who is below the level of his time, shall also be possible. One does not occur without the other.[9]

Visionaries such as Socrates, Christ, Galileo and Tukaram take shape from a shadowy world of ideas and dreams outside the accepted parameters of society. According to Durkheim, it is this very space that also spawns the criminal. It may be necessary therefore to portray this outer region to understand violence.

The dream world of violence is netted by the crisscrossing strands of latent temptations and terror: there is the wordless possibility of the fulfillment of lust and the temptation of boundless enjoyment of power and economic gain and the haunting terrors of impotence and of death. Rape, exploitation of women, sexual abuse of minors can be listed under the category of sexual violence. With these may be counted the spurts of ordinary anger leading to barbarism, abusive language that describes either the desire for physical violence or sexual violence against the mother/sister of the person who has roused one's anger. If theft, dacoity, murder, arson, plunders fulfill lust for money, then the violence that destroys particular sections of society constitutes lust for power. But the begetters and supporters of such violence are constantly devoured by a fear of their own impotence. A bully or *dada* is, from the psychological perspective, a person living in constant dread of losing his own manhood. This instinctual apprehension of impotence troubles not only individuals, but also suppressed cultures and societies. Beset by this anxiety, they take to extreme violence. The man, who without a strong economic motive kills his wife, is in all likelihood, obsessed with the fear of impotence. Similarly, leaders who push a society into unnecessary violence can also be seen to be deeply troubled by the same fear. Common bullies who set up non-government 'armies' and threaten innocent citizens into advancing protection money live in extreme fear of individual debilitation. There is considerable disparity between the fear of impotence and actual sexual incapacity. This state of mind has a basis not in actual physical defect but is the result of a mental makeup, as "the impotence is clearly psychological when the anamnesis reveals its selective occurrence". [10]

Individuals afflicted by this violence generating anxiety, initially start using extremely powerful verbal feats in order to influence. Quite a few among these develop into forceful influential orators and create an oratory that invades, seizes and hypnotises the listening community. In their field of consciousness the dividing line between reality and fantasy becomes more and more hazy and the self-created, novel, dream-like reality is the one they begin to live. Consequently, their sympathy for the suffering of others diminishes. The road to mass slaughter, the torture of millions without scruple or qualm is now clear: Adolf Hitler was one such leader.

Hitler spent his childhood in wretched conditions. In his youth he joined the German army and during the First World War fought on the front. When Germany lost the war and the young boys of the army were let loose without employment or wherewithal, Hitler began to live as a menial in Vienna. He actually wished to be a painter, but circumstances had forced him onto a different path. In despair, Hitler began to identify himself with the defeat of Germany. From this identification was born Hitler, the political aspirant. He began to turn the focus of the anger and hatred that he felt for his own life towards the communists and Jews. This was the source too for his singular oratorical skills. The unprecedented philosophy of violence, which he developed, emerged from these factors. The hatred for human species is seen in his own words:

> The psyche of the broad masses is accessible only to what is strong and uncompromising. Like a woman whose inner sensibilities are not so much under sway of abstract reasoning but are always subject to the influence of a vague emotional longing for the strength that completes her being, and who would rather bow to the strong man than dominate the weakling — in like manner the masses of the people prefer the ruler to the suppliant and are filled with a stronger sense of mental security by a teaching that brooks no rival than by a teaching which offers them a liberal choice...They feel very little shame at being terrorized intellectually and they are scarcely conscious of the fact that their freedom as human beings is impudently absurd... They see only the ruthless force and brutality of its determined utterances, to which they always submit.[11]

These conclusions that compare the people with a woman, projecting the image of woman as weak and powerless, and finally, that see a woman as enjoying brutal terrorization are an example of a philosophy that reflects Hitler's perverse sexual imagination. This is Hitler at the beginning of his political career. When he had accepted the leadership of his newly formed National Socialist (Nazi) party, there began clashes between the 'non-government' army, which he had established, and the police troops of the contemporary weak government. In 1923 he was imprisoned in the Landresburg prison for his role in the well-known Munich

Beer Hall revolt. During the year of his imprisonment, the young Hitler wrote *Mein Kamf* which is, in effect, a treatise of his political philosophy. In this book is clearly perceived the maturing of his violent scheme of thought. The readers of those times in Germany understood Hitler's ideas to be only political propaganda. No one believed that he himself considered these ideas with any seriousness, or that he would really implement them once he had secured power. Had that happened, perhaps the entire history of the twentieth century would be different. But Hitler himself felt that the destructive dream world of his thoughts was the real thing. Not only this, he believed implicitly that this fantasy was the new spiritual guiding force of life. The convergence of faith and violence is seen to constantly generate upheavals in history.

> When sheer force is used to combat the spread of a doctrine, then that force must be employed systematically and persistently. This means that the chances of success in the suppression of a doctrine lie only in the persistent and uniform application of the method chosen. The moment hesitation is shown and periods of tolerance alternate with the application of force, the doctrine against which these measures are directed will not only recover strength but every successive persecution will bring to its support new adherents who have been shocked by the oppressive methods employed.[12]

The basic principle of Hitler's politics was violence and his image of society was feminine. That the masses in any country are feminine in character and that they are attracted by a show of violent strength were the most important principles in his discourse. Thus violence became the crucial means of getting and keeping power. No one who was not ready to inflict violence had the right to come to power. Moreover Hitler's assumption was that he who wished to live must fight:

> He who would live must fight. He who does not wish to fight in this world...has not the right to exist. [13]

The youth of the vanquished Germany were attracted by Hitler's philosophy of violence. Germany between the two world wars is an excellent example of how an entire society, beset by the fear of impotence, becomes brutal. A whole section of despairing young population, smarting under the humiliation following defeat in the war, was lured into believing Hitler's strident propaganda. Increasingly, reality and fantasy mingled insidiously with each other in Hitler's dream world. Towards the end of his hegemony, even when the fall of Germany was certain and the Allies were on the threshold of Berlin, Hitler was still sending written orders to the fragmented divisions of his annihilated army. Another important fact of his philosophy was the belief in the glory of untruth. His words in the German tongue are: *In der Groesse der Leregeliegt immer ein Faktor des Geglaubt-werdens* which may be translated as, "in every big untruth inheres a confidence begetting quality". The greater the proportion of untruth, greater is its ability to evoke trust. As the range of the lie expands, so too does the probability of that land of fantasy. Hitler presumed that the understanding of the common people, especially the minimum common denominator of their collective intelligence, was very low. Such deficient understanding comprehends only the dangerously easy language of violence. The message that he gave to wartime Germany was couched in similar simple words. And it was: Do or die. Those who would not surrender to this apostle of violence would have to accept death. In the name of genetic identity, for the sake of retaining the purity of race, Hitler's forcible transgression of civil society originating from a fear of castration was the most shameful of all the orgies of violence unleashed in history by a power hungry leader. Obviously, there continue to be, even after Hitler, many such orgies of violence, unknown to history in the small by-lanes of every big city.

2

Fear of Death: East and West

Not all violence stems from the fear of impotence however. Much stronger is the fear of death. When conflicts and differences arise between families or communities, even ordinarily peaceful individuals are likely to turn violent. The main cause for this appears to be the fear of mortality. In the name of self-defense, human beings have kept up with their business of killing other animals. Though acquainted with a bookish knowledge of snakes, if a person was to be confronted with a non-venomous reptile, his first uncontrollable instinct would be to kill it. Such instances of the fear of death may be observed in violent behaviour.

When Aristotle was critically evaluating tragedy, the most dominant form of literature in ancient Greece, he came upon the understanding that the watching spectators keenly felt two predominant emotions: fear and pity. When spectators see that even the powerful and mighty, such as a God or a king, fall in the end to death, they become deeply uneasy at the realization that there can be no escape from death for anyone. At the same time, however, they also feel a sense of relief that the loss suffered by the hero is not their own loss.

As capitalism developed, Western society increasingly privileged youth. Youth became important because it is in all senses, productive. Correspondingly old age and death held more dread. Earlier in medieval Europe, Hercules, Atlas, King Lear and such characters of advanced age used to appear as heroes in literature and mythology. But since the utmost value was placed on youth, a new literary custom evolved of projecting the hero as youthful. The hero of Oscar Wilde's *The Picture of Dorian Gray*, who hankers after perennial youth, is but a representative of a capitalist society's dread of old age and death.

The reverberations of the increasing fear of death were felt by Western medical science too. The central preoccupation of Western medicine since the end of the last century has been the attempt to defeat death. Surgical operations—a medical treatment making violent, if curative, incisions on the body, gained both acceptance and impetus. This violence on the human body in Western surgery together with the violent use of nature in Western technology are both, clearly, projections of the deeply embedded fear of death.

In Western theology, particularly in Christianity, it is believed that humankind tainted with original sin is born with the seed of mortality. Western systems of knowledge founded on such a theology, have developed on the most strenuous attempts to obtain victory over death, and as such, violence is woven into the very fabric of these systems. If physical sciences were ceaselessly utilized to take possession of as much land as possible, to refine arms and weapons, to cross the limits of time and place, seize new regions and societies and castrate them, the main purpose of sociology, economics, and anthropology was to extend the limits of human freedom. In an individualistic society, a system is generated whereby every individual is safe from any kind of division. The word 'individual' in English is at its root connected to the indivisible. A capitalist society inevitably depends on all kinds and manner of violence to preserve and keep safe an individual's indivisibility.

Western systems of knowledge, political structure, aesthetics and psychology have evolved from that basis of Christian theology focusing on the fear of death and the concept of original sin. All facets of Western life and its intellectual progress are coloured dark by violence. Behind the nineteenth century colonization undertaken world wide by the European countries was the support of its philosophy of violence.

As opposed to this, a culture that believes death to be an ordinary, natural event and whose philosophy establishes the possibility of an after-life, will perhaps, lay down a different equation with violence. This different equation may be seen in Indian philosophy in the times of the Mahabharata. Every epic narrates a violent confrontation. But it is difficult to find anywhere in world literature the several different kinds of violence and the profound philosophic thought relating to it that is discussed in the Mahabharata.

The dialogue which the armed and war-weary Arjuna has with Krishna right on the battlefield is embodied in the Bhagawad Gita—a systematic body of all the ideas and notions of violence that have prevailed in Indian culture. In it, especially in the first two chapters, are discussed several ideas of violence reflected in Western culture and philosophy. Bow and arrow in hand, Arjun says to Krishna, "Take me right to the middle of these two seas of army so that I may clearly see all the violent deeds of these warriors" (*Senayor ubhayor madhye sthapayati me Achuta*)[1]

The first two chapters contain repeated references to the endless stretch of the columns of soldiers due to which the reader can never lose sight of the fact that the entire dialogue of the Gita takes place on the actual battlefield. When Krishna drives Arjuna's chariot to the centre of the two armies, Arjuna's eyes fall on Bhishma, Dronacharya and the other commanders of the army. He can also see the warriors of the entire Kaurava clan. On seeing all these warriors, his own relatives, kith and kin, Arjuna asks, "What is the use of killing them? The only thing that will come about is the ruin of this clan".

Thinking about such a violent end, Arjuna becomes dejected. The thought of this imminent destruction sets his body trembling and he felt as if his bow, the Gandiv, would drop from his nerveless fingers. He says to Krishna:

> O Janardan, even if these people, out of greed, do not in the least care that the family will be destroyed, why should we who can think, take part in this massive violence? The loss of family means the loss of family dharma. And I have got ready to commit this enormous sin! The root

> of this violence lies in the greed for power. I do not wish the power or the violence. It would be better if the sons of Dhritarashtra slay me in an unarmed state: that may be more proper.

Looking at Arjuna in such a condition Krishna says:

> This despair does not suit you. Shake off this debility.

Arjuna replies:

> It might be better to beg for my living than kill my guru and gain a kingdom, because if I kill him and win the kingdom, every luxury and joy will be stained with his blood.

In the entire conversation the subject of violence is structured in the context of desire, the will to power, impotence and the fear of death. But violence as opposed to non-violence is not the main subject of the Gita. Knowledge as against ignorance is the main theme. Standing between the two armies, looking at Arjuna's limp figure, Krishna says,

> Though your words seem to be knowledgeable they are really a product of ignorance. The enlightened one does not fall prey to such shallow sorrows. The truth is that, what is not the truth will not last and that which is eternal will never be destroyed.
>
> No warrior can possibly kill what is eternal. That is why both the one who inflicts hurt and the one who is hurt, are removed from real knowledge. Because that which is without end is neither destructive nor capable of being destroyed.
>
> Hence, O Parth, examine deeply your thoughts on death. Do not fall into a false duel of the killer 'you' and the slain 'they'; though you do not kill them, what is mortal will die. Therefore, without taking credit for any success perform your duty. You cannot destroy them by killing only their physical bodies for within them too are the eternal.
>
> On the contrary, if you learn to recognize the eternal truth in all the animal species your sorrow will vanish in a moment. And without crediting success to yourself if you

> fight and win then happiness will be gained, if you lose you will enter heaven.

It must be noted that in Krishna's advice there is no glorification of violence. Nor does he tell Arjuna that the body is perishable, so there is no harm in violence. The gist of his advice is: violence, which is a product of ignorance, is as ignoble as the non-violence that is a product of ignorance. It is equally deplorable, both if non-violence were to be practiced just out of a fear of destroying the family, and if violence were to be committed out of a desire to preserve the family. Instead, if an individual out of the knowledge of living creatures and the regular functioning of the universe were to go about his duty in a spirit of detachment, then even necessary violence will be as noble as that necessary non-violence. The important issue is not violence but consciousness. On this Arjuna enquires, "How may a being full of enlightenment be described?"

In the words of Krishna, the one who holds joy and sorrow alike, stays aloof from desire and can avoid both fear and anger—he is the enlightened one. The one who can separate sense feeling from sense gratification is the conscious one.

Western knowledge, political system and social structure have grown around the necessity of satisfying the senses. The violence necessary for such satisfaction has been considered acceptable there. In ancient Indian culture however, the place of knowledge was understood to be higher than that of physical happiness. Western science and technology, attracted by sense gratification, have been hunting till today for ways of triumphing over death, over nature and other living creatures. As opposed to this, Indian sciences, philosophy and technology, without considering death the final experience, without claiming nature to be separate from human consciousness or other societies to be alien to one's own, and most importantly, without considering physical gratification to be greater than knowledge, have made their way through the ages. Accordingly, in Western culture, the innate tendency to violence in the human mind forged an open and external path. Violence, in Indian society, turned inwards and the coveting of physical joys was suppressed. Therefore in

Indian society various forms of violence directed towards the self are present at different levels.

At the beginning of the twentieth century the Gita underwent several new translations, and there were many new commentaries made on it. Of these, the two most important commentaries are Lokmanya Tilak's *Gita Rahasya* and Aurobindo's *Essays on the Gita.* Tilak believed that the Gita teaches a philosophy of action. Previously, scholars had interpreted the main significance of the Gita to be renunciation or knowledge. Though Tilak's commentary did not make an objection to such an interpretation, he took exception to the view that the Gita focused only on renunciation or that its predominant meaning is knowledge

> I do not say that the Gita has not preached Vedanta or Devotion or the Patanjali Yoga at all. But the combination of these three subjects which has been made by the Gita must be such that thereby Arjuna, who was on the horns of a terrible dilemma of conflicting principles of morality, and who had on that account become so confused about his proper duty as to say: 'Shall I do this, or shall I do that?' could find a sinless path of duty and feel inclined to perform the duties enjoined on him by his status as a warrior. In short, it is perfectly clear that the proper preaching in this place would be of Energism (*pravritti*) and that, as all other things are only supporting Energism, that is, as they are all auxiliary, the purport of the Gita religion must also be to support Energism, that is, to support action.[2]

Tilak based his argument on several fields of scholarship looking at the Gita as a whole: its location, its principal theme, its effect and its originality and a theory of existence that could be garnered from it.

Shri Aurobindo attempted to formulate a theory that would enable the human being to find spiritual evolution from the three-streamed unification of the paths of knowledge, renunciation and action. Arjuna asks Krishna the question, "Is the violence committed by me pardonable?" Aurobindo's discussion takes into account this question by addressing two issues. The first is that Arjuna'a warfare is in conformity with the dharma of his caste.

The second is that Arjun's nature was consistent with his duty. Aurobindo's Krishna answers Arjuna thus,

> This high and great knowledge, this strenuous self-discipline of the mind and soul by which it is to rise beyond the clamour of the emotions and the delusion of the senses to true self-knowledge, may well free us from grief and delusion, it may well cure us of the fear of death and the sorrow for the dead, it may well show us that those whom we speak of as dead are not dead at all nor to be sorrowed for, since they have only gone beyond, it may well teach us to look undisturbed upon the most terrible assaults of life and upon the death of the body as a trifle...[3]

In order to completely erase Arjuna's dejection, to make steady his mind stunned by the violence that was taking place before his eyes, Krishna further says,

> If you are not satisfied with your social duty and the virtue of your order, if you think that leads you to sorrow and sin, then I bid you rise to a higher and not sink to a lower ideal. Put away all egoism from you, disregard joy and sorrow, disregard gain and loss and all worldly results; look only at the cause you must serve and the work that you must achieve by divine command; so thou shalt not incur sin.[4]

Contained in the thought of the Gita is the philosophy of control of the senses. The philosophy of sense-gratification, which is a characteristic of Western culture, is diametrically opposite to this. But just as a philosophy of sense-gratification gives rise to an illusory, fantasy-ridden world of violence, structured by desire and fear; in like manner the philosophy of sense-control subtly creates another world of violence. In such a world, the realities of life are frozen. The reality of this dream world becomes more important than the empirical reality. As a result, both positive and negative aspects of violence, and non-violence come to be negated. This means, in this dream world, whether there is violence or whether there is no violence, it makes no difference. Hence, in the actual reality of living, violence gets a free rein. Once this stand is accepted, the moral perspective on killing of the body turns lax.

3

Death by Order

A highly interesting volume by historian Upendra Thakur *The History of Suicide in India* analyzes the typology of suicide in different regions of India and comes to the following conclusions:

> What do these instances point to? Why this colossal indifference towards the most precious thing on earth - life? They clearly show that when there was enough attachment to persons or even to ideas, people ceased to have all interest in life and were prepared to sacrifice it as if it were a trifle.[1]

In the twenty-first century, the number of suicides in India has increased significantly:

> But the staggering figure for suicide in modern India as we know it through daily newspaper and periodicals and other such sources in the absence of any authoritative official statistics collated, collected and compiled for the purpose beat all the previous records hollow.[2]...But if we take into account all reports on suicides hitherto published in English and other dailies in Indian languages all over the country, the number would be so staggering and horrifying so as to make us shudder. [3]

Like suicide, looting and killing of people, the burning of young brides, sacrificing human beings in order to propitiate the gods, giving away girl children to temples and later making them prostitutes, murdering for trivial enmities, burning the houses of

Muslims and Dalits, blinding of the Dalits by responsible government officials, the cutting away of an ear or nose of members of one's own family as a 'minor' punishment, self-immolation as a protest—examples of such violent deeds are plenty in India. Just as the fear of death may be the moving force behind violence, so too the understanding that death is not the final and real experience and the lesser importance paid to physical, sensual reality may trigger off a different kind of self-absorbed violence. Treason against one's own people, the privileging of the spiritual at the cost of suppressing the sensual and the continuous caste-strife seen in social life are forms of violence in India.

Medical science has attempted to analyze the psychological tendency to inflict violence on the self. Just as violent thoughts increase with the decreased flow of serotonin to the brain, suicidal tendencies too gain strength with a limited supply of this chemical. J. John Mann of the Columbia Presbyterian Medical Center has propounded this theory after examining several patients.[4] Serotonin keeps the intensity of feelings under check and as a result an individual has more control over his behaviour. As and when the flow of serotonin inside the brain decreases by 20 to 25 per cent, an individual starts experiencing either violent or suicidal thoughts. If such individuals are naturally prone to depression, then the possibility of suicide is definitely enhanced. Such individuals may also conceal their thoughts from doctors. Dr. Mann analyzed the psychological states of mind of patients from Finland and England who had attempted to kill themselves, and after verifying that it was the lack of sufficient serotonin that was the chief medical reason for suicide, and in order to lessen the incidence of suicide, he put into effect a new method of treatment— PET (Positron Emission Tomography). When he was making use of this treatment, Dr. Mann realized that if misery and deprivation are faced for long periods in childhood, the capacity of the brain to produce serotonin is reduced, and such reduced capacity later becomes a permanent genetic feature of that patient. That is, such unsound states of mind pass from one generation to the next generation. A whole class of people characterized by decreased production of serotonin comes into being in a society wracked by poverty, and wretched and deprived childhoods. In addition, suicidal thoughts may become an integral part of common social behaviour. In course of time such social behaviour and thought find cultural acceptability. In other words, ecological, material and economic factors contribute in a major way to the emergence and increase of violence, and also in violence gaining cultural status.

The practice of *sati*, the custom of several widowed women collectively immolating themselves in a common pyre on the death of the king, giving up a tactical warfare to commit *harakiri* on knowing the certainty of defeat in war, came into being as cultural practices and attained spiritual status in Rajasthan, the region that experiences scarcity of fresh fruit and vegetables. The customs of any society that are given cultural approval initially evolve from the degree of fertility of the soil, the climatic conditions and the availability of food grains. Subsequently, as a result of the cyclical and recurrent nature of history these customs turn into cultural values, and still later, a philosophy that upholds and nourishes these values gradually forms itself.

At this point one can shift to another track and examine anthropology that has made numerous attempts to search for the roots of violence in social and economic conditions, in individual mental makeup, in philosophic and spiritual formations and the political system of community. There are thinkers who believe it necessary to examine episodes of violence in order to understand violence, to classify, grade and arrange them in numerical charts. A specialist in criminal law, Hans Torov has published a scholarly book *Violent Men: An Inquiry into the Psychology of Violence*,[5] which makes a study on these lines. He lists nine types of violence in this book. Violence arises out of the tendencies to subdue by force, the implementation of rule and law, shame and disgrace, self-defense, domination, plunder and robbery, bullying and the eruption of suppressed feelings. Categories based on such descriptions have their own limitations; they are built on the examination of instances of violence within a particular society, at a particular period of time. In such cataloguing, prisoners locked up in jails, patients with mental problems in hospitals and people in the streets of cities are interviewed, questioned in a specific method and then, the information so received is classified. Such studies may benefit the police and judiciary, or those who administer jails or treat the mentally diseased; but beyond this, they are not very useful in understanding the origins and roots of violence. Psychology examines why certain persons treat their own selves with hostility, inflict torture on themselves, or behave in a diabolical fashion towards others. More particularly it gauges the mysterious relation between the unconscious and the sense perception. The main premise on which psychology and sociology base themselves is that tendencies towards violence are caused because of external circumstances, and these suppressed feelings rise to the surface, again, due to the force of circumstances. But there is also an exactly opposite analysis of violence that has emerged from the life sciences. This view holds that as the human species evolved gradually from the less intelligent organism, the human species must have picked up the natural instinct for violence from the less developed species. This involves a sub-principle too: though nature has endowed man with the most powerful weapon of reason, it has given man no sharp nails and teeth, pointed horns, strong tail, heels that enable the owner to run like lightening, the ability to change in a moment the colour of the skin, no poisonous fangs or any other physical means to protect himself. As the human mind developed, violence became the only weapon at its disposal so that man might protect himself. The main argument that can be put forward to support this principle is as follows: very few animals practice killing other members of their own kind; but in human communities, not only is the killing of other human beings accepted, but it is considered inevitable, and even honorable. Therefore, it is believed that the human species, which kills its own brethren, is the most brutal and violent of all the living creatures in nature.

Though this argument seems reasonable, it is not very difficult to locate its faulty logic. It is true that men kill other men, but it is also true that human beings run hospitals for others of their kind, find new medicines, shelter the destitute, evolve philosophies to lessen pain and sorrow, create concepts of divinities, and generate religious institutions based on them. One does not see wild animals doing any of these things. But it is also not right to conclude from the above that the human species is of a more patient nature than other animals. The truth is that violence in the minds of human beings and in society, and the violence in the consciousness of wild animals cannot be measured on the same scale. Because of the gift of language, man is able to speak about his own and other bodies; and as a result there is a deep chasm between the human point of view of looking at human bodies, and the perspective of developed, but language-less, animals. Whenever a new word is coined for a thing or an experience in human society, a new distance is created between the object or experience and the one who experiences. Until that moment, there were only two entities in nature: the thing itself and the experiences of that thing; but after the inception of the word there comes into being a triangular relation among the thing, the experiences, and in the absence of the thing itself, its representative word. Our own names are only words. But with the word our body (and mind) presents itself before us. That is, a new body/being outside of our body enters our consciousness. As a result, the acute sensitivity to the body gets divided into the actual body and the word-body. There is, therefore, a very profound difference between the violence in human interactions and the violence in the animal world. The process of evolution is not only continuous, but also one of incessant transitions. Sometimes these transitions are of such magnitude that the newly created thing may be radically different from its substance prior to the transition. Since language is central to human society, the evolution of violent tendencies in nature will have to be fitted in this framework of continuity as well as transition.

Two important points arise out of the above reflections. The first is, it is important to be aware that violence appears in different images in every age; second, when violence is set free in the medium of language, violent feelings, violent deeds and the means to tolerate violence—aspects involving sense experience, change to a new structure altogether. In short, during the natural evolutionary process, and particularly in the progress of the human society, violent emotions and experience emerge out of actual oppression and suffering, but progressively transform into commercial products; and a society that is able to create and tolerate violence comes into being. In our time it is now routine to produce violence in a symbolic form and suppress it too in an equally symbolic manner. A political party issues a statement in the newspaper and declares a *bandh*, and the government mans the streets with gun-toting policemen who do not have to fire a single bullet! Such rituals are an indication of the symbolic transaction of the production and management of violence. The killing of a person, thousand of miles away through a mere phone call, carried out by hired mercenaries, is an indication of the commodification of violence.

4

Distanced Violence

In very ancient times violence was an experience of actual infliction and suffering. Today it can be bought and sold. Even if it is a reality at the experiential level, its material nature has become more encompassing. The indicators of the sale/bargaining/marketing of violence in every society and every epoch vary. They have their own particular identity. It may also be claimed that as newer and newer shapes and forms are produced in the text of violence, society too changes into newer forms. From this perspective it is very difficult to say which comes first: the structure of the society or the rhythm and encasing of violence; because though violence is a constant feature of human civilization, the type of violence and the society of that time are tangled very intricately together. If one were to look at the history of ideas, it may appear as though camps of human society have settled themselves on the banks of violence; from the point of view of law it seems as though the secret paths of violence have always surprised the world by making sudden social appearances. Physiology and medicine only declare the exact moment when violence was inflicted on the body, while economics and political science reiterate its inevitability. Psychology has made the closest study of violence, yet since there is general confusion in this discipline about what constitutes a 'normal' state of mind, there exists the expected confusion in its understanding of violence.

Moreover it is clear that psychology will not be able to throw much light on the material aspects of violence. Perhaps it may be more appropriate to speak through metaphor and simile, and describe violence in the way the Brahma of Advaita is defined in terms of *neti neti*, or in terms of what it is not.

The French Revolution of the eighteenth century attempted to overthrow the exploitative rule of the Louis dynasty. Soon after, women, men and children of this family, as well as the nobles and aristocrats faithful to them were publicly put to death by the guillotine. In a few years, taking advantage of the unstable political situation caused by the Revolution, Napoleon Bonaparte, a young army officer, rose to power and conquered Austria, Prussia, Italy and other countries. For twenty-five years between 1789 and 1815, as a result of Napoleon's ambitions there were a number of wars fought in Europe, in which thousands of innocent people lost their lives. During the Revolution and later, when the wars were fought, the French people dreamt of a new world, and to set up this new reality they were ready to take to violent means wherever necessary.

During the Middle Ages, Christian and Muslim soldiers battled each other for centuries in the Crusades. The soldiers on both sides believed profoundly that they were the messengers of a new world. Towards the beginning of the twentieth century in India, particularly in the ten to fifteen years after the partition of Bengal in 1905, there were a number of small and big organizations busy in the attempt to end the British rule through revolutionary means. Their aim was to create a new nation, which they dreamt would be a temple to Mother India. Whenever violent means are undertaken, there is an attempt to fundamentally change established systems and create a new order of reality. When exploitative governments make use of their power to suppress or torture opposing ideologies or persons, the violence of those in power is also an obstinate desire to perpetuate the reality of their making. Every act of violence has the purpose of asserting one's claim over a given establishment or to establish a new order. Whether the levels of serotonin in the brain have lessened or not, when individuals feel they cannot change the world around them by accepted ways and find it impossible to bear the agony of an existing order of reality, even ordinarily meek persons take recourse to violence. School- and college-going youth casually pelt stones at the window panes of their libraries and classrooms during agitations; parents beat up their own offspring without the slightest awareness of their action; while walking on the street, an already desperate person abuses and curses when he is accidentally jostled around; these people experience a feeling that all ways to construct a framework of the reality they wish to have, are closed to them. To construct a different reality, at least to assert one's right to do so is one of the impelling drives behind violence.

But it is precisely this force with which social reformers, thinkers, seers and inspired artists also perform their work. There is an intimate relation between every creative act and every violent deed. Just as with the creation of every god there is bound to be the creation of a corresponding demon, just as the gods do not have any significance without the demons, for any constructive worker to emerge, there is the need, according to Durkheim's theory alluded to earlier, for people with violent tendencies.

If the motives behind violence are to create a new structure of reality then violence will compare well with artistic creativity. The poet, the painter, the sculptor and artists of every hue are troubled by the established conventions of the world; they are in search of ways to change it. According to Sigmund Freud the world of the artist is peopled with daydreams. Within the censorious regime of the social code, a creative way of channeling the individual's suppressed desires, perversities, and individuality, is through art. Freud thought that every work of literature clearly reveals the criss-crossing weave of the poet's desires, dreams, fears, frustrations, hate and jealousy. What is not possible in the actual and established reality, art attempts to make possible through the medium of words, colour, and rhythm. The reality of the art world is significantly different from ordinary everyday reality. Nevertheless since both have similarities, art reality was termed "virtual reality" by Susan Langer.[1] Such a virtual reality is sought to be created through violent acts as well. Persons who participate in violence have the satisfaction of at least momentarily changing reality.

Moreover, just as an artist experiences a feeling of being invaded by an unseen force at the time of creating his work, a violent person may behave as if possessed at the time of committing violence. Great writers and painters create a new language, colour or style while creating their work, which means that though a writer uses known language such as English or Marathi, or a painter uses blue, red and other known colours, still the power of the language, its style and rhythm is something that has never been expressed before. Within the confines of the available expanse of space on the canvas, the painter constructs a new world. Violent persons too create new and different kinds of relationships, other than those which society establishes as social relations. When the hands that normally join in a greeting on meeting somebody, are used to strangle the throat of the person in front, the attempt is to establish a new relationship, which goes beyond expected social relations. The only difference is that a writer creates this relation in language systems, the painter in the space on the canvas, while the violent person uses the medium of other people's bodies as the medium for this action. Violent individuals who use the medium of the body and actual physical reality in order to fulfill their dreams are some kind of perverse artists. If aesthetics had the tools to test the chemistry of creativity, perhaps anthropology would have found it possible to evolve its own tools of understanding the chemistry of violence. Unfortunately even in aesthetics it has not been possible to have a clear understanding of creation of art. Therefore, the act of violence has remained, as are the divinely inspired arts, an eternal and unsolvable riddle in human life.

Ashis Nandy has made an insightful study of violence in the modern world.[2] According to him the texture and quality of violence in the twentieth century are completely different from that in all earlier times. Whenever violence occurred in earlier times, there was awareness that the killer and the killed were both human creatures. Whatever the degree of rage in the slayer and even if his cruelty was inhuman, the acts of violence were accompanied with the recognition that the slain could also be in a fury, that he too could be equally cruel. In other words, it was not denied that those who fell prey to violence were also human. But in the twentieth century, people are killed systematically and in cold blood. Just as a farmer sprinkles insecticides in his fields to wipe out germs and insects without the least anger, in fact with a peaceful mind and dutiful feelings, scientists, political leaders, soldiers and police officials in the twentieth century are seen to annihilate groups holding opposite views with pride in being dutiful, not letting human sympathies disturb them emotionally. Ashis Nandy notes that in the last hundred years there has been genocide of nearly one hundred and ten million entirely due to human volition. But merciless killing done out of a feeling of duty, or done so as to implement law leads to a dehumanization of the killer. According to Nandy, a police officer like K. P. S. Gill may be able to control insurgencies in a state like Punjab; but in the process the police officials in his department, all unawares, gradually acquire demonic tendencies.

In June 1994, the Supreme Court ordered the hearing of fifty-eight police officers of Uttar Pradesh. These officers had, in the previous year, arrested and later killed ten innocent youth on the allegation of their being terrorists. The reality, however, was that they had no connection with terrorism in Punjab, and they were on a pilgrimage to Huzoorsahib and other religious places of Maharashtra. The police nabbed them on a bus and killed them. The death of these youth fortunately became widely known, and the Supreme Court asked the guilty police officers for an explanation; but in many states of India and in many other countries, hundreds of people fall victim every day to similar police 'encounters'. Violence too has become an industry during the twentieth century. The architects of political violence are able to manipulate the genocide of countless innocent people without a drop of blood on their hands. A political leader like Hitler can sit in his own private chamber and bring about the death of innumerable people. In the twentieth century, violence has come to be sold and bought by people as if it is like so many sanitized factory products, nicely wrapped in colourful paper.

In the twentieth century, violence has enveloped every aspect of human affairs. Just as human violence that manifests in words is different from the wordless violence of wild animals, the marketable violence of the twentieth century is different from the violence of the preceding centuries. It is possible to control through medical means the violence stemming from the defective production of chemicals in the brain, a diseased psychological state of mind and the anger produced from a fear of impotence, but not, however, violence emerging from religion, nation, language or race. The violence set in motion by a particular ideology can be countered by putting forward an opposing philosophy. The incidence of crime in society may be put under some check by undertaking programmes to eradicate poverty. But it is impossible to stop the marketable and inhuman violence of the twentieth century by these traditional solutions. To do so it may be necessary to discover radically new routes of human progress. Until now, all the studies on violence have put the responsibility of violence on the individual and the responsibility of such violent individuals on the inequality in society. We might ask if violence emerges from the notion of progress that has been upheld for the last two or three centuries. Of the few visionaries who thought and spoke on these lines are Aurobindo Ghosh, Mahatma Gandhi and J. Krishnamurti, all Indian thinkers. In 1909 Mahatma Gandhi in his short but radical book *Hind Swaraj* questioned the established goal of progress in the modern world. Today, a century later, while thinking about the violence in our times, it is imperative that this question be raised once more. Among the issues raised by Gandhi, education, the relation of progress with power, and with social morality are the most important. Though the context of violence has changed in our time, any attempt to understand the essential nature of violence must take a fresh look at these issues.

5

The End of Innocence

If we believe that violence is caused by the procedures of socializing then it becomes necessary to examine the system of upbringing of children in a given society. The psychology of the members of any society is determined by the kind of schooling that is available to it. Today, children are required to attend school in most societies; it is considered a desirable practice. If we look at school-going children in India, we will notice that we may well be producing a generation of young people with broken backs. School weighs heavily on children in more ways than one. Such a generation may carry a psychological burden of violence throughout its life. And this is but an outward symptom of a process submerged in the psyche of children. In ancient societies knowledge was transferred from one generation to the next in an informal, non-institutionalized form. One did not have to go to formal schools in order to learn or to get a document certifying learning. Today if children do not go to schools they are refused certificates confirming their education and they are rejected by society as useless. Jobs, economic advantages and social acceptance evade them. In a sense, this certificate, an official stamp of education, has become a synonym for normalcy. In contemporary society there is no room for children who do not want to attend school. Society today compels all children to be 'normal'; it is in the business of turning all children into normal children. And it may not make room for extraordinary children either. It may be practical to insist on uniformity in education and on certifying the normalcy of children, but it is not the most ideal way of educating children.

A related phenomenon in India is the dramatic increase in the number of schools. However those who educate children are not necessarily competent to take care of young minds. The once noble profession of teaching has become, today in India, a nexus between greed and insensitivity. The teacher, who has, in all possibility, paid a hefty bribe for his recruitment, attempts to recover this amount by providing tuitions. He has no other way and he cannot be blamed for this. Tuitions look for ways of providing incentives to attract students, and the incentive normally is the promise of easy success. The children who join the tuition classes are given slightly better marks than those who do not join the tuition. It is a simple and practical transaction. The consequence is that the child learns from a very early age to purchase success. In the world outside the school it is necessary to have specialized skills in order to perform specialized jobs, which are generally in short supply. There is little room for all the degree holders in that competitive market of skilled labour and this is underlined during adolescence with a stupendous pressure to succeed in that environment of scarce opportunity. Children who have had experience of getting better results by paying for them will expect the same in the competitive market for employment. One immediate result is that children enter the competitive world with a degree of cynicism and violence rather than with a sense of confidence.

In larger towns, very often adolescent students give vent to their cynicism and violence by forming peer groups, which then, as a way of self-expression, begin to indulge in petty crime. Since there are a large number of such gangs in all the big towns of India, a general ethos of violence is forged. Violence as a social substance receives a certain tacit sanction. This ethos is reflected in all forms of dreams that Indian society sees. The cinema and television are the two most pervasive forms of such social dreams. The scale and degree of violence in Indian cinema is a result of the turmoil within the minds of the young.

The structure of violence in mainstream cinema is as follows.

The main participant in that world of illusions has to undergo some acid tests in the form of violent physical engagements and emotional gestures. When he passes these acid tests he is certified as the newborn hero. The becoming of a hero in commercial cinema is based on his being violent; his new identity is a manifestation of the latent violence and cynicism. The process begins in school and concludes with the collective dream of our society.

Together with such dreams grows an attendant political ideology, which translates the dream world of violence into a programme for action. Political ideologies of hatred by themselves do not have the capacity to attract mass support unless the masses have nurtured the emotion of hatred for long years. In India there is a nexus between faulty education, the adolescent dreams that we dream collectively, and the politics of crime, which is the last and the visible consequence of that larger alliance.

An important question that needs to be asked at this point is how much knowledge do human beings really require. The answer will be that they require knowledge just enough to perform in their respective fields of activity. The present system of education loads the minds of children with huge quantities of excess information, far beyond their requirement. The cruel competition in the areas of employment and this heavy pressure to internalize knowledge may lead to a national genetic disorder. At no time in the past have we trained children in this manner? In no period of our history have we loaded the school bags and minds of our children with such an excess of knowledge. There was always space for leisure, this space has been rapidly shrinking. In its place instead, we find the dream world of violence which occupies the imagination of the young generation. Even parents are sucked into the educational system as surrogate children. The system involves them in the child's admission interview, preparation for studies and exams and other activities. The educational system occupies much of the social space and the privacy of homes. On the one hand it reduces the period of childhood but at the same time substantially increases the period for which a child is required to stay in the educational track. In the past there was a correspondence between the biological and psychological period of childhood and adolescence. With the years of education a middle class person receives today, the actual period of childhood is reduced drastically while the period of education has increased substantially. Therefore, there is an unhealthy disagreement between the body and the social practice that children have to bear.

Obviously something is wrong with this kind of education. Education is meant for emotional and intellectual growth of children. Yet it denies them their very childhood. In such situation, neither emotion nor intellect can develop. Instead, such education creates in the child a vacuum, a national psychological disorder. India has the second largest population in the world but its achievement in practically every area has been relatively poor. The responsibility must, in the final analysis, rest in the flawed education that is given to our children. If as a nation our collective dreams are frustrated in the international arena, they may give rise to extremely violent international conflicts. All Indian thinkers of significance during the twentieth century have tried to focus attention on this issue. Gandhi, Tagore, Aurobindo, Vinoba Bhave, J. Krishnamurti have made serious attempts to understand the discordance between human nature and the knowledge cultivated in schools. The nation, however, has failed to take their warnings with sufficient seriousness. In the manner of Blake one can say today, "Is it a holy thing to see so many children tortured in school?"

During the last two hundred years the aesthetics in India has perhaps been the aesthetics of conflict. The model of education perpetuated by the British colonial rule, post Macaulay, basically to train Indians for employment in the British government is the model followed by independent India these last fifty years. A second model of education, which hoped to address the spiritual and creative potential in the child was evolved by visionaries like Tagore, Aurobindo and Krishnamurti. Throughout the history of independent India, these two models have worked at cross-purposes. This conflict is at the core of our vision of education in this country. The attempt to make children normal by straitjacketing them in the first model does not sanction space for room to be oneself in the mode of the second model. It does not result in the maximum fulfillment of potential which was the aim set out by all the Indian thinkers of the twentieth century. The poverty today in the fields of philosophy and social thought has lowered the guard against the tendency to violence that the education system generates.

If the West through capitalism and industrialization has hurt natural resources, we in India have exploited and harmed our human resources. There is no term still to describe the destruction of childhood in the name of education in this country. In the West education has produced knowledge, which encourages the exploitation of nature; in India we have produced an educational system which results in violence. Though huge resources are expended in funding education, India has perhaps only managed to convert creativity to violence; all it has managed to create is spiraling machinery of violence.

In this connection, the Vora Committee Report deserves to be read as a serious warning to the nation. It is an indepth study of the dynamics of crime and its close link with politics. The brief of this committee was to investigate the nature of violence in the country. The investigation revealed a fairly repetitive pattern of violence beginning with the small town school dropout forming a gang engaged in small-time crime. The gang then graduates to buying police protection for larger offences such as smuggling and drug trafficking. At this stage the gang leader may buy political patronage and become an extension of the political network. Gradually he gravitates towards active politics. From this legally established position he is free to facilitate the smooth functioning of his criminal activities and the further infiltration of criminals into decision-making positions. This pushes one to the realization that the raw material for political decision-making is drawn from the unruly edges of the violent school system.

6

The Masculine State

It is necessary at this point of time to think about the state that India has visualized, accepted and perpetuated in order to understand the nature of violence. During the Indian freedom movement the Indian National Congress gave shape to the dream of independent India as a strong and united nation, united in spite of its amazing diversity, which would be a shining example to the rest of the world. This goal of the freedom struggle of a reconstructed united India took its inspiration from the philosophy of nationalism that European political history had generated. The Congress also accepted the model of British parliamentary democracy to govern the federation of such a large variety of traditional administrative units. It is important to understand that in his *Hind Swaraj*, among many other issues pertaining to the future of India, Gandhi discusses precisely the question of the parliamentary form of government for India. This book presents his thought in the form of a dialogue with Indian revolutionaries. Gandhi's argument is that driving the British out of India by itself does not change anything if India is to merely replicate Britain in administrative matters. Shocking his contemporary society, Gandhi said in no uncertain terms that the parliament was like a prostitute, a statement that he refused to change even thirty years later when the book was going in for a reprint. He justified his epithet by reasoning that the elected representatives of the parliament are encouraged by the nature of the very system; they never do any good for its own sake and only do what the people want them to do. Not right things but things that please. The parliament depends on the mercy and the pleasure of the people. Nor does it transact any useful business. Gandhi further pointed out that the members of parliament hardly attend the sessions unless the whip directs them to do so. Even when there is attendance, it is more often than not unruly or the members attend only to claim privileges. This is not an argument against democracy. Rather it is a caution against thinking of the parliamentary government as the essence of democracy.

After accepting democracy and the parliamentary form of government, independent India created a federation of Indian states, on the pattern of the United States of America, by merging all princely states. Many cultures were merged into the federation. Further it was accepted that India as a nation had to have armed forces to defend it; and since it was surrounded by some hostile nations it had to have well maintained armed forces. The parliament has the final control over the army, the navy, the air force, the police and the para-military forces. It thus becomes the law-enforcing agency and a very powerful one. Political power supported by an army and police can only have the face of a man. It can only be masculine. The armed forces are also seen as a mechanism for stabilizing external relations with other countries.

Most citizens today want to be close to the parliament, the seat of power. Even if becoming a minister or member of the parliament is out of reach, a desired ambition is to climb up the ladder of power, which gravitates towards the parliament. The process may not be immediately visible but when a small segment of any activity in the national life is examined it is immediately clear that schools, *panchayats*, corporate bodies, all aspire towards the centre of this masculine political power. In this country most of us live in a dream world crowded by metaphors of power; we secretly desire to be a presence in the power structure. In a sense, a majority of Indians aspire to wear the mask of masculinity. Since all power in this country emanates from the parliament, and since the parliament is formed in the image of man, all of us have accepted the mask of masculinity as a desirable identity marker.

In this process we are losing an extremely significant and valuable part of our cultural personality. The several cultures of India, which have over these many centuries evolved the delicate and humane, the feminine part of the national personality, are in grave danger of being lost. This is the second source of violence in the Indian psyche. We have created a powerful centre of authority, which is sucking all of us into its masculinity taking us away from our femininity, taking away from us our real federal structure. Perhaps the kind of change that is taking place in the personality of India would not have taken place if India had not accepted the parliamentary system of government and if India had not become a nation-state. Had we retained our status of many nations there would perhaps have been no shift to this all-male identity. Indian culture is a culture of variety. It is a culture of heterogeneity. But the nature of the state in India is not in agreement with the nature of Indian culture.

If the scale of violence has gone up in India after independence there must be some correspondence between the nature of the state that we have created and the incidence of violence. We have become parts of a political machine, which has created an imbalance of personality in us, of which we are perhaps unaware. There is need to create an alternative political system, and therefore, there is need to rethink what Gandhi said about the parliament. We must think of *swaraj* rather than the *raj*. *Swaraj* is self-discipline and for self-discipline one must be in touch with one's own self. What we have tried to create in India is a large-scale copy of Britain. We must now try to be India. Gandhi's alternative to the parliamentary democracy was the governance by people in small communities without a powerful centre. He advocated the principle of local self-government which provides for minute regional variations within the general framework of a national democracy.

The aspiration to enter the power circle, and the resolve to make India a nation has compelled us to homogenize the widely different ways of life and cultures. In the process we have lost our varied cultural personalities. The system of governance after independence does not agree with our cultural *prakruti* or self-hood. A fall out of this phenomenon is that as soon as a government is elected to power, a sense of disillusionment sets in. Due to the clash between our desire to have a government that we need and the government that we elect, tremendous pent-up violence is built into our psyche, which surfaces at the slightest provocation. It is not enough to think of just riots, assassinations and insurgencies. It is not enough to think about the import of arsenals from Sweden or France. It is not enough to think about atrocities on Adivasis and nomads, or gender discrimination. Though all these are real manifestations of violence, what is more real is what we are doing to children in schools and the kind of government we have accepted.

If India has to tackle the problems of violence at its roots then it is necessary to re-think the form of state we have chosen. It is then that India can dream of a society free of violence. However, this change cannot be brought about through violence. All violent revolutions, which begin with the idea of changing the state, always end in creating greater violence. Violence produces nothing but counter violence. Therefore pacifist ways of changing the present form of state will have to be invented. One way to do this is to encourage femininity, which is opposed to the kind of state we have today. It can be drawn from the sources of Indian traditions. Femininity is devotion, love and art. The present state encourages a parallel set of values, such as craftiness, not craft. It does not encourage love, it encourages hatred. It divides us as Hindu against Muslim, rich against poor, upper caste against lower caste, rural against urban people. And instead of devotion, the state encourages a selfish loyalty to power. Devotion does not admit greed but the state encourages attachment to power. We have to choose between these two sets of values: loyalty, hatred and craftiness, or devotion, love and art. To make this choice is the most pointed political statement against violence that an ordinary Indian citizen can make.

7

Social Structure

One more important factor contributing to violence is the social structure in India. I have had the opportunity of speaking to a number of men who have burned their wives and been convicted. One of them had secured an M.A. in English Literature and he happened to be a former student of the University where I used to teach. Another was a school teacher from north Gujarat. There was a third who hailed from Bulsar in southern Gujarat. I met them on a number of occasions and spoke to them at length. They were all very young, and I could not imagine them killing their wives. The one from Bulsar had failed in his matriculation exam and had started working as a salesman in a pharmaceutical company having furnished a fake certificate. He lost his job when he was found out, after which he asked his father-in-law for some capital to start a business of his own. His father-in-law refused to pay up and this young man, with the help of his mother, burned his wife so that he could marry again for dowry. His father-in-law went to the police and this man was sentenced to rigorous life imprisonment. In India, a life sentence does not mean the entire life, but only fourteen years and on the condition of good behaviour it can be further reduced. He killed his wife when he was twenty-three years. When he comes out of jail at the age of thirty-two or so, his family and society will accept him and take him back. In fact, his mother, also without remorse, has already arranged for a second marriage. He had no doubt about his acceptance since his justification was that he committed the crime on advice from his parents. He was doing it for his parents, it was his duty, and the responsibility was not his. It was, for him, a sacrifice.

The schoolteacher's wife was not very well educated. It appeared that there was a girl student in his school with whom he became a little too friendly. His defense was that the girl was interested in studies and he was encouraging that interest. His wife objected to this friendship. At this, the teacher took a wooden block and hit his wife with it. Even after she fell down, he kept hitting her with the block till her head was crushed to a pulp. Her parents lodged a complaint with the police when the village was preparing for the funeral. He too was awarded a fourteen-year term. When I asked the schoolteacher who his most favourite person in the world was, he said it was Mahatma Gandhi because Gandhi never told a lie. He said that he had never lied in his life; he had confessed his actions immediately to the policemen. He quoted from the Ramayana, and comparing himself with Rama, said there was a long tradition, which sanctioned the kind of act he had committed.

There are a number of such cases, and these provide us with sufficient material to describe the structure of violence involved in the practice of wife-killing in India. In the first case, the parents seem to have accepted the killing of a young bride as a perfectly normal social practice. In the second case, the murderer justifies his deed as sanctioned by a cultural practice. This is a reflection of the confused state of moral and social values in India today. A large majority of Indians live in an ethos in which crime can be excused if it conforms to certain accepted social and moral norms. Simultaneously, the modern capitalist economy has created new material desires in the psyche of individuals; in fact the individual is almost defined in terms of desires and not spiritual attributes. The market celebrates freedom to desire and the need to succeed. The huge machinery of media, entertainment and advertisement grounds every human emotion in the world of material things. Most emotions seem to culminate in the desire for success in work or erotic love. The individual is thus a victim of this network of desires, especially erotic desire. Most criminals in our society are victims of the huge market of desires. Within it, all human actions have lost their significance except in terms of gratification of the senses. The general atmosphere of greed and craving for material success encourages a culture of violence. All modern communication contributes to a rise in the human instinct for greed. An already oppressive social system has become unbearably exploitative and in this system there is unprecedented violence against women and children.

Similarly the instances of violence against the lower castes, the Dalits and the economically disadvantaged have increased in recent times. The Bhagalpur blinding and the killing of tribals in a rally at Nagpur some years back are some of the more known instances. All available statistics show that atrocities are rampant in India. There is clearly a link between crimes committed by individuals and the violence caused by social groups. At the basis of both is the desire for material possession and wealth, which drives our collective minds, again on an unprecedented scale. Never before in the entire history of India had desire become the centre of the social order. Material wealth is sought in order to acquire 'a new body' (as discussed earlier in connection with the cinema) which is resistant to violence, which transcends violence. It is a body hungry for consuming all the pleasures sold in the market of desires. The desires that are sold as commodities have in fact turned violence too into a commodity, which in a way helps in the acquisition of the other commodities. In short there is a nexus between violence and desire, which is even more fearful than the nexus between crime and politics. The traditional social structure with its history of caste, tribal and gender discrimination creates a neatly available space for the circulation of desire as violence. Violence is the inevitable mediator in the social conflicts that traditionally existed in Indian culture. Contemporary society is a tragic social scenario: a result of the rapid breakdown of dialogue between the upper caste and Dalit, the Adivasi and non-Adivasi, the rich and the poor, the urban and the rural. Thus India today is an extremely violent country with an unprecedented scale of violence generating due to the institutions of knowledge, the political structure and social inequality.

8

Countering Violence

The aim of legal systems is to deter violence by punishing those who transgress the law. But it is always difficult to decide whether a person acts violently because he has no respect for law or because he is not in full control of his faculties. That is, it is difficult to determine if violence emerges from a psychic disorder or deviation from a given social norm. Is it subversion of established practice or perversion in the human mind? The legal system only classifies the cases of individual violence in an arbitrary way. The legal way of understanding violence is guided by its classification in terms of arson and looting, suicide and murder, assault and crime, war, acts of insanity and so on. This, it must be admitted, is somewhat crude. Since we do not understand violence we have been unable to come to terms with it and to counter it. There have been occasional efforts by people like Jesus Christ and Mahatma Gandhi: but these have not sunk into the collective psyche of humanity. Gandhi understood violence to be essentially a result of greed, both in the field of an individual life as well as in the public domain. Freedom from desire is non-violence not just in terms of acts of violence but also with regard to concepts and feelings. That is, violence lies in deeds but perhaps more importantly in thoughts. He considered it as a force residing in the human mind. He interpreted violence as an excess of masculine qualities. In his *Intimate Enemy*, Ashis Nandy analyzes Gandhi's opposition of British colonial masculinity by privileging femininity. Passive resistance, Satyagraha, non-cooperation were Gandhi's weapons of fighting the aggressive British rule. His entire struggle against colonial rule took the form of a struggle of '*stritva*' against the British '*purushatva*'. But such efforts of understanding violence do not sink very deep in the human psyche. It is one thing to understand that violence arises out of desire, it is quite another to create a society free of desire. Human history for the last three centuries is an epic story of the creation of desire. Ever since the great philosophers of Enlightenment such as Galileo, Kepler, and Copernicus made discoveries in astronomy, the human being has become the centre of the universe. The right to exploit natural resources for the material progress of human beings evolved during this period. Increasingly sophisticated machines that reduce labour and produce commodities that gratify desire have been created reducing the dignity of labour and enhancing desire. To have more and to have the ability to have more is considered an indication of human progress. This ideology is concurrent with a certain moral framework that is indifferent to the needs of ecology. Industrialization has rarely cared for the well-being of nature; industrial society perceives nature as a mute entity without life or language.

In a sense the history of the last three centuries has been a tyranny of speech over silence: it is the history of the self-obsessed language of oppression. The social space that used to be occupied by silence is erased. At present progress is measured in terms of the ability to produce more, to possess more and to consume more than what we really need. This is the new ethic, the new *dharma*. The rhetoric of modernity and the ideology of progress boiled down to what Gandhi called violence. No world organization ever attempts to persuade people to improve their conscience. The ones that teach thus have become obsolete and irrelevant. The entire ethos is engaged in building a world of desires. Those who oppose this, such as the church and other religious organizations are today redundant. The reason is that they still invoke the idea of the good in the name of God. It is difficult to believe that God exists in any form of existence that we can know. The medieval saint-poet Kabir knew this. He had no hesitation in stating that whoever created the fish also created the net, which caught it. God in fact was not a very reliable proposition: he claimed that the guru was far superior to Govinda. If God was a mere maker of existence, the guru was the one who had understood it, the one who had knowledge about it. Perhaps we need to revive Kabir's understanding of God as a passive agency if we have to get out of the trap set by fundamentalist religious groups.

In the space vacated by religion, secular institutions like WTO, WHO, World Bank, etc., have stepped in and have made it their business to spread the message of material acquisition. The failure of the last three centuries has been the failure to create a force counter to the ideology of industrialization and material advancement.

As the most important thinker to counter the materialism entailed in modernism, Gandhi attempted to combine politics with religion, to create spiritual buffers. Because the ethical framework surrounding technological civilization is unquestioned, violence is the order of the day. Nature and people who are termed backward are routinely destroyed so as to gratify multiplying desires. Modern civilization is based on unrestricted violence. There have been few attempts to change this situation: for instance, communism was one such attempt. However, it tried to control the greed of individuals without removing the source of it. It failed to understand that the solution to violence is not counter violence. Gandhi's answer was to counter violence with non-violence.

It may be interesting to examine this position closely. Implicit in non-violence is a certain degree of passivity. No defense of non-violence can rule this element out. Gandhi, one must not forget, also stated that the violence of a courageous person is preferable to the non-violence of a coward. I should like to argue that the true alternative of violence is not non-violence, but a dynamic constructive activity. The constructive action should be for our time and our society and not just an imitation of what great minds have done in the past. When we think of the opposition between violence and non-violence, the Gita necessarily surfaces to the mind. It is a text that springs out of an intense moment of violence. It is a poem in the form of advice for action. In India there are these two counter points when we think of violence: one is Gandhi who preferred non-violence to action, and the other is the Gita, which advocates violence to non-action.

To carry forward the discussion made a little earlier, the Gita became a crucially important text at the beginning of the twentieth century when India was evolving a new political identity for herself. A number of philosopher leaders worked on it. Sri Aurobindo wrote *Essays on the Gita*, Tilak composed *Gitarahasya*, Gandhi translated the Gita and also wrote a series of letters commenting on his translation. These three interpretations of the Gita are important because the three thinkers were among the makers of the destiny of modern India. These interpretations emerge from a very deep contemplation of the political activity that they were involved in. Tilak's essays have to be located in the context of a tradition of philosophy, which dates back to the thirteenth century, a tradition that originates from Jnanadev's commentary on the Gita. These essays offer reflections on the long continuing debate as to whether the Gita teaches action, *pravrutti*, or detachment, *nivrutti*. The debate has focused on the concept of a *sthitapragny*a: a person who retains his equanimity in the midst of turmoil and suffering. The second chapter of the Gita discusses the detached person, the *sthitapragnya*, in elaborate detail. Krishna charts the daily routine of such a person as also the quality of his inner world, and sets out the much-quoted comparison of the lotus blooming in the muddy pond. This leads Krishna to the definition of the soul: it does not get drenched in water, not burn when set afire, nor dry in the wind; the definition rests on its description of detachment. This has led to a philosophical debate about the opposition between action and inaction. The Gita states that the desire attached to action leads to sorrow and so, often before Tilak's time the Gita had been interpreted as a text advocating passivity. Tilak's persuasive argument was that above everything else, the Gita teaches a sense of responsibility towards the action expected of man and the failure to act amounts to failing in his duty, a sin. His interpretation of the Gita is known as the *karmamarga*.

Sri Aurobindo offers a very different interpretation of the Gita, though there is little doubt that his essays are influenced by Tilak's interpretation. Tilak and Aurobindo were contemporaries and had worked together for a while in the Indian National Congress. Aurobindo understands the Gita to be knowledge, *jnana*. He himself had formulated a philosophy of evolution from matter to mind and from the mind to the super mind. In his opinion the Gita corresponds to this theory of spiritual evolution; it provides knowledge about this evolutionary process. He focused on the Gita's interpretation of the Sankhya philosophy, a system of philosophy that is characterized by its discussion of a cyclic progress from *tamasa* to *sattva*. His reading was that the Gita unfolds an image of the world known through the medium of thought. Therefore his discussion of the text privileges knowledge over devotion as well as over action. It is important to recall that Tilak and Aurobindo were active contemporaries in national politics. Hence their understanding of the Gita is not just a philosophical exercise. Their ultimate objective was freedom for the millions of Indians. Their understanding of the Gita was a means of seeking freedom. Their attempt was to make the Gita relevant to modern India.

Gandhi entered the national political scene soon after Tilak and Sri Aurobindo. His interpretation of the Gita is particularly interesting given his views on violence. Gandhi's translation of the Gita probably was not much appreciated and his followers raised some questions about his interpretative translation. In order to defend it, he wrote seven letters, which were published independently. The first of these letters persuades the reader to begin reading the translation with the fifth chapter of the *Gita*, which sees Arjuna as a *bhakta*. Thus, for him the *Gita* is about devotion, love and compassion. Gandhi wished to focus on the fact that though Krishna speaks of war and action, Arjuna is primarily a devotee and an undue emphasis on action is to misinterpret the Gita. Krishna himself stresses on *bhakti* when he says knowledge and action without devotion are not of much value. Thus Gandhi claimed that devotion is the essence of the Gita.

The Gita is essentially a poem; it is to be understood as philosophy only after it is appreciated as a poem and hence open to several readings. The above discussion shows its different interpretations as *karmamarga, jnanamarga* and *bhaktimarga* by the three great nationalists who shaped the destiny of India during the twentieth century. If one can think of the history of India as an unfinished, still to be resolved story, and of Tilak, Aurobindo and Gandhi as characters in this story, perhaps one can look at the question of violence from a fresh perspective. The history of India in the early part of this century is dominated by the philosophy of non-violence. At the same time it has been a history tremendously interested in the question of violence as discussed in the Gita. If the story has to be brought to some conclusion, how shall we face the question of violence again? The conclusion can only be this: that non-violence is not the opposite of violence. Its opposite is constructive action. We must also realize that to read the Gita in terms of action alone, or knowledge alone, or only devotion is not to understand it in its entirety. One hesitates to say this, for those three leaders emphasizing *karmamarga, jnanamarga*, or *bhaktimarga* were without doubt great thinkers. It is perhaps more appropriate to understand the Gita as an integration of all the three. And with this understanding if we invite Lord Krishna and Mahatma Gandhi into a dialogue once again in our presence, perhaps we will know why it is necessary to think of action of a certain kind as the countering force to violence.

Today the significance of *jnanamarga* is not in seeking knowledge about God alone but in seeking to reform, and radically reform, the institutions of knowledge. Which means, to put the Gita into practice, *jnanamarga* would involve making our educational system more responsible and more humane. *Bhaktimarga* today lies in rethinking the network of loyalties, *bhakti*, in which we are bound. It does not mean only thinking of devotion to God: that path has not succeeded in producing an alternative to the technological civilization. Today, there is a network of *bhakti* to the institutions, which pervade our lives, with the state at its apex and all routes of devotion leading to that apex. The modern form of devotion has substituted God with the political state. It is important to rethink the nature of this *bhakti* to the state. Perhaps we need to look at small communities, at commitment to the local as against the pan-national or global.

Karmamarga today would mean restructuring political ethics in our collective life to improve society to the best of one's ability, not just accumulating spiritual virtue in an individual fashion.

If *bhakti, jnana* and *karma* can be integrated in these forms, the task that the generation of Tilak, Aurobindo and Gandhi began, but which we need to take to its fruition, will perhaps be completed. We may be able to evolve a viable alternative to violence in the form of constructive action through such integration. We must learn to look at Krishna as a statesman, not an avatar, see the Gita as talking about man and not God. We need to combine Gandhi without his non-violence and the *Gita* without its God. It is then that one may understand the core of violence in modern Indian society and be able to counter it. This will be the true antithesis of violence.

Notes and References

1. Violence

1. Edwin H. Sutherland and Donald R. Cressey, *Criminology*, J. B. Lippincott Company, 1970, p. 3. Also see, Edwin Sutherland and Donald R. Cressey, 'Differential Association Theory', in *Deviant Behavior: Readings in the Sociology of Deviance*, ed. Delos H. Kelly, St. Martin's Press, New York, 1979, pp. 93–99.
2. Hans J. Eysenck and Leon Kamin, *Intelliegence: The Battle of the Mind*, Macmillan, 1981.
3. Karl A. Menninger, *The Crime of Punishment*, Penguin Books, New York, 1978.
4. *The New Scientist*, February 1994, p. 33.
5. Hannah Arendt, 'On Violence', *Crises of the Republic*, Harcourt Brace & Co., San Diego, 1969; 'Antisemitism', *The Origins of Totalitarianism*, Part I, Harcourt Brace & Co., San Diego, 1972.
6. Robert Merton, 'Social Structure and Anomie', *American Sociological Review*, Vol. III, reprinted in *Deviant Behavior*, ed. Delos H. Kelly, St. Martin's Press, New York, 1979, pp. 110–21 (117).
7 Emile Durkheim, *The Rules of Sociological Method*, translated by Sarah A. Solovay and John H. Mueller and edited by George E. C. Catlin, 1938, reprinted in *Deviant Behaviour*, ed. Delos H. Kelly, St. Martin's Press, New York, 1979, p. 51.
8. *Ibid.*, p. 53.
9 *Ibid.*, p. 54
10. Entry on 'Impotence', *Encyclopedia of Psychology*, Continuum International Publication Group, 1972.
11. Adolf Hitler, *Mein Kampf*, Jaico Print, 1988, p. 48.
12. *Ibid*, p. 152.
13. *Ibid.*, p. 242.

2. Fear of Death

1. In the original Maraṭhi essay, Jnanadeva's celebrated translation of the Gita, the *Jnaneshwari* is used. Here, the translation used is from the Ramakrishna Mission edition of the Gita, together with the commentary by Sankara and Swami Vivekananda. Translation used in some of the subsequent passages is drawn on the Bhagavad Gita as rendered by Swami Gambhirananda, Advaita Ashram, Calcutta, second edition, 1991.

2. *Bal Gangadhar Tilak, Srimad Bhagvadgita-Rahasya or Karma-Yoga-Sutra*, translated by Bhalachandra Sitaram Sukthankar, Seventh Edition, Gita Printers, Pune, p. xxviii.
3. Sri Aurobindo, 'The Creed of the Aryan Fighter', *Essays on the Gita*, Sri Aurobindo Birth Centenary Library, Vol. 13, 1972, pp. 58–59.
4. *Ibid.*, p. 61.

3. Death by Order

1. Upendra Thakur, *The History of Suicide in India: An Introduction*, Munshiram Manoharlal, Delhi, 1963, p. 61.
2. *Ibid.*, p. 73.
3. *Ibid.*, p. 77.
4. *The New Scientist*, February 1994.
5. Hans Torov, *Violent Men: An Inquiry into the Psychology of Violence*, Aldine Publishing Co., Chicago, 1969.

4. Distanced Violence

1. Susanne Langer, *Feeling and Form: A Theory of the Arts*, Routledge and Kegan Paul, 1953.
2. Ashis Nandy, (Ed.), *Science, Hegemony and Violence: A Requiem for Modernity*, The United Nations University, Japan, 1988, reprinted by Oxford University Press, Delhi, 1990; 'The Discreet Charms of Indian Terrorism', *The Savage Freud*, Oxford University Press, 1995, pp. 1–31.

Index